PLATO
GORGIAS

and

ARISTOTLE
RHETORIC

PLATO

GORGIAS

and

ARISTOTLE

RHETORIC

Translation, Glossary, and Introductory Essay

Joe Sachs
St. John's College, Annapolis

Focus Publishing
R. Pullins Company
PO Box 369
Newburyport, MA 01950
www.pullins.com

The Focus Philosophical Library

Plato: Sophist • E. Brann, P. Kalkavage, E. Salem • 1996
Plato: Parmenides • Albert Keith Whitaker • 1996
Plato: Symposium • Avi Sharon • 1998
Plato: Phaedo • E. Brann, P. Kalkavage, E. Salem • 1998
Empire and the Ends of Politics • S. D. Collins and D. Stauffer • 1999
Four Island Utopias • D Clay, A. Purvis • 1999
Plato: Timaeus • P. Kalkavage • 2001
Aristotle:Nicomachean Ethics • Joe Sachs • 2002
Hegel: The Philosophy of Right • Alan White • 2002
Socrates and Alcibiades: Four Texts • David M. Johnson • 2003
Plato: Phaedrus • Stephen Scully • 2003
Plato: Meno • George Anastaplo and Laurence Berns • 2004
Spinoza: Theologico-Political Treatise • Martin Yaffe • 2004
Plato: Theaetetus • Joe Sachs • 2004
Aristotle: Poetics • Joe Sachs • 2005
Plato and Xenophon: Apologies • Mark Kremer • 2006
Plato: Gorgias • James Arietti and Roger Barrus • 2007
Plato's Republic • Joe Sachs • 2007
René Descartes: Discourse on Method • R. Kennington, P. Kraus & F. Hunt • 2007

Cover image by Wendy Braithwaite

ISBN 10: 1-58510-299-0
ISBN 13: 978-1-58510-299-0

This book is published by Focus Publishing, R. Pullins Company, PO Box 369, Newburyport MA 01950.

10 9 8 7 6 5 4 3 2 1 0

0908TS

CONTENTS

INTRODUCTION

There is a widespread belief that the teachings of Plato and Aristotle on most if not all subjects are opposites. A famous image at the center of a famous painting depicts the two philosophers locking eyes with stern expressions as the one points up and the other spreads his hand in a level gesture over the earth. The supposition that anything written by one of these authors will be arguing for an opinion at the opposite extreme from whatever the other has said on the same subject can become a principle of interpretation, invariably confirming the judgment the interpreter has made in advance about the relation between Platonic and Aristotelian teachings. This approach to interpretation rests, of course, on the further presupposition that one comes to one author already understanding the other. All in all, it is an interpretive strategy that never arrives anywhere except at the spot on which the interpreter is already standing, facing Raphael's highly perspectival painting of the *School of Athens* from the apex of an isosceles triangle, just far enough away to see its symmetrical balance without being able to put it into any larger framework. This book has been brought into being in the conviction that more can be learned from Plato and Aristotle when one wanders off that conventional standpoint and tries out other points of view.

The writings of the two philosophers on rhetoric offer a useful example of the way the thinking of Aristotle is related to that of Plato. The *Gorgias* is a famous attack on rhetoric, and the *Rhetoric* contains a classic defense of it. The situation is similar to that involving poetry, and tragic poetry in particular, which Socrates attacks in Plato's *Republic* and Aristotle defends in the *Poetics*. But the *Republic* is large and complex, and one must come to terms with the way the criticisms of poetry fit into its whole intention. The *Gorgias*, though, is focused on rhetoric just as much as is the work of Aristotle that bears that name, and the pair of works is clearly a conversation. The fourth word of the *Rhetoric*, following those that mean "Rhetoric is a," is taken from the *Gorgias*, and the sentence ends with a direct denial of the corresponding claim made there by Socrates. As the *Gorgias* begins by setting up a confrontation of Gorgias by Socrates, the *Rhetoric* begins by setting up a confrontation of Plato by Aristotle. But some confrontations are quarrels and some are not. We need to look beneath the surfaces of the two writings before we can understand exactly what the one is attacking and the other defending. When we do, I suggest we will find more continuity than contention between the two authors. The discussion in the *Gorgias* of what is wrong with rhetoric is always pointing to the question of what makes it right, and that is the question Aristotle takes up.

But why, in the first place, is rhetoric a subject worthy of serious philosophic attention? A glance at the literary forerunners of Plato and Aristotle may bring to sight an answer that would extend beyond literature and beyond the century and country in which they worked and wrote. Behind them and their readers stands, first of all, the first work of western literature, the poem that was often said to have educated Greece. Homer's *Iliad* is thought to have been written about four centuries before the time of Plato, and is set long before that in the Trojan war; it contains a long and elaborate presentation of the participants who came from all over the known world to fight that war. But the characters in the poem are not introduced until after we have seen those on the Greek side interacting, and that interaction is predominantly of a certain kind. Homer begins the introductory "catalogue of ships" in the middle of Book II, and in the thousand or so lines that precede it, I count no less no less than seven separate occasions when some speaker addresses an appeal of some kind to some group of others. A priest asks a favor from the assembled Greek army; they assent but their commander turns it down. A prominent and powerful warrior calls an assembly that leads to a lasting division within the army. One of the lesser deities on Olympus makes an appeal that averts a similar division among the gods. A council of chieftains called by the Greek commander-in-chief is followed by another assembly of the whole army to test its resolve to stay and fight. In the chaos that ensues, one resourceful leader restores order by running around to exhort the other commanders to hold their men together, then by reassembling all the men, and in this seventh gathering one of the speakers is the most despised man in the ranks of foot-soldiers who has no hesitation about attacking the character and motives of his commanders. There is no democracy in the *Iliad*, where the ordering of political authority is the farthest thing from it, but there is more than one king, and even among their own people Homer's kings listen to the arguments of those who rise to make those arguments in public.

The *Iliad* had a great influence on the self-understanding of its Greek hearers for centuries to come. A character in the *Gorgias* quotes the *Iliad* (458D) without having to name either the poem or its author, to add weight to his claim that manly excellence is displayed in public life, where skill at speaking is indispensable. And Aeschylus's *Oresteia*, the only complete tragic trilogy that has come down to us from ancient Greece, depicts the resolution of a bloody cycle of private murders by the establishment of a court of law, where the supreme power will forever be Persuasion, personified as the goddess Peitho (*Eumenides* 885, 971). In Thucydides' *History of the Peloponnesian War*, the recreated speeches play a larger role in letting the reader draw conclusions about what happened than do the reconstructions of events. Whether ruled monarchically, oligarchically, democratically, or in some mixed form, every city involved in the conflict is shown making and reassessing decisions by listening to speeches. The eighth book of Thucydides' work was never completed, and a reader whose expectations have been formed by the previous seven books may find it unsatisfactory as history; it is full of events but contains no speeches. The common life of the Greeks, as we see and feel it in these prominent works of poetry and prose, gives a central place to speaking that is organized, persuasive, and public.

But is this predilection for giving and hearing speeches merely a peculiarity of a particular place and time? The emphasis some writers place on the fact that democracy emerged in ancient Greece may obscure something deeper, more universal, and more revealing. In the writings we possess from ancient Greece, it is possible to see the emergence of political life itself. The most important distinction among human communities is not how many within them rule but how they rule. One place to see something of this is in the first work of what we call history, the *History*, or inquiries, of Herodotus of Halicarnassus. Herodotus traveled in countries east of Greece, and inquired, among other things, into the Persian wars. It was in those wars that Greeks began to discover what they had in common in all their independent cities, when those cities were under a common threat from outside. Xerxes, the Persian emperor who leads the largest invasion of Greece, cannot believe any army of men accustomed to freedom could stand up to the united force of his slaves, fighting under the compulsion of the lash. (VII, 103) He echoes the sentiment of the first Persian emperor, Cyrus, who said he had no fear of any men who gathered in the centers of their cities to tell lies (I, 153), and he was referring both to free market commerce and to the commerce of political speech. But Xerxes' opinion begins to change when his massive and united force confronts a handful of Spartans in a narrow pass at Thermopylae, and he realizes that he has many *anthropoi* but few *andres* (VII, 210), or as David Grene translates it, many men but few *men*. We might think of the distinction as being between human material and humans whose capacities have been formed and put to work. And if the capacity to become fully human remains unrealized among slaves of a despot, perhaps it is the civic institutions in place among the Greeks that make room for it to emerge. When Athena establishes the lawcourt in the *Oresteia*, her explicit purpose is to avoid the despotic rule of a master over slaves (*Eumenides* 696) and replace it with the rule of Persuasion. Herodotus inquires into how and why the Greeks schooled in the latter fashion withstood and drove out a massively superior force of fighters who were not.

It is well known that, in his *Politics*, Aristotle said that a human being is a political animal by nature (1253a 2-3), but what is given by nature can be neglected or thwarted, and may not emerge if it is not cultivated. The social lives of bees and herding animals are present by mere nature, Aristotle goes on in the same passage, because they communicate about what is pleasant and painful. But their communication is not speech, and it is upon speech that he claims political life depends. The power of speech, he says, is what reveals that some things that are pleasant—and that means some things toward which we are led by nature—may not be advantageous, or may not be just. Aristotle claims that it is a shared perception of the good, the advantageous, and the just that constitutes a *polis*, a city that is not a mere hive or herd but a locus of political life. The cities represented in the *Iliad* all have kings, but they are genuine cities by Aristotle's test, because we see the subjects ruled by those kings listening to speeches that refer to the ends to which their common life is a means. The invading hordes ruled by the Great King of Persia appear by contrast to have been forced into subhuman lives.

The making and hearing of speeches, then, are not only prominent features of the place and time in which Plato and Aristotle wrote but activities worthy of attention as common features of human nature, through which people anywhere at any time cultivate one of the highest possibilities of that nature. But we may seem to have answered the wrong question. We asked why philosophic attention was merited by rhetoric. With the necessities of life, with instrumental goods of any kind, the best way of providing them may be a division of labor. A farmer, a carpenter, a weaver may produce better goods with better efficiency by concentrating all his time and effort on one of the things people need, and spare others from paying any attention to it at all. But those goods that consist in activity cannot be farmed out. You will not become fit by paying someone to do your running or walking. And what should we make of the following facts? I have known two people who briefly had jobs doing someone else's reading, one who prepared a "read board" for a general with summaries of articles and reports, and one who wrote summaries and evaluations for a professor of philosophy, of books related to one he was then writing. I found the former fact surprising but understandable and the latter merely depressing. I know people who read more acutely or more imaginatively than I do, but I would never want any of them to do my reading for me. I like hearing them speak about things they have read, but only when I have read them too. There are also certainly people who are better than the rest of us at public speaking, but if that activity is left to them as a specialty or even a profession, may we not be neglecting a matter that ought not to be professionalized? And what exactly is it that such specialists profess to be skilled at doing? Should we regard rhetoric as something that contributes to political life or tends to undermine it?

A simple analogy may shed some light on what may be wrong with misguided professionalism. We all know that some teachers are better at what they do than others are. But what makes them better? Do they have a technique? Some think they do, and they may even claim to have an expertise in pedagogy. I engaged in teaching for some decades, and opinions were mixed about how well or badly I did at it, but I was always made uneasy when others claimed to have any special pedagogical knowledge. Teaching, as distinct from training or instructing, has always seemed to me to be a natural outgrowth of learning. There is no technique for the latter, and the adoption of one for the former undermines its very sources. Learning depends on desire and effort, and those who know learning from the inside, and have kept it alive in themselves, can recognize its beginnings in others in all their unpredictable shapes and try to invite, encourage, and assist them. Pedagogical techniques always seem manipulative to me, as though the learner were some neutral material for the teacher to mold, but anyone who has experienced it knows that learning has to follow its own course and cannot be manipulated. Learning can be coaxed, or stimulated, or inspired, but in such matters one size does not fit all. So the very word "pedagogy" puts me on alert for something that is unlikely to be what it claims to be. Now it happens that this analogy is not original with me, but taken from a more complex analogy Socrates makes in the *Gorgias*. In ancient Greece, those who claimed to be specialists not in some teachable art but in teaching itself were called sophists, and they gave even wisdom a bad name. Socrates says in 465C that a specialization in rhetoric is so much like sophistry that those who practiced them could make no clear distinction of themselves from each other. But their reputations were as different as could be: sophists were looked down on by popular opinion, but rhetoricians carried a certain glamour.

This situation, in which names draw strong public reactions, but the things named are not clearly understood, is in itself worthy of investigation. And when one of those vaguely understood activities claims to be the dominant power in public life, a thoughtful scrutiny of what it is and does might be very much needed. Plato designs the *Gorgias* to display rhetoric as a subject that cannot be understood apart from an inquiry into the human good and as an object of choice that can be no less than a matter of life and death. In the dialogue, Socrates confronts, one after another, three men whose lives are absorbed in rhetorical pursuits, and demands that they articulate what they do and why. Gorgias is an old show-off, an international celebrity who complacently offers to teach people how to dominate their cities with rhetoric. Polus is a younger follower of Gorgias, a cheerleader for rhetoric and for a tyrannical approach to life. Callicles is younger still, on the verge of making life choices, and sold on the possibilities that rhetoric offers. It is the presence of Callicles that brings out the ultimate seriousness of the conversation. This is partly because he does not shy away from bringing all his opinions into the open, but even more the case because of who he is. Nearly all the participants in Plato's dialogues are people who were known to have lived in or visited Athens during the life of Socrates. In a handful of dialogues there are invented characters, such as the unnamed philosopher from Elea who takes the lead in the discussions in the *Sophist* and *Statesman*. But Callicles is presented in the *Gorgias* with a wealth of detail about his friends and the part of town he lives in, and yet he is entirely unknown from any other source. The likeliest explanation for this anomaly seems to me to be that he was someone known to Plato who entered political life in Athens with exactly those brutal aims he announces in the dialogue, and that he did not live long enough to accomplish any of them.

If this interpretation of Callicles' fate is correct, then Plato's contemporary readers would have been aware of a background to the dialogue that would enhance its tone of seriousness. The effect would be comparable to the dramatic framing of the *Theaetetus* as a conversation recounted while Theaetetus was dying. But the fact of Callicles' early and helpless death would reflect badly on his confidence in the power of rhetoric without providing confirmation of anything for which Socrates criticizes it. Polus and Callicles do recommend rhetoric as an art of self-preservation (473C, 511A-513C), but Socrates does not disagree with that assessment; what he argues is that the way a life is lived matters more than how long it lasts. The explicit criticism Socrates makes of rhetoric is that it panders to the crowd and presupposes that the things that matter most in life are the goods the crowd approves of and can provide. Buying into rhetoric, according to Socrates, ultimately means buying into a conception of a tyrannical life as the highest to which a human being can aspire. Gorgias and Polus are content to stand on the sidelines of politics, to enable and applaud those who adopt tyrannical goals, but Callicles is deadly serious about pursuing such a life. And if Callicles is a figure brought before us to display the potentially fatal consequences of a commitment to a certain kind of life, his outcome has to be paired with that of Socrates, whose manner of dying was, and is, well known to every reader of the dialogue, ancient and modern. Plato shows Socrates to us in the *Apology*, refusing to play to the crowd in the trial for his life, in the *Crito*, refusing to escape from prison when his friends had it all arranged, and in the *Phaedo*, accepting his death without complaint after spending his last day in philosophic conversation. The *Gorgias* brings together two men who apparently died the way they chose to live.

But the original confrontation and pairing in the dialogue is of Socrates with Gorgias, and it is this juxtaposition that brings to sight a deeper level of Socrates' opposition to rhetoric. The central claims of the dialogue may be said to revolve around the singular and plural forms of a single word. Gorgias announces that what he has a knowledge of and a power over are speeches, *logoi* (449E), and shortly thereafter (453C) Socrates begins to pound away at the singular of that word, as he says over and over again that what he wants to do and they need to do is to follow the *logos* where it leads. In this translation, that word is translated as *speech* even when "argument" or some other choice might fit the context more smoothly. In his conversation with Gorgias, Socrates does everything he can to let us recognize that we have a choice between thinking of speech as an instrument of coercion that we control, or a power of the revelation of meaning that we can follow. The criticism implied by this alternative may appear unrelated to the charge of pandering, but the two have much in common. The speaker who plays to the crowd accepts their opinions and preferences as governing his interaction with them, and has to assimilate himself to his audience by giving at least the appearance of sharing them. The speaker who believes himself to be superior to the crowd, and to be manipulating them by manipulating words, has made the assumption that his own opinions need no exploration or revision. In neither attitude is the rhetorician open to discovering anything about the things he speaks about. In neither way of using speeches is speech regarded as the medium through which understanding comes into being. Socrates' deepest criticism of rhetoric is that it is a perversion of our relation to the power of speech.

But we noted earlier the argument in Aristotle's *Politics* to the effect that the human power of speech is what makes our cities more than herds or hives. At least potentially, our political life is an opportunity for a common understanding of the good, the advantageous, and the just to be achieved. What Aristotle says the political life of every city in fact rests on is a common perception (*aisthesis*) of those things. But could rhetoric play a role in allowing a community to advance in its common understanding of the perceived goals of its common life? Again, Socrates makes a shift in the meaning of a word that says more about the possible uses of rhetoric than do his explicit arguments. Explicitly, his discussion with Polus leads to the conclusion that there is little or no use for rhetoric among decent people who are not trying to get away with anything dishonest (481B), but the way he goes about discussing it shows such a use. From the very beginning of the dialogue, the word everyone chooses for what Gorgias does is *epideiknunai*: he makes displays. But when Socrates has been talking for a while with Polus, who attempts to ridicule him and tell him that no one agrees with him, Socrates asks him to stop doing those things and instead to display to him that he is wrong (467C). Polus is unable to oblige, and the word drops out of the dialogue, never to be used again. But with all three of the men he argues with, Socrates is continually displaying evidence from their own words that suggests they are wrong. It is a common remark of readers that in the *Gorgias* Socrates himself becomes a rhetorician, because he eventually drops his usual question-and-answer style, and makes long and sometimes impassioned speeches. But he never drops his characteristic way of pursuing the implications of other people's statements. One can follow the *logos* not only for the sake of one's own understanding, but to display connections of thought that another person might be obliged to recognize, and one can put these on display for any audience that might be present.

It would seem to be a stretch to call Socrates' exploration of the implications of the words of others rhetorical, but there is at least enough affinity and overlap between the two uses of speech to allow a reader to measure rhetorical practices by comparison with Socratic ones. But Socrates himself raises the possibility of a rhetoric that would be the extreme opposite of the prevalent one, and that form of it he certainly does practice. The word he uses for pandering is *kolakeia,* servile flattery used by someone who wants to get something advantageous to himself out of others who have what he wants. Its opposite would be authoritative rebuke, used by someone who wants to provide something advantageous to another person. This is not the sort of thing Socrates usually does, but he does it with Polus and Callicles. The word for discipline, for corrective restraint or punishment, is *kolasis*, and forms of it are used frequently when Socrates speaks to and about those two men. And with those two, Socrates at times abandons his usual protestations that he knows nothing, and makes emphatic pronouncements that he knows better than they do what is good for them. He adopts a form of rhetoric we are all familiar with, used by parents and judges who are trying to persuade children or criminals that their punishment is for their own good. It might be called kolastic rhetoric. If the prevalent, pandering or kolakic rhetoric is meant to be seductive or wheedling, the kolastic variety is instead like a splash of cold water in the face. It would seem that its utility is limited, but Socrates offers it as the standard for judging political leaders. In a passage beginning at 515C, Socrates argues that there has been no example, not even Pericles, of an Athenian politician who used rhetoric to make the citizens better. Callicles takes this claim almost as fighting words (515E), and since Socrates clearly intends to provoke such a reaction, this is itself an instance of kolastic rhetoric.

Now Socrates is setting the bar for political rhetoric very high. He is demanding not only that a politician not pander to the crowd but that he go to the opposite extreme to discipline it. And he judges the politicians of the past not by any worthwhile policies they may have pursued, but solely by whether they left their fellow citizens better human beings than they found them. Even by these standards, Pericles would not have been judged a complete failure by everyone. Thucydides sums him up as a leader who did restrain the multitude as long as he was alive, and could speak to them in ways that did not please them but made them angry. (*Pelopponesian War*, II, 65) But Thucydides also presents a funeral oration in which Pericles reveals what he considered good citizenship to be. He tells the Athenians that there is no shame in being poor as long as one is trying to get rich, and urges them to keep their eyes on their city's power and develop a lust for it. (II, 40, 43) He encourages them to take as their right the imperial supremacy that allowed them to enjoy the good things that flowed into their city from all over the world. (II, 38) Thucydides does not comment directly on the assumptions underlying Pericles' rhetoric, but he places immediately following the funeral speech an account of a plague that Athens suffered a few months later, an epidemic that was deadly to vast numbers and devastating as well to the characters of the people who survived; and Thucydides points out that the plague flowed north from upper Egypt and into Athens through its port. (II, 48) Socrates says that Pericles neglected the temperance and justice of the citizens, and "filled the city up with harbors and shipyards and walls and tribute and nonsense like that." (519A) Virtues of character would have given the people a better defense against misfortune than all the money and power in the world, and it is not likely that Thucydides would have disagreed with Socrates about that. But Thucydides compares Pericles to those who came after him, and gives him credit for a moderating influence they lacked.

But Socrates claims that he himself is the only man of his time to have a beneficial role in political life (521D). So how well does he fare by his own standards? He, like Pericles, is clearly willing at times to tell an Athenian audience things it does not want to hear, and in his case one can point to people who believe he has made their lives better. At the beginning of Plato's *Symposium*, for example, a certain Apollodorus gives Socrates credit for having transformed his life for the better, though at the end of the same dialogue we have a glimpse of the undisciplined life led by Alcibiades, whose disastrous effect on Athens was blamed by many on Socrates' failure to transform him.

But a more interesting instance might be Plato, who turned a talent for writing toward philosophic ends as a result of hearing Socrates speak to others. Socrates spoke in public, but his speech was directed almost always toward one person at a time. It is hard enough to tell what lasting effect he had on anyone we see encountering him in a dialogue and impossible to know what his words might have initiated in the soul of any silent listener. But we do have a succession of people to whom he speaks about rhetoric in the *Gorgias*, in a context in which it is impossible not to think of his words as having a rhetorical aspect, and we can see something of what he is doing by comparing the ways he speaks to them. There is no question that Socrates handles the three men very differently, and it is clear that all three are aware that they are in public and that the listeners will be judging them by the way they stand up to his challenges. Each of the three becomes a public advocate of some kind—Gorgias advising a course of action as advantageous, Polus praising an activity as the most beautiful of human pursuits, and Callicles accusing Socrates of spreading opinions that pervert justice—and all three end up having to defend themselves. We shall see when we discuss Aristotle's *Rhetoric* that the *Gorgias* gives us a display of the three main objects rhetoric seeks to be persuasive about, those that are ordinarily considered in public assemblies, on ceremonial occasions, and in courtrooms. In the dialogue there is no such formal occasion that calls for speakers to defend or attack any opinion. Wherever Socrates goes, a conversation breaks out, some issue worth thinking about is brought into focus, and those who are in earshot gather to listen.

The conversations Socrates engages in are always dialectical, in the sense that they follow up the presuppositions and consequences of the other person's stated opinions, and always philosophic, in that they expose the need for opinions to be grounded in ultimate convictions and for actions to be guided by ultimate ends, about which all human beings need to inquire, and his conversations in the *Gorgias* are no exceptions. And a rhetorical component is never absent from Socrates' conversations, at least in the sense that he suits the level of the discussion to the abilities of the other person; in the *Theaetetus*, for instance, Theaetetus is taken through intricate arguments while Theodorus is engaged on a more chatty, sometimes even gossipy, level. The way Socrates talks in the *Gorgias* is distinctive only in that three such conversations take place side by side while questions about rhetoric are directly in front of everyone who speaks and listens. And Socrates often engages in mild flattery, though not of a servile kind and not for any advantage to himself but to turn the other person's vanity to use in persuading him to pursue an argument; he does this with Gorgias in 449D, with Polus in 473A, and with Callicles in 487A-B. If a good use of rhetoric is on display in the *Gorgias*, it is nothing other than Socrates' usual mode of conversation, and it lies between the two extremes we have called kolakic and kolastic. It neither wheedles nor browbeats. Socrates can draw someone forward without pandering to him, and pull someone back without rebuking him. The power, of both attraction and compulsion, that Socrates taps into has its source in the *logos*.

We noted earlier that the deepest criticism Socrates makes of the rhetoric of Gorgias is that it perverts our relation to the power of speech. If this observation is correct, then we would expect the rhetoric practiced by Socrates himself to straighten out that relation. Gorgias thinks of speeches as the contents of a toolbox, or box of tricks, by which he makes other people his slaves (452E). We do not have to rely on the accuracy of Plato's portrayal to know this. We possess two complete speeches of Gorgias, one of which, the *Encomium of Helen*, speaks directly about rhetoric in a passage alluded to in the dialogue (483E). In it, Gorgias says that persuasive speakers mold speech into deceptions of opinion and perversions of the soul in their listeners. Socrates, we have seen, repeatedly urges the alternative of following the *logos* "in order that it might move forward in a way that would make whatever is being spoken of evident to us as much as possible." (453C) Even Gorgias, once he is off the hot seat and Polus or Callicles is on it, wants to see where the speech that has emerged will lead (463D-E, 497B, 506A-B). The *logos* that unites speaker and listener and underlies human language is not merely logic, though it includes logical relations. It includes content also, the intelligible meaning of things that are said, which can become more evident if they are unfolded. It is often said that when Socrates asks a question such as "What is rhetoric?" he is looking for a definition, but his interest is not in a word or in any formulation of its meaning. It is the thing named that is the matter of concern. Any articulation of it that is discussed is for the sake of revealing to the participants in the conversation more than they saw when they named it. The formal definitions of rhetoric that Socrates offers in the dialogue, that it is pandering to the ignorant, a simulation of a part of politics, a counterpart for the soul of cooking tasty food, and so on, are merely starting points of a *logos* that moves beyond them to make something entirely different evident.

But if what Socrates did was simply to take an opinion stated by another person, reason from it, and display evidence for what something is, his turn to the *logos* would leave behind the human interaction out of which it began. We hear in the *Symposium* from two of his companions that Socrates sometimes turned his thoughts inward for as long as twenty-four hours at a time (175B, 220C-D), and we have a brief glimpse in the *Theaetetus* (192A-D) of Socrates as he runs through seventeen logical possibilities so rapidly that a young man skilled in mathematics cannot follow him. But the consistent and overwhelming picture in Plato's dialogues shows Socrates to us always talking to someone in particular, and always trying *not* to leave that person behind. Socrates turns to the *logos* determined to take along with him others who may be unready or unwilling to go along. The causes of that resistance are varied and they can have great strength; the task of Socratic rhetoric is to find and overcome them. The question we considered earlier of whether Socrates has made anyone a better person may now be sharpened to the question of whether he has made anyone begin to inquire about anything he does not know, which may in turn require making him see that there is something important he does not know; in the *Meno* (86B-C), Socrates declares, as a conviction he would fight for, that anyone who makes any step in that direction is already, by that very fact, a better person. The aim of Socrates in the dialogues is never to teach something by making evident the reasons for believing it, but to move some particular person toward doing that for himself. Socratic rhetoric is the taking up of the challenge Socrates makes to Polus (467C): *epideixon hoti pseudomai*, "show me that I'm wrong."

Now the arguments Socrates makes are always interesting in ways that transcend their immediate occasions, partly because we see something of ourselves in those he argues with, or at least feel a resistance of our own to what he is saying, and partly because we want to refute those others and do not know how to do so. A mixture of contradictory motives in these matters is not uncommon. And at times one of Socrates' arguments may be almost entirely detachable from its context. Some of the arguments in the *Gorgias* to the effect that neither power nor pleasure is good in itself have a universality and rigor that cannot be denied. But the presuppositions of such arguments are always open to challenge, and Socrates in one way or another always seeks to provoke those challenges. There is always an example that doesn't quite fit, a supporting argument with a dubious premise, or a conclusion stated in an extreme or even outrageous form. The structure of the *Gorgias* is built on Socrates' failed attempts to get first Gorgias, then Polus, to try to say what is wrong with his arguments, attempts which finally succeed in provoking that response from Callicles. Socrates' goal is not to make his arguments conclusive or even persuasive, but to make them impossible to ignore, and the best way to do that is to make them hit close to home.

The particular aspect of rhetoric that Gorgias emphasizes is the mastery it gives him, over speech and over people. What Socrates does with him is to put him, gently but firmly, into a position in which he cannot fail to see his own helplessness. In a long and successful rhetorical career in which he has not encountered for many years a question which he had not handled before (448A), Gorgias seems never to have acquired the habit of spotting flaws in an argument and constructing a counter-argument. At any rate, in the stretch of dialogue from 460A to 461B, Gorgias's contributions become hesitant, brief, uncertain, and finally nonexistent. Polus steps in to defend Gorgias, but the aspect of rhetoric *he* has emphasized from the first has been that it is the most beautiful of human activities (448C), and the focus of Socrates' arguments shifts with this change of partners in the discussion. Socrates' elaborate presentation of the array of arts and counterfeit arts that minister to and pander to the body and the soul is in fact built on the fundamental example of fostering beauty. Those who spoil themselves with an unhealthy diet and a lack of exercise depend on a cosmetic art to display the illusion of a beauty they do not possess (465B), and rhetoric is defined by its place in an analogy between body and soul. Polus's response is that the reputation of rhetoricians matches that of tyrants (466C), and Socrates' arguments with him then focus on getting him to acknowledge that the activities of tyrants are ugly things. Polus himself paints the ugliest of pictures of what can happen to someone who attempts to gain a tyranny and fails (473C), and this picture seems to stay with him and govern his response when he unhesitatingly replies that doing injustice, while better than suffering it, is an uglier thing (474C). One of Socrates' later arguments, to the effect that the same attributes must belong to both the infliction and the suffering of any action (476B-D), may not have universal validity, but Polus's own graphic description of tortures that are ugly to suffer seems to taint his earlier praise of rhetoricians for having the tyrannical power to kill and rob whomever they please. The issue at stake is not a matter of logical inconsistency but of whether Polus on reflection really wants the things that have so far seemed good to him (466D-E). He has wanted to have the power of a tyrant in a sanitized and civilized form, and Socrates gives him a chance to see that more clearly.

It is Callicles who makes the strongest and most sustained counterattack on behalf of rhetoric, and the aspect of it that he singles out most of all is its manliness. He speaks the first words of the dialogue, and they are a playful accusation that Socrates is a coward. By the time he makes his long speech in the middle of the dialogue, he has stopped playing and his accusation that Socrates is unmanly is explicit (485D). Natural justice, he argues, demands that the manliest men should rule (491B) for the sake of nothing but their own unrestrained enjoyment of pleasure (491E-492A). He is confident that he has life all figured out, but his tone begins to change when Socrates' arguments have made him look at the question of whether it is the manly or the cowardly men on a battlefield who are more devoted to pleasure. His reply is made contemptuously (499B), but that cannot disguise the fact that he has given up ground at the heart of his defenses. Once Socrates has compared rhetoric to swimming or piloting a ship, menial skills for saving lives without regard to the worth or worthlessness of those lives, he confesses in a wondering tone to being partly persuaded (513C). The crucial moment for Callicles seems to me to arrive when Socrates asks him once again if he is still recommending the servile pandering that the rhetoric he is advocating requires. In a burst of angry honesty, Callicles says, in effect, I don't care if you call it by the unmanliest of names, I still see no other means to survive in a turbulent political environment (521B). In the rhetorical contest over rhetoric, the scales have tipped at that moment, and the dispute itself has drawn even. By accepting the name Mysian, the name of a race considered to be the least manly in the world, Callicles has not only abandoned the claim of manliness on which all his arguments were based, he has also said the matter is too important to be treated rhetorically. Along the way, Callicles has been shown that pleasures are always measured by some standard other than pleasure, and at the end of the line he himself is insisting that rhetoric be judged by speech that is not rhetorical. Call it by any name you please, he says, color it with any appeal to disapproval, but tell me how else to live in Athens.

Now at such a moment one might expect Socrates to deliver a knockout punch of some sort, but that would be appropriate only if he were competing for victory or trying to impose some opinion on others. What he does is admit that his own life is by no means secure in Athens, claim that he is undisturbed by that fact, and then tell a myth about an afterlife. An inexperienced reader of Plato might conclude that everything Socrates has said rests on a faith in a supernatural reward. A more experienced reader will notice that Socrates tells many such myths, and that they all differ in what they describe. In the *Phaedo* (61B), he says he is no teller of myths (*muthologikos*), but he tells an elaborate one of his own invention later in the dialogue, before concluding that no one with any sense would insist things were really that way (114D). In the *Phaedrus* he says he believes all the commonly accepted myths because it is not worth his time to quarrel with them, since the only thing he really wants to understand is what kind of being he himself is (229E-230A); later in that dialogue, Phaedrus tells him he makes up mythical stories at the drop of a hat and pretends they are things he has heard (275B). Socrates mythologizes with the lightest touch imaginable, making the ultimate destiny of the human soul the subject of an assortment of disposable and replaceable narratives. We can take them or leave them or hold them in the imagination as things that are neither true nor false. Telling a myth can be a way of making invisible things visible; what is envisioned can offer confirmation of something one has already "seen" in the understanding, or it can invite an effort to understand as a way of getting the point. And paradoxically, even when it is not taken as literal truth, a myth can inspire action. For this reason, Jacob Klein, in *A Commentary on Plato's Meno* (University of North Carolina Press, 1965, p. 171), has written that "Myth-telling is indeed the paradigm of all rhetorical art."

The myth Socrates tells in the *Gorgias*, unlike any of his other pictures of an afterlife, and almost certainly unlike any myth any other human being has ever conceived, presents the place of the last judgment of souls as a gymnasium. It was the custom of the Greeks to exercise naked, and the analogy to the conversation that has just unfolded in the *Gorgias* is evident enough. It is emphasized throughout the discussion with Callicles that opinions are being stated with all the conventional disguises of shame and politeness stripped away (487B, 492D), and that the people who are stating them are themselves being exposed to judgment (514D-515C). To the listeners surrounding Socrates and Callicles, and to the readers of the dialogue, this myth is like an epilogue that universalizes what the preceding conversation has put on display, and does so not by interpreting it for us but by offering it up in a rhetorical image. But we have all along been looking at Socratic rhetoric as something designed for, and addressed to, the one person Socrates is speaking to, and from that perspective it appears to be the worst rhetorical tactic anyone would ever think of choosing for Callicles. In 493A-494A, Socrates has already tried out a little myth-telling on Callicles that met with nothing but disdain, and Socrates says at the end of his long final myth that he expects Callicles to dismiss it as the sort of thing old women say (527A). If a man has declared that the source of the highest praise he knows how to give is manliness, why would someone who clearly has some rhetorical adroitness address him the way an old woman would? The answer seems to me to be found in a brilliant suggestion made by a late colleague of mine, Hugh McGrath. The final display that Socrates leaves Callicles with is the picture of Socrates himself as a man brave enough to stand up in public and endorse the sort of things that old women tell children. Callicles has already been stung by the accusation that his concern for saving his own skin above all else is unmanly. He now has the opportunity to see an image of a manliness he never imagined. If he sees it, it cannot fail to reflect on his image of himself, and that could lead to some radical rethinking of his firmest opinions. There can never be any assurance that anyone led to the brink of such questioning will undertake it, and in the case of Callicles we have seen reasons to suspect that he never did, but a failure at that stage cannot be blamed on anyone but himself. Socratic rhetoric has done everything that could be done to get him headed in that direction.

The *Gorgias*, then, contains an attack on one sort of rhetoric, a recommendation of another sort, and a display of yet a third. It attacks the prostitution of speech to pander to a crowd for ulterior motives of the speaker, recommends the coercive use of speech to impose discipline on a person or a city, and displays the use of speech tailored to the predispositions of a single hearer to invite and provoke that hearer to follow the *logos* on his own. What we have not yet addressed here is the question of what is common to the three activities that makes us recognize them all as varieties of one species that we have unceremoniously been calling rhetoric. The dialogue seems to me to offer us the means to answer this question in the central distinction between speeches and speech itself. It may seem at first to support Socrates' claims that all rhetoric is inherently bad, and to suggest that this is because it is not a disinterested pursuit of understanding. This might in turn suggest that rhetoric is the making of speeches devoid of all rational content. It surely looks that way when we witness Gorgias's inability to offer even the slightest argument in favor of the claims he asserts. And Polus gives us no grounds to abandon that view as he attempts to support his claims by invoking the weight of popular opinion, conjuring up the image of pain and death, and heaping ridicule on anyone who disagrees with him, tactics that Socrates points out at 471E, 473D, and 473E. Gorgias and Polus have their conclusions and seem to expect to be able to persuade people of them by means other than argument. Gorgias in fact takes this view of rhetoric to be a compliment to his skill. It makes life a lot easier if one can persuade people by means of gimmicks, without having to take the trouble to learn or understand anything (459C). Now the elimination of *all* rational content from a speech would be impossible. Gorgias speaks in intelligible sentences, and he uses the particle *gar* the way all his contemporaries do, to assert that one sentence or clause gives a reason for what is said in the preceding one. But if his reasoning is more apparent than real, and still persuasive, his own power must surpass that which is the common human lot (456A). Gorgias is not only willing but proud to represent that extreme at which speeches are completely divorced from the rational power of speech itself.

Callicles' long speech at 482C-486D, with its distinction between arguments from nature and arguments from convention, presents an understanding of things that seems to go beyond anything found in the speeches Gorgias and Polus make, but the difference may again be more apparent than real. To support his own claims about natural justice, Callicles does not use arguments at all, but historical examples (483D-E), a vivid image, and quotations from Pindar and Euripides (484B, E). Xerxes and Darius and Heracles took whatever they wanted, and that made it right for them to have it, he says. But the examples can have no effect unless the audience is familiar with them, and those who pause for even a moment to recollect them will notice that Xerxes and Darius did not succeed in getting what they wanted in the instances Callicles cites, and Heracles did not want what he got, but had to get it for someone else. Zethus, a character in a play by Euripides who chose the manly life of action his brother Amphion rejected, ended up needing his brother's help to hold on to the things they cared about in common. This superficial use of examples that show something entirely different from what he is claiming must mean that Callicles has not considered it worth his while to think through any reasons for his conclusions. Between his historical and poetic examples he puts an image of a young lion that throws off all restraints of law and convention, to make his conception of natural justice "shine forth" with an immediacy that needs no argument to justify it. But again his rhetoric may show something he did not intend. Any of his contemporaries, presented with an image of a marauding lion, would be likely to think of a famous simile of a lion that appears twice in the *Iliad* (XI, 547-556; XVII, 657-666). Homer's lion is powerful in its strength and in its desire, but it is no match for the weaker dogs and country folk who cannot kill it, but can protect their cattle from it all night; it goes away at dawn having accomplished no single thing that it desired, with a heart filled with nothing but regrets. The sorrowful lion, that cannot understand why it could not, for all its strength, fulfill any of its desires, may in the end be a pitiful image of Callicles' own life. The roar of his rhetoric is ferocious, but no one will ever use him as an example of a man who saw what he wanted and got it.

There seems to be no denying that in the *Gorgias* it is Socrates' rhetoric alone that is potent, or that it draws its effectiveness from combining rather than separating the rational and non-rational elements in speech. Socrates claims to want to persuade those with whom he speaks that it is better to suffer injustice than to do it, that happiness is possible only in an orderly life and never in the life of a tyrant, and that political life cannot flourish unless it is grounded in philosophy. He does not persuade any of them of any of those things, but he does show them that they do not know how to show that those opinions are wrong (509A, 527A-B). If we get absorbed in the dialogue, Plato may be able to show us the same thing. The purpose of the dialogue is not to drive home any of the points Socrates asserts, but to show Socrates to us as he shows things to others. The arguments are the heart of the rhetoric of both Socrates and Plato, and those arguments will succeed at their rhetorical task only if they are not good enough to demonstrate their conclusions but too good to be dismissed. Their complete rhetorical success would mean that someone turned to the pursuit of philosophy, but they are still successful if all they do is make people a little more moderate and thoughtful, a little less sure of what they thought they knew, and a little more inclined to reflect on the ends they are seeking. Thucydides tells us that Pericles was able to exert a moderating influence on the Athenian people as long as he was alive, but that he had no lasting effect on them. If Socratic rhetoric has a moderating influence, it is one that takes root in the people around him and grows only in his absence. And since Plato practices the same rhetorical restraint, the same refusal to settle things for anyone else, that Socratic influence has maintained some of its power through all the centuries between his time and ours.

The Socratic rhetoric we witness in the *Gorgias* is of a very specific kind, and its aims are for the long term. Plato practiced it, and some teachers may do so, but does its example get us anywhere in thinking about the ordinary uses of rhetoric that happen all the time? We noted earlier that Aristotle identifies the kinds of places where rhetoric is typically used as three: courtrooms, public assemblies, and ceremonial gatherings. In the first two, decisions need to be made on the spot, and in the third, most audiences want the speaker to do the work and finish it on the spot. Having a lasting effect, large or small, on the members of the audience is not the principal aim, which is simply to persuade people to adopt one opinion in preference to another for long enough to conclude the business at hand in the way the speaker thinks best. But the way Socratic rhetoric does its job is by making arguments primary, and using them to show something to others, and this *is* possible in all the customary places rhetoric is used. And according to Aristotle in the first chapter of his *Rhetoric*, this is the one and only thing that is intrinsic to the rhetorical art. In the first words of that work, Aristotle declares that rhetoric is a counterpart of dialectic; this is a pointed replacement of Socrates' assertion that rhetoric is the counterpart of the sort of cooking that panders to childish bodily tastes. But that shift is one that Socrates himself has tacitly made in the *Gorgias* by showing us a rhetoric with an affinity to dialectic. Aristotle begins his *Rhetoric* not by rejecting the *Gorgias* but by taking up where it leaves off.

Aristotle does take an adversary position in the first chapter of the *Rhetoric*, but his opponent is not Plato or Socrates but the whole array of earlier books on rhetoric *other* than the *Gorgias*. There were apparently many such books, for which Aristotle uses the generic title *Art of Speeches* (*technê tôn logôn*). Socrates uses the same phrase in Plato's *Phaedrus*, and makes fun of these books and their authors (260D, 261B-D, 266D-267E), who include Gorgias, Polus, and the Thrasymachus who appears in the *Republic*. Socrates says in the *Phaedrus* that a speech needs to have a body, like a living thing, and Aristotle declares in the first chapter of his *Rhetoric* that the body of persuasion is made up of arguments. His complaint about the earlier treatises is that they provide no part of the art of rhetoric but only its accessories, the secondary matters of arousing prejudice and passion. Aristotle discusses such matters himself at length in the *Rhetoric*, as factors that influence the way a speech and its speaker are received, but all as means to the end which governs all persuasive speaking, the *showing* of something as factual or true, or at least as worthy of belief (1354a 26-28, 1356a 1-20). Like Socrates in the *Gorgias*, Aristotle considers the rhetoric Gorgias and Polus practise and teach to be no art at all. Like Socrates in the *Gorgias*, Aristotle says that a rhetorician cannot achieve his end solely by manipulating feelings, but needs to show evidence for a conclusion.

The word Aristotle chooses for the showing that is the one central task of rhetoric is *deixis*. It marks out a range that lies between two extremes: the *epideixis* characteristic of Gorgias, a showiness that makes an empty display, and the *apodeixis* characteristic of mathematics, reasoning that demonstrates something rigorously and conclusively. Rhetoric has rational content but cannot have proof, and this according to Aristotle is what defines it, by analogy to and contrast with dialectic. The notion of dialectic is prefigured in the *Gorgias* when Socrates contrasts rhetoric with having a conversation (*dialegesthai*) to find out what something is (448E). In the *Phaedrus*, Socrates describes an extension of that conversational process into an art of finding the natural distinctions among things, the way a good butcher carves a body at its natural joints, and he says that a dialectical preparation of that sort would be needed to make rhetoric an art (265D-266C). Aristotle devotes the work called the *Topics* to dialectic, which he takes to be strict and rigorous reasoning that is not demonstration because it does not proceed from self-evident starting points. It reasons from opinions that are accepted by many people or by eminent thinkers, in order to test them, and it makes secure progress toward knowledge either by rejecting those opinions through a process of elimination, or by establishing them on some firm and clear basis. Aristotle's own theoretical works, such as the *Metaphysics*, the *Physics*, and *On the Soul*, are works of dialectic, ascending in stages from commonly held popular and philosophic opinions to secure an understanding of the way things are. Dialectic itself, as explored in the *Topics*, is the study of the kinds of arguments that can show the way from opinion toward the starting points of knowledge.

In calling rhetoric a counterpart (*antistrophos*) of dialectic, Aristotle means that the two are analogous activities. In the performance of a tragedy, one stanza of a choral ode, the strophe, is chanted by a chorus as it dances across the stage, and it is followed by an antistrophe, a stanza with the same number of lines, in the same metric pattern, sung as the chorus dances the same steps again the other way across the stage. In the *Gorgias*, when Socrates lays out a two-by-two array of arts that minister to the body and soul to promote or restore a healthy condition, with a corresponding array of types of pandering, he uses the word *antistrophos* for one of the match-ups within the second array. What Aristotle matches up are the tools used in dialectical reasoning with a whole array of rhetorical counterparts: dialectic uses syllogisms and induction, based on necessary or contingent premises, while rhetoric uses enthymemes and examples, based on likelihoods and signs (1356b 10-11, 1357a 30-33). What makes them different is that, while dialectic reasons from opinions, it reasons with strict necessity about matters that admit of knowledge, but rhetoric reasons about things that must remain matters of opinion always, because they inherently admit of going different ways (1357a 24, 35-36). This is in part because the past and future matters of fact judged by juries and political assemblies can never be fully known (1356b 32-33), in part because the general notions about the advantageous, the just, and the beautiful shared by the communities of human beings who seek those ends are variable. They cannot be determined by experts, and must be agreed upon by people who do not have the leisure to develop the skill of following long or complex arguments (1357a 1-4). Rhetoric, according to Aristotle, is an outgrowth of dialectic into politics (1356a 25-27). The dialectical pursuit of the things that are knowable about politics, such as the advantages and disadvantages of the various forms of government, is contained in the work he calls the *Politics*, but the content of political life, all the things that must be argued about every day by the human beings who live in political communities, because such things can never be definitively settled, can be studied as well, in a manner analogous to dialectic, and that study is the heart of what Aristotle means by the art of rhetoric.

The *Rhetoric* is not, as is sometimes said, a manual for winning arguments. It is a preparatory exploration of the things one would need to show in order to make persuasive arguments about the common concerns of practical life. Before one can show anything, one must see it, and recognize its aptness to the purpose, and therefore Aristotle calls rhetoric a power of *theorein*, of recognizing or beholding (1355b 25-26). In the full and strict sense of *theoria*, or contemplative knowing, Aristotle recognizes only three kinds of subject matter that have the stability to permit theoretical study: those pursued by metaphysics, physics, and mathematics. But in the same way that rhetoric is dialectical in character without being dialectic, it is also theoretical in character without being contemplative. What rhetoric sees is evidence that makes conclusions persuasive, and this evidence is shown to others by means of arguments that have the same formal structure as syllogisms; Aristotle calls them *enthumêma*. There is no good way to translate *enthumêmon* except as enthymeme, but to the extent this has become an English word it is likely to be misleading. It is usually understood to mean a truncated syllogism, with one premise either lacking or omitted for rhetorical effect, but this is not at all what Aristotle means by it. The misunderstanding comes from the purely formal approach to logic that is now prevalent. If I said "I believe the *Bugle* had a favorable review of that book, and they're usually reliable, so it's probably worth reading," current usage could call that a syllogism, but Aristotle would not. Two premises and a valid conclusion are all present, but this is still an enthymeme because the premises are not demonstrable and the conclusion is not demonstrated. Rhetoric dwells among arguments of this kind, in which the premises are mere likelihoods, the inferences merely by signs, and the conclusions at best persuasive. At the end of an enthymeme, a reason has been given for an opinion, but nothing in the argument rules out finding a more persuasive reason for an opposite opinion. And Aristotle has no interest in making rhetoric into logic by introducing "modal" distinctions of possibility or probability into its propositions. He is interested in studying everything that does and can go into the way we think about the decisions we make. That thinking does not need to be shallow and scanty, but it is limited by the imprecision of the things about which it thinks.

Two of the primary things rhetoric deals with are pleasure and happiness. The injustices people commit are generally for the sake of pleasure, and the actions governments undertake are justified by their contribution to the happiness of the citizens, so speakers in courtrooms and public assemblies are always presupposing something about those ends. What they are is discussed at length in Aristotle's *Nicomachean Ethics*, a work in which he warns the reader at the beginning of Bk. I, Chap. 3 (and repeatedly thereafter) not to expect greater precision than the subject admits. But his discussions of these same subjects in the *Rhetoric* have distinctly less precision than he attains in the *Ethics*. When commentators speak of Aristotle's definitions of pleasure and happiness, they mean the ones he arrives at in the *Nicomachean Ethics*. Pleasure is the unimpeded being-at-work of an active condition in accord with nature (1153a 14-15), and happiness is a being-at-work of the soul in accordance with the best and most complete virtue, in a whole life (1098a 16-18). Clearly those formulations do not speak for themselves. Each is arrived at by way of a dialectical process involving numerous stages at which faulty notions are rejected and subordinate ones are clarified. To carry over those definitions into the *Rhetoric* would be useless without the development of thought that gives them meaning, and still useless with that fullness of reasoning, since it could never be brought into any rhetorical occasion in a way that an audience could take in. In the *Rhetoric*, Bk. I, Chap. 11 deals with the subject of pleasure as it might enter into courtroom speeches of accusation or defense, and that discussion is entirely governed by a definition of pleasure that Aristotle explicitly rejects in the *Ethics*. Some scholars conclude that the *Rhetoric* must have been written earlier, before Aristotle figured out what he thought pleasure was. They do not grasp what Aristotle understands, that the study of rhetoric must take place where its audiences are, and not above their heads. At 1360b 14-18, in discussing advisory speeches for public assemblies, Aristotle lists four notions of happiness, saying that everyone pretty much agrees that happiness is somewhere on that list. The first item listed is roughly equivalent to the definition in the *Ethics*, in simpler terms, but the next three descend from there to become progressively more crude, ending up by identifying happiness with having a lot of money and slaves. Here the metaphor of an antistrophe becomes almost visual: we can practically see the steps of the strophe, the upward dialectic in the *Ethics*, being danced in reverse in the *Rhetoric*.

This combination of the metaphor of a reversal of steps with the conception of philosophic activity as a dialectic ascending toward the most precise understanding of the sources and causes of things suggests another way in which Aristotle and Plato are engaged in the same endeavor. One of the most famous similes in Plato's dialogues is the cave analogy in Book VII of the *Republic*. A philosophic education is compared there to an ascent into the sunlight, but the demands of being a human being require that anyone who makes the ascent return to the cave, in which our common life has to be lived by the firelight of opinion. Socratic rhetoric, which we have analyzed as a summons to begin the upward journey, must take its beginnings from the common ground the one whose education has already begun shares with those who are summoned. Aristotle generalizes his discussion to take in all the occasions that call for rhetoric, and begins by exploring the opinions that form the basis of civic life. Book I of the *Rhetoric* is a study of our shared perceptions of the advantageous, the just, and the beautiful, the goals for the sake of which we live in communities, and it can be seen as an orderly assembling of all the assumptions Socrates singles out in the dialogues as starting points of discussions. But while Socrates' purpose is to show one person at a time that those assumptions need examination, Aristotle's interest is in showing groups of people that their assumptions have consequences. When a community needs to determine whether or not to punish someone accused of injustice or whether or not to adopt some measure proposed for its advantage, or when it is invited to take some person or group as a model of the best life to which it can aspire, such judgments can be made at random, according to the skills of those who persuade it, or they can be made as a result of seeing the way they contribute to and follow from the goals to which they are already committed. The firelight in the cave is still light, and torches can be held up in places that show us what we are doing. The *Rhetoric* is Aristotle in the cave, bringing as much light as possible into all its corners.

Aristotle says, though, that rhetoric, like most good things, can be used to do great harm (1355b 2-7). This may seem to be an echo of Gorgias's "don't blame me" speech in the *Gorgias* (456C-457C), in which he compares rhetoric to skill at fighting. There are in fact commentators who claim that unlike Socrates, Aristotle agrees with Gorgias that rhetoric is a "morally neutral" instrument, but this is far from accurate. Aristotle also says that "human beings are adequately directed toward what is true by nature, and for the most part hit upon the truth" (1355a 15-18), and a few lines later, the first reason he gives for studying rhetoric is that, while things that are true or just are inherently more persuasive than their opposites, weaker arguments often prevail. His point, which he makes with moral indignation, is that it is only a *lack* of rhetorical art that permits this to happen. If there are people present on a rhetorical occasion who have taken the time and effort to see the available means of persuasion, then arguments can be shown on both sides, and the audience will have a chance to use its best judgment in the light of those arguments. Aristotle is firmly on Socrates' side in this matter too, in the belief that following the *logos* is bound to make our lives better. Book I of the *Rhetoric* outlines the basis on which arguments can be made and displayed, and that kind of display is nowhere to be found in the kinds of speeches Gorgias makes. But between the reasons that audiences are shown and the judgments they form, stand the passions, prejudices, and preferences they bring with them, and no speaker can afford to ignore them. Book II of the *Rhetoric*, then, begins by turning to these matters which inevitably influence the way the rational content of a speech will be received. Chapters 2-11 of Book II constitute a treatise on the passions. It is not a discussion of tactics for manipulating passions, but an inquiry into fourteen of the most important of them, seven pairs of opposites, to see what sort of feeling each of them is, what sorts of people it is directed at, and what occasions give rise to it.

These chapters on the passions are probably read more often than any other parts of the *Rhetoric*. Readers of the *Poetics* or the *Nicomachean Ethics* who want to find out more about Aristotle's understanding of pity or fear or *hubris* turn to them as to a reference work. What they find is in no way tailored to rhetorical situations, but is solely an attempt to see clearly what is at work in us when any of these temporary and irrational motives takes hold of us. And it is striking to find, despite the differences of customs and language, how much of ourselves we can see illuminated by Aristotle's discussion. The operation of shame (II, 6), for example, may seem to be less a factor in our lives than it was among Aristotle's contemporaries, but one may find that every observation he makes still rings true, even if our peer groups may govern their disapproval by notions different from those Aristotle is thinking of. And if his description of anger (II, 2) seems narrower than one might have expected, one might find this justified when Chapter 9 argues that righteous indignation is a very different feeling, or when in Chapter 4 Aristotle observes that we want someone we are angry with to suffer, but we want someone we hate not to exist (1382a 13-15). The distinctions he makes are valuable to the extent they show us something about motives that are in us but are ordinarily obscure to us. Our image of Aristotle bringing light into murky places may apply to these chapters as much as to his exploration of common opinions in Book I, and here there can be no illusion that the artful rhetorician is superior to his audience. What the study of the passions offers a speaker is not a bag of tricks by which to manipulate others, but power to see more of what he may need to show others. At the end of II, 4, a chapter that discusses the liking and disliking people may feel for others they do not know, Aristotle sums up its usefulness to a public speaker by saying it will make it possible to show people who their friends and enemies are, to show claims to that effect to be wrong, and to lead people out of disputes based on hostility alone, and bring them over to one side or the other. Even where irrational motives are at work, arguing from evidence can have an effect, though as with all rhetorical matters, persuasive arguments can be made on opposite sides. What rhetorical art, understood by Aristotle as the prior study of all the things that go into persuasion, can bring into rhetorical occasions is a use of rationality to combine with and moderate the passions. And this is once again a wholly Socratic endeavor.

What is not Socratic about the rhetoric Aristotle deals with is the fact that one does not know what will matter most to one's hearers, or whether their preferences and predispositions will have anything in common. Socrates talks to one person at a time, and listens to each of them, and in the *Gorgias* we see him take the discussion of the same subject in three very different directions, as he discovers what each of three men cares most about. In the ordinary situations in which juries, political assemblies, and public gatherings need to be addressed, arguments must be tailored to a more generic pattern. And one cannot expect all segments of a community to have convergent desires, even though that did happen at least once in Athens, as reported by Thucydides (VI, 24). Sixteen years into the Peloponnesian war, Alcibiades urged the Athenian populace to undertake a major invasion to conquer Sicily and got an enthusiastic reception. The older men thought the campaign would be easy and safe, the younger ones thought the adventure would be fun, and the poor saw an opportunity for paid work both during the conquest and afterward in the occupation. Nicias, who opposed the venture, warned that a massive army would be needed, and the people gladly accepted his assessment, thinking their numbers would make the enterprise foolproof. Nearly everyone, Thucydides says, was caught up in a lust for this expansion of Athens' imperial power. But such unity of feeling is rare and unreliable, and in this case it led only to disaster. In the ordinary course of the ordinary life of a community, what a speaker can do is pay attention to the differing groups that may make up an audience. Rhetorical art of the Aristotelian kind would be pursued by a preliminary study of the differing motives that would tend to prevail with these groups. Chapters 12-17 of Book II of the *Rhetoric*, then, explore the prevalent motives at work in the young, the old, the rich, and a few other groups. Generalizations are risky when one tries to apply them to particular people, but there is no question that the young and the old typically do not think alike, and Aristotle's chapters on what it is like to be young and to be old have always been of interest even to readers who are not concerned about rhetoric. For the student of rhetoric, this is one more area of shared life into which some light can be brought.

The second half of Book II returns from considerations about the hearers of speeches to the arguments themselves that are the body of persuasion. This may make the *Rhetoric* appear to be an awkward patchwork, with pieces tucked in as afterthoughts. I think it is easiest to understand the way the work is arranged by noting that, while Book I deals with the opinions that form the basis of rhetorical arguments, Book II deals with everything involved in designing arguments on the basis of those opinions. The passions that might obstruct or assist the reception of such an argument and the considerations most likely to be important to the particular types of people in the audience are two factors that would influence the design of a speech, but there are also varying strategies of argumentation that a speaker needs to be familiar with. Historical examples, analogies, and fables all have their uses; those weighty and terse statements of principles called maxims are sometimes effective; refutation of an opponent can be accomplished by counter-argument or more briefly by a well-chosen objection; and one's own enthymemes can be more or less artfully constructed. A speaker who has given prior thought to his options in these matters stands a better chance of getting his point across to an audience, and that goal is the common concern that unites Book II. It is in this third section of that book, Chapters 18-26, that one begins to get the flavor of the kinds of speeches Aristotle is talking about. He gives an abundance of examples of rhetorical arguments he considers well made, especially in Chapter 23, which is a compilation of what he calls topics. In general, this translation avoids the use of technical terms that do not have transparent meanings in today's English, but "topic," like "enthymeme," is an exception. These two words are part of the texture of the *Rhetoric*, and the only direct English equivalents to them would be phrases cumbersome to keep repeating. A topic (*topos*) is a ready-made argument that can be adapted to a variety of similar situations, a place to turn when such a situation is at hand. It can be a bit confusing to read in Chapter 26 that something is *not* a topic but rather the subject matter of an argument (the sort of thing he would have examined in Book I); the *topic* is a particular way of getting to a conclusion on that subject. One can get accustomed to this antique sense of the term by reading through the twenty-eight topics collected in Chapter 23 and the nine counterfeit topics in Chapter 24 that have the look and sound of enthymemes but do not show what they purport to. For Aristotle's contemporary readers, those same chapters would help accustom them to spotting misleading arguments that need to be exposed, while having at hand a stock of better arguments that might apply to matters that come up for consideration. Aristotle intends all of Books I and II of the *Rhetoric* to be a preparation for active citizenship.

The notion that the *Rhetoric* is a handbook for persuasion stems mainly from Book III, where Aristotle turns to the wording and arrangement of speeches. The second of these concerns is certainly a Socratic one; in the *Phaedrus* (264A-E), when Socrates makes the remark noted earlier, comparing a good speech to a living thing, he also makes fun of a speech by Lysias by claiming that it could be scrambled into any order without becoming any the worse or better in any rearrangement. It might appear that the first concern of Book III is not Socratic, since it is common in the dialogues for Socrates to make fun of language that is sonorous and impressive, but unclear, by calling it *tragikôs*, "in the tragic manner." In the *Meno*, Socrates makes this complaint (76E) about a pretentious definition of color that could mean anything or nothing; he also calls it an answer of the sort Gorgias would give (76C). In the *Republic* (413B), Socrates applies the same adverb to a formulation of his own which happens to be strung together out of language Gorgias uses in his *Encomium of Helen* (see note to *Gorgias*, end of 483E). What Socrates objects to is wording that impresses an audience with an elevated tone and an illusion of profundity, wording that attempts to use style to disguise a lack of content. One should not be surprised to learn that Aristotle does not disagree. He begins Chapter 2 of Book III by observing that the virtue of wording (*lexis*) in a speech is to be clear and appropriate to its subject, not elevated, not tasteless, and not sounding like poetry. One of the rhetoricians Aristotle quotes most often and with most approval is Isocrates, who learned his style from Gorgias but learned everything else from Socrates; the examples Aristotle gives from his speeches display an elegant style that has distinction without pretentiousness. Elegance (*asteiotês*) is connected by Aristotle with wording that makes us learn something quickly and easily, especially by means of vivid visual metaphors and balanced antitheses (1410b 20-36). The latter was a technique that Gorgias made famous, but the examples Aristotle gives are all from Isocrates (1409b 33-1410a 25); one of them is his pithy summation of Xerxes' plan "to sail across the mainland and march across the sea, bridging the Hellespont and dredging Athos." Phrases and clauses put together in this way are pleasing to us, Aristotle says, because contraries are easy to grasp and to remember, and easier still when put right next to each other.

Aristotle credits elegant wording with making a speaker be well-thought-of (*eudokimos*). This last point seems to me to offer a way to think about the whole of Book III, and hence the whole of the *Rhetoric*. Public speaking is all about showing something to an audience, on the basis of opinions most of the members of that audience will be likely to accept. The common opinions that unite political communities, about the matters of advantage that bring them together in the first place, the matters of justice that hold them together, and the models of a beautiful life to which they aspire, are explored in Book I. These opinions supply the premises of arguments that cannot be demonstrations, but can be more or less persuasive. But constructing a persuasive argument requires taking into account the particular people who will be hearing it. Book II explores the passions that obstruct or assist persuasion, the considerations likely to be most persuasive to the typical members of various groups, and the varying tactics of argument that can go into the design of a speech. In Book I Aristotle addresses the reader as "you" only once, and in Book II only twice. But in Book III, which deals with style rather than content, Aristotle's own style changes. There are at least a dozen distinct places in the third book in which Aristotle talks about what "you" should do in various situations. Not all translations can be relied on to reflect this difference accurately. In the first two books, Aristotle frequently uses verbal adjectives in the neuter, an impersonal construction that means something like "what needs to be done," or "the thing that fits the situation," but some translators turn this into "you should..." or "we must..." This carelessness makes a study that is designed for seeing and understanding sound like a handbook for arguing. But for a reader who has seen the available means of persuasion outlined in Books I and II, and wants to compose a speech, Book III is all about "you," because a speech, Aristotle says (1358a 37-1358b 1), is necessarily comprised of three things: that about which one speaks, those to whom one speaks, and the speaker. This threefold division, broadly interpreted, broadly structures the three books of the *Rhetoric*. And Aristotle, in highly qualified language, says that one might say that just about the most decisive factor in persuasion is the speaker himself (1356a 4-13). He is speaking there of character, of the kind of person the speaker seems to be, and whether the audience trusts his judgment.

Book III introduces a new consideration into the work, one that Aristotle says no one before his time thought worthy to write about: every speech is a performance (1403b 22). To neglect this fact, he says, is to forget that rhetoric dwells in the medium of opinion, and needs to address the imagination as well as the understanding. The Greek word for opinion (*doxa*) is related to the verb for seeming (*dokein*). The three books of the *Rhetoric* would then be dealing with, first, the opinions already accepted, second, the consequences of those opinions relevant to a particular audience and occasion, and third, the way those opinions and their consequences make their appearance in a particular speech. In the imagination of a listener, that appearance will be inseparable from the way the speaker himself seems. Most important of all, his handling of the arguments, his own and those of his opponents, will give an audience a sense of whether he is trustworthy, judicious, and fair. But a speaker has to know when to back off from argument just as much as when and how to use it. Near the end of the work, Aristotle describes several circumstances in which enthymemes do more harm than good (1418a 6-17). An inept speaker may put together too many enthymemes in succession, and spoil their effect; he may try to demonstrate something the audience already accepts, on the basis of things that are less clear; he may fail to recognize moments when appropriate feelings have been aroused, and undercut them by adding unnecessary arguments; and worst of all, he may think he can reveal someone's character by reciting that person's reasoning. Socratic rhetoric follows the *logos*, and Aristotle follows Socrates in insisting that enthymemes form the body of persuasion. But a body has limbs, and extremities, and even clothing. The rational content of a speech has to get across to others, and elegance in its wording has the double advantage of getting it across more smoothly and making the audience think well of the speaker. And Aristotle seems not to worry about speakers who are slick and unscrupulous. As with the fallacious enthymemes reviewed in Book II, the remedy for persuasion that depends only on style is more rhetorical art and not less. A speaker like Gorgias is all show and shows nothing. A speaker like Isocrates makes just as pleasing a showing and has something to show. At the end of the *Phaedrus* (279A-B), Socrates predicts that Isocrates will raise rhetoric to a higher level, because his thinking has some philosophy in it. In Book III of the *Rhetoric*, Aristotle studies the ways Isocrates and other elegant speakers produce their most successful effects. Having studied Book III would help someone with a talent for speaking be better prepared to stand up against impressive but vapid opponents. The final judgment of rhetoric is made by the public, and it will always be better able to see through illusion when it is on display next to artful speech that shows reasons to adopt certain opinions in preference to others. In practice, for showing something that may have an impact on the life of a political community, a big voice may sometimes be more important than precision of formulation (1414a 15-17). In the *Rhetoric*, that offshoot of dialectic into politics, Aristotle does not disdain to say so.

In the *Gorgias*, Socrates does not mention anything that pertains to the delivery or performing involved in speech-making, but he is not above a little mockery of such tactics, in ways that incidentally show that he is no slouch at them himself. In 487B he permits himself to indulge in some throwaway wordplay that shows how easily he can outdo both Polus and Callicles at their own game. And after Callicles has been incautious enough to patronize him as brash (482C), Socrates gives him a few lessons in how to make that charge stick (508D, 509A, 527D). But Socrates is interested in a motion away from a concern with style. Socratic rhetoric, since it is an encouragement to dialectic, seeks to leave rhetoric behind. Aristotle, on the other hand, remains interested enough in the ordinary persuasive uses of rhetoric to dwell with that subject in all its detail. He intends his *Rhetoric* to be the first example of a study of persuasive speech as an art, and hence as a cousin to dialectic. If Socrates provides a rhetorical preparation for the pursuit of dialectic, one may say that Aristotle provides a dialectical preparation for the practice of rhetoric, if "dialectical" is taken to mean proceeding in the manner of dialectic to the extent the subject at hand permits. We know that Aristotle considers rhetoric an antistrophe to dialectic. This means that rhetoric which is turned by study into art occupies the same stage as philosophy. This is not a contradiction of Socrates' claim that rhetoric occupies the same stage as cookery and cosmetics. It is Aristotle's response to Socrates' implied invitation at 481B of the *Gorgias* for someone to find and justify a worthwhile use for rhetoric. That was the point at which Callicles entered the discussion to give a rhetorical justification for the rhetoric of Gorgias. The *Rhetoric* of Aristotle is a product of the second half the dialogue could have had if an Aristotle had been present.

*****

The *Gorgias* first captured my interest when I was a freshman at St. John's College. The seminar leader I first read it with was Robert Bart, who was also one of my examiners when I wrote on it at the end of that year. I chose to write on it again three years later for what was called my senior thesis, on which one of my examiners was Hugh McGrath. Both were men of subtle intelligence and unfailingly elegant speech, and both knew how to practice a salutary and bracing kind of kolastic rhetoric. I was fortunate to have them both as teachers, colleagues, and friends. In graduate school, I believe the first paper I wrote was an attempt to track down Callicles' sources, for which I spent an exhilarating day sending employees of the central New York City Public Library on repeated trips to the stacks. St. John's once had a dean who argued that there was nothing new for students to discuss or learn from the *Gorgias* after they had studied Book I of the *Republic*. Suffice it to say he was both mistaken and unpersuasive.

The *Rhetoric* is a work I had neglected until just a few years ago, when it appeared on a list of subjects students had requested for intensive classes. I was familiar only with bits and pieces of its second book, and read the whole of it for the first time with a small group of juniors and seniors. It was as fresh, and sometimes puzzling, to me as to them, and we went on to read some famous speeches, ancient and modern, to see if it helped us get more out of them. It definitely contributed something to our ability to read them thoughtfully, but my return to studying the *Rhetoric* was occasioned more by an interest in its connections with Aristotle's other works than by a desire to think about persuasive speech. The *Rhetoric* turned out, for me, to be an opening into Aristotle's thinking about political life, and a way to deepen my grasp of what he means by dialectic. The latter is his characteristic mode of thinking and writing, though this fact is appreciated neither by the tradition that regards him as an expounder of "sciences" nor by the assortment of scholars who see him as an early analytic philosopher, playing around with the various meanings of Greek words.

The *Gorgias* and the *Rhetoric* proved more revealing to me when studied together than when read independently, and this book is meant to encourage that study. There are other good versions of the *Gorgias* available, notably that of Arieti and Barrus. Their 2007 translation in this Focus series came to my attention only when my own was well advanced, and came into my hands only after mine was complete. I admire their work; their book contains valuable material not present in mine, and represents translation choices always at least as good. As for the *Rhetoric*, the choice has been between earlier versions that are easy to read but somewhat loose and the recent, overly literal translation by George A. Kennedy. The translation offered here aims always at the needs of the general reader, while striving for a high degree of fidelity to the Greek. The context of greatest interest to me has always been the other writings of Aristotle and Plato rather than the tradition of commentary on them or the vocabulary of other classical works on rhetoric.

The Greek text used for the *Gorgias* was that of E. R. Dodds (Oxford U. P., 1959); departures from his editorial judgment are rare, and noted where they occur. His annotations were always valuable. The *Rhetoric* was translated from the Oxford Classical Text of W. D. Ross, published by the same press in the same year as Dodds' *Gorgias*. The notes in Kennedy's *Aristotle on Rhetoric: A Theory of Civic Discourse* (Oxford U. P., 2nd ed. 2007) provided valuable references of all kinds. In addition to the introduction, the book you are reading contains a glossary of important terms, or terms with meanings not transparent in English translation. It is brief, and can be read through as additional introductory material. The index is keyed to the standard pagination in the margins of the primary texts, and is intended to be selective rather than comprehensive. Because the content of the *Rhetoric* is so varied, summaries of its chapters are given at the beginning of that work for the reader's convenience. They should not be regarded as definitive, but only as guides to reading or subsequent discussion.

I owe a large debt of gratitude to Eric Salem once again. He read through the translation of the *Gorgias* and caught numerous errors, including a couple of real howlers. His unfailingly intelligent and perceptive suggestions have improved this translation, as they have improved so many before it. Any faults remaining are due to my own obstinacy. My thanks go also to Michael Dink, who found the time to read the introduction with a sharp eye, and to give me the benefit of a number of criticisms. His disagreements and suggestions have strengthened it both dialectically and rhetorically. And I am grateful to David Levine, who used the translation of the *Rhetoric* in a class in Santa Fe; he and his students informed me of many errors, in both typography and judgment, that you will be spared. The fact that all the parts of this book overlapped with current interests and projects of colleagues of mine is the sort of coincidence that can become a likelihood in a community of learning such as the one that survives on the two campuses of St. John's College; the generosity of those colleagues is a sign of the life of learning itself.

Annapolis, Maryland
January, 2008

PLATO
GORGIAS

447A–448C	**Introductory Conversation**
448D–461B	**Socrates and Gorgias**
461B–481B	**Socrates and Polus**
481B–486D	**Callicles' Interruption and Speech**
486D–523A	**Socrates and Callicles**
523A–527E	**Socrates' Concluding Speech**

Note

There are five people involved in the dialogue. Socrates arrives with an old friend and follower, Chaerephon, at a house in Athens where a distinguished guest, Gorgias, is accompanied by a younger associate, Polus. The former two are native Athenians, the latter two from Sicily. The fifth person, who greets Socrates on his arrival, unlike the other four, is entirely unknown outside this dialogue. He may be one of the handful of fictional characters in Plato's dialogues, or more likely, as a young man entering on a public career at a chaotic period in Athenian political life, he simply disappeared. There may or may not be significance in the fact that his name ("famed for visible excellence") resembles Plato's given name, which was Aristocles ("famed for highest excellence"). Callicles eventually becomes the primary participant in the conversation with Socrates. He also speaks the dialogue's first words.

447A *Callicles:* In war and battle, Socrates, this is the way to do your part, they say.

Socrates: Oh my. Did we show up too late—after the feast, as the saying goes?

Callicles: And very much of a stylish feast at that, because Gorgias laid out a display of many beautiful things for us a little while ago.

Socrates: Well, Callicles, Chaerephon here is to blame for that, since he made us waste our time in the marketplace.

B *Chaerephon:* It's no big thing, Socrates, since I'll provide the cure too, because Gorgias is a friend of mine. So he'll put on a display for us now, if that seems good, or some other time if you want.

Callicles: What, Chaerephon? Does Socrates have a desire to hear Gorgias?

Chaerephon: That's the very thing we're here for, in fact.

Callicles: Then come to my place whenever you want, because Gorgias is stopping off with me, and he'll give a display for you.

Socrates: That's good of you to say, Callicles, but would he be willing
C to have a conversation with us? Because I want to find out from
him what power belongs to the man's art,[1] and what it is that he
lays claim to and teaches; as for the other thing, the display, let
him do that some other time, as you say.

Callicles: There's nothing like asking the man himself, Socrates, because this too was one part of his display. At any rate, he was just now urging any of the people inside to ask whatever they might want, and saying he'd give an answer on every subject.

Socrates: Beautiful! Chaerephon, you ask him.

Chaerephon: What am I going to ask?

D *Socrates:* Who he is.

Chaerephon: How do you mean?

Socrates: The same way, if he happened to be a craftsman who made shoes, he'd presumably answer you that he's a leatherworker—or don't you understand how I mean it?

Chaerephon: I do understand, and I'll ask him. Tell me, Gorgias, is Callicles here telling the truth, that you claim to answer whatever anyone asks you?

---

1 The Greek word translated "art" (*technê*) is a common one; its meaning ordinarily includes three elements, and refers to any sort of know-how that involves some theoretical understanding, some practical skill at carrying it out, and some experience with particulars to guide its application. The first two examples given below, shoemaking and doctoring, give an idea of the span of things it takes in, but it is even wider, and can apply to ditch-digging at one extreme and the theory of numerical ratios (as exhibited in Book VII of Euclid's *Elements*) at the other. Socrates will later raise a question about what activities deserve to be called arts, and one should not prejudice or preempt that discussion by translating it as "science" or "craft"; it is truer to the text, and not difficult, to accustom ourselves to recapture the general sense that was once present in English in phrases like fine arts, useful arts, liberal arts, arts of understanding, and so on. Some notion of an artful approach to achieving one's ends underlies all such phrases, and conveys to us the living meaning of an English word very close to this Greek word; meanings directly grasped in this way are prior to any attempts at definition.

Gorgias: It's true, Chaerephon; I was just now making that very claim, and I tell you, for many years, no one has ever asked me anything new. 448A

Chaerephon: Then I suppose you give answers with ease, Gorgias.

Gorgias: It's open to you to put that to the test, Chaerephon.

Polus: If that's what you want, Chaerephon, test me, by Zeus! Gorgias seems to me to be worn out, since he's just gone through a lot of answers.

Chaerephon: What, Polus? Do you suppose you'd give answers more beautifully than Gorgias would?

Polus: What does that matter, as long as I answer well enough for you? B

Chaerephon: It doesn't. Since you want to, then, you answer.

Polus: Ask.

Chaerephon: I'm asking: if Gorgias happened to be knowledgeable in the same art his brother Herodicus is, what would we justly name him? Wouldn't it be the same as that one?

Polus: Certainly.

Chaerephon: Therefore we'd be speaking beautifully in declaring him to be a doctor.

Polus: Yes.

Chaerephon: But if he were experienced in the same art as Aristophon, the son of Aglaophon, or as *his* brother, what would we rightly call him?

Polus: A painter, obviously. C

Chaerephon: But as it is, since he's knowledgeable in some art, by calling him what would we be calling him rightly?

Polus: There are many arts among human beings, Chaerephon, that have been discovered experientially from experiences, for experience makes our lifespan pass along the path of art, but inexperience along the path of chance. And of the sorts of arts, various people partake of various ones in various ways, the best partaking of the best. Gorgias here is one of these, and partakes of the most beautiful[2] of the arts.

---

2 Polus introduces the highest term of praise, by calling Gorgias's art best not only in the sense of what is most excellent (*ariston*) but of that which visibly displays the standard of excellence. The excellence of something beautiful is spelled out by Socrates below (474D-475B) as its being especially well suited to the pleasure of another or to its own ends. In the latter sense, a beautiful body is visibly well formed to be the kind of thing it is, and a beautiful action or activity is manifestly an end in itself, capable of no higher justification. As something beautiful (*kalon*) evokes admiration, its opposite (*aischron*) evokes shame. (See the note to 458D.) Translators tend to shy away from translating *kalon* in the natural way as "beautiful" in the belief that it now connotes only a bodily appearance related to pleasure, but the English word has not lost the full range of meaning present in the Greek, as evidenced whenever we say "that was a beautiful thing to do." The word translators most often resort to is "fair," as in the obsolete English usage found in Dryden's line "None but the brave deserves the fair." This sidesteps such translators' embarrassment with the word "beautiful," but affords no opportunity to think about the beauty of actions.

D *Socrates:* Polus appears to be beautifully prepared for speeches, Gorgias, but he's not doing what he'd promised Chaerephon.

Gorgias: What's that, Socrates?

Socrates: He doesn't appear to me to be answering what was asked at all.

Gorgias: Then you ask him, if you want.

Socrates: Not if it's possible that you yourself want to answer; it would be much pleasanter to ask you instead, because it's clear to me even from what he's said that Polus has taken more care over what's called rhetoric than over engaging in conversation.

E *Polus:* How's that, Socrates?

Socrates: Because, Polus, when Chaerephon asked what art Gorgias is knowledgeable in, you praised his art as though someone was blaming it, but you didn't answer what it is.

Polus: Well, didn't I answer that it was the most beautiful one?

Socrates: You sure did. But no one asked what *sort* of thing Gorgias's
art might be, but *what* it is, and what one ought to call Gorgias.
The same way Chaerephon set out examples for you before, and
449A you answered him beautifully and with few words, now too say
in that way what the art is and what we should call Gorgias. Or
rather, Gorgias, tell us yourself what we should call you, for being
knowledgeable in what art.

Gorgias: Rhetoric, Socrates.

Socrates: Then we should call you a rhetorician?

Gorgias: A good one too, Socrates, if you want to call me what I "flaunt myself to be," as Homer says.

Socrates: I do want to.

Gorgias: Then call me that.

B *Socrates:* And shall we say that you're capable of making others rhetoricians too?

Gorgias: I make exactly that claim, not only here but also in other places.

Socrates: Then would you be willing, Gorgias, to go on conversing the way we are now, one asking questions and the other answering, and put off to another time this length of speeches that Polus started? But don't make a lie out of what you're promising; just be willing to answer what's asked with one short reply at a time.

Gorgias: There are some answers, Socrates, that are necessarily made
C with long speeches, but still, I'll try anyway to be as brief as possible. Because even this is also one of the things I claim, that no
one could say the same things in fewer words than I.

Socrates: That's what's needed, Gorgias: make a display for me of this very thing, brief talk, and the lengthy talk some other time.

Gorgias: That's just what I'll do, and you'll say you've heard no briefer talker.

Socrates: Then let's get to it: you claim you're knowledgeable in the art of rhetoric and could make another person a rhetorician too. D
What exactly, among the things there are, is rhetoric about? The same way weaving is about cloth-working—isn't it?

Gorgias: Yes.

Socrates: And music is about tune-making?

Gorgias: Yes.

Socrates: By Hera, Gorgias, I marvel at your answers, the way you answer in the fewest possible words.

Gorgias: Yes, Socrates, I guess I do a pretty fair job of that.

Socrates: You put it well. Come, then, and tell me about rhetoric the same way: which of the things there are is it a knowledge of?

Gorgias: Of speeches. E

Socrates: What sort of them, Gorgias? The ones that point out to sick people how to lead their lives so they can become healthy?

Gorgias: No.

Socrates: So rhetoric *isn't* about *all* speeches.

Gorgias: No indeed.

Socrates: But it does make people capable of speaking.

Gorgias: Yes.

Socrates: So does it also make them have sound judgments about the things they're speaking of?

Gorgias: How could it not?

Socrates: Well, does the medical art that was just now mentioned make 450A
people be capable of having sound judgments and speaking about sick people?

Gorgias: Necessarily.

Socrates: So it looks like the medical art is also about speeches.

Gorgias: Yes.

Socrates: The ones that have to do with diseases?

Gorgias: Especially those.

Socrates: And so the art of gymnastic training is also about speeches, the ones having to do with good and bad condition in bodies?

Gorgias: Quite so.

Socrates: And surely Gorgias, the rest of the arts are the same way; B
each of them is about just those speeches that have to do with the subject matter concerning which it is the art.

Gorgias: So it appears.

Socrates: So why in the world don't you call the rest of the arts rhetorical, since they're about speeches, if indeed you call that art which is about speeches rhetoric?

Gorgias: Because, Socrates, all the knowledge involved in the rest of the arts, one may say, is about handicrafts and actions of that sort, while in rhetoric there is no such work of handicraft, but its whole action and exertion of mastery are by means of speeches. For these C reasons I hold that the art of rhetoric, rightly speaking, is about speeches, as I claim.

Socrates: But am I understanding what sort of art you want to call it, then? Maybe I'll get to know it more clearly. Just answer me this: we have arts, right?

Gorgias: Yes.

Socrates: And among all the arts, I suppose the major part of some of them consists of working and they need little speech—some of them none—but what pertains to the art could be accomplished even in silence, as with painting and sculpture and many others.
D It's arts such as these that you seem to me to be speaking of as those you claim rhetoric has no concern with; isn't that it?

Gorgias: You draw the inference quite beautifully, Socrates.

Socrates: But there are others among the arts that accomplish everything by means of speech,[3] and have, one may say, either no additional need of work, or very little, such as arithmetic, the study of numerical ratios,[4] geometry, and even checkers, as well as many other arts, of which some have the speeches about equal in number to the actions, while many have more speeches, and with them
E absolutely all the action and exertion of mastery are by means of speeches. You seem to me to be saying that rhetoric is one of the arts of this kind.

Gorgias: What you say is true.

Socrates: But I don't suppose you want to call any of *those* rhetoric, even though you said it that way in your wording—that the art that has its exertion of mastery by means of speech is rhetoric—and if someone wanted to wanted to be picky about *your* speeches he might come back with "Therefore, Gorgias, you're saying arithmetic is rhetoric?" But I don't suppose you mean either arithmetic or geometry is rhetoric.

---

3 This contrast with arts that use little speech introduces into the dialogue the word *logos* in the singular. It is a word with a vast array of possible meanings, but here it takes its primary sense from its relation to the plural. The speeches made by rhetoricians occur in a medium that connects the speaker and hearers, and that medium is speech. The contrast between *logoi* plural and the single *logos* will soon become emphatic as the crux of the difference between Gorgias and Socrates. For this reason, this translation attempts to render *logos* as "speech" virtually always, even in phrases such as *kata ton logon* or *logon didonai*, conventionally translated, respectively, as "according to the argument" and "giving an account." One exception is the mathematical meaning of *logos* mentioned in the next footnote.

4 The last phrase translates *logistikê*, which other translations render as "calculation." In later Greek authors, it did routinely refer to the art of calculation, the application of the theoretical side of arithmetic, but this is not the distinction Socrates makes just below. Consistently in Plato's writings, *logistikê* and *arithmetikê* are both understood as arts that span theory and practice, as discussed in the note to 447C above. This is shown by Jacob Klein in *Greek Mathematical Thought and the Origin of Algebra* (MIT Press, 1968, Chap. 3). In mathematics, the word *logos* means ratio; the use here of the example of *logistikê* puts together the notions of art and *logoi* in a way very different from what Gorgias had in mind.

Gorgias: Your supposition is right, Socrates, and your comeback is 451A
just.

Socrates: Come on now, you too finish off the answer to what I asked.
Since rhetoric happens to be one among those arts that use speech
for the most part, while others also happen to be of that sort, try
to tell what it *is* about which rhetoric has its exertion of mastery in
words.[5] It's the same as if someone were to ask me, about any one
of the arts whatever that we were just now speaking of, "What *is*
the art of arithmetic, Socrates?" I'd tell him, just the way you did B
just now, that it's one of the arts that have their exertion of mastery
by means of speech. And if he were to go on and ask me, "The one
among them that's about *what*?" I'd tell him that it's the one among
them that's about the even and the odd, and exactly how much each
is. And if he were to ask in turn, "What art do you call the study of
numerical ratios?" I'd tell him that this is one of those that exert all
their mastery through speech. And if he were to go on and ask me,
"The one about *what*?" I'd tell him, like people drafting a motion in C
the assembly, that whereas in other respects the study of numerical ratios corresponds to the art of arithmetic—since they're about
the same thing, the even and the odd—they differ to this extent,
that the study of numerical ratios studies the way the odd and the
even are related to themselves and to one another in multitude.
And if someone were to ask about astronomy, and if, when I said
that it too exerts its mastery in all respects by speech, he were to
say, "What are the speeches of astronomy about, Socrates?" I'd tell
him that they're about the way the motions of the stars, the sun,
and the moon are related to one another in speed.

Gorgias: And you'd be quite right in saying it, Socrates.

Socrates: You come on then too, Gorgias. Rhetoric is precisely one of D
the arts that accomplish everything and exert all their mastery by
speech, isn't it?

Gorgias: That it is.

Socrates: So tell me, the one among them that's about *what*? What is it, among the things there are, that these speeches that rhetoric employs are about?

Gorgias: The greatest of human concerns, Socrates, and the best.

Socrates: But, Gorgias, even in this you're saying something open to
dispute, and it's still not clear at all. I imagine you've heard people E
at drinking parties singing that round-song in which they count
them off, singing that "having your health is best, being beauti-

5 Reading this speech as an actor or director would, one might suspect that there is a pause at this point, and that Socrates proceeds as he does only after Gorgias has failed to reply. It is worth thinking about this, in connection with the growing length of some of Socrates' speeches. There are similar moments with Polus below, in 468C and D, and another in Plato's *Meno* just before 75A; Meno, who there fails to reply, is another admirer of Gorgias who endorses his opinions.

ful second best, and third best," according to the composer of the round, "being rich without being crooked."

Gorgias: I've heard it, but what's your point in saying this?

452A *Socrates:* That if the craftsmen responsible for these things the poet
praises in the round-song were standing here right now, a doctor
and a trainer and a businessman, the doctor might say, first,
"Socrates, Gorgias is fooling you, because his art isn't about the
greatest good for human beings; mine is." If I were then to ask
him, "Who are you to say so?" he'd probably say that he's a doctor.
"And what are you saying? That the work of your art is the greatest good?" He'd probably reply, "How could it not be, Socrates?
B It's health. What greater good is there for human beings than
health?" And if, after him, the trainer in turn were to say, "I'd be
surprised myself as well, Socrates, if Gorgias has a greater good to
show you from his art than I have from mine," I'd say back to him
too, "And who are you, fellow? What's your job?" "A trainer," he'd
reply, "and my job is to make human beings beautiful and strong
in body." And after the trainer, the businessman would speak,
C having complete disdain for everyone: "Just consider, Socrates,
whether anything that's a greater good than wealth shows itself
to you, around either Gorgias or anyone else at all." We'd say to
him, "What? Are you a craftsman responsible for that?" He'd say
so. "Who are you?" "A businessman." "What?" we'd say; "do you
judge wealth to be the greatest good for human beings?" "How
could it be otherwise?" he'll reply. "And yet Gorgias here contends
that the art at his disposal is a cause of a greater good than yours,"
D we'd say. It's obvious that after that he'd reply, "And what *is* this
good? Let Gorgias answer." So come on, Gorgias; make believe
you've been asked by them and by me, and answer what this is
that you claim is the greatest good for human beings, and claim
that you're a craftsman of.

Gorgias: It's the very thing that is in truth the greatest good, Socrates, and the thing that's responsible not only for being free for human beings themselves but also for their ruling others, each in his own city.

Socrates: So what are you saying that is?

E *Gorgias:* *I'm* saying it's being able to persuade people by speeches,
jurors in a lawcourt, legislators in a council chamber, and those
assembled in a deliberative assembly and in every other gathering,
whatever civic gathering may occur. And in fact, with this power
you'll have the doctor as a slave, and the trainer as a slave, and
that businessman will be shown up as doing business for someone
else and not for himself, namely for you, the one with the power
to speak and persuade the multitudes.

Socrates: Now, Gorgias, you seem to me to have come closest to reveal-
453A ing rhetoric for the sort of art you take it to be, and if I'm under-

standing at all, you're saying that rhetoric is a crafter of persuasion, and the whole concern and sum total of it ends with that. Or do you have anything further to say that rhetoric has the power to do beyond producing in its hearers persuasion in the soul?

Gorgias: Nothing whatever, Socrates; you seem to me to be defining it sufficiently, because that is the sum total of it.

Socrates: Then listen, Gorgias, because you can be sure about me, as
I persuade myself, that if anyone engages in conversation with B
someone else wanting to know the very thing that our speech is about, I too am one of these, and I consider you to be one also.

Gorgias: What about it, then, Socrates?

Socrates: I'll tell you right now. You can be sure that I don't know clearly what in the world the persuasion you speak of as coming from rhetoric *is*, or what things the persuasion is about, even though I have a suspicion of what I imagine you're speaking of and what it's about. Nevertheless, I'll ask *you* what in the world you say the
persuasion that comes from rhetoric is and what things it's about. C
Now for what purpose am I going to ask you and not say it myself, when I have my own suspicion? It's not for your sake but for the sake of our speech, in order that it might move forward in a way that would make whatever is being spoken of evident to us as much as possible. Now consider whether I seem to you to be questioning you justly: the same way as if I happened to ask you who Zeuxis is among painters, and you told me that he was a painter of living figures, wouldn't it be just if I were to ask you what sort of living figures he was a painter of and where?

Gogias: Very much so.

Socrates: And for this reason, that there are also other figure painters D
who paint lots of different figures?

Gorgias: Yes.

Socrates: But if no one other than Zeuxis was a painter, your answer would have been beautifully put?

Gorgias: How could it not?

Socrates: Come on and tell me about rhetoric, then. Does it seem to you that only rhetoric produces persuasion or that other arts do too? I mean something like this: when anyone teaches any subject whatever, does the one who teaches it persuade? Or do you think he doesn't?

Gorgias: Oh no, Socrates; persuading is what he does most of all.

Socrates: Then let's go back to the same arts we were speaking of just E
now. Don't arithmetic and the person skilled at arithmetic teach us as many things as have to do with number?

Gorgias: Very much so.

Socrates: Then they also persuade?

Gorgias: Yes.

Socrates: Therefore arithmetic too is a crafter of persuasion?

Gorgias: So it appears.

Socrates: Then if someone should ask us what sort of persuasion, and
about what, presumably we'd answer him that it's of the instructive
454A sort, about how much the even and odd are. And with all the other
arts we were just now speaking of, we'll be able to demonstrate that
they're crafters of persuasion, and what sort they are, and about
what; isn't that so?

Gorgias: Yes.

Socrates: Therefore it's not only rhetoric that's a crafter of persuasion.

Gorgias: You're speaking the truth.

Socrates: Then since not only it accomplishes this work, but other arts
do too, we might justly go on to ask the person speaking, as we did
about the painter: Of what sort of persuasion, and of persuasion
B about what, is rhetoric the art? Or doesn't it seem to you to be a
just thing to go on asking?

Gorgias: It does to me.

Socrates: So answer, Gorgias, seeing as how it seems that way to you too.

Gorgias: Well then, Socrates, I say it's the art of that persuasion that goes on in lawcourts and in other crowds, as I was in fact saying just now, and that's about those things that are just and unjust.

Socrates: I suspected as well that you were speaking of that persuasion and about those topics, Gorgias, but don't be surprised if I ask
you some other question of that sort a little later, that seems to be
C obvious, but I go ahead and ask it anyway. Because exactly as I'm
saying, I'm asking for the sake of carrying our speech to completion in an orderly way, not for your sake but so that we don't get
in the habit of guessing and snatching up the things said by one
another too quickly, in order that, in whatever way you want, you
might carry the things said by yourself to a conclusion that follows
what's been set down.

Gorgias: And it seems to me you're doing so quite rightly, Socrates.

Socrates: Come on, then, and let's examine this point: do you call a certain condition "having learned?"

Gorgias: I call something that.

Socrates: And what about "having believed?"

D *Gorgias:* I do.

Socrates: And do they seem to you to be the same thing—having learned and having believed, or learning and belief—or different?

Gorgias: I certainly imagine they're different, Socrates.

Socrates: You're imagining it beautifully, and you'll recognize that from this: if someone were to ask you, "Gorgias, is there a false belief as well as a true one?" I imagine you'd say there is.

Gorgias: Yes.

Socrates: And what about this? Is there a false knowledge as well as a true one?

Gorgias: By no means.

Socrates: Therefore it's obvious that they're not the same.

Gorgias: You're speaking the truth.

Socrates: But surely those who've learned something are persuaded of E
it, and so are those who've come to believe something.

Gorgias: These things are so.

Socrates: Then do you want us to posit two forms of persuasion, one that provides belief without knowing, another that provides knowledge?

Gorgias: Very much so.

Socrates: Then which sort of persuasion does rhetoric produce in lawcourts and other crowds about things that are just and unjust? Is it the one from which believing comes without knowing, or from which knowing comes?

Gorgias: It's obvious, I presume, Socrates, that it's the sort from which believing comes.

Socrates: Therefore it looks like rhetoric is a crafter not of persuasion 455A
that teaches but of persuasion into belief about what's just and
unjust.

Gorgias: Yes.

Socrates: And therefore the rhetorician is not someone who teaches the lawcourts and other crowds about things that are just and unjust, but only someone who's persuasive, since presumably he wouldn't be able to teach so big a crowd in so little time about such great matters.

Gorgias: Certainly not.

Socrates: Come on then, let's see what in the world we're in fact saying
about rhetoric, because I can't even tell yet what I'm saying myself. B
Whenever there's a meeting in the city for choosing doctors or
shipbuilders or any other confraternity of public workers, is there
any doubt that the rhetorician won't be giving any advice then?
Because it's obvious that in each choice, it's necessary to choose
the person most skilled at the art. And he won't when it's about
building walls either, or about equipping harbors and shipyards,
but the engineers will. And also not when there's a deliberation
about choosing generals, or about some battle plan against enemies, C
or about capturing territory; skilled military men will give advice
then, but not rhetoricians. What do you say about things like that,
Gorgias? Since you yourself claim to be a rhetorician, and to make
other people rhetoricians, it's a good idea to find out the things that
have to do with your art from you. And regard me now as keenly
promoting your interest, because probably someone among those
in the place happens to want to become a student of yours, since I
notice some, quite a few even, who'd probably be shy about asking

D you. So when you're asked the question by me, regard it as also being asked by them: "What will we get out of it, Gorgias, if we associate with you? What will we be able to give advice to the city about? Will it only be about just and unjust, or also about the things Socrates was just talking about?" So try to give them an answer.

Gorgias: I will try, then, Socrates, to reveal the whole power of rhetoric to you clearly, and you yourself have pointed the way beautifully.
E Because you know, I presume, that these shipyards and walls of the Athenians, and the equipage of their harbors, came about thanks to the advice of Themistocles, and some to that of Pericles, and not thanks to the workmen.

Socrates: So it's said, Gorgias, in the case of Themistocles. I myself heard Pericles when he was giving us advice about the wall down the middle.[6]

456A *Gorgias:* And whenever there's any choice about the things you were just speaking of, Socrates, you see that the rhetoricians are the ones who give the advice and carry the motions about these issues.

Socrates: It's from being amazed at these things too, Gorgias, that I've been asking all along what in the world the power of rhetoric *is*. Because when I look at it this way, the greatness of it has the appearance of some supernatural power.

Gorgias: Oh, if you knew it all, Socrates—that it holds all powers, if I
B may put it so, rounded up in subjection to itself. I'll tell you a big sign of this: often before now I've gone along with my brother and with other doctors to some sick person who wasn't willing to drink his medicine, or to allow the doctor to do any cutting or burning, and when the doctor wasn't able to be persuasive I did persuade him, with no art other than rhetoric. And I tell you, if a rhetorically skilled man and a doctor went into any city you want, and had to compete in speech in the assembly or in any other gathering over
C which of the two should be chosen as a doctor, the doctor would clearly get nowhere, and the one with the power to speak would be chosen if he wanted to. And whatever other sort of workman he might be in competition with, the rhetorician would be more persuasive than anyone else whatsoever at getting himself chosen. Because there is nothing at all about which the rhetorician would not speak more persuasively among a multitude than any of the other workmen whatsoever. So that's how great the power of the

---

6 Themistocles and Pericles were political figures who held the highest elected office in Athens. Thucydides (*The Peloponnesian War*, Bk. I, Ch. 93) credits the former with making Athens a naval power by recognizing the potential of the Piraeus as a port, and persuading the citizens to protect it with a pair of long walls extending at an angle from the city to the sea. The latter persuaded them to add a third wall some years afterward, within and parallel to the long wall to Piraeus, to produce a fortified military road, then later argued that they had nothing to fear from war with Sparta. A speech by Pericles on this subject on the brink of the Peloponnesian War is recounted by Thucydides in I, 139-146.

art is, and what it's like. Mind you, Socrates, rhetoric has to be
used like every other skilled combat. Because one ought not to D
make use of another combat skill against all people either, just on
account of the fact that one has learned boxing or no-holds-barred
wrestling or fighting in armor so well as to be overpowering to
friends and enemies alike—one doesn't have to go around hitting
and killing one's friends just for that reason. By Zeus, suppose
somebody who's gone regularly to a wrestling school, has his
body in good shape, and has become a skilled boxer, should then
hit his father and mother, or any of his other relations or friends;
that wouldn't be any reason why one should hate the trainers or E
those who teach people to fight in armor, or should throw them
out of the cities. They passed on the skills to be used in a just
manner against enemies and people who do injustice, by those
who are defending themselves, not starting anything, and those 457A
who pervert their strength and their art aren't using them rightly.
Their teachers aren't the ones who are corrupt, and the art is not to
blame and is not corrupt on that account; by my thinking, it's the
ones who don't use it rightly. Now the same argument also applies
to rhetoric, because the rhetorician is in fact capable of speaking
against everyone and about everything in such a way as to be more
persuasive among the multitudes about, in a word, whatever he B
wants. But there's not one bit more reason on that account why he
has to steal the doctors' reputation—just because he has the power
to do that—or the reputation of any other workmen; he has to use
his rhetoric justly too, the same as a combat skill. By my thinking,
if somebody who's become rhetorically skilled should then do
injustice with this power and art, it's not right to hate the teacher
and throw him out of the cities. He passed it on for use in a just C
manner; the other person is using it the opposite way. The just
thing is to hate the person who doesn't use it rightly, and to exile
him or put him to death, but not his teacher.

Socrates: I imagine that you're experienced too, Gorgias, with lots of
speeches, and that you've noticed this fact about them, that people
are not easily able to delineate what they're trying to converse with
one another about, and to learn and to teach themselves, and settle D
their interchanges in that way, but if they disagree about something
and one claims the other isn't speaking rightly or isn't speaking
clearly, they get angry and imagine the person is speaking out of
malice against themselves, from a desire to come out on top, rather
than inquiring after the thing that's in front of them in their speech.
Some of them end up breaking things off in the ugliest way, with
name-calling, and after saying and hearing the sort of things that
make even the other people present sorry on their own behalf that
they deigned to be an audience to such persons. Now what's my E
point in saying these things? It's because you seem to me now to

be saying things that don't entirely follow from or harmonize with
the things you were saying at first about rhetoric. So I'm afraid to
refute you, in case you might get the idea that I'm speaking not
from a desire to get on top of the matter at hand by making it clear
458A but to come out on top of you. So if you're the same sort of person
I am, I'd be glad to go on questioning you, but if not I'd let it go.
And what sort of person am I? One who's glad to be refuted if I say
anything that's not true, and glad to do the refuting if anyone says
anything that's not true, and no less glad to be refuted than to do
the refuting. Because I consider that a greater good, insofar as it's
a greater good to be set free oneself from the greatest evil than to
set someone else free, since I can imagine no evil as being so great
B for a human being as a false opinion about precisely those things
that our speech is now about. So if you too claim to be that sort of
person, let's have a conversation, but if it seems we need to let it
go, let's tell it goodbye right now, and call off our speech.

Gorgias: I do indeed claim that I myself am the sort of person you
indicate, Socrates; maybe we should give some thought to the
preference of those present, though. Because I tell you, before you
two even got here, I gave those present a display of many things
C for a long time, and now we'll be drawing things out too far if we
have a conversation. It's only right to consider their preference too,
so we don't detain any of them who want to do something else.

Chaerephon: Well, Gorgias and Socrates, you yourselves hear the racket these men are making, because they want to hear anything you might say. And for my own part, far be it from me to be so busy that doing *anything* else becomes more important than speeches of this sort spoken in this way, for me to pass them up.

D *Callicles:* By the gods, Chaerephon, I too have been present at many
speeches before now, and I don't know when I've ever enjoyed
myself so much as right now. So for me, even if you want to go on
with the conversation all day long, you'll be doing me a favor.

Socrates: Well, Callicles, nothing on my side prevents it, so long as Gorgias is willing.

Gorgias: It would be a shameful[7] thing indeed after that, Socrates, for
me not to be willing, when I myself promised that anyone could
E ask whatever he wants. So if that seems good to these people here,
go on with the conversation and ask whatever you want.

Socrates: Listen, then, Gorgias, to what I'm surprised at in the things said by you. Because it may well be that you're speaking rightly and I just don't get it rightly. You claim you're able to make someone a rhetorician if he wants to learn from you?

Gorgias: Yes.

7 The superlative of this same word (*aischron*) was translated "ugliest" just above (457D). One might almost translate it the same way here: "It would be ugly of me indeed..."

Socrates: So as to be persuasive in a crowd about all subjects, not
teaching but persuading? 459A

Gorgias: Quite so.

Socrates: You were surely saying just now that the rhetorician will be more persuasive about what's healthy than the doctor.

Gorgias: I was saying he would be—in a crowd, anyway.

Socrates: And the "in a crowd" amounts to this: among the ignorant? Since presumably he won't be more persuasive than the doctor among those who have knowledge.

Gorgias: You're speaking the truth.

Socrates: So if he'll be more persuasive than the doctor, he becomes more persuasive than the one who has knowledge?

Gorgias: Quite.

Socrates: Even though he's not a doctor, right? B

Gorgias: Yes.

Socrates: But presumably someone who's not a doctor is lacking in knowledge of the things the doctor is knowledgeable about.

Gorgias: Clearly.

Socrates: Therefore, every time the rhetorician is more persuasive than the doctor, the one without knowledge will be more persuasive among people without knowledge. Is that what follows, or something else?

Gorgias: In this case, anyway, that does follow.

Socrates: But the rhetorician is in the same condition with respect to
all the other arts too, and so is rhetoric. There's no need at all for
it to know how things stand with the subjects themselves; it just
needs to have discovered some contrivance of persuasion to make C
it appear to those who don't know that it knows more than those
who do know.

Gorgias: Well doesn't that make it a lot easier, Socrates, for someone who hasn't learned the rest of the arts but just this one to be no worse off than the artisans?

Socrates: Whether the rhetorician is worse off or not worse off than
the others for being in that condition, we'll look into shortly, if it
has any bearing on our speech, but for now let's examine this first: D
is the rhetorician in exactly the same condition with respect to the
just and the unjust, the shameful and the beautiful, the good and
the bad, as he is with respect to the healthy and the other matters
belonging to the other arts, that he doesn't know them, what's good
or what's bad, what's beautiful or what's shameful or just or unjust,
but contrives persuasion about them so that without knowing
he seems, among those who don't know, to know more than the E
one who does know? Or is it a necessity to know them, and does
the person who's going to learn rhetoric from you have to arrive
knowing these things already? And if the one who arrives doesn't
know them, are you, as the teacher of rhetoric, going to teach him

nothing about these things—because it's not your job—and are you going to make him seem among the masses to know such things when he doesn't know them, and seem to be good when he isn't? Or will you be totally unable to teach him rhetoric, if he doesn't already know the truth about these things? How does it go with
460A things like that, Gorgias? And in front of Zeus, make the revelation you were just now saying you would, and tell us what in the world the power of rhetoric is.

Gorgias: Well, I suppose, Socrates, if he doesn't happen to know these things, he'll learn them too from me.

Socrates: Hold it right there, because you're putting it beautifully. If you make someone a rhetorician, it's a necessity for him to know the things that are just and unjust, either beforehand, or afterward by learning them from you.

B *Gorgias:* Quite so.

Socrates: What about this? Someone who's learned matters of carpentry is a carpenter, is he not?

Gorgias: Yes.

Socrates: And someone who's learned matters of music is a musician?

Gorgias: Yes.

Socrates: And someone who's learned matters of doctoring is a doctor, and so on for the rest? According to our same speech, each one who's learned each thing is the sort of person his knowledge turns him into?

Gorgias: Quite so.

Socrates: So according to our same speech, it's also the case that someone who's learned matters of justice is just?

Gorgias: Totally so, I presume.

Socrates: And presumably the just person does just things.

Gorgias: Yes.

C *Socrates:* Then it's a necessity that the rhetorician is just, and that a just person wants to do just things?

Gorgias: So it appears.

Socrates: Therefore the just person will never want to do injustice.

Gorgias: Necessarily.

Socrates: And from our speech it's a necessity that the rhetorician is just?

Gorgias: Yes.

Socrates: Therefore the rhetorician will never want to do injustice.

Gorgias: It appears not, anyway.

Socrates: Well do you remember saying a little while ago that one ought
D not to lay the blame on the trainers, or throw them out of the cities, if a boxer uses his boxing skill and commits injustice, and so in the same way if a rhetorician uses his rhetorical skill unjustly one ought not to lay the blame on the person who taught him or exile

him from the city, but the person who's doing the injustice and isn't using his rhetoric rightly? Were those things said or not?

Gorgias: They were said.

Socrates: But now it's shown that this same person, the rhetorician, E
never does injustice, isn't that so?

Gorgias: So it appears.

Socrates: And in the first speeches that were made, Gorgias, it was said that rhetoric would be about speeches not on the even and the odd but on the just and the unjust, is that right?

Gorgias: Yes.

Socrates: So in view of that, when you said those things then, I assumed that rhetoric, which always makes speeches about justice, could never be an unjust thing. But since you were saying a little later
that the rhetorician might also use his rhetoric unjustly, I got so sur- 461A
prised, thinking the things that had been said weren't in harmony, that I made those statements to the effect that if you would count it a gain to be refuted, the way I would, it would be worthwhile to have a conversation, but if not, to tell it goodbye. And now further along, when we've examined it, you see for yourself that we agree once again that the rhetorician is incapable of using his rhetoric unjustly or of being willing to do injustice. What in the world is
going on with these things, Gorgias —by the dog![8]—is something B
it will take no small communal effort to look into adequately from all angles.

Polus: What gives, Socrates? Do you really think about rhetoric the way you're now talking about it? Or do you imagine—because Gorgias was ashamed not to grant you that the rhetorically skilled man knows the things that are just and beautiful and good, or if someone came not knowing them on his own, he'd teach him himself, and then from this concession maybe some contradiction ended up in
his speeches, just what you love, when you yourself were leading C
him on with such questions!—well who do you imagine would deny either that he knew what's just or that he'd teach it to others? But it's terribly uncouth to draw the talk into such matters.

Socrates: Polus, you most beautifully-mannered gentleman, surely it is with good reason that we get ourselves companions and sons, so when we ourselves have gotten too old and go off the straight and narrow, you youngsters standing by can straighten our lives out again in our deeds and in our speeches as well. And now if in
any respect Gorgias and I have gone out of bounds in our speeches, D
you stand by and do set us straight—it's the just thing for you to

8 This was an oath frequently used by Socrates in Plato's dialogues, but rarely found elsewhere. At 482B below, he reveals that the dog in question is Anubis, an Egyptian god corresponding to the Greek god Hermes. Eva Brann (*The Music of the Republic*, Paul Dry Press, 2004, pp. 118-119) argues that it is particularly the role of Hermes as guide of Heracles that the oath invokes, for the truly Herculean labor of self-examination.

do—and on your say-so, I'm willing take back whatever you want from among the things that have been agreed, if any of them seem to you not beautiful things to have agreed to, as long as you'll guard against just one thing for me.

Polus: What do you mean by that?

Socrates: That you keep a limit, Polus, on that lengthy speaking that you tried to use at first.

Polus: What? Won't I have the right to say as much as I want?

E *Socrates:* You'd certainly be suffering something dreadful, most excellent fellow, when you've come to Athens, where there's the greatest
right to speak in Greece, if you alone were then to fail to get that
here. But just put it a different way: if you're speaking at length
and aren't willing to answer what you're asked, wouldn't I be suffering something dreadful on my side if I'm not going to have the
462A right to go away and not listen to you? But if anything said in our
speech troubles you, and you want to straighten it out, then speak
the way I did just now, putting it a different way that seems good
to you, and by asking and answering questions in your turn the
way Gorgias and I did, refute and be refuted. Because presumably
you claim to know the same things Gorgias does, isn't that right?

Polus: I do.

Socrates: And do you also urge people on each occasion to ask you whatever anyone wants, claiming to know how to answer?

Polus: Very much so.

B *Socrates:* Now, then, do whichever of these two things you want: ask
or answer.

Polus: I'll do just that. Answer me, Socrates: what do *you* claim rhetoric is, since Gorgias seems to you to have no clue about it?

Socrates: Are you asking me what sort of art I claim it is?

Polus: I am.

Socrates: None at all, it seems to me, Polus, to tell you the truth.

Polus: Then what *does* rhetoric seem to you to be?

Socrates: A thing that you claim, in the book I was reading recently,
C *makes* art.

Polus: What's that you're talking about?

Socrates: A certain kind of experience, I'd say.

Polus: So rhetoric seems to you to be experience?

Socrates: It does to me, unless you say it's something else.

Polus: Experience at what?

Socrates: At bringing about a certain gratification and pleasure.

Polus: So rhetoric seems to you to be a beautiful thing, then, since it's able to gratify people?

Socrates: What's this, Polus? Have you already learned from me what
D I claim it *is*, so you can ask the question that follows that, about
whether it doesn't seem to me to be beautiful?

Polus: Well haven't I found out that you claim it's a certain kind of experience?

Socrates: Then since you have a high regard for gratifying, would you like to gratify me in a small way?

Polus: I would.

Socrates: Ask me now about the cooking of tasty food,[9] what sort of art that seems to me to be.

Polus: I ask you, then: what sort of art is cooking tasty food?

Socrates: None at all, Polus. Say "But what is it?"

Polus: I say it.

Socrates: A certain kind of experience. Say "At what?"

Polus: I say it.

Socrates: At bringing about gratification and pleasure, Polus. E

Polus: So cooking tasty food is the same thing as rhetoric?

Socrates: Not at all, just a part of the same pursuit.

Polus: What's that you're speaking of?

Socrates: Telling the truth might be too uncouth; for Gorgias' sake, I'm reluctant to say it, in case he imagines I'm making fun of his pursuit. But I don't really know whether this is the rhetoric Gorgias 463A
pursues—from our speech just now nothing became clear to us about what in the world *he* thinks it is—but what *I* call rhetoric is part of a certain matter that's not one of the beautiful things.

Gorgias: Part of what, Socrates? Speak; don't be ashamed on my account.

Socrates: Well it seems to me, Gorgias, that it's not an artful pursuit at all, but belongs to a soul that's good at guessing, brave, and clever by nature at dealing with people. The crux of it I call pandering. B
It seems to me that there are many other parts of this pursuit as well, and that one of them is cooking tasty food, which seems to be an art, but, the way my speech has it, isn't art but a matter of experience and repetition. I call rhetoric a part of this too, as well as cosmetology and sophistry, these four parts to deal with four matters. Now if Polus wants to learn something, let him learn it, because he hasn't learned yet what kind of part of pandering I claim C
rhetoric is, but without noticing that I haven't answered that yet, he goes on to ask whether I consider it a beautiful thing. But I'm not going to answer him whether I consider rhetoric to be a beautiful thing or a shameful one before I first answer what it is. That wouldn't be a just thing, Polus. If you do want to learn it though, ask what kind of part of pandering I claim rhetoric is.

Polus: I'm asking: answer what kind of part it is.

9 The Greek word means the preparation of *opsa*, all the things other than bread that people eat. Some of the older British translations settled on translating the word as "cookery," for its belittling tone, or chose "pastry cooking," to draw upon that especially British form of passion for empty calories.

D *Socrates:* Now would you understand it when I've answered? By my speech, rhetoric is a simulation of a part of politics.

Polus: What about it, then? Are you saying it's beautiful or shameful?

Socrates: Shameful, I call it—I do call bad things shameful—since I'm obliged to answer you as if you already knew what I'm talking about.

Gorgias: By Zeus, Socrates! I don't understand what you're talking about myself.

E *Socrates:* That's likely, Gorgias, because I'm not saying anything clear yet, but this Polus is a headstrong young thing.

Gorgias: Pay no attention to him, then, and tell me how you mean that rhetoric is a simulation of a part of politics.

Socrates: I'll just try to put into words what rhetoric appears to me to
464A be, and if that's not exactly what it is, Polus here will refute me. You call something a body, presumably, and something a soul?

Gorgias: How could it be otherwise?

Socrates: And do you imagine that there's a certain good condition for each of these?

Gorgias: I do.

Socrates: And what about this? Is there something that seems to be good condition but isn't? I mean this sort of thing, for example: there are many people who seem to have their bodies in good shape, whom someone other than a doctor or a gymnastic trainer could not easily detect are not in good condition.

Gorgias: You're telling the truth.

Socrates: I'm speaking of that sort of thing as being present both in a body and in a soul, which makes the body and the soul seem to
B be in good condition, but not be so any the more.

Gorgias: There are such things.

Socrates: Come along, then, and if I have the power, I'll display to you more clearly what I mean. Since there's a pair of matters of concern, I say there are two arts; the one applying to the soul I call politics, and while I'm not able to give you a name that way for the one applying to the body, I say that ministering to the body is one thing with two parts, gymnastic training and doctoring. In politics, there's lawmaking in place of gymnastic training, and
C justice corresponding to doctoring. Now each of the two pairings overlaps within itself, inasmuch as its parts are concerned with the same thing, doctoring overlapping with gymnastic training and justice with lawmaking; all the same, they differ from one another in a certain way. So there are these four, which always minister to what's best, the one pair to the body, the other to the soul; the aptitude for pandering, noticing this—not by discernment, I mean, but by guesswork—dividing itself up four ways and slipping into
D the guise of each of the parts, passes itself off as being that very

thing it has slipped its way into; it has no concern at all for what's best, but using what's most pleasant in each case, sets a trap for foolishness and entices it, with the result that it seems to be of the highest worth. So cooking tasty food has slipped into the guise of doctoring, and passes itself off as knowing the best foods for the body, so that, if there had to be a contest between a cook and a doctor among children, or among men as foolish as children, over which of the two has an understanding of desirable and worthless
foods, the doctor or the cook, the doctor would die of starvation. E
So I call it pandering, and I claim that sort of thing is shameful, 465A
Polus—yes, I'm saying this to you—because it makes guesses about what's pleasant in the absence of what's best. And I say it's not art but a matter of experience, because it has no speech to give about the nature of the things it makes use of or what it uses them on, whatever they may be, and therefore it can't state the cause of any of them. I don't call any proceeding that's irrational an art. But if you want to take issue with these things, I'm willing to submit to the test of speech.

So as I say, cooking tasty food is pandering disguised as doctor- B
ing, and in this same manner, the guise of gymnastic training is worn by cosmetology, a harmful, deceitful, low-class thing unfit for free people, that tricks people by shaping, coloring, smoothing, and clothing, so as to make them wrap an extraneous beauty around themselves, to the neglect of the native kind that comes through gymnastic exercise. Now to avoid making a long speech, I'm willing to say it for you the way geometers do, since you're probably C
already following this, that as cosmetology is to gymnastic training, so is cooking tasty food to doctoring—or more precisely, like this: as cosmetology is to gymnastic training, so is sophistry to lawmaking, and as cooking tasty food is to doctoring, so is rhetoric to justice. However, as I say, while these things differ in this way by nature, since they're closely akin, sophists and rhetoricians get mixed together in the same place dealing with the same subjects, and they themselves have no more notion of what use they are than
other people have about them. In fact, if the soul wasn't in charge of D
the body but the body depended on itself, and cooking tasty food and doctoring weren't overviewed and distinguished by the soul, but the body itself did the judging, evaluating the things pertaining to itself by the gratifications they gave, then, Polus my friend, the saying of Anaxagoras[10]—since you're experienced with these things— would be very apt: all things would be mixed up together

10 A philosopher who wrote that all material things contain all natures, and are named for whatever predominates in the mixture. He claimed that Intellect alone is unmixed, and orders all things, but according to Socrates (*Phaedo* 97B-99D), he made no use of that claim in any account of causes.

in the same place, with health-restoring and health-promoting and tasty things being indistinguishable.

E So you've heard what I claim rhetoric is, the counterpart for the soul of cooking tasty food, working the way that does on the body. Now maybe I've done something absurd, since, when I'm not letting you speak in long speeches, I've drawn out a copious speech myself. But it's something I deserve to have your forgiveness for, because you weren't understanding me when I spoke briefly, and you were unable to make any use at all of the answer that I gave
466A you and needed a detailed explanation. So if I too have no way to make use of something you answer, then you too draw out your speech, but if I have a way, then let me make use of it; that's the just thing. And now, if you have any way to make use of this answer, make use of it.

Polus: So what are you claiming? Rhetoric seems to you to be pandering?

Socrates: Well, I said it's a part of pandering. Can't you remember at your age, Polus? What will you do later?

Polus: So the good rhetoricians seem to you to be regarded in their cities as disreputable panderers?

B *Socrates:* Are you asking this as a question or stating it as the beginning of some speech?

Polus: I'm asking.

Socrates: To me, they don't seem to be regarded period.

Polus: How not regarded? Don't they have the greatest power in their cities?

Socrates: No, not if you mean that having power is a good thing for the one who has it.

Polus: That's exactly what I do mean.

Socrates: Then it seems to me the rhetoricians have the least amount of power in the city.

C *Polus:* What? Don't they put to death anyone they want, the same as tyrants, and seize property, and expel anyone it seems good to them from the cities.

Socrates: By the dog, Polus, I truly can't decide about any of the things you say whether you're saying them yourself and exposing your own opinion, or asking me.

Polus: Well, I'm asking you.

Socrates: Okay, my friend; in that case, are you asking me two questions at the same time?

Polus: How two?

Socrates: Weren't you just saying something to this effect: "Don't the
D rhetoricians put to death anyone they want, the same as tyrants, and seize property, and force anyone it seems good to them out of the cities?"

Polus: I was.

Socrates: Then I say to you that these are two questions, and I'll give you an answer for both. Because I claim, Polus, that both the rhetoricians and the tyrants have the smallest amount of power in their cities,
as I was saying just now, since they do next to nothing of what they E
want, although they do whatever seems to them to be best.

Polus: So isn't that having great power?

Socrates: No, not as Polus claims anyway.

Polus: I claim it's not? I claim it is.

Socrates: By the—no you don't, since you claim that having great power is a good thing for the one who has it.

Polus: I do claim that.

Socrates: So do you imagine it's a good thing if someone does these things that seem to him to be best when he doesn't have any sense? And that's what you call having great power?

Polus: Not I.

Socrates: Then will you demonstrate that rhetoricians have sense and 467A
that rhetoric is an art and not pandering by refuting me? But if you leave me unrefuted, the rhetoricians who do what seems good to them in their cities, and the tyrants as well, will have attained nothing good by that. But power is a good thing, as you claim, while you also agree that doing what seems good without sense is a bad thing—don't you?

Polus: I do.

Socrates: So how can rhetoricians or tyrants have great power in their cities unless Socrates has been refuted by Polus and they do what they want?

Polus: This man— B

Socrates: I claim they don't do what they want; just refute me.

Polus: Weren't you just agreeing that they do what seems to them to be best?

Socrates: I agree to it now too.

Polus: Then don't they do what they want?

Socrates: I claim they don't.

Polus: When they do what seems good to them?

Socrates: That's what I claim.

Polus: You're making appalling and monstrous statements, Socrates.

Socrates: Don't cast aspersions, drollest Polus—so that I might give
you a salutation in your own style. But if you have things to ask C
me, display the fact that I'm mistaken, and if you don't, answer questions yourself.

Polus: I'm quite willing to answer questions, so I can know what you're talking about too.

Socrates: Then does it seem to you that human beings want that thing which they do on each occasion, or that for the sake of which they do the thing which they do? Take for example people who drink medicines they get from doctors; do they seem to you to want that very thing which they're doing, drinking medicine and having the unpleasantness of it, or do they want that thing, being healthy, for the sake of which they're drinking it?

D *Polus:* It's obvious that it's the being healthy.

Socrates: Then too, take the case of people who make voyages and engage in other money-making business; what they want is not that which they do on each occasion. (Who wants to go to sea and take risks and have trouble?) Instead, I imagine they want that for the sake of which they go to sea, to get rich, because it's for the sake of riches that they make the voyages.

Polus: Certainly.

Socrates: So is it any other way with everything as well? If anyone does anything for the sake of something, he wants not that thing which
E he does but that for the sake of which he does it?

Polus: Yes.

Socrates: Now of the things there are, is there any which is not either good or bad or in between, namely neither good nor bad?

Polus: That's a great necessity, Socrates.

Socrates: And do you say that wisdom and health and riches and other things of that sort are good, and that the opposites of these are bad?

Polus: I do.

Socrates: And do you say that things that are neither good nor bad are
468A the ones that sometimes have a share of good, sometimes a share of bad, and sometimes of neither, such as sitting and walking and running and voyaging, and also such as stones and sticks and other things like that? Aren't these the things you mean? Or are there some other things you call neither good nor bad?

Polus: No, it's those.

Socrates: Well, do people do these in-between things for the sake of the good ones whenever they do them, or the good for the sake of the in-between?

B *Polus:* Presumably the in-between for the sake of the good.

Socrates: Therefore it's in pursuit of the good that we walk whenever we walk, imagining it to be better, and on the other hand stand still whenever we stand still, for the sake of the same thing, the good, isn't that right?

Polus: Yes.

Socrates: Then also we put people to death, if we do put anyone to death, and exile people and seize property, imagining it's better for us to do these things than not to?

Polus: Certainly.

Socrates: Therefore those who do these things do them for the sake of the good?

Polus: I affirm that.

Socrates: And we've agreed that the things people do for the sake of something are not the things they want, but they want that for the sake of which they do them? C

Polus: Most assuredly.

Socrates: Therefore we don't simply want to slaughter people or throw them out of our cities or seize their property in that sense, but if these things might be beneficial we want to do them, and when they're harmful we don't want to. Because, as you affirm, it's the good things that we want, while we don't want the ones that are neither good nor bad or the bad ones. Is that right? Do I seem to you to be telling the truth, Polus, or not? Why don't you answer?

Polus: It's true.

Socrates: Then if we're in agreement about these things, if anyone puts someone to death or exiles him from a city or seizes his property, whether he's a tyrant or a rhetorician, imagining that it's better for himself when it happens to be worse, that person is doing what seems good to him, right? D

Polus: Yes.

Socrates: Well is he also doing what he wants, if these things happen to be bad? Why don't you answer?

Polus: He sure doesn't seem to me to be doing what he wants.

Socrates: So is there any way such a person can have great power in that city, if, by your own admission, having great power is something good? E

Polus: There's not.

Socrates: Therefore I was telling the truth when I said that it's possible for a human being to do what seems good to him in a city without having great power and without doing what he wants.

Polus: Yeah, right, Socrates, as if you wouldn't accept free rein to do what seemed good to you in the city rather than not, and wouldn't be envious when you saw someone putting to death anyone that seemed good to him or seizing his property or locking him up.

Socrates: Justly, you mean, or unjustly?

Polus: Whichever way he might do it! Isn't he someone to envy either way? 469A

Socrates: Watch what you say, Polus.

Polus: Why's that?

Socrates: Because one shouldn't envy those who are unenviable or miserable but pity them.

Polus: What? Is that the condition the people I'm talking about seem to you to be in?

Socrates: How could it be any other way?

Polus: Then whoever puts to death anyone it seems good to him, and puts him to death justly, seems to you to be miserable and pathetic?

Socrates: Not to me, but not enviable either.

Polus: Weren't you claiming just now that he's miserable?

B *Socrates:* The one who puts someone to death unjustly is, my comrade, and pathetic on top of it; the one who does so justly is not to be envied.

Polus: I'd suppose it's the one who's put to death unjustly who's pathetic and miserable.

Socrates: Less so than the one who puts him to death, Polus, and less so than someone who's justly put to death.

Polus: How can that be, Socrates?

Socrates: In this way, that *the* greatest of evils is committing injustice.

Polus: That's the greatest? Isn't suffering injustice a greater one?

Socrates: That least of all.

Polus: So you'd rather suffer injustice than commit it?

C *Socrates:* I wouldn't want to do either one, but if it were necessary either to commit injustice or suffer it, I'd choose to suffer it rather than commit it.

Polus: So you wouldn't accept being a tyrant?

Socrates: Not if you mean the same thing by being a tyrant that I do.

Polus: I mean the very thing I was speaking of just now, having free rein to do whatever seems good to oneself in one's city, putting to death and exiling people and doing it all as one takes the notion.

Socrates: You blessed fellow! I'll just describe something; you can
D make objections. If I were in the marketplace when it was crowded, and took a dagger from under my sleeve and said to you, "Polus, an amazing and tyrannical power has just come over me, so if it seems to me that any of these people you see here really ought to die this very moment, that person—whomever I see fit—will be dead; and if it seems to me that any of them should have his head split open, it will be thoroughly split open this very moment, or
E his cloak will be ripped to pieces if that seems good. That's how great my power in this city is." And if you were incredulous and I showed you the dagger, when you saw it you might perhaps say, "Everybody could have great power that way, Socrates, since by that method any house that seemed good to you could be burned down, as well as the Athenian shipyards and warships, and the whole fleet, both public and private." But then that's not having great power, just doing what seems good to oneself, or does it seem so to you?

Polus: No, certainly not the way you describe it.

470A *Socrates:* Then can you tell me why you find fault with that sort of power?

Polus: I can.

Socrates: Why do you, exactly? Tell me.

Polus: Because it's inevitable that someone who acts that way will be punished.

Socrates: And isn't being punished a bad thing?

Polus: Very much so.

Socrates: Well then, you amazing fellow, you've come back around and now it appears to you that if it ends up working out advantageously for the person who does what seems good, it's a good thing, and that, it looks like, is having great power; but if it doesn't end up that way, it's a bad thing, and that's having scant power. But let's consider this point as well: would we do anything other than agree that sometimes it's better to do those things we were just talking about—putting people to death and forcing them into exile and seizing their property—but sometimes it's not? B

Polus: That's certainly the case.

Socrates: So it looks like this is a point of agreement on both your side and mine.

Polus: Yes.

Socrates: When, then, do you claim it's better to do these things? Tell me what line you'd draw.

Polus: You answer that, Socrates.

Socrates: Well then, Polus, if it pleases you more to hear it from me, I claim that whenever someone does those things justly, it's better, and whenever he does them unjustly, it's worse. C

Polus: Wow, it's a tough thing to refute you, Socrates. Even a child could come up with a refutation showing that you're not speaking the truth, couldn't he?

Socrates: Then I'd be most grateful to the child, and equally so to you, if you refute me and rescue me from my fatuousness. And see to it that you don't get tired of doing a favor for a man who's your friend, but refute me.

Polus: Well, Socrates, there's certainly no need to go back to ancient goings-on to refute you. Why, those things that happened just yesterday or the day before are enough to prove you wrong and to demonstrate that lots of unjust people are happy. D

Socrates: What sorts of things are those?

Polus: I suppose you see Archelaus,[11] that son of Perdiccas, ruling over Macedonia.

Socrates: If not, at least I hear it.

Polus: Well, does he seem to you to be happy or miserable?

Socrates: I don't know, Polus; I've never been around the man.

Polus: What? You need to be around him to tell? You can't tell otherwise, here and now, that he's happy? E

Socrates: I certainly can't, by Zeus.

11 As Polus spells out in lurid detail below, Archelaus came to power by violence. He sought to legitimize his rule by inviting prominent Athenians to pay him visits. Euripides and others had gone, but Socrates had refused the invitation. The phrase Great King used below was the Greeks' way of referring to the supreme and absolute ruler of the vast Persian empire.

Polus: Obviously, Socrates, you'll claim next that you can't even tell whether the Great King is happy.

Socrates: And I'll be telling the truth, because I don't know how he's doing in education and justice.

Polus: What? That's where all happiness is?

Socrates: That's what I say, anyway, Polus, since I claim that a man or woman with the beauty of goodness[12] is happy, and one who's unjust and corrupt is miserable.

471A *Polus:* So on your say-so, this Archelaus is miserable?

Socrates: If indeed he's unjust, my friend.

Polus: Well how could he not be unjust? He had no right at all to
the ruling position he now holds, since his mother was a slave
of Perdiccas's brother Alcetas; so according to what's just he was
Alcetas's slave, and if he wanted to do the just thing he'd be slaving
away for Alcetas, and be happy by your speech. And how amaz-
ingly miserable he's become now, since he's committed the greatest
B injustices. First, he sent for this very master and uncle of his, as if
to give him back the ruling position Perdiccas had robbed him of,
and entertained him and his son Alexander—his own cousin, and
about his own age—as guests, and when he'd gotten them drunk,
he bundled them into a cart, hauled them away after dark, slit both
their throats, and hid their bodies. He failed to notice that committing these injustices had make him utterly miserable, and they
C caused him no regret; and a little later he had no wish to become
happy by bringing up his brother, Perdiccas's legitimate son, a
boy of about seven to whom the ruling position would have come
as a matter of justice, and restoring the rule to him, but flung him
into a well and drowned him, and told the boy's mother Cleopatra
that he fell in and died chasing after a goose. So now assuredly,
inasmuch as he's committed the greatest injustices of anyone in
Macedonia, he's the most miserable person of all the Macedonians,
not the happiest, and maybe among the Athenians there's someone,
D you to start with, who'd prefer to become any other Macedonian
at all rather than Archelaus.

Socrates: Right at the beginning of our speeches, Polus, I commended you, saying that it seems to me you've been well educated for rhetoric, but that you haven't paid attention to conversing. And now this is the speech, is it, by which a child could refute me? You imagine that I've now been refuted by you by this speech, for declaring that the person who commits injustice is not happy? On what basis, my good man? Why, I don't agree with a single one of the things you're claiming.

---

12 *Kalos kagathos*, literally "beautiful and good," was a standard phrase used by the Athenian aristocracy to express its opinion of itself. Socrates transforms that usage here and in other dialogues by taking the meaning of the words seriously, and by taking the phrase as applying equally to women.

Polus: You don't want to, since the way it seems to you is the way I say it is. E

Socrates: You blessed fellow, you're trying to refute me rhetorically,
doing what people in the lawcourts consider refuting. There too,
those on one side have the impression they're refuting those on the
other when they bring up lots of well-regarded witnesses in favor
of the speeches they're making, while the opposing speaker brings
up maybe one or none. But that sort of refutation is worth nothing
for getting at truth; at times someone can even be destroyed by 472A
large numbers of false witnesses who seem to have something to
them. Now too, for the things you're talking about, little short of
everybody, Athenians and foreigners alike, will join you in saying
the same things, if you want to bring up witnesses against me to
say I'm not telling the truth. Nicias the son of Niceratus, and his
brothers along with him, will be witnesses on your side, if you
want, they whose tripods are standing in a row at the temple of
Dionysus, and if you want, so will Aristocrates the son of Scellias, B
who dedicated that beautiful offering at the temple of Pythian
Apollo, or, if you want, there's the whole household of Pericles
or any other family you want to pick from those around here.[13]
But I, who happen to be one person, do not agree with you. You
can't force me to, although by bringing in many false witnesses
against me you're trying to oust me from my birthright, which is
the truth. But if I don't bring you yourself forward as one witness
to agree with the things I'm saying, I consider myself as having
accomplished nothing worth speaking of in regard to the things
our speech may be about. And I consider that you haven't either C
unless I, only one though I am, am a witness for your side, and you
let go of all these others. So there's that one style of refutation, as
you and many others imagine, and there's another, which I for my
part envision. Now that we've set them alongside one another, let's
examine whether there's any difference between them. Because the
things about which we're in dispute happen to be no small matters
at all, but just about the ones it's most beautiful to have knowledge
about, and most shameful to lack it, since what they boil down to is
recognizing or being ignorant of who's happy and who's not. First D
of all, the immediate issue, the one with which our speech is now
concerned, is that you regard a man who commits injustice and
is unjust as being able to be blessedly happy, if indeed you regard

13 The examples Socrates chooses reflect the diversity of Athenian political styles. Nicias was a traditionalist, Aristocrates an oligarch, and Pericles a leader of the democracy. Even the two temples mentioned point to the diversity of Athenian styles of worship, with the Apollonian and Dionysian observances resembling something like a high-church/low-church distinction, though both sorts were incorporated into the common public celebrations each year. The offerings dedicated at temples were a way of showing off wealth and laying claim to prestige. Polus can look in any direction, Socrates grants, and find the "opinion leaders" of Athens on his side.

Archelaus as being unjust but happy. There's no other way for us to think you consider the matter, is there?

Polus: None at all.

Socrates: But I claim that's impossible. That's one thing we're in dispute about, then. Okay: say the unjust person will be happy. Will that still be the case if he gets his just due and punishment?

Polus: Then least of all; that way he'd be the most miserable.

E *Socrates:* So therefore, by your speech, if someone who commits injustice doesn't get his just due he *will* be happy.

Polus: So I claim.

Socrates: Well, by my opinion, Polus, someone who commits injustice and is unjust is thoroughly miserable, but still more miserable if he doesn't pay a just penalty and get punishment when he commits injustice, and less miserable if he pays a just penalty and gets his just due from gods and humans.

473A *Polus:* Well, Socrates, the things you're trying to say are bizarre anyway.

Socrates: And I'll also try to make you say the same things with me, my comrade—because I consider you a friend. Now, then, these are the things we differ about; you examine them too. I believe I said in the earlier discussion that committing injustice is worse than suffering it.

Polus: You certainly did.

Socrates: And you said suffering it is.

Polus: Yes.

Socrates: And I claimed that those who commit injustice are miserable, and got refuted by you.

Polus: By Zeus, yes!

B *Socrates:* So you imagine, Polus.

Polus: Imagining what's true.

Socrates: Maybe. But you said in turn that those who commit injustice are happy, if they don't pay a just penalty.

Polus: Very much so.

Socrates: While I'm claiming they're the most miserable, and the ones who pay a just penalty are less so. Do you want to refute that too?

Polus: Oh, yeah, Socrates; that's even harder to refute than the other thing.

Socrates: Not only that, Polus; it's impossible. The truth never gets refuted.

Polus: What are you talking about? If a fellow gets caught committing
C an injustice, plotting a tyranny, say, and after he's caught is broken on the rack and castrated and has his eyes burned out, and after suffering many other severe mutilations of all sorts himself and watching his children and wife suffer them, he's at last nailed up on stakes or covered in tar and set on fire, that guy's going to be

happier than if he got away with it and was set up as tyrant and lived out his life ruling over the city, doing whatever he wanted, being envied and considered happy by his fellow citizens and D
everyone else, foreigners and all? That's what you're saying is impossible to refute?

Socrates: This time, Polus you high-class fellow, instead of refuting me you're scaring me with bogeymen; last time you were citing witnesses. But leaving that aside, help me remember a little something. "If he were committing an injustice, plotting a tyranny, say," were you saying that?

Polus: I was.

Socrates: Then neither one of them is ever going to be any happier than the other one, neither the one who achieved the tyranny by committing injustice nor the one who paid the just penalty—out of a pair of miserable people, there couldn't be a *happier* one—but E
the one who gets away with it and becomes a tyrant will certainly be more miserable. What's this, Polus? You're laughing? Is this still another form of refutation, when someone says something, to laugh it down without refuting it?

Polus: Wouldn't you assume you've been refuted, Socrates, when you say things of a sort that no human being would lay claim to? Just ask any of the people here.

Socrates: I'm not a politician,[14] Polus. Last year, in fact, when I was chosen by lot to be on the council, and, since my tribe held the presidency, I had to put a question up for votes, I came in for some 474A
laughter—I didn't know how to put it to a vote. So don't urge me now either to take the votes of the people around us, but if you have no better refutation than that, then as I was just now saying, give it up for me to take a turn, and test out a refutation of the sort I imagine it ought to be. Because as I say, I know how to bring forward a witness who's one person, the very one with whom the speech with me is taking place, but I let the many witnesses go; and I know how to take the vote of one person, but with many I don't B
even have a conversation. See, then, whether you'll be willing in your turn to give a chance for a refutation by answering my questions. Because I imagine that you and I and the rest of humankind believe it's worse to commit injustice than to suffer it, and worse not to pay one's just due than to pay it.

Polus: And I say neither I nor any other human being believes that. You'd choose then to suffer injustice rather than commit it?

Socrates: And so would you and everybody else.

---

14 This assertion should be compared with one Socrates makes below, in 521D. The allusion he goes on to make here is a classic example of Socrates' self-effacing irony. As he describes more fully in the *Apology* (32B-C), Socrates had refused, at risk of imprisonment or even death, to permit a vote on an illegal motion to put a group of generals on trial *en masse* for not bringing back the bodies of the dead after a naval battle.

Polus: Not by a long shot; neither I nor you nor anyone else would.

C *Socrates:* So you'll answer?

Polus: Certainly, because I can't wait to find out what in the world you're going to say.

Socrates: Well, so you can find out, tell me, as though I were asking it to start with: which seems worse to you, Polus, committing injustice or suffering it?

Polus: To me, suffering it.

Socrates: But what about this? Which seems uglier,[15] committing injustice or suffering it?

Polus: Committing it.

Socrates: So it's also worse, if it's an uglier thing?

Polus: Not in the least.

D *Socrates:* I understand. Very likely you believe beautiful and good aren't the same thing, and bad and ugly aren't either.

Polus: Certainly not.

Socrates: But what about this? With all beautiful things, such as bodies, colors, shapes, sounds, pursuits, is there nothing you're looking to when you call them beautiful in each case? For instance, in the case of beautiful bodies first, don't you say that they're beautiful either as a result of the fitness each has for some end it's fitted to, or as a result of some pleasure, if upon being beheld they cause the beholders to feel delight? Do you have anything to say about beautiful bodies that goes beyond these things?

E *Polus:* I don't.

Socrates: So is it that way with everything else too, and do you refer to shapes and colors as beautiful either on account of some pleasure or on account of contributing to an end or both?

Polus: I do.

Socrates: And is it the same way with sounds and with everything that has to do with music?

Polus: Yes.

Socrates: And the things that have to do with laws and pursuits, beautiful ones that is, presumably don't go beyond these bounds, of being beneficial[16] or pleasant or both.

475A *Polus:* It doesn't seem so to me.

Socrates: And is the beauty of learnable things of the same sort?

---

15 See the footnote to 458D. The ugly scene described in 457D, behavior that makes people cringe just to watch it, that occasions the first use of any form of the word *aischros* in the dialogue, is perhaps a suitable model to display the kind of ugliness of actions that becomes synonymous with shamefulness. It is important to judge whether Polus's answer to this question expresses an honest opinion; Callicles will claim later (482E) that Polus is experiencing shame about telling the truth in public.

16 Socrates has gotten to this criterion of the beautiful in three steps, from (visible) fitness to an end (*chreia*), to the quality of contributing to an end (*ôphelia*), to being beneficial (*ôphelimos*).

Polus: Quite so, and now at any rate you're laying things out beautifully, Socrates, in defining the beautiful by pleasure and good.

Socrates: And the ugly by the opposites, pain and bad?

Polus: Of necessity.

Socrates: Therefore, whenever one of a pair of beautiful things is the more beautiful, it's more beautiful by means of one or the other, or both, of this pair, by means of either pleasure or contributing to an end, or both.

Polus: Certainly.

Socrates: And whenever one of a pair of ugly things is the more ugly, B
it will be uglier by exceeding in either pain or badness—isn't that a necessity?

Polus: Yes.

Socrates: Now then, what was being said just now about committing injustice and suffering it? Didn't you say that suffering injustice is worse but committing it is uglier?

Polus: That's what I said.

Socrates: So if committing injustice is uglier than suffering it, then either it's more painful, and it would be uglier by exceeding in pain, or it's uglier by exceeding in badness, or in both? Isn't that too a necessity?

Polus: How could it not be?

Socrates: First, then, let's consider this: does committing injustice C
exceed suffering it in pain, and do people who commit injustice suffer more pain than those who suffer injustice?

Polus: That's not the way it is at all, Socrates.

Socrates: Therefore it doesn't exceed it in pain, at least.

Polus: It sure doesn't.

Socrates: So if it doesn't exceed it in pain, it couldn't exceed it in both ways either.

Polus: It doesn't appear that it could.

Socrates: So what's left is that it exceeds it in the other way.

Polus: Yes.

Socrates: In badness.

Polus: It looks that way.

Socrates: So by exceeding it in badness, committing injustice would be worse than suffering it.

Polus: Evidently it would.

Socrates: And isn't it the case that it's agreed by most human beings,[17] as D
it was agreed by you with us a while ago, that committing injustice is an uglier thing than suffering it?

Polus: Yes.

Socrates: And it's come to light that it's worse.

Polus: It looks that way.

---

17 Note that it was Polus who earlier (471C-D, 473E) set himself up as an authority on what most people believe.

Socrates: Well, would you prefer what's worse and uglier when it's more so rather than less? Don't shy away from answering, Polus; you won't get hurt. Just answer with some class by submitting to
E the speech as you would to doctor, and either concur in what I'm asking or deny it.

Polus: I certainly wouldn't prefer it, Socrates.

Socrates: Would any other human being?

Polus: It doesn't seem so to me from this speech anyway.

Socrates: Therefore what I was saying is true, that neither I nor you nor any other human being would prefer to commit injustice rather than suffer it, precisely because it's a worse thing.

Polus: So it appears.

Socrates: So you see, Polus, when refutation and refutation are laid out side by side, there's no resemblance at all, but in your case everybody else agrees except me, and in my case it's good enough that
476A you alone, though you're only one person, are in agreement and stand as a witness, and I put the question up to your vote alone and dismiss everyone else. So let that be the way that point goes. Next let's examine the second thing we were in dispute about, whether it's the greatest of evils for someone who commits injustice to pay a just penalty, as you imagined, or a greater one for him not to pay it, as I imagined instead. Let's consider it this way: do you call paying a just penalty when one commits injustice the same thing as being justly disciplined?

Polus: I do.

B *Socrates:* Well, can you say that it's not the case that all just things are beautiful to the extent that they're just? Tell me after you've thought it over carefully.

Polus: No, Socrates, it seems to me they are.

Socrates: Then consider this too: if anyone does anything, is it necessary for there also to be something it's done to by the one who's doing it?

Polus: It seems that way to me.

Socrates: And is it also necessary for what the doer does to the thing it's done to to be of such a sort as the doer does? I mean something like this: if someone hits, it's necessary for something to *be* hit?

Polus: It's necessary.

C *Socrates:* And if the one doing the hitting hits hard or quickly, that's also the way the thing that's hit is hit?

Polus: Yes.

Socrates: Therefore what happens to the thing that's hit is of the sort that the one doing the hitting makes it?

Polus: Certainly.

Socrates: And if anyone does any burning, it's necessary for something to be burned?

Polus: How could it be otherwise?

Socrates: And if he burns in a severe or painful way, what's burned is burned the way the one doing the burning burns it?

Polus: Certainly.

Socrates: And if someone cuts, the same speech applies? Because something is cut.

Polus: Yes.

Socrates: And if he makes the cut big or deep or painful, the thing cut D
is cut with the sort of cut by which the cutter cuts it?

Polus: So it appears.

Socrates: So putting it together, see if you agree with what was said just before, that for everything, the way the doer does something is the way it's done to the thing it's done to.

Polus: I do agree.

Socrates: Now with these things agreed, is paying a just penalty having something done to one, or doing something?

Polus: By necessity, Socrates, it's having something done to one.

Socrates: And done by someone who does it?

Polus: How could it not be? By the one doing the disciplining, of course.

Socrates: And someone who disciplines rightly disciplines justly? E

Polus: Yes.

Socrates: Doing things that are just, or not?

Polus: Things that are just.

Socrates: So the one who's disciplined by paying a just penalty has just things done to him?

Polus: So it appears.

Socrates: And it's agreed, presumably, that just things are beautiful?

Polus: Certainly.

Socrates: Therefore, one of these people does beautiful things, and the other, the one who's disciplined, has beautiful things done to him.

Polus: Yes.

Socrates: And if they're beautiful things, they're good things? Because 477A
they're either pleasant or beneficial.

Polus: That's a necessity.

Socrates: Therefore, someone who pays a just penalty has good things done to him?

Polus: It looks like it.

Socrates: Therefore he's benefited?

Polus: Yes.

Socrates: By contributing to the end I suspect it does—that he becomes better in his soul if he's justly disciplined?

Polus: Likely so.

Socrates: Therefore someone who pays a just penalty is set free from badness of soul?

Polus: Yes.

B *Socrates:* And thus set free from the greatest evil? Look at it this way: do you observe any sort of badness in the monetary possessions a human being is equipped with other than poverty?

Polus: No, only poverty.

Socrates: What about in the body he's equipped with? Would you claim its badness to be weakness, disease, ugliness, and that sort of thing?

Polus: I would.

Socrates: And do you believe there's also some bad condition in a soul?

Polus: Of course.

Socrates: And don't you call this injustice, stupidity, cowardice, and that sort of thing?

Polus: Quite so.

C *Socrates:* So for monetary possessions, body, and soul, which are three things, you've mentioned a trio of bad conditions—poverty, disease, and injustice?

Polus: Yes.

Socrates: Then which of these bad conditions is the ugliest? Isn't it injustice, and bad condition of the soul altogether?

Polus: By a long way.

Socrates: So if it's the ugliest, it's also the worst?

Polus: How do you mean that, Socrates?

Socrates: Like this: from the things that were agreed in what went before, what's ugliest is always ugliest by having in it the greatest pain or harm or both.

Polus: Most assuredly.

Socrates: And just now it was agreed by us that injustice, and the bad
D condition of a soul in totality, is the ugliest thing?

Polus: It was indeed agreed.

Socrates: Then either it's the most grievously painful, and is the ugliest of these by exceeding in grievous pain, or it exceeds in harmfulness or in both?

Polus: That's a necessity.

Socrates: Well, is it more painful to be unjust, dissipated, cowardly, and stupid than it is to be poor and sick?

Polus: It certainly doesn't seem that way to me, Socrates.

Socrates: Therefore it's from exceeding the others in some harm that's
E prodigiously great and astoundingly bad that the bad condition of the soul is the ugliest of them all, since, as your speech has it, it doesn't exceed them in painfulness.

Polus: So it appears, at least on the basis of these things.[18]

---

18 The last phrase is transposed from the end of Polus's previous reply, in accord with a nineteenth-century editor's conjecture. Consistently through this whole section, it is only the logical conclusions that Polus seeks to distance himself from, not any of the separate pieces of evidence from which they follow.

Socrates: But presumably what exceeds in the greatest harm would be the greatest evil among the things there are.

Polus: Yes.

Socrates: Therefore injustice and inability to control oneself, and the rest of the bad condition of a soul, make up the greatest evil in the things there are?

Polus: So it appears.

Socrates: Now which art sets one free from poverty? Isn't it skill at business?

Polus: Yes.

Socrates: And which from disease? Isn't it doctoring?

Polus: Necessarily. **478A**

Socrates: And which from badness and injustice? If you're not equipped to say right off, consider it this way: where and to whom do we take people who are sick in their bodies?

Polus: To doctors, Socrates.

Socrates: And where do we take those who commit acts of injustice and dissipation?

Polus: Do you mean to judges?

Socrates: And that's so they pay a just penalty?

Polus: I'd say so.

Socrates: And isn't it by using a certain art of justice that those who discipline them discipline them rightly?

Polus: Clearly so.

Socrates: Therefore, skill at business sets people free from poverty, **B**
doctoring from disease, and justice from the inability to control oneself and from injustice.

Polus: So it appears.

Socrates: So which of these things is the most beautiful?

Polus: What things are you talking about?

Socrates: Skill at business, doctoring, justice.

Polus: Justice stands out by far, Socrates.

Socrates: So then in turn, if it's the most beautiful, it produces either the greatest pleasure or the greatest contribution to an end, or both?

Polus: Yes.

Socrates: Well, is it pleasant to get cured, and do those who are being cured enjoy it?

Polus: It doesn't seem so to me.

Socrates: But it certainly is beneficial, right?

Polus: Yes. **C**

Socrates: Because one is set free from a great evil, so that it pays off to endure the pain and be healthy.

Polus: Of course.

Socrates: And would a human being be happiest in this condition as far as his body's concerned, being cured, or not being sick in the first place?

Polus: Obviously not being sick.

Socrates: Because it seems likely that happiness never was a release from an evil, but avoiding acquiring it in the first place.

Polus: That's what it is.

D *Socrates:* What about this? Of a pair of people who have an evil in either body or soul, which is the more miserable, one who gets cured and is set free from the evil, or one who isn't cured and has it?

Polus: It appears to me it's the one who isn't cured.

Socrates: And paying the just penalty was a release from the greatest evil, the bad condition of a soul?

Polus: It was.

Socrates: Presumably because the judicial process moderates people and makes them more just, and acts as a medical art for the bad condition of a soul.

Polus: Yes.

Socrates: Therefore the happiest person is the one who has no evil in
E his soul, since that showed itself to be the greatest of evils.

Polus: Clearly so.

Socrates: And presumably the second happiest is the one who's set free from it.

Polus: It looks like it.

Socrates: And that was the person who's reprimanded and chastised, and pays a just penalty.

Polus: Yes.

Socrates: Therefore it's the person who has a bad condition of the soul and isn't set free from it who lives the worst life.

Polus: So it appears.

Socrates: And this is precisely the person who, while committing the greatest unjust acts and making use of the greatest injustice,
479A so arranges things that he's not reprimanded or disciplined and doesn't pay the just penalty, the very way you claim Archelaus made his provisions, and the other tyrants and rhetoricians and dictators?

Polus: It looks like it.

Socrates: I suppose, most excellent fellow, it's because these are people who've arranged things in pretty much the same way as if someone suffering from the greatest diseases would arrange not to pay the doctors the just penalty for his mistreatment of his body, and not get cured, being afraid of the burning and cutting, as if he were a
B child, because it hurt. Doesn't it seem that way to you?

Polus: To me, it does.

Socrates: It looks as though he'd be ignorant of what the health and virtue of a body are like. Because, based on the things that are now agreed by us, Polus, people who seek to escape justice are liable to be doing the same sort of thing, looking to the painfulness of it but being blind to the way it contributes to an end, and ignorant of how

much more miserable than living with an unhealthy body it is to
live with a soul that's not healthy but decayed, unjust, and impious; C
that's why they do everything to avoid paying the just penalty and
not be set free from the greatest evil, equipping themselves with
money and friends and the means to be as persuasive as possible
at speaking. But if what we've agreed is true, Polus, do you notice
the conclusions that follow from our speech? Or do you want us
to gather them up?

Polus: Only if you intend to in any case.

Socrates: Well, does it follow that injustice and committing unjust acts
are the greatest evil? D

Polus: So it appears, anyway.

Socrates: And paying the just penalty showed itself to be a release from that evil?

Polus: It's liable to be.

Socrates: But not paying it is clinging to the evil?

Polus: Yes.

Socrates: Therefore committing unjust acts is second in magnitude among evils; what is by nature the first and greatest of all evils is for the person who commits unjust acts not to pay the just penalty.

Polus: It looks like it.

Socrates: Well, my friend, wasn't it on this point that we were in dispute, when you regarded Archelaus as happy for committing the
greatest unjust acts and paying no penalty at all, and I imagined the E
opposite, that if either Archelaus or anyone else at all among human
beings did not pay the just penalty when he committed injustice, it
would be his lot to be miserable to a degree surpassing the rest of
humankind, and that the person who commits injustice is always
more miserable than the one who has injustice done to him, and
the person who doesn't pay a just penalty is always more miserable
than the one who pays it? Weren't these things said by me?

Polus: Yes.

Socrates: And hasn't it been demonstrated that they were said truly?

Polus: So it appears.

Socrates: Okay. Now if these things are true, Polus, what great use is 480A
there for rhetoric? Because, based on the things now agreed, one
ought to guard himself most of all against committing injustice,
seeing as how he'd get plenty enough evil out of it, isn't that so?

Polus: Quite so.

Socrates: But if he does commit injustice, either himself or anyone else
he cares about, he ought to go willingly to the place where he'll pay
the just penalty as quickly as possible, hurrying to the judge as he
would to the doctor, so the disease of injustice won't become chronic B
and make his soul fester with hidden sores and be incurable. What
else can we say about it, Polus, if the things we said before are still

agreed to by us? Isn't it a necessity that these things be this way and no other if they're to harmonize with those others?

Polus: Yeah—what assertion can we make, Socrates?

Socrates: Therefore, for making a defense of one's own injustice, or
that of one's parents or comrades or children or fatherland, when
it commits injustice, rhetoric is of no use to us, Polus, unless some-
C one were to take it the opposite way—that one ought most of all
to bring accusations against oneself, and in the next place against
his relatives and against whomever else among those dear to him
happens at any time to commit injustice, and not hide the unjust
deed but bring it out into the open so he can pay the just penalty
and become healthy; that he ought to force himself and the others
not to be cowards but to close their eyes and submit to it in good
and brave fashion, as they would to a doctor to cut or burn them,
pursuing what's good and beautiful without taking account of the
D pain; that if the injustice he's committed deserves lashes, he ought
to take his beating, if imprisonment, submit to being locked up, if a
fine, pay it, if exile, go away, if death, die, being himself the first to
accuse himself and the rest of his relatives and using his rhetoric
for that, so that when their injustices have become manifest they
may be set free from the greatest evil, injustice. Shall we assert
that or deny it, Polus?

E *Polus:* It seems crazy to me, Socrates, but all the same, you know, it
agrees with the earlier statements.

Socrates: So either those things have to be refuted or it's necessary for these to follow?

Polus: Yes—that's the way it is.

Socrates: But also, turning it around the opposite way, if it's right to do
harm to anyone, an enemy or whomever, as long as it's not oneself
suffering the injustice from the enemy—that's something that
still needs to be guarded against—but if it's someone else that the
enemy is treating unjustly, one needs to be prepared in every way,
481A by using deeds and speeches, to make sure he doesn't pay the just
penalty or even come before a judge. And if he does come before
one, a means needs to be contrived for the enemy to get away and
not pay the just penalty; and if he's plundered a lot of gold, for him
not to give it back but keep it and spend it on himself and those
around him, unjustly and in a godless way, or if he's committed
injustices deserving death, for him not to be put to death, best of
all not ever, so he'll be immortal while being corrupt, but if not
B that, so he'll live the longest possible time being that way. It's for
things like that, Polus, that rhetoric seems to me to be useful, since
for someone who has no intention of committing injustice there
doesn't seem to be any great use for it, if in fact there's any use at
all, since in the previous discussion, anyway, no way for it to be of
use showed up anywhere.

Callicles: Tell me, Chaerephon, is Socrates serious about these things or is he playing games?

Chaerephon: It seems to me, Callicles, that he's prodigiously serious. However, there's nothing like asking the man himself.[19]

Callicles: By the gods, that's just what I'm bursting to do! Tell me,
Socrates, should we take you as being serious now or playing C
games? Because if you *are* serious, and if these things that you're saying turn out to be true, would our life as human beings not be turned upside down, and would we not, as it seems, be doing everything that's opposite to what we ought to do?

Socrates: If human beings didn't have any experience that was the same, Callicles—one for one sort of people, another for others—but one of us had some private experience apart from the rest, it
wouldn't be easy to make one's own experience known to anyone D
else. What I have in mind in saying this is that you and I now happen to be experiencing something that's the same: we're a pair of lovers, each of us in love with two things, I with Alcibiades, Cleinias' son, and with philosophy, you with a pair of Demuses, the Athenian populace and Pyrilampes' son.[20] Now I notice that, even though you're formidably clever, you don't have the ability on any occasion to contradict anything your darlings say, whatever
they may claim is the case, but you keep turning yourself upside E
down. When you say something in the assembly, if the Athenian populace denies that it's the case, you turn around and say what it wants, and other things like that happen to you around that beautiful young son of Pyrilampes. Because you aren't able to oppose the intentions and speeches of your darlings, so if, any time you were saying the things you do on account of them, anyone was surprised at how bizarre they were, maybe, if you wanted to tell
the truth, you'd tell him that unless someone makes your darlings 482A
stop saying these things, you won't ever stop saying them either. So accept the fact that you have to hear other things things like that from me too, and don't be surprised that I'm saying these things, but stop my darling, philosophy, from saying them. Because, dear

19 Chaerephon gives Callicles back his own words from 447C. This has the effect of separating the dialogue into two main sections. In the first, Gorgias was challenged to defend the power of his rhetorical skill; now Socrates has to stand up to a challenge to the seriousness of his philosophic pursuit. It is the primary commitments of the two men's lives that are under scrutiny and under attack.

20 Sexual attachments between older, usually married, men and younger men were common and even fashionable in Greece at the time. A conventional view of the practice may be found in Plato's *Symposium* in the speech of Pausanias (180C-185C). Later in that dialogue (212D-223A), Alcibiades reveals that he and Socrates had two different ideas about what was going on between them. Alcibiades was gifted and handsome, and later played a disastrous role in Athens' political fortunes. The name of Callicles' beloved, Demus, was also the word for "populace," the lower order of society that held the ultimate power in democratic Athens. Demus was a relative of Plato's, and was reputed to be handsome and not very bright.

comrade, what you're hearing now from me is what she always
says, and she's much less capricious with me than other darlings.
That son of Cleinias is taken over by different speeches at differ-
B ent times, but philosophy by the same ones always; she says the
things you're now surprised at, and you were even present yourself
while they were being said. So either refute her, as I was saying
just now, by showing that committing injustice without paying
the just penalty for committing it is *not* the ultimate extreme of all
evils, or else, if you leave that unrefuted, then by the dog, the god
of the Egyptians, Callicles, *Callicles* won't agree with you; he'll be
out of tune in every bit of his life. And yet I imagine, most excellent fellow, I'd be better off with my lyre inharmonious and out of
C tune, or a chorus that I'd sponsored in public, or with masses of
people disagreeing with me and saying things that contradict me,
than with me, one person, being out of harmony with myself and
saying contradictory things.

Callicles: Socrates, you seem to me to be full of brash talk in your
speeches like the true demagogue you are, and you're demagogu-
ing up these things now because Polus has had the very same
experience happen to him that he accused Gorgias of having had
with you. Because he said, I believe, that when Gorgias was asked
by you whether, when someone came to him wanting to learn
D rhetoric but not knowing what's just, he'd teach him, Gorgias
was ashamed and claimed he'd teach him, on account of people's
habit of taking offense if anyone wouldn't say that. So on account
of that concession, he was forced to say things in contradiction
with himself, and you just loved that. Polus laughed at you then,
and rightly as it seemed to me, but now he himself has had this
same experience happen to him all over again. And I don't think
highly of Polus on this very issue, that he went along with you in
saying that committing injustice is an uglier thing than suffering it,
E because it's from that concession in turn that, having gotten himself
wrong-footed by you, he got his mouth gagged in the midst of his
speeches, since he was ashamed to say what he was thinking. The
reality of it is, Socrates, that while claiming to be pursuing the
truth, you lead things into such disgusting demagoguery about
what's beautiful not by nature but by convention. For the most
part, these things are the opposites of each other—nature and
483A convention. So if someone is ashamed and doesn't have the nerve
to say what he's thinking, he's forced to say contradictory things.
And it's exactly by understanding this ingenious trick that you do
the damage in your speeches: if anyone says things according to
convention, you respond with a question about things according
to nature, and if he says natural things, you question him about
conventional ones. And that's just the way it went in these present
statements about committing and suffering injustice; when Polus

spoke of what was an uglier thing according to convention, you went after his speech in accord with nature. Because by nature, everything is uglier that's also worse, as suffering injustice is, but committing it is uglier by convention. This suffering of injustice B
isn't an experience that belongs to a *man* at all, but to some slave who's better off dead than alive, anyone who's subjected to injustice and insults and isn't able on his own to defend himself or anyone else he cares about. But I imagine those who make the laws[21] are weak people, and the majority. It's with a view to themselves and what's advantageous to them that they make the laws, praise the things they praise, and blame the things they blame; to intimidate C
the more vigorous among humankind, the ones with the power to have more, and prevent them from having more than they do, they say that getting too much is an ugly and unjust thing, and that that's what committing injustice is, striving to have more than other people, since they themselves are well pleased to have an equality when they're inferior.

So for these reasons, this striving to have more than most people do is spoken of by convention as unjust and ugly, and people call it committing injustice. But nature itself, I should think, declares that the very thing that's just is for the one who's better to have D
more than the one who's worse, and the more powerful more than the less powerful. It's obvious in many areas that these things are the case, both among the other animals and among whole cities and tribes of human beings—that what's just is decided this way: by the stronger's ruling the weaker and having more. Otherwise, what sort of justice was Xerxes going by when he led an army against Greece, or his father against the Scythians?[22] Or take the E
tens of thousands of other such examples one might speak of. I should think these people in these cases are acting in accord with nature—the nature of justice—and yes, by Zeus!, in accord with law too—the law of nature[23]—though maybe not in accord with the one we make. We mold the best and most vigorous among ourselves

21 The word for convention (or custom) is the same as the word for law (*nomos*); one might translate the phrase "those who set up the conventions." The tacit legislation of approval and disapproval may be the strongest pressure by which any group of people controls its members.

22 Xerxes, the Great King of Persia, personally led a campaign against Greece in 480 BC with hordes of fighters, so many that he appeared to have brought all Asia into Europe. His father Darius had similarly led a large invasion to the east into the interior of what is now Russia. (See Herodotus, *History*, Book IV, Chapters 1-142, and all of Bks. VII and VIII.) The odd thing about Callicles' choice of these two examples from among the tens of thousands he claims there are is that both were failures.

23 This is the first known use of this phrase in literature. Callicles intends it as a surprising juxtaposition of terms conventionally regarded as contradictory, a paradox comparable to that in Heracleitus' fragment 62 (Diels numbering), "immortals are mortal; mortals are immortal."

by catching them young, as people do with lions, and make slaves
484A of them by casting spells and bewitching them,[24] telling them they should have an equal position and that this is what's beautiful and good. But I imagine that if a man having a strong enough nature came along, he'd shake off all these things, break out, and escape, trampling underfoot all our writings and charms and enchantments and laws, all contrary to nature, and our slave would rise up
B and reveal himself as our master, and there what's just by nature would shine forth. And it seems to me the very things I'm saying were pointed out by Pindar in the ode in which he says that

Law is king of all,
Mortals and immortals,

and that this, he claims,

Brings with it the most extreme violence, justifying it
By its supreme hand; I take as proof
The deeds of Heracles, for, without purchase money...

he says something to that effect—I don't know the poem—but he says that he drove off the cattle that he hadn't been sold and Geryon
C hadn't given him, since this was by nature the just thing, for cattle and all other possessions of worse and lesser people to belong to the one who's superior and greater.[25]

So that's how the truth is, and you'll recognize it if you go on to greater things and leave philosophy aside from here on out. Because I'll tell you, Socrates, philosophy is a charming thing if someone dabbles in it to a modest extent at the right time of life, but if he wastes more time on it than is fitting, that's the downfall of human beings. Even if one is very gifted by nature, if he engages in philosophy much past the right time in life, it's inevitable for
D him to end up unacquainted with all the things one needs to be acquainted with if he's going to be a fine figure of a man[26] and one who'll be well thought of. Such people end up unacquainted with the laws that apply to the city, with the kinds of speech one has to use to negotiate with people in private and public business, and with the pleasures and desires belonging to humankind; in short,

24 The three vivid and uncommon verbs used here for molding, casting spells, and bewitching are all forms of words used near each other in one of the two speeches of Gorgias of any length that we possess, the *Encomium of Helen* (Sections 10-11), in a passage extolling the power of rhetoric.

25 We have only a fragment of the poem, but we have enough to know that Callicles breaks off before revealing that Heracles was driving the cattle off to Eurystheus, his king, a lesser man than himself to whom he was in subjection through the trickery of the goddess Hera, and for whom he had to perform his twelve famous labors. Pindar probably means that the theft was justified not because might made it right, but because a decree of Zeus was an unbreakable law, binding even upon Zeus himself.

26 *Kalos kagathos anêr*; see the note to 470E.

they end up totally unacquainted with people's characters. So
whenever they venture into action of any private or political kind, E
they make laughingstocks of themselves, the same way, I imagine,
the politicians are laughingstocks when they in turn venture into
your pastimes and speeches. It turns out to be the way Euripides
says,[27]

> Each is a shining light in that, presses on to that,
> Gives the greatest part of the day to that,
> At which he happens to be his best,

but what he's no good at, he keeps away from and runs down, 485A
while he praises the other pursuit from his good opinion of himself, thinking of that as a way to praise himself. But I imagine the
thing that's most right is to get something of both. It's a beautiful
thing to get just enough of philosophy for the sake of an education, and there's no shame in engaging in philosophy when one's
a young man; but when a person who's already along in age still
pursues philosophy the matter becomes ridiculous, Socrates, and
I feel toward those pursuing philosophy very similarly to the way B
I feel about people who talk baby talk and act playful. Whenever I
see a child, for whom it's appropriate to talk that way, talking baby
talk and playing around, I enjoy it and it appears charming to me,
free-spirited, and suited to the child's age, and when I hear a little
child talking distinctly, it seems to me to be a piercing thing that
grates on my ears—it seems to me to be something fit for a slave;
but when one hears a man talking baby talk, or sees him playing C
around, it appears ridiculous and unmanly, and something that
deserves a beating. Now this is the same way I feel also toward
those who pursue philosophy. I admire philosophy when I see it
in a young adolescent, and it seems fitting to me, and I consider
him to be a free-spirited person, while one who doesn't engage in
philosophy is unfit for freedom and will never consider himself
worthy of any beautiful or noble deed; but when I see someone D
along in age still pursuing philosophy and not giving it up, it
seems to me that at that point, Socrates, that man needs a beating.
Because as I was saying just now, even if that person is very gifted
by nature, he's bound to become unmanly by keeping out of his

27 This is the first of several references in the dialogue to Euripides' lost play *Antiope*, of which many fragments survive. It concerns the twins Amphion and Zethus, the former a musician, the latter an outdoor type who cultivated his strength. The lines here seem to be Amphion's response to his brother's reproaches, of which we will hear much more. When a crisis needing action came, the two brothers prevailed together, and Amphion's music charmed the stones around Thebes into forming a wall as a lasting protection for them and those they cared for. Since Socrates' first response when Callicles stops speaking contains a reference to stones, he probably means to bring that aspect of the story to mind in his hearers, and stones will become an important metaphor later in the dialogue.

city's centers and marketplaces, in which the poet[28] says men gain
"highest distinction"; it's his lot to spend the rest of his life slunk
E away in a corner, whispering with three or four teenagers, and
never utter a thing that's free or great or rises to the occasion.

But I'm pretty friendly toward you, Socrates, so I'm probably feeling now the way Euripides' Zethus, whom I mentioned, did toward
Amphion. And it occurs to me to speak some such words to you
as the former did to his brother, saying "You're being neglectful,
Socrates, of things you ought to be paying attention to, and though
you're blessed with a soul so noble in nature, you put it on display
486A in the shape of some teenager, and you could neither add to the
counsels of justice a speech rightly made, nor declaim in ringing
tones anything probable or persuasive, nor advise any striking new
plan for anyone else." And yet, Socrates my friend—and don't get
mad at me, because I'm speaking with your good in mind—doesn't
it seem shameful to you to be in the condition I imagine you're in,
along with the others who are always pushing far on into philosophy? Why if anyone were to grab you now, or anyone else at all of
your sort, and drag you off to prison, claiming you'd committed an
injustice when you'd committed none, you know that you'd have no
B clue how to handle yourself, but your head would swim and your
mouth would hang open while you had nothing to say, and when
hauled into court, even if your accuser happened to be someone of
the lowest and most corrupt sort, you'd be put to death if he wanted
to set death as your penalty. So "how wise can that be," Socrates,
"any art that took a gifted mortal and made him worse off," when
he has no power either to help himself or to save either himself
C or anyone else at all from the greatest dangers, left to be stripped
by his enemies of all he has and is, to live in his city as someone
literally worthless? To say it a little crudely, anyone is free to slap
such a person upside the head without paying any penalty. But
good fellow, take my advice, stop your refuting, "train yourself in
the beautiful music" of practical life, and train where "you will be
reputed to have good sense; let others keep these fancy subtleties,"
whether one ought to call them frivolities or nonsense, "from which
you'll come to dwell in vacant rooms." Don't seek to rival men who
D engage in refutation over these minuscule matters, but those who
have the means of life, and good repute, and an abundance of other
good things.

Socrates: If I happened to have a soul made of gold, Callicles, don't
you imagine I'd be well pleased to find one of those stones people
rub against gold to test it, the best one, so that if I went ahead and
applied my soul to it, and it confirmed to me that it had been nur-

28 Homer, *Iliad*, IX, 441, from Phoenix's advice to Achilles to get back into the war.

tured in a beautiful way, I'd know for sure at that point that I was
in good enough shape and had no need of any other test?
Callicles: For what purpose, exactly, are you asking that, Socrates? E
Socrates: I'll tell you right now: I'm thinking that in meeting up with
you, I've run into just such a stroke of luck.
Callicles: How so?
Socrates: I know for sure that if *you* agree with me about things my soul
holds as opinions, then without more ado these things are the exact
truth, because I realize that anyone who's going to test adequately 487A
whether a soul is living rightly or not needs, after all, to have three
things, all of which you have: knowledge, goodwill, and frankness.
Now I meet up with lots of people who are unable to test me because
they aren't wise the way you are, while others are wise, but aren't
willing to tell me the truth because they don't care about me the
way you do, and as for our two visitors, Gorgias and Polus, though
the pair of them are wise and are my friends, they're too lacking in B
frankness and too susceptible to feelings of shame—more so than
is right and proper. How can that not be the case, when the pair of
them are so far advanced in shame that, from being ashamed, each
one himself has the audacity, himself, to contradict himself to his
own face, in the face of many people,[29] and about the greatest matters at that! But you do have all these things the others don't have,
because you've received what many of the Athenians would assert
is an adequate education, and you are well-intentioned toward
me. What evidence do I draw on for that? I'll tell you. I know, Cal- C
licles, that there are four of you who've become a partnership in
wisdom—you, Tisander of Aphidna, Androtion's son Andron, and
Nausicydes of Cholarges—and I once overheard you deliberating
about how far a training in wisdom should be taken. I know that
an opinion of the following sort prevailed among you, that one
shouldn't be eager to go on in philosophy to achieve any precision,
but you urged one another to be cautious not to become excessively D
wise beyond what's right and proper, in order that you not ruin
yourselves without realizing it. Now since I hear you giving the
same advice to me as to your closest companions, that's sufficient
evidence to me that you're truly well-intentioned toward me. And
surely, as for the fact that you're the sort to speak frankly and not
be ashamed, you claim this yourself and the speech you made a
little while ago backs you up. So it's clear that this is how it stands
right now about these matters: if you agree with me on any point E

29 The words "from...people" attempt to capture the style of *dia to aischunesthai tolma hekateros autôn autos hautô enantia legein enantion pollôn anthropôn*, a more resounding echo of Gorgias's manner of speaking than Polus's repetitions of the word "various" in 448C, and a bit of rhetorical one-upmanship directed at Callicles. When the latter said (482D-483A) that Polus contradicted himself out of shame, he pounded repetitively at the words "nature" and "convention," and in 483E he jammed the same two words together into a paradoxical pairing as Socrates does here with audacity and shame.

in our speeches, then without more ado that point will have been
sufficiently established by me and you together, and there won't be
any need to take it up again for any further test. Because you would
never have gone along with it from either a lack of wisdom or an
overabundance of shame, and you wouldn't have gone along with
it to deceive me either, since you're my friend; you say so yourself.
In reality, then, our agreement, yours and mine, will contain the
complete fulfillment of truth. And the inquiry into those things
for which you reproached me, Callicles, is the most beautiful one
488A of all, concerning the sort of person a man ought to be, and what
he ought to pursue, and to what extent, both when he's older and
when he's younger. Because you can be assured of this, that if I'm
acting in any way that's not right in my own life, I'm not slipping
up willingly but from my ignorance. So in just the way you began to
rebuke me, don't give up, but make it sufficiently plain to me what
this is that I need to pursue, and by what means I could get hold
of it; and once I've agreed with you now, if you catch me at a later
time not doing those things I agreed to, consider me a complete
B imbecile, and don't give me any more rebukes ever again, since I
wouldn't be deserving of any.

But take it from the beginning again for me. How does it go, what you and Pindar claim is the just thing by nature? That the one who's greater should carry off the things that belong to those who are lesser, and the superior should rule the inferior, and the better should have more than the worse? You don't say what's just is anything else but that, or am I remembering rightly?

Callicles: That's exactly what I was saying then, and also what I say now.

Socrates: And is it the same person you're calling "superior" and
C "greater"? Because I really couldn't understand then what in the
world you mean, whether you're calling stronger people greater,
and saying those who are weaker have to obey someone who's
stronger, which is the sort of thing it seems to me you were pointing to then, that for big cities to attack little ones is just by nature
because they're greater and stronger, since the greater and stronger
and better are the same thing; is it possible to be superior while
being lesser and weaker, and to be greater while being more
D depraved, or is the definition of superior and greater the same?
Distinguish that exact point for me clearly: are the greater, the
superior, and the stronger the same or different?

Callicles: Well, I'm telling you clearly that they're the same.

Socrates: So according to nature, is the multitude greater than a single person? They're the ones who impose laws on that one person, as you were also saying just now.

Callicles: How could they not be?

Socrates: Therefore the things regarded as lawful by the multitude
come from those who are greater?

Callicles: Quite so.

Socrates: So they come from those who are superior? For presumably E
according to your speech the greater are the superior.

Callicles: Yes.

Socrates: So the things they regard as lawful are beautiful according
to nature, since they come from those who are greater?

Callicles: I'm claiming that.

Socrates: Well isn't it this way of considering things that the multitude
regards as lawful, as you were saying just now as well, that having
an equal position is just, and committing injustice is an uglier thing
than suffering it? Is that so or not? And watch out here that you 489A
too don't get caught feeling ashamed. Do the masses customarily
hold, or do they not, that it's just to have an equal position and not
to have more, and that it's an uglier thing to commit injustice than
to suffer it? Don't be grudging about answering me that, Callicles,
so that if you agree with me, I'll have it established by you right
away, as something that's been agreed to by a man competent to
resolve the matter.

Callicles: Well, the masses *do* customarily think that way.

Socrates: Therefore it's not only by convention that committing injustice
is an uglier thing than suffering it, or that having an equal position B
is just, but by nature as well. So you're liable to have been saying
something that's not true in your earlier remarks, and there's a
chance that your accusation against me wasn't correct when you
were saying that convention and nature are opposed, and that I'm
aware of that and do the damage in my speeches by leading things
over to convention if anyone speaks in accordance with nature, and
over to nature if anyone speaks in accordance with convention.

Callicles: This man here just won't stop spewing nonsense. Tell me,
Socrates, aren't you ashamed at your age to be catching at words,
and if anyone slips up in his phrasing, to make a stroke of luck C
out of that? Do you imagine that I mean anything else by "being
greater" than "being superior"? Haven't I been saying all along that
I claim the superior person and the greater person are the same?
Or do you imagine I mean that if a motley collection of slaves and
every sort of human being who's worth nothing except for maybe
being strong in body, gets together and declares something, that
these are lawful things?

Socrates: Oho, superlatively wise Callicles, that's what you're
saying?

Callicles: Very much so.

Socrates: Well, you strange fellow, I too have been guessing all along D
myself that you mean something like that by "the greater," and I've
been asking questions tenaciously to know clearly what you do

mean. Because, presumably, you don't consider two people superior to one, or your slaves superior to you just because they're stronger than you are. But tell me again from the beginning, what in the world *do* you mean by "the superior" since they aren't the stronger? And, you amazing fellow, give me my preparatory schooling in a more gentle way, or else I might stop going to you for lessons.

E *Callicles:* You're being ironic, Socrates.

Socrates: Am I really, Callicles, by Zethus,[30] whom you made use of just now to heap a lot of irony on me? Just come on and tell me, who do you say are the superior people?

Callicles: I say they're the better ones.

Socrates: And do you see that you yourself are speaking mere words and making nothing clear? Won't you say whether, by people who are superior and greater, you mean those who are smarter or somebody else?

Callicles: Yes, by Zeus, I mean exactly them, emphatically so.

490A *Socrates:* Therefore, by your speech, one person who's smart is often greater than tens of thousands who aren't, and it's right for that person to rule and the others to be ruled, and for the ruler to have more than those he rules. Because that's what it seems to me you want to say—and I'm not catching at your phrasing—if the one person is greater than the tens of thousands.

Callicles: That's exactly what I'm saying, because I should think that's the thing that's just by nature, for the one who's superior and smarter to be the ruler and to have more than the inferior people.

B *Socrates:* Hold it right there. What in the world do you mean now? If many of us are congregated in the same place, as we are now, and a lot of food and drink belongs to us in common, but we're people of all sorts, some strong, some weak, and one of us is smarter about these matters since he's a doctor, while he, as is likely, is stronger than some and weaker than others, does anything else follow than that he, being smarter than we are, will be superior and greater on these matters?

Callicles: Of course that follows.

C *Socrates:* Then does he have to get more of that food than we do because he's superior, or should he hand it all out by virtue of ruling, but in

30 Socrates puts a twist in the name of Zeus to swear by the character Callicles was quoting in 485E-486D. The word irony did not yet have full range of use it later came to have, partly as a result of reflection on the depth of the way Socrates commonly spoke. The Greek word for irony applied especially to the gracious modesty of his frequent pretenses of ignorance, but there was more than mere politeness in that attitude, which was rooted in an underlying conviction that all of us need to recognize our ignorance if we're ever to make any progress toward understanding. Callicles, with a superficially similar ironic tone, had adopted a pose of giving friendly advice for Socrates' own good. Socrates is saying, in effect, "if you want me to drop my mask, you have to drop yours."

the consumption and use of it not take an excess of it into his own body, if he doesn't want to pay the penalty for that, but get more than some people and less than others? And if by chance he's the weakest of all, is it right for the most superior person to have the least, Callicles? Isn't that how it is, good fellow?

Callicles: You're talking food and drink and doctors and nonsense. D
That's not what I mean.

Socrates: Aren't you saying the smarter person is superior? Declare yes or no.

Callicles: I am.

Socrates: But not that the superior person should have more?

Callicles: Not more food and drink anyway.

Socrates: I understand. Maybe clothes, then, and the most skillful weaver should have his cloak the biggest, and have the most of them, and go around wearing the most beautiful ones?

Callicles: What have clothes got to do with anything?

Socrates: But as for shoes, it's clear that the person who's the smartest
and most superior on that score ought to get more. Maybe the one E
who cuts the leather should walk around with the biggest shoes on his feet, and have the most of them.

Callicles: What have shoes got to do with anything? You keep on talking nonsense.

Socrates: Well then, if you don't mean things of that sort, maybe you mean things like this: a man skilled at farming, say, who's intelligent about the land, and a fine figure of a man—maybe *he* should get more of the seed, and use as much seed as possible on his own land.

Callicles: You do go on, always saying the same things, Socrates.

Socrates: Not only that, Callicles, but about the same things too.

Callicles: By the gods! You're literally always talking nonstop about 491A
leather workers and drycleaners and cooks and doctors, as if our speech had anything to do with *them*.

Socrates: Then will you tell me who it does have to do with? What is it that the greater and smarter person, who has more, justly gets more *of*? Or are you neither going to let me make suggestions nor say it yourself?

Callicles: But I am saying it, and have been all along. In the first place, the greater people I'm talking about are those who aren't leather
workers or cooks but are smart about practical matters having to B
do with the city, about the way they might be well managed, and they're not only smart but also manly, capable of accomplishing what they intend and not get fainthearted on account of softness in the soul.

Socrates: Most superior Callicles, do you see how the things you blame me for are not the same ones I blame you for? You claim I'm always saying the same things and make that a reproach against me, but I

claim the opposite about you, that you never say the same things
C about the same things, but at one time you define the superior and
greater people as the stronger ones, and then in turn as the smarter,
but now again you've come up with something else: it's some sort
of "manlier" people who are being described by you as the superior
and better ones. But, good fellow, say who in the world you mean
by the superior and greater people, and in connection with what,
and get it over with.

Callicles: But I've said it's those who are smarter about practical matters
D having to do with the city, and more manly. They're fit to rule the
cities, and that's the thing that's just, for them, the rulers, to have
more in comparison with the others, the ruled.

Socrates: What about in comparison with themselves, my friend?

Callicles: What about *what*?

Socrates: Rulers or ruled?

Callicles: How do you mean?

Socrates: I'm talking about each one himself ruling over himself—or is there no need for that, for one to rule oneself, just to rule others?

Callicles: What do mean by someone's ruling himself?

Socrates: Nothing elaborate, just what most people do: being moder-
E ate and in control of oneself, ruling over the pleasures and desires
in oneself.

Callicles: How droll you are. By "moderate" people you're talking about stupid ones.

Socrates: How's that? There's no one at all who wouldn't recognize that that's *not* what I'm saying.

Callicles: You most emphatically are, Socrates. How could a human
being become happy if he's enslaved to anyone at all? This, I now
tell you frankly, is what's beautiful and just according to nature:
that someone who's going to live rightly needs to let his own desires
492A be the greatest possible and not discipline them but be up to the
task of ministering to them when they're the greatest they can
be, by being manly and smart, and always providing satisfaction
of whatever the desire happens to be for. But I imagine this isn't
possible for most people, which is why they censure people of that
sort, out of shame, to cover up their own powerlessness, and they
claim self-indulgence is an ugly thing, doing exactly what I was
saying before, enslaving those human beings who are superior by
nature; and since they themselves lack the power to provide for
B the satisfaction of their own pleasures, they praise moderation and
justice because of their own lack of manliness. Because, for all those
who have the advantage from the start either of being kings' sons,
or of being capable by their own nature of providing themselves
with some ruling position, a tyranny or a place in a dictatorial
group, what could be truly more shameful and a greater evil than
moderation and justice in such people, who, since they can enjoy

good things with no one to stand in their way, would themselves be imposing as a slavemaster over themselves the law, the word, and the censure of the masses of humanity? How could they not become miserable under the thumb of that lovely thing that consists C
of justice and moderation, when they can pass out nothing more to their friends than to their enemies, and that's happening while they're the rulers in their own cities? But in truth, Socrates, and that's what you claim to be pursuing, it's like this: luxury and self-indulgence and freedom, if they have force to defend them—that's what virtue and happiness are—and everything else is window dressing, agreements made by people in contravention of nature, and worthless nonsense.

Socrates: The frank way you go through things in your speech is cer- D
tainly not lacking in nobility, Callicles, because you're now saying clearly what other people think but are unwilling to say. So I beg of you not to let up in any way, so that it may genuinely become crystal clear how one ought to live. And tell me, you're claiming that one's desires ought not to be disciplined if one is to be the sort of person he ought to be, but he should provide satisfaction for them from wherever he can get it after he's let them be as great as possible, and that this is virtue? E

Callicles: That's what I'm claiming.

Socrates: Therefore it's not rightly said that people are happy when they're in want of nothing?

Callicles: No, because in that case stones and corpses would be happy.

Socrates: Yes, but the life of the people you're talking about is pretty strange too, and I wouldn't be at all surprised if Euripides was telling the truth in the lines where he said,

> Who knows whether to be alive is to be dead,
> And to be dead is to be alive?

Maybe in reality we're the ones who are dead, because once in 493A
fact I heard from someone, one of the wise people, that we're now dead and the body is our tomb,[31] while that part of the soul that our desires are in happens to be the sort of thing that can be per-

31 "The body, a tomb" (*sôma sêma*) was a Pythagorean saying, which would have been especially current in the Greek cities of Italy and Sicily. The lines of Euripides above are from a lost play. The fable below is Socrates' own invention, starting from the words *pithanos* (easy to persuade) and *pithos* (vat or urn) and incorporating a pun on *amuêtos* (uninitiated, from *mue-o*; leaky, from *mu-o*); Socrates had a habit of referring to unspecified wise men and women when he was about to make up a parable (see Plato's *Meno*, 81A-D, and *Phaedrus* 252B-C, 274C-275C). Because the word *pithanos* meant "persuasive" (as above at 457A, 458E, etc.) as well as "easily persuadable," the image here unites the two halves of the dialogue, alluding to Gorgias's opinion of his own power and Callicles' vision of human happiness as two sides of one human weakness.

suaded around and turn upside down, and so some elaborately
clever man—maybe some Sicilian or Italian—told a fable about this,
and with a play on words he named this part, because it's easily
persuadable and quick to turn, an urn, and named unintelligent
B people uninitiates, and he said that the self-indulgent element in
this part of the soul, where the desires are in unintelligent people,
since it's not water-tight, would be an urn full of holes, making
that image of its insatiability. So just the opposite of you, Callicles,
this man indicates that the most miserable ones in the realm of
Hades—by which I mean the invisible[32] place—would be these
uninitiates, and he says they'd be carrying water to the hole-filled
urn with another thing similarly full of holes, a sieve. And he meant
C the sieve, in turn, as the one who told it to me said, to be the soul,
and he likened the soul of the unintelligent to a sieve as a soul
full of holes, since it's powerless to keep anything in because of its
unsteadiness of belief and its forgetfulness. And while these things
are getting on for being fairly absurd, they make clear what I want
to get across to you, in any way I possibly can, to persuade you to
change course, and instead of a life in an insatiable and dissipated
condition, to choose a life in an orderly condition that's always in
a state of sufficiency and contentment with the things it has. But
D am I persuading you at all and are you changing to the opinion
that orderly people are happier than self-indulgent ones, or would
you not change course any the more even if I were to tell you lots
of other fables of this kind?

Callicles: What you've said now is more the truth, Socrates.

Socrates: Come on anyway, I'll relate to you another image from the
same school as the present one. See if you mean something like
this about the life of each of the two, that of the moderate and that
of the self-indulgent person: suppose each one of the pair had a lot
E of urns, and one of the two had his intact and full, one of wine, one
of honey, one of milk, and many others filled with many things,
and the influx of each of these things was meager and hard to
come by, and took a lot of hard work to provide. Now one of the
two people, once he's got them filled, wouldn't pipe in any more or
worry about it, but would stay tranquil as far as those things are
concerned; for the other person, the influx would be just as possible
and just as difficult to provide as for the first, but his containers
are full of holes and decayed, and he'd be forced to keep filling
494A them constantly, night and day, or be afflicted with the extremity
of pain. If that's the sort of life each one has, do you say it would
be a happier one for the self-indulgent person than for the orderly
one? Am I persuading you at all by saying these things, to accept

32 The word for "invisible," in the masculine and feminine nominative, differs from Hades' name only by the position of the accent. This was a common pun; what Socrates means by it here emerges in the myth he tells at the end of the dialogue (523-527).

along with me that the orderly life is better than the self-indulgent one, or am I not persuading you?

Callicles: You're not persuading me, Socrates, because there's no longer any pleasure at all for the person who's filled up, and that's what I was just now saying is living like a stone, when one has been filled B
and isn't feeling any more joy or pain. But living pleasantly consists in this: in having the greatest possible amount flowing in.

Socrates: Well isn't it a necessity, if there's a lot flowing in, for there also to be a lot that's running out, and for there to be some big holes for the outflows?

Callicles: Of course.

Socrates: Then you're talking now about some sort of life of a plover[33] instead of a life of a corpse or a stone. And tell me, are you talking, for example, about something like being hungry, and eating when you're hungry?

Callicles: I am.

Socrates: And being thirsty, and drinking when you're thirsty? C

Callicles: I'm saying also that someone who has all the rest of the desires and has the power to fulfill them lives happily in enjoying them.

Socrates: Great, you superlative fellow! Now go on to the end in just the way you've begun, and don't be ashamed. And it looks like I'd better not hold back out of shame either. First of all, then, tell me whether someone who has an itch and wants to rub it, and be uninhibited in his rubbing and spend his life rubbing away at it, is living happily.

Callicles: How outrageous you are, Socrates, an absolute dema- D
gogue.

Socrates: Well sure, Callicles, and I shocked Polus and Gorgias and made them ashamed, but you won't be shocked and you won't be ashamed because you're manly. So just answer.

Callicles: Well, I claim that even the person who's rubbing himself would be living pleasantly.

Socrates: And if pleasantly, then happily too?

Callicles: Of course.

Socrates: Is that if it's only his head he's rubbing—or what else shall E
I ask you? See what you'll answer, Callicles, if someone asks you one step at a time about all the things that follow from these. And what brings these sorts of things to a head is the life of kept

33 The particular species of plover Socrates apparently has in mind is a shore bird with the habit of emitting a stream of excrement while it's feeding.

boys[34]—isn't that a dreadful and ugly and miserable life? Or will you have the nerve to say these people are happy too, if they get what they want unstintingly?

Callicles: Aren't you ashamed to be leading our talk into such things, Socrates?

Socrates: Am I really the one leading them there, you noble fellow, or is it the person who's claiming in this unrestrained way that people

495A who have pleasure, however they have pleasure, are happy, and doesn't distinguish which sorts of pleasures are good and bad? But go on and say that now too: do you claim the pleasant and the good are the same thing, or is there any pleasant thing that isn't good?

Callicles: In order that my speech may not be inconsistent if I claim they're different, I claim they're the same.

Socrates: You're undermining your first speeches, Callicles, and you couldn't any longer adequately assess the way things are along with me, if you're going to say things contrary to the way they seem to you yourself.

B *Callicles:* You do that too, Socrates.

Socrates: Then I'm not doing the right thing, if I'm doing that, and neither are you. But consider this, you blessedly happy fellow, that the good may not be having pleasure in any and every way, since these many ugly things implied just now would be obvious consequences if that's the way it is, and lots of others.

Callicles: The way *you* imagine it, Socrates.

Socrates: And you, Callicles, insist that this is how it really is?

Callicles: I do.

C *Socrates:* Shall we therefore take up the speech as something you're serious about?

Callicles: Most emphatically.

Socrates: So come on then, since it seems that way, and delineate the following for me: presumably you call something knowledge?

Callicles: I do.

Socrates: And weren't you saying just now that there can be a certain manliness along with knowledge?

Callicles: I was saying that.

Socrates: And did you mean these as anything other than two things, manliness a different thing from knowledge?

Callicles: Emphatically so.

Socrates: And what about this? Are pleasure and knowledge the same or different?

---

34 Catamites, perhaps something close to "sex slaves," would not include privileged young men like Demus or Alciabiades (see 481D and note) who might attract lovers. Since this moment in the dialogue corresponds to those at which Gorgias and Polus succumbed to shame, it is important to decide whether Callicles' resistance to the example is caused by the directness of the sexual reference, by the idea of a life narrowed to a single form of pleasure, by any suggestion of approval of the passivity and unmanliness of the boys in question, or by some combination of these.

Callicles: Unquestionably different, you paragon of wisdom. D

Socrates: And manliness is also different from pleasure?

Callicles: How could it not be?

Socrates: Come on then, so we may memorialize these things: Callicles the Acharnian[35] says pleasant and good are the same thing but knowledge and manliness are different from each other and from the good.

Callicles: And Socrates from Alopece does not agree with these things, or does he agree?

Socrates: He does not agree, and I imagine that Callicles won't either when he comes to see himself rightly. But tell me, don't you regard people who are doing well as having an experience opposite to that of people who are doing badly? E

Callicles: I do.

Socrates: Well then, if these are experiences opposite to each other, isn't it a necessity that people be in the same condition with regard to them as they are with regard to health and sickness? Because, presumably, a human being can't be healthy and sick at the same time, or be getting rid of health and sickness at the same time.

Callicles: How do you mean?

Socrates: Take any part of the body you want as an example and consider it. Presumably a human being gets sick in the eyes, and the name for that is eye-inflammation? 496A

Callicles: Certainly.

Socrates: And doubtless he's not also healthy at the same time in those same eyes?

Callicles: In no way whatsoever.

Socrates: And what about when he's getting over his eye-inflammation? Is he getting rid of the health of his eyes too at that time, and does he end up rid of both at the same time?

Callicles: Not in the least.

Socrates: Because I imagine that would be a surprising and unaccountable thing to happen, wouldn't it? B

Callicles: Emphatically so.

Socrates: Instead, I imagine, he's getting and losing each of the two in turn?

Callicles: I'd say so.

Socrates: So it's also the same way with strength and weakness?

Callicles: Yes.

Socrates: And speed and slowness?

Callicles: Quite so.

Socrates: And as for good things and happiness, and their opposites, bad things and misery, does one get and get rid of each pair in turn?

---

35 Socrates, as though drawing up a legal affidavit, includes the district of Athens Callicles lives in.

Callicles: Totally, no doubt about it.

C *Socrates:* Therefore, if we discover certain things that a human being gets rid of at the same time and has at the same time, it's clear that these things at any rate could not be the good and the bad. Are we agreed on that? Think it over very carefully and then answer.

Callicles: Oh, it's extraordinary how much I agree.

Socrates: Now go back to the things that were agreed earlier. You were speaking of being hungry—as something pleasant or painful? I mean being hungry itself.

Callicles: I say it's painful, though eating when one is hungry is pleasant.

D *Socrates:* Me too; I understand. But being hungry itself at any rate is a painful thing, isn't it?

Callicles: I'd say so.

Socrates: And being thirsty too?

Callicles: Emphatically so.

Socrates: So shall I keep asking about more cases, or do you agree that all lack and desire are painful?

Callicles: I agree; don't keep asking.

Socrates: Okay. And are you claiming anything other than that it's a pleasant thing to drink when one is thirsty?

Callicles: That's what I'm claiming.

Socrates: And by this "when one is thirsty," presumably you mean when one is in pain?

E *Callicles:* Yes.

Socrates: And drinking is a filling up of the lack, and a pleasure?

Callicles: Yes.

Socrates: So you're saying one is having pleasure during the drinking?

Callicles: Very much so.

Socrates: When one is thirsty?

Callicles: So I claim.

Socrates: When one is in pain?

Callicles: Yes.

Socrates: So do you see what follows, that you're saying that someone who's in pain has pleasure at the same time when you speak of drinking when one is thirsty? Or does this not happen at the same time in the same place—whether soul or body, as you prefer, since I imagine it makes no difference—is this how it is or not?

Callicles: It is.

497A *Socrates:* But surely you claim it's impossible for someone who's doing well to be doing badly at the same time.

Callicles: I do claim that.

Socrates: But you've agreed that it's possible to have pleasure while one is in pain.

Callicles: So it appears.

Socrates: Therefore to have pleasure is not to be doing well, and to be in pain is not to be doing badly, and so it turns out that the pleasant is different from the good.

Callicles: I don't know what kind of tricky arguments you're making, Socrates.

Socrates: You know, Callicles, but you're playing dumb. Just continue on to the next step.

Callicles: Why do you keep being so asinine?

Socrates: So you'll know how wise you're being to rebuke me. Doesn't B
each of us stop being thirsty at the same time he stops feeling pleasure at drinking?

Callicles: I don't know what you mean.

Gorgias: None of that, Callicles. Just answer him, for our sakes too, so that the speeches may be brought to an end.

Callicles: But Socrates is always like this, Gorgias. He asks little questions of little importance and makes a refutation out of them.

Gorgias: But what difference does that make to you? There's nothing here that's a matter of your honor, Callicles. Just submit to Socrates, to refute you however he wants.

Callicles: Go on and ask these shriveled little questions of yours, since C
that's the way Gorgias likes it.

Socrates: You are a happy one, Callicles, to be initiated into the great mysteries[36] before the small ones; I didn't imagine it was permitted. Answer where you left off, then, whether each of us doesn't stop being thirsty and having pleasure at the same time.

Callicles: I'd say so.

Socrates: And does one also cease from hunger and from the other desires at the same time as from the pleasures?

Callicles: That's how it is.

Socrates: And so one ceases from pains and pleasures at the same D
time?

Callicles: Yes.

Socrates: But surely, as you agreed, one does *not* cease from good things at the same time as from bad; do you not agree with that now?

Callicles: I do; so what?

Socrates: So, my friend, good things turn out *not* to be the same as pleasant ones, and bad things not the same as painful ones, because one ceases from the one pair at the same time but not from the other pair, indicating that they're different. How, then, could pleasant things be the same as good or painful things be the same as bad?

But if you'd like, examine it in this way as well, because I imagine
it's not conceded by you on that ground. Consider: don't you call E

36 The reference is to the stages of initiation into the Eleusinian religious rites. The word "mystery" is derived from the word for initiation, the same word that, with a negative prefix, had the second meaning "leaky" in the image of the urns above (493A).

good people good because of the presence of good things, just as you call people beautiful because beauty is present in them?

Callicles: I do.

Socrates: And what about this? Do you call good men foolish and cowardly? You didn't just now at any rate, but were saying they're the manly and smart ones. Or do you not call them good?

Callicles: Very much so.

Socrates: Well, haven't you ever seen a foolish child having pleasure?

Callicles: I have.

Socrates: But you've never seen a foolish man having pleasure?

Callicles: I imagine I have, but what about it?

498A *Socrates:* Nothing; just answer.

Callicles: I've seen that.

Socrates: What about a person with good sense being in pain or having pleasure?

Callicles: I'd say so.

Socrates: And which ones have more pleasure and more pain, the smart ones or the stupid ones?

Callicles: I imagine there's not a lot of difference.

Socrates: Well, even that's sufficient. Now in war, have you ever seen a man be a coward?

Callicles: How could I not?

Socrates: And what about when the enemies went away? Which ones seemed to you to enjoy it more, the cowards or the manly ones?

B *Callicles:* Both sorts seemed to me to enjoy it; maybe the former more, or if not, pretty much the same.

Socrates: It makes no difference. So the cowards have pleasure too?

Callicles: Emphatically so.

Socrates: And it's likely the stupid people do too.

Callicles: Yes.

Socrates: And when the enemies come toward them, are the cowards the only ones pained at that, or the manly ones too?

Callicles: Both sorts.

Socrates: To a similar degree?

Callicles: Maybe the cowards more.

Socrates: But when they go away the cowards don't feel more pleasure?

Callicles: Maybe they do.

Socrates: So the stupid ones and the smart ones, and the cowards and
C manly ones, feel pain and pleasure about the same, as you claim, but the cowards more than the manly ones?

Callicles: I'd say so.

Socrates: But surely the smart and manly ones are good, and the cowardly and stupid ones are bad?

Callicles: Yes.

Socrates: Therefore, good and bad people feel pleasure and pain about equally?

Callicles: I'd say so.

Socrates: Well, are good and bad people about equally good and bad? Or are the bad ones in fact even more good?

Callicles: By Zeus, I don't know what you're talking about! D

Socrates: You don't know that you're claiming that good people are good by the presence of good things, and bad people are bad by the presence of bad things, and that pleasures are the good things and pains the bad things?

Callicles: I do.

Socrates: So then good things are present in people who are having pleasure, so long as they're having pleasure?

Callicles: Of course.

Socrates: So then, because good things are present in them, people who are having pleasure are good?

Callicles: Yes.

Socrates: And what about this? Aren't bad things, pains, present in people who are in pain?

Callicles: They're present.

Socrates: But it's by the presence of bad things that you claim bad E
people are bad—or do you no longer claim that?

Callicles: I do.

Socrates: Therefore, those who have pleasure are good, and those who are in pain are bad?

Callicles: Certainly.

Socrates: And those who are more so are more that way, those less so less, and those about the same about the same?

Callicles: Yes.

Socrates: And you claim that smart and stupid people, and cowards and manly ones, have pleasure and pain to about the same degree, or else the cowards even more so?

Callicles: I do.

Socrates: Then in cooperation with me, gather up what follows from the things agreed to by us, because people say it's a beautiful
thing to say beautiful things even two or three times over, and 499A
to examine them too. We claim that a smart and manly person is good, don't we?

Callicles: Yes.

Socrates: And a stupid and cowardly person is bad?

Callicles: Very much so.

Socrates: And also that someone who's having pleasure is good?

Callicles: Yes.

Socrates: And someone who's having pain is bad?

Callicles: That's a necessity.

Socrates: And the good person and the bad have pain and pleasure to a similar degree, or maybe the bad person more?

Callicles: Yes.

Socrates: So then a bad person turns out to be bad and good to a simi-
B lar degree as a good person, or to be even more good? Don't these
things, as well as those previous ones, follow if anyone claims that
pleasant things and good things are the same? Isn't that a necessity, Callicles?

Callicles: You know, all the time I've been listening to you, Socrates, responding with agreement, I've been taking note of how, if anyone gives in to you on any point, even as a joke, you hang on to it with glee the way teenagers would. As if you could imagine that I or anyone else at all of humankind didn't consider some pleasures better and others worse!

Socrates: Ohoho, Callicles, what an amoral[37] fellow you are! You're
C treating me just like a child, declaring the same things are now one
way, now another, to play tricks on me. And yet never did I imagine
from the start that I'd be tricked by you on purpose, thinking you
were my friend. But now I've been duped, and it seems necessary
for me, as the old saying goes, to make the best of what's at hand,
and take whatever is given by you. So what you're now saying, it
seems, is that some particular pleasures are good but others are
bad—is that it?

D *Callicles:* Yes.

Socrates: And that the beneficial ones good and the harmful ones are bad?

Callicles: Of course.

Socrates: And those that do something good are beneficial, while those that do something bad are bad pleasures?

Callicles: I'd say so.

Socrates: Now do you mean, say, those sorts of pleasures we were just
talking about that apply to the body, those involved in eating and
drinking, and that the ones that produce health in the body, or
strength, or some other excellence of the body, are good, but the
E ones that produce effects opposite to these are bad?

Callicles: Certainly.

Socrates: And the same way with pains, some are worthwhile and others worthless?

Callicles: Of course.

---

37 The Greek word is *panourgos,* one who'll do anything, in the sense of stop at nothing. The word has a certain grandeur, equivalent to the bravado of Callicles' long speech, in which he announced his disdain for all the rules and restrictions society imposes on its natural superior, but in the context of Callicles' condescending rebuke of Socrates for being petty and childish in the argument, the choice of word carries a weight of irony, since Callicles has presented himself as someone above any sort of deception himself. The self-proclaimed amoralist has been caught weaseling out of his own brave words.

Socrates: And so the worthwhile pleasures and pains are to be chosen and taken on?

Callicles: Certainly.

Socrates: But not the worthless ones?

Callicles: Obviously not.

Socrates: Because it seemed to us, no doubt, that all actions are to be undertaken for the sake of good things, if you recall, to Polus and me that is. Does it seem that way to you too in common with us, that the good is the end of all actions and that one ought to undertake
all other things for it's sake and not it for the sake of anything else? **500A**
Do you cast your vote along with us too from a third precinct?

Callicles: I do.

Socrates: Therefore one ought to take on everything else, even pleasures, for the sake of good things, and not good things for the sake of pleasures.

Callicles: Certainly.

Socrates: And is it in every man's power to pick out from among pleasant things which sorts are good and which sorts bad, or is there a need for someone with an art for each case?

Callicles: Someone with an art.

Socrates: Then let's recall again precisely those things I happened to be saying to Polus and Gorgias, because, if you remember, I was
saying that there could be some arrangements that extend as far **B**
as pleasure and provide that very thing alone, ignorant of what's better and worse, while others discern that there's a good and a bad. And among those concerned with pleasures, I placed cooking—a matter of experience but not of art—while among those concerned with the good I placed the art of doctoring. Now in the name of Friendship, Callicles, don't imagine it's right for you yourself to joke with me, don't answer something at random contrary to the way
things seem, and don't take what comes from me either as though **C**
I were joking. Make sure you see that our speeches are concerned with this matter—and what matter should any human being with even a little bit of sense be more serious about than this?—of the way one ought to live one's life: whether it's the way you exhort me toward, of doing those things befitting a *man*, speaking among the populace, training in rhetoric, and getting into politics in this way that you people engage in it nowadays, or this life spent in philosophy, and whatever it is about this life that differs from that
one. So maybe it's best to set them out in contrast, as I tried to do **D**
a little while ago, and once we've set them in contrast and agreed with each other whether there is this twofold division of lives, to examine what is to be distinguished from each other in the pair, and which of the pair is to be lived. But maybe you don't yet know what I mean.

Callicles: I sure don't.

Socrates: Then I'll tell you more clearly. Since you and I have agreed
that there's something good and something pleasant, and what's
pleasant is a different thing from what's good, and that there's a
certain way of attending to each of the two and arranging to get
hold of it, one hunting for what's pleasant and the other for what's
E good—but first assent to just this point for me, or deny it. Do you
assent?

Callicles: That's how I'd say it is.

Socrates: Come then, and agree with me on the things I was also saying
to these folks here, if I seemed to you to be speaking the truth then.
I believe I was saying that cooking tasty food didn't seem to me to
501A be an art but a matter of experience, while as for doctoring, I was
saying that it looked into the nature of the person it ministers to
and the cause of the things it does, and has a speech to give about
these things; that's doctoring, but the other is about pleasure, on
which all its ministration is focused, and the way it goes after that
is completely lacking in art, since it isn't looking into the nature or
cause of pleasure at all, and totally devoid of speech, since it makes
virtually no distinctions, merely keeping a memory of what usually
B happens by routine and experience, which are the means by which
it provides pleasures. First, then, consider whether it seems to you
that this is said adequately, and whether there are also certain other
similar concerns dealing with the soul, artful ones that have some
forethought for what's best in regard to the soul, and other ones
that have contempt for that, but, again as in the other case, they've
looked only into the soul's pleasure for how it might come to it, but
as for which of the pleasures are better or worse, they don't look
into that or bother themselves about anything, for better or for
C worse, other than the mere gratifying. Because, Callicles, it seems
to me there are things of this sort, and *I* claim such a thing is pandering, in the case of both the body and the soul, and of anything
else whatever, if one ministers to pleasure in disregard of what's
better and worse. So do you put in together with us in the same
opinion about these things, or do you challenge it?

Callicles: Not I. I go along with it so the speech may be brought to an
end by you, and I may gratify Gorgias here.

D *Socrates:* And is this so for one soul but not for two or many?

Callicles: No, for two and for many as well.

Socrates: And is it possible to gratify masses of people at the same
time without looking out for what's best?

Callicles: I imagine so.

Socrates: Then can you say what endeavors do that? Or rather, if you
like, when I ask about them, say yes if something seems to be one
E of these or say no if it doesn't. First let's consider flute playing.
Doesn't it seem to you to be one of the endeavors of this sort, Cal-

licles—one that pursues only our pleasure and gives no thought to anything else?

Callicles: It seems that way to me.

Socrates: And everything like that as well, such as harp playing in competitions?

Callicles: Yes.

Socrates: And what about the designing of choreography and the composition of dithyrambs?[38] Isn't it obvious to you that they're of that sort? Or do you think Meles' son Cinesias gives any thought to how he says anything so that his hearers could become better from it, rather than how he's going to gratify the crowd of spectators? **502A**

Callicles: That's certainly clear, Socrates, at least as far as Cinesias is concerned.

Socrates: And what about his father Meles? Did he seem to you to be looking toward what's best in singing with his harp? Or in his case, was he not even looking to what's most pleasant, since when he sang it was a pain to the audience? But just consider whether all singing with the harp and composing of dithyrambs doesn't seem to you to have been devised for the sake of pleasure.

Callicles: To me it does.

Socrates: And what about that awesome and wondrous thing, the **B**
composition of tragic poetry? What is it so solemn about? Does its effort and seriousness seem to you only to go into gratifying its spectators or, if there's something that's pleasant and gratifying to them, but debasing, does it also struggle to find a way not to say that, while if there happens to be something unpleasing but beneficial, will it speak and sing that, whether people get any enjoyment from it or not? In which way does the composing of tragic poetry seem to you to turn its efforts?

Callicles: This at least is definitely clear, Socrates, that it exerts itself
more toward pleasure and gratifying the spectators. **C**

Socrates: And it's such a thing, Callicles, that we were claiming just now is pandering?

Callicles: Quite so.

Socrates: Come along, then: if one peels away the melody and rhythm and meter from all poetry, does what's left turn out to be anything other than speeches?

Callicles: That's a necessity.

Socrates: And these speeches are spoken to a big crowd and populace?

---

38 Dithyrambic poetry was chanted by a group of dancers as part of the worship of Dionysus. The examples Socrates gives form a progression. The flute (an instrument resembling our recorders) was part of the customary entertainment at dinner parties. Competitive playing of the *kithara*, an instrument larger than a lyre but smaller than modern concert harps, took place at public festivals. The dithyramb, less sedate than other choral odes such as the nomes in honor of Apollo, evolved by stages into the tragedy.

Callicles: I'd say so.

Socrates: Therefore poetry is a certain kind of public speaking?

D *Callicles:* So it appears.

Socrates: And it would be rhetorical public speaking—or don't the poets seem to you to use rhetoric in the theaters?

Callicles: To me they do.

Socrates: Therefore we've now discovered a kind of rhetoric directed to a populace of a sort that consists of children, women, and men together, slaves as well as free, a kind that we don't quite respect, since we declare it to be pandering.

Callicles: Quite so.

Socrates: Okay. What about the rhetoric directed to the Athenian
E populace or to the other populations of free men in the cities? What in the world do we make of that? Do rhetoricians seem to you to be speaking always with a view to what's best, aiming at that with their speeches so the citizens will be the best they can possibly be, or do they too exert themselves toward gratifying the citizens, and place a low value on the common good for the sake their own private interest, talking to the populace like they were children, trying only to gratify them without giving any thought
503A to whether they'll be better or worse from that?

Callicles: This is no longer a simple question you're asking, because there are some who say the things they say out of care for the citizens, and some who are the sort you're speaking of.

Socrates: That's good enough, because if this is also twofold, one part of it would presumably be an ugly pandering and demagoguery while the other would be a beautiful thing, turning its efforts to the way the souls of the citizens would be the best they can possibly be, and struggling to say the best things, whether they're more
B pleasing or more unpleasant to those who hear them. But you've never seen this sort of rhetoric; or if you have any such rhetorician to mention, why haven't you told me who it is too?

Callicles: But by Zeus, *I* don't have a single one to mention to you, at least among the rhetoricians of today.

Socrates: What about those of the old days? Do you have any to mention through whom the Athenians are held to have become better, from the time he first started his public speaking, when they'd been worse in the preceding time? Because I don't know who that would be.

C *Callicles:* What about Themistocles? Don't you hear that he was a good man, and also Cimon and Miltiades[39] and that very Pericles who died recently and whom you even heard speak?

39 Miltiades and his son Cimon were the most influential political and military leaders in Athens between the time of Themistocles and that of Pericles. The four of them presided over a half-century or so of vast expansion of Athenian power and wealth.

Socrates: Yes, Callicles, if what you were saying virtue is before is true virtue, namely satisfying the desires of oneself and of others; if it's not that, but it's what we were compelled to agree it is later in our speech—fulfilling those desires whose satisfaction makes a human being better and not those that make him worse, and **D** there's a certain art to this—I certainly couldn't say how any of these was that sort of man.

Callicles: But if you do a beautiful job of searching, you'll find out.[40]

Socrates: So by considering it without anxiety, as we are, let's see whether any of these people was of that sort. Come along then: the good man, whose speech is directed to what's best, wouldn't say the things he does in a random way, would he, but with his **E** eye on some end? It's the same way as with all the other craftsmen: each one looks to his own work and brings to bear on it not what he chooses at random, but what will make what he works on have a certain form to it. For instance, if you want to look at painters, housebuilders, shipbuilders, all the rest of the craftsmen, whichever one of them you want, each of them puts each thing he handles into some arrangement and constrains one thing to be **504A** suited to and harmonious with another until the sum of them all is organized into an end result that's arranged and ordered. And so do the other craftsmen as well, even the ones we were just talking about who deal with the body, the trainers and doctors; presumably they give the body order and arrangement. Do we agree that this is how it is or not?

Callicles: Let it be so.

Socrates: Therefore, a house that attains an arrangement and ordering would be a serviceable one, but one that falls into disarray would be in a deplorable state?

Callicles: I'd say so.

Socrates: And the same way with a ship?

Callicles: Yes. **B**

Socrates: And do we claim it's the same with our bodies?

Callicles: Certainly.

Socrates: And what about the soul? Will it be serviceable if it falls into disarray, or rather if it attains a certain arrangement and ordering?

Callicles: Based on the previous things, it's necessary to agree with this too.

Socrates: And in the body, what's the word for what comes from its arrangement and ordering?

40 There is inconsistency in the manuscripts here, and disagreement among editors. Dodds, the editor whose version this translation generally follows, puts this line at the end of Socrates' speech, but it is not Socrates who thinks high repute in the political realm would always be a sign of virtue. The assignment of speakers followed here is that of Burnet, which gives the sequence "I can't...You will...Let us."

Callicles: You're probably speaking of health and strength.

C *Socrates:* I am. And what in turn for what comes into the soul from its arrangement and ordering? Try to find and state the word as in the former case.

Callicles: Why not say it yourself, Socrates?

Socrates: Well, if that's more pleasing to you, I'll state it, but if I seem to you to say it beautifully, you say so, and if not, refute me and don't let me get away with it. Because it seems to me that the word for arrangements of the body is "healthy," and that from them health comes to be present in it, as well as the rest of the virtue of the body. Is that so or not?

Callicles: It is.

D *Socrates:* And for the arrangements and orderings of the soul, it's "law-abiding" and law, from which souls become law-abiding and orderly. And these conditions are justice and moderation. Do you say so or not?

Callicles: Let it be so.

Socrates: Then that rhetorician, the one who's artful and good, will be looking toward these things and will bring them to bear on our souls in the speeches he makes and in all his actions. And if he gives us any gift or takes anything from us, he'll give it or take it
E having his thoughts on this: on how justice may be brought into the souls of his fellow-citizens and injustice may be eliminated, on how moderation may be brought in and self-indulgence eliminated, and how the rest of virtue may be brought in and vice expelled. Do you go along with that or not?

Callicles: I go along with it.

Socrates: Because what benefit is there, Callicles, in giving a diseased body that's in deplorable shape a lot of the most pleasant foods or drinks or anything else whatever when there's no way that's going to make it any better off, or on the contrary, on a just account of the matter, will make it even worse off? Is that how it is?

505A *Callicles:* Let it be so.

Socrates: Because I don't imagine it's any profit for a human being to live with a deplorable body, since in that way it's a necessity for him also to live a deplorable life. Or isn't that so?

Callicles: Yes.

Socrates: So fulfilling one's desires, such as eating or drinking as much as one wants when hungry or thirsty, is something the doctors allow, for the most part, when someone is healthy, but when he's sick they allow him to fill up on things he desires, in a word, never; do you go along with that or not?

Callicles: I do.

B *Socrates:* And concerning the soul, most excellent fellow, isn't it the same way? As long as it's in a worthless condition, and is thoughtless and self-indulgent and unjust and impious, one needs to keep it back from its desires and not trust it to do any other things than those as a result of which it will be better; do you assert this or not?

Callicles: I assert it.

Socrates: Because presumably that's the way that's better for the soul itself?

Callicles: Quite so.

Socrates: And keeping it back from things it desires is disciplining it?

Callicles: Yes.

Socrates: Therefore being disciplined is better for the soul than a lack of discipline, which you imagined was better a little while ago.

Callicles: I don't know what you're talking about, Socrates; just ask C
someone else.

Socrates: This man can't stand to be benefited or to undergo himself what our speech is about: accepting discipline.

Callicles: And nothing *you* say is of any concern to me either; I've been giving you these answers to please Gorgias.

Socrates: Okay. So what should we do? Do we break off the speech in the middle?

Callicles: Decide for yourself.

Socrates: But they say it's not right even to leave off stories in the D
middle; they should have heads put on them so they don't go around without a head. So answer the questions that are left too, so that our speech will get a head.

Callicles: How forceful you are, Socrates. But if you're persuaded by me, you'll tell this speech goodbye, or else have the conversation with someone else.

Socrates: But who else is willing? Surely we can't abandon the speech incomplete.

Callicles: Couldn't you go through the speech on your own, either speaking by yourself or answering your own questions?

Socrates: So the words of Epicharmus[41] would come true for me, "what E
two men were saying before this," I must become sufficient for, though I'm only one. Well, it's probably unavoidable. But we'll do it in the following way. I think all of us need to be in eager rivalry for knowing what the truth is about the things we're speaking of, and what's false, since it's a good thing for everyone in common
for it to become evident. So in the speech, I'll go through the way 506A
it seems to me to be, but if it seems to any of you that the things I'm agreeing with myself about are not so, you need to grab hold of them and refute them. Because I'm certainly not saying the things I'm saying with any complete knowledge, but I'm inquiring in common with you folks; so if, when someone disputes me,

41 An early comic poet, possibly the first to write dialogue for actors rather than recitations of ridicule. Only fragments of his work survive.

there's manifestly something in what he says, I'll be the first one to go along with it. But I say these things assuming it seems right to bring the speech to completion; if you folks don't want that, let's tell it goodbye right now and go away.

B *Gorgias:* But it doesn't seem right to me to go away yet, Socrates, but instead for you to go on through the speech, and it appears to me to seem that way to the others as well. I myself certainly want to hear you go through the things that are left yourself.

Socrates: Well, Gorgias, I myself would have been pleased to be still conversing with Callicles here, until I'd given him back an address by Amphion in return for that of Zethus. But since you, Callicles, aren't willing to join in bringing the speech to completion, at least,
C as you listen to me, interrupt if I seem to you not to be speaking in a beautiful manner. And if you refute me, I won't be annoyed with you the way you were with me, but you'll be engraved in my memory as my greatest benefactor.

Callicles: Speak, good fellow, yourself, and get it over with.

Socrates: Then listen as I take up the speech again from the beginning. Are the pleasant and the good the same thing? Not the same, as Callicles and I agreed. Is what's pleasant to be done for the sake of the good, or what's good for the sake of the pleasant? What's
D pleasant for the sake of the good. And the pleasant is that at the coming of which we're pleased, and the good is that by the presence of which we're good? Of course. But we and everything else that's good are good because some virtue has come to be present? That seems necessary to me at any rate, Callicles. But surely the virtue of each thing, of a piece of equipment or a body, or also of a soul and of any living thing, doesn't come to be present most beautifully just at random, but by an arrangement and a rightness and by whichever art is given over to each of them; is that so? I
E say it is. Therefore, the virtue of each thing is something arranged in an arrangement and made orderly? I'd surely say so. Therefore a certain orderliness that's native to each thing, when it comes to be present in it, is what makes each of the things there are good? It certainly seems that way to me. Therefore in the case of a soul too, one that has the orderliness that belongs to it is better than a disorderly one? Necessarily. But surely the one that has an orderli-
507A ness is an orderly soul? How could it fail to be? And an orderly soul is moderate? That's a great necessity. Therefore a moderate soul is good. I have no other things to say counter to these, Callicles my friend, but if you do, instruct us.

Callicles: Speak on, good fellow.

Socrates: Well, I say that, if a moderate soul is good, one with an experience opposite to a moderate one is bad, and that would be an unreasonable[42] and self-indulgent one. Of course. And surely a moderate person would do what's appropriate in regard to both gods and human beings, since he wouldn't be moderate if he did inappropriate things. It's a necessity that these things be so. And **B** if he does what's appropriate in regard to human beings, surely he'd be doing just things, and pious things in regard to gods; and someone who does just and pious things is necessarily a just and pious person. That's so. And in fact it's a necessity that he be manly as well, because it's characteristic of a moderate man not to pursue or avoid things that are inappropriate but to pursue or avoid what one should, actions and people as well as pleasures and pains, and to be steadfast in enduring whatever one should; so it's a great necessity,[43] Callicles, for this one who's moderate, **C** since he is, as we've gone over, just and manly and pious, to be a completely good man, and for this one who's good to do what he does well and beautifully, and for this one who does well to be blessed and happy, while someone who's worthless and does badly is miserable, and that would be someone in the opposite condition to a moderate person, namely the self-indulgent person whom you were praising.

So I set these things down in this way, and I claim that they're true. And if they *are* true, it looks like the thing someone who wants to be happy needs to pursue and make a practice of is moderation, **D** and the thing each of us needs to run from as fast as his feet can go is self-indulgence; at best one needs to manage things so as to have no need for discipline to be imposed, but if he himself or any other private person close to him, or his city, does need it, a just penalty needs to be enforced and discipline needs to be imposed, if they're going to be happy. This seems to me to be the target one ought to live with his eye on, bending all his own efforts and those of his city toward this, toward acting in such a way that justice and **E** moderation will be present for a person who's going to be blessedly happy, not toward letting his desires be undisciplined and trying

42 The word "moderate" (*sophrôn*), used for someone who recognizes and does what is appropriate, particularly between the extremes of self-indulgence and self-denial, has the literal meaning "maintaining good sense," or "reasonable," and is precisely negated by *aphrôn*, "lacking good sense."

43 Throughout this paragraph, the necessities asserted are necessary implications of the conventional language used for qualities conventionally praised. The very name for moderation implies courage, and its name is *andreia*, the manliness Callicles admires. Moderation, justice, courage and piety were often regarded as constituting the whole of virtue, so to act in accordance with all four would be to do everything rightly and well, and doing well is a conventional way to speak of being happy. None of this is proof of anything. Socrates is doing what he has repeatedly said he is doing, following the *logos*. Callicles has made a rhetorically vivid speech rejecting moderation and endorsing manliness. Socrates is challenging him to think that through, and see whether he can give a consistent and intelligible speech to the same effect. If not, he will have choices to face.

to give them their fill, a trouble that has no end, while he lives the life of a plunderer. For that sort of person would not be dearly loved by any other human being or god, since he's incapable of sharing anything, and where no single thing is shared there can be no friendship. Those who are wise declare, Callicles, that heaven and
508A earth and gods and humans are held together by the shared bond of friendship, and by orderliness, moderation, and justice, and for this reason, my comrade, they call this whole a cosmos,[44] not a disorder or a dissipation. But as for you, Callicles, even though you're smart about these things, you don't seem to me to pay attention to them, and it's escaped your notice that geometrical equality has great power among gods and human beings; you imagine one ought to make a practice of getting more because you neglect geometry.[45]
B Okay. Either this speech has to be refuted by us, and it's not by the possession of justice and moderation that the happy are happy, and by the possession of vice that the miserable are miserable, or else, if this speech is true, we need to examine what its consequences are. Those earlier consequences all follow, Callicles, the ones you asked me if I was serious about when I stated them, saying there would be a need to accuse oneself, or one's son or comrade, if he committed any injustice, and to make use of rhetoric for that. And the things you imagined Polus was going along with out of shame would be true after all, that to whatever extent committing injustice
C is an uglier thing than suffering it, to that extent it's worse, and that someone who's going to be a rhetorician in the right way will need

44 The Greek word *kosmos*, the root of all the words translated here as order, ordering, orderly, and so on, was used by various earlier writers as a name for the ordered whole of all things. The word *taxis*, translated here as arrangement, was more neutral, while *kosmos* carried the sense of something deserving admiration and praise. The latter is the first word of Gorgias's *Encomium of Helen* (see note to 483E), which begins: "*Kosmos* in a city is manliness, in a body beauty, in a soul wisdom, in an action virtue, and in a speech truth." In 503D, Socrates began following the *logos* from artfulness to arrangement to the rhetorically overpowering array of meanings gathered in the word *kosmos*.

45 Geometrical equality can mean proportionality, equality of ratios. Commentators generally point to Aristotle's discussion of distributive justice in Bk. V, Chap. 3 of the *Nicomachean Ethics*, but the issue here is not the relative distribution of common resources but the choices of each human being that lead to maximum satisfaction. More to the point here is the discussion of the mean that begins in Bk. II, Chap. 6 of the *Nicomachean Ethics*. In all things that vary in quantity, Aristotle says, there is a greater, a less, and an equal, where equality is determined not by matching some other quantity but by matching up with the qualitative nature of the thing that has the quantity. In 503E above, Socrates had said that artful work is never random, but looks to an end in order to bring an appropriate form to its result. Proportionate equality is called geometrical because it is present in every aspect of similar figures, those that are the same in form. Socrates is both playful and serious in suggesting that the recognition of form that governs geometry is the antidote to the blind quantitative principle of always wanting more. Human happiness may be recognizable in one's own experience and in the lives of others as a geometrical magnitude, as suggested at 509C below.

to be just, and knowledgeable about what's just, after all, which
Polus in turn said Gorgias had agreed to on account of shame.

Now since that's how these things are, let's consider what if
anything there is in the criticisms you made of me, whether it is or
isn't beautifully said that I'm unable to come to the aid of myself or
of any of my friends or relations, or to save them from the greatest
dangers, that like the dregs of society I'm at the mercy of anyone
who so chooses if he wants—in that brash phrase of yours— to D
give me a slap upside the head, or to take away my possessions or
expel me from the city, or in the extreme case to kill me. And to be
in that condition is the most shameful of all things, as your speech
has it. What mine is has been said repeatedly already, but nothing prevents its being said yet again: I claim, Callicles, that being
unjustly slapped upside the head is not the most shameful thing,
and neither is having either my body or my pocket cut open, but E
hitting and cutting me or what's mine is both more shameful and
worse, and by the same token stealing, enslaving, housebreaking,
and in short, committing any injustice whatever upon me or what's
mine is both worse and more shameful for the one who commits
the injustice than for me who suffers it. The fact that these things
are the way I say, back there in the previous speeches, was plainly
fastened down and locked up, if it may be put rather crudely, in 509A
ironclad and diamond-hard arguments—at least that's the way it
would seem—and if you, or someone more brash than you, doesn't
unfasten them, it won't be possible for anyone who says otherwise
than what I'm now saying to be speaking beautifully. Because as
for me, what I say is always the same, that I don't know how these
things are, but that none of the people I've run across, present company included, is able to say otherwise without being completely
ridiculous. So I for my part hold these things to be this way, and B
if they are this way, and injustice is the greatest of evils for the
person who commits it, and a still greater evil than this one that's
the greatest, if that's possible, is for someone to commit injustice
without paying the just penalty, then what sort of help would it
truly be ridiculous for a human being not to have the power to
give himself? Wouldn't it be whatever sort of help would turn the
greatest harm away from us? And it's a great necessity that this
would be the most shameful sort of help *not* to have the power to
give oneself and one's friends and relations; second would be the
sort of help that turns away the second greatest evil, third the third, C
and so on with the rest. As the magnitude of each sort of evil is by
nature, so is the beauty of being powerful enough to help against
each, and the shamefulness of not being powerful enough. Is it
otherwise, Callicles, or is it that way?

Callicles: Not otherwise.

Socrates: So out of this pair, committing injustice and suffering it,
we claim committing injustice is a greater evil and suffering it
is a lesser one. What preparations, then, should a human being
D make so he can help himself, in order to have both these benefits,
that of not committing injustice and that of not suffering it? Is it
a matter of power or of wanting it? I mean this: will someone not
suffer injustice because he doesn't *want* to suffer it, or because he
prepared himself with a power to avoid suffering it?

Callicles: That's obvious; because of a power.

Socrates: And what about committing injustice? If someone doesn't
want to commit injustice, is that sufficient—since he won't commit
E it—or in this case too does one need to prepare oneself with some
power and art, on the grounds that he will commit injustice if he
doesn't learn and practice certain things? Why don't you answer
me just this point, Callicles, whether it seems to you that we, Polus
and I, were rightly compelled or not to agree in the earlier speeches,
when we agreed that no one commits injustice because he wants
to, but all those who commit injustice do so unwillingly?[46]

510A *Callicles:* Have it your way, Socrates; let this be that way so you can
finish off the speech.

Socrates: For this too, therefore, it looks like there's a need to prepare oneself with some power and art so that we don't commit injustice.

Callicles: Quite so.

Socrates: So what art might there be for the preparation for suffering no injustice, or the least possible amount? See whether it seems to you the same way it does to me, because to me it seems like this: one ought to be a ruler in the city oneself, or even be a tyrant, or else be a comrade of the regime that's already there.

B *Callicles:* Do you see, Socrates, how ready I am to praise you when
you speak beautifully in any way? On this point you seem to me
to have spoken very beautifully.

Socrates: Then see whether I seem to you to be speaking well on this point too: it seems to me that each with each is a friend to the greatest possible degree in the way the wise people of ancient times said, like with like. Don't you think so too?

Callicles: I do.

Socrates: So where the ruler is a savage, uneducated tyrant, if there
were anyone in the city who was much better than he, the tyrant
would presumably be afraid of him and would never be capable
C of becoming his friend with all his heart?

46 What Polus agreed to at 468D was that injustice is always committed as a means to an end, and is done unwillingly *if* its result is in fact harmful to the one who commits it. Socrates has just claimed that the "if" has now been removed, unless and until Callicles can show otherwise. That no one does evil willingly was a paradox often asserted by Socrates; see for example Plato's *Meno*, 77B-77B.

Callicles: That's how it is.

Socrates: And if there were someone much worse, he couldn't be a friend either, since the tyrant would despise him and could never look at him seriously as a friend.

Callicles: That's true too.

Socrates: So the only one left worth mentioning as a friend to such a person is someone similar to him in character, who blames and praises the same things, and is willing to be ruled and be subordinate to the ruler. He'll have great power in that city; no one will D
get any joy out of doing *him* an injustice. Isn't that how it is?

Callicles: Yes.

Socrates: Therefore, if any of the young people in that city were to reflect, "What's the way I could get great power and have no one do me any injustice?" it looks like this would be the path for him: to get accustomed straight from youth to being delighted and annoyed by the same things himself as his boss, and prepare himself to be as much like that person as possible. Isn't that so?

Callicles: Yes.

Socrates: So for him, not suffering injustice and having great power, E
in the sense you people speak of it, will have been attained in his city.

Callicles: Entirely so.

Socrates: And not committing injustice either? Or far from it, if he's going to be like a ruler who's unjust, and have great power at his side? I imagine his preparation will be all in the opposite direction, toward being able to commit the greatest possible number of injustices and not pay the just penalty for committing them, won't it?

Callicles: So it appears.

Socrates: So the greatest evil will befall him when he's depraved in 511A
soul and maimed by imitation of his boss and by his power.

Callicles: I don't know how you manage to turn the speeches upside down every time, Socrates; or else you're unaware that this imitator will put that non-imitator to death if he wants to, and take away his property.

Socrates: I know it, good Callicles, if I'm not deaf, from listening to B
both you and Polus just now, over and over, and to little short of everyone else in the city; but you listen to me too, saying that he will put him to death if he wants to, but it will be someone who's worthless taking a beautiful and good life.

Callicles: And isn't that exactly what makes it so galling?

Socrates: Not to anyone with any sense; that's what our speech implies. Or do you imagine that this is what a human being ought to prepare himself for, to live as long as possible a time, and study those arts that save us from dangers in every situation, like the one you're C
exhorting me to study, the sort of rhetoric that gets people off safely in the lawcourts?

Callicles: Yes, by Zeus! And I'm giving you the right advice.

Socrates: What about swimming, then, most excellent fellow? Does it seem to you the knowledge of swimming is anything awe-inspiring?

Callicles: By Zeus, not to me.

Socrates: And yet that saves human beings from death, whenever
they've fallen into any situation of the sort that requires that
D knowledge. But if that seems to be a petty thing, I'll tell you one
greater than that, helmsmanship, which saves not only our souls
but also our bodies and our possessions from the most extreme
dangers, the same way rhetoric does. And this one is self-effacing
and orderly, and doesn't have an exalted air about it as though it
were accomplishing some high and mighty feat; but when it does
accomplish the same things as lawyering, if it gets someone here
safely from Aegina, I think it charges a couple of cents, or if it's
E from Egypt or from the Black Sea, for this great benefit of saving
the things I was just speaking of—oneself and one's children, possessions, and women—when it lands them in the harbor it charges,
at the very most, a couple of dollars.[47] And the one himself who has
the art and has accomplished these things steps off at the seaside
and stretches his legs next to the ship with a modest air about
him; I imagine that's because he knows that it's an unclear thing
to figure out which of the passengers he's done a favor to by not
letting them sink under the sea, and which ones he's done harm,
512A since he knows that he's put them off the ship no better sorts of
people than they were when he took them on, in either body or
soul. So he reasons that, if someone afflicted in body with great
and incurable diseases hasn't drowned, and that person is miserable because he hasn't died, and isn't benefited at all by him, it's
therefore not the case when someone has many incurable diseases
in something more valuable than his body, his soul, that his life is
worth living and he'll be doing him a favor if he saves him either
B from the sea or the lawcourt or from anything else whatever. He
knows that it's not better for a depraved person to live, since it's a
necessity that he'll live a bad life.

That's why it's not the custom for a helmsman to exalt himself,
even though he saves our lives, or, you amazing fellow, for a maker
of war machines either, and he sometimes has the power to save
no fewer lives than a general, much less a helmsman or anyone
else, since there are times when he saves whole cities. He doesn't
seem to you to rank with a lawyer, does he? Yet if he wanted to
C speak the way you people do, Callicles, making something exalted

47 The words translated "dollars" and "cents" are literally drachmas and obols. In purchasing power they were more substantial sums than the translation would suggest, but they were the smallest named divisions of the currency, and the translation is intended to convey something of Socrates' tone.

out of his concerns, he could deluge you with speeches, speaking in exhortation about how people need to become war-machine makers, since nothing else is any big deal, because he'd have enough to say. But you look down on him and on that art of his nonetheless, and would toss the name "mechanic" at him as if in reproach, and wouldn't be willing to let your daughter marry his son or accept his daughter for your own son. Yet on the basis of the things you praise your own specialty for, what reason do you have with any justice to it for looking down on the war-machine maker or the others I was just speaking of? I know you'd claim to D
be better and to come from better stock. But if better isn't what I say it is, and virtue is just this saving of oneself and one's things, whatever sort of person one happens to be, your fault-finding becomes ridiculous when applied to a war-machine maker, to a doctor, or to any of the other arts that have been devised for the sake of saving people. But, you blessedly happy fellow, see whether what's high-born and good isn't something other than saving and being saved. Because *that*, just living for some length of time, is E
something to be disdained by anyone who's truly a *man*; being in love with life on any terms is not for him. He turns over concern for those things to the god instead, and believes what the women say, that no single person can escape what's allotted; on that view, the thing that needs to be considered is in what manner he can live this time he's going to live in the best possible way. Is it by turning himself into a likeness of that regime in which he happens to have 513A
his home? Therefore in the present instance you'd need to become exactly like the Athenian populace if you're going to be loved by it and have great power in the city. See if this is profitable for you and for me, you strange fellow, so that we don't suffer the same fate they say the Thessalian women do when they pull down the moon; our choice of that power in the city will be in exchange for the things we love most.[48] If you imagine that any human being whatsoever is going to hand over to you any kind of art that will B
make you have great power here in this city while you're *un*like its regime, for better and for worse, then the way it seems to me, Callicles, is that you're not being given the right advice. Because you can't be an imitator, you have to *be* like them in your very nature, if you're going to work your way into any genuine friendship with the Athenian populace, and yes, with Pyrilampes' son too, by Zeus![49] So whoever is going to turn you into the most complete likeness of these is the one who'll make you a politician in the way you want to be a politician, and a rhetorician, because people of each type take C

48 Witches were thought to gain their powers, such as that of causing eclipses, at the price of losing loved ones, their own sight, or something else precious to them.

49 See 481D and footnote.

delight in speeches made in accord with their own character, and are put off by speeches meant for anyone else's character—unless you say something different, dear heart. Do we say anything in response to this, Callicles?

Callicles: Something about the way you're speaking seems good to me, Socrates—I don't know what it is—but I'm having the experience most people do: I'm not entirely persuaded by you.

Socrates: That's because the love of the populace that's there in your
soul, Callicles, is resisting me, but if we examine these same things
D over and over, and better, you'll be persuaded. Anyway, remember
that we were claiming there are two kinds of preparation for taking
care of each thing having to do with the body and the soul, one that
goes about its business with a view to pleasure, the other doing so
with a view to what's best, and not giving in but struggling for it.
Weren't these the things we distinguished then?

Callicles: Quite so.

Socrates: And one of them, the one looking toward pleasure, is of base lineage and turns out to be nothing other than pandering, right?

E *Callicles:* Have it your way, if you want.

Socrates: While the purpose of the other is that the thing we're caring for, whether it happens to be a body or a soul, will be the best it can be?

Callicles: Quite so.

Socrates: And shouldn't we attempt to care for the city and its citizens
in that way, to make the citizens themselves the best they can be?
Because failing that, as we discovered in the earlier discussion,
514A it's of no benefit to perform any other service if the people who
are going to get a lot of money, or a position of rule over anyone,
or any other power whatever, aren't beautiful and good in their
thinking. Shall we set this down as being so?

Callicles: Quite so, if that's more pleasing to you.

Socrates: So, Callicles, if we were going to enter into action in public
in political matters, and we exhorted one another toward matters
pertaining to building walls or shipyards or temples, for the great-
B est building projects, would we have to examine and test ourselves
first to see if we're knowledgeable or not about the art of building,
and who we learned it from? Would we have to do that or not?

Callicles: Quite so.

Socrates: And then, second, this: if we'd ever built any building privately for any of our friends or our own selves, and whether that
building is beautiful or ugly? And if we found out after consider-
C ing it that our teachers had been good and reputable, and many
beautiful buildings had been built by us along with our teachers,
and many private ones also by us after we'd left our teachers, those
would be the circumstances in which it would be appropriate for
people with any sense to go in for public works. But if we had no

teacher of ours to point to, and either no buildings or a lot of worthless ones, in that case, presumably, it would just be senseless to
attempt public works or to exhort one another toward them. Shall
we set these things down as being rightly said or not? D

Callicles: Quite so.

Socrates: And is it that way with everything else too? If we'd tried to
go into public life and were urging one another to it as competent
doctors, no doubt I would have examined you and you me: "Come
now, before the gods, how is Socrates himself doing in regard to
health in his body? Or has anyone else, slave or free, gotten free of
disease before now because of Socrates?" And I imagine I'd have
looked into other things of that sort about you. And if we discovered that no one had become better in body because of us, none of E
the foreigners or townspeople, no man and no woman, then before
Zeus, Callicles, wouldn't it be truly ludicrous that human beings
could go so far in senselessness that before doing a lot of private
work, however we might do at that, correcting a lot of our errors
and getting adequate training in the art, we tried, as that saying
goes, to learn pottery on an urn and go into public life ourselves
and exhort others to do that sort of thing? Doesn't it seem senseless
to you to act that way?

Callicles: To me, yes.

Socrates: Now then, most excellent of men, since you yourself are 515A
just starting to take an active part in the affairs of the city and
urging me to, and blaming me for not taking an active part, shall
we not examine one another: "Come now, Callicles, which of the
citizens have you made better before now? Is there anyone who
was depraved before, unjust and self-indulgent and stupid, who
became beautiful and good in character because of Callicles, any
foreigner or townsman, slave or free?" Tell me, Callicles, if some- B
one puts you to the test on these matters, what will you say? What
human being will you claim you've made better by his association
with you? Are you reluctant to answer, if there is in fact any deed
of yours, while still in private life, prior to your attempting to go
into public life?

Callicles: You just love to win arguments, Socrates.

Socrates: I'm not asking the question out of a love of winning arguments, but truly wanting to know how in the world you imagine
you ought to behave in politics among us. Or will you, after you
go into the affairs of the city with us, really be putting your effort C
into something *other* than how we, the citizens, might be the best
we can be? Haven't we already agreed repeatedly that that's the
way a political man ought to act? Have we agreed to that or not?
Answer me. We *have* agreed; I'll answer in your place. So if that's
what a good man ought to provide for in his own city, recalling
now, tell me about those men you were speaking of a little while

ago, whether they still seem to you to have been good citizens,
D Pericles, Cimon, Miltiades, and Themistocles.

Callicles: To me, yes.

Socrates: So if they were good, it's obvious that each of them used to make the citizens better instead of worse. Is that what they used to do, or not?

Callicles: Yes.

Socrates: So when Pericles began speaking among the populace, the Athenians were worse than when he spoke for the last times?

Callicles: Maybe.

Socrates: No maybe about it, most excellent one, but by necessity, based on the things that have been agreed, if in fact he was a good citizen.

E *Callicles:* So, what then?

Socrates: Nothing. But tell me this on that point, whether the Athenians are said to have become better because of Pericles or completely the opposite, to have been corrupted by him. Because what *I* hear is this: that Pericles made the Athenians lazy, cowardly, babbling money-lovers, by having first brought in fees for public service.[50]

Callicles: You hear those things from guys with cauliflower ears, Socrates.[51]

Socrates: But the following are no longer things I hear but things I know clearly, and you know as well as I: that at first Pericles used to be well thought of, and the Athenians didn't vote any shameful penalty against him at the time when they were worse; but when
516A they'd become beautiful and good in character thanks to him, at the end of Pericles' life, they voted him guilty of theft, and they were little short of condemning him to death, obviously on the grounds that he was a reprehensible person.

Callicles: So what, then? Pericles was bad because of that?

Socrates: Well, it would seem that someone in charge of asses or horses or cattle was bad if he was like that—if they weren't kicking or butting or biting him when he took them over and he gives them back doing all those things because of wildness. Doesn't it seem to
B you that anyone, whoever it may be, is a bad caretaker of an animal

---

50 Pericles introduced the policy of paying the people for days spent on jury duty or military service. These were democratic reforms, permitting all citizens to participate in public life. The policy was extended after his time by fees for attendance at the legislative assembly.

51 The dialogue is set at an indeterminate date; various events that happened years apart are referred to as recent and vivid in the participants' memories. But all these events took place during the period when Athens was at war with Sparta. Callicles is making a not-so-veiled accusation of Spartan sympathies, since boxing was a favorite Spartan sport. The kind of government Socrates considered best, described at length in Plato's *Republic,* is sometimes taken as similar to that of Sparta, but Socrates in fact criticizes the Spartan regime in that dialogue (547E-548C) for one of the same faults he attributes here to Pericles.

if he takes it over tamer and gives it back wilder than he took it? Does it seem that way or not?

Callicles: Quite so, in order that I may gratify you.

Socrates: Then gratify me on this point too by answering whether a human being is also one of the animals or not.

Callicles: Of course he is.

Socrates: And Pericles was in charge of human beings?

Callicles: Yes.

Socrates: So what, then? Shouldn't they have become more just, as we agreed just now, instead of more unjust because of him, if in fact
he had charge of them and was good at political matters? C

Callicles: Quite so.

Socrates: And the just are gentle, as Homer said.[52] What do you say? Isn't it that way?

Callicles: Yes.

Socrates: But surely he turned them out wilder than the sort of people they were when he took them over, and toward himself at that, what he'd least have wanted.

Callicles: Do you want[53] me to agree with you?

Socrates: Only if I seem to you to be speaking the truth.

Callicles: Let it be so.

Socrates: And if wilder, more unjust and worse?

Callicles: Let it be. D

Socrates: Therefore, on the basis of this speech, Pericles was not good at political matters.

Callicles: *You* claim he wasn't.

Socrates: By Zeus, you do too by the things you've agreed to. And tell me again about Cimon; didn't the people he took care of ostracize him, so they wouldn't have to hear his voice for ten years? And didn't they do the same things to Themistocles, and punish him with exile on top of it?[54] And Miltiades, who was at Marathon,
didn't they vote to throw him down a chasm, and if it hadn't been E
for the presiding official, wouldn't he 've gone into it? And yet, if these men were good at what you claim they were, they'd never have suffered those things. Good charioteers certainly don't keep from falling out of the chariots at first, but then fall out of them after they've taken care of their horses and become better charioteers.

52 Scholars worry over the fact that this is not in our texts of Homer, though the phrase "wild, not just" occurs a few times in the *Odyssey*. Socrates is probably making a mild joke at the expense of people who, like Gorgias in 449A, quote Homer in support of the simplest, briefest, and most obvious remarks.

53 The immediate repetition of the word may make one begin to wonder whether Socrates has turned Callicles any tamer than when he took him over, and whether that's what he wants.

54 Ostracism was not a punishment, but a measure to remove from the city someone who was becoming too powerful. Themistocles was first ostracized, then exiled permanently when certain crimes of his came to light.

That's not the way it is in charioteering or in any other work. Or does it seem to you it is?

Callicles: Not to me.

517A *Socrates:* Therefore it looks like the earlier speeches, to the effect that we don't know of any man who's been good at political matters in this city here, were true. You agreed that none of those here now are, although from those here before you picked out these men; but these have been shown up as being on an equal footing with those here now, so if they were rhetoricians, they weren't using the true rhetoric—or they wouldn't have been driven out—or the pandering sort either.

Callicles: But surely, Socrates, any of those here now falls far short of accomplishing deeds of the sort those men accomplished, which-
B ever one of them you want to take.

Socrates: You strange fellow, I'm not blaming them either, at least not in their capacity as servants of the city; they seem to me to have been of more service than those here now, and more capable of providing the city with the things it desired. But as for guiding those desires in a different direction rather than giving way to them, by persuading or compelling them toward what will make
C the citizens be better, there's no difference to speak of between them, and that's the only job there is for a good citizen. I even agree with you too that they were more formidable than these are at providing ships and walls and shipyards and lots of things of that sort. So you and I are doing a comical thing in our speeches, because in all the time we've been having a discussion we've made no end of circling around always to the same point in ignorance of what each other is saying. At any rate, I imagine that several
D times you've agreed and understood that this business concerned with both the body and the soul is something twofold after all, and that one side is fit for service, whereby, if our bodies are hungry, it's capable of providing food, if thirsty, drink, if cold, cloaks, bed coverings, footwear, and other things that bodies come to desire. I'm deliberately speaking to you with the same illustrations so you may understand more easily.[55] Because someone skilled at providing these things is either a retailer, an importer, or a craftsman of
E one of the items themselves, a baker, a cook, a weaver, a leather-worker, a tanner, and there's nothing surprising when someone of that sort seems to himself and to others to be a caretaker of a body, to everyone who doesn't know that there's any art beyond all these of gymnastic training and doctoring, which precisely are in reality the caretaking of a body, and which have the fitting position of ruling over all these arts and using their products on account of knowing what among food and drink is serviceable or

55 See 490E-491A.

worthless toward the virtue of a body, while all these others are 518A
ignorant of that. That's exactly why these other arts are slavish
and menial and don't pertain to freedom, while gymnastic training and doctoring, according to what's just, are their masters.[56]
Now sometimes you seem to me to understand, when I'm saying
it, that these same things also apply to the soul, and you agree as
though you know what I mean, but here you come a little later
saying that people have been beautiful and good citizens in our B
city, and when I ask you who, you seem to me to hold out people
involved in politics who are exactly the same sort as if I'd asked
you who had been or are good caretakers of bodies in matters
of gymnastic training, and you told me in all seriousness that
Thearion the breadmaker, and Mithaicus, the writer of Sicilian
cookbooks, and Sarambus the shopkeeper had been wonderful
caretakers of bodies, one providing wonderful loaves, one tasty C
food, and one wine.

Now probably you'd get mad if I said to you, "You don't understand anything about gymnastic training, man; you're talking to
me about servants and people who provide for desires but don't
understand anything beautiful and good about them, who, if it so
happens, stuff people's bodies full and add fat to them, and get
praised by them, and on top of that ruin the flesh they had originally. But they for their part, because of inexperience, won't blame D
the people who feasted them for being the causes of their ailments
and of the ruin of their original flesh. But those who happen to be
around them and give them any advice at the time when the gorg-
ing they got then, because it happened without regard to what's
healthy, comes back on them bringing an ailment a long time later,
they're the ones they'll blame and criticize and do some harm to
if they're able, while they sing the praises of those earlier ones
who were the causes of their troubles." And now you, Callicles, E
are doing something exactly like that: you're singing the praises
of people who've feasted these citizens with a lavish supply of the
things they desired. And people claim they've made the city great,
but they don't recognize that the city is swollen and festering with 519A
hidden sores on account of those people of earlier times. Because
without temperance and justice they filled the city up with harbors
and shipyards and walls and tribute[57] and nonsense like that. Then,
when that attack of feebleness comes, they'll blame the advisors
present at the time, but go on singing the praises of Themistocles
and Cimon and Pericles, the ones who caused the troubles. And
maybe they'll attack you, if you're not careful, and my companion

56 See 484A-B.

57 Money or gifts extorted from the cities on Aegean islands and on the coast of Asia Minor for protection by the Athenian navy.

B Alcibiades, when they're losing what they had originally as well as the things they acquired, even though you're not the causes of the troubles, except possibly as accessories.[58]

And in fact I see and hear a senseless thing going on now that has to do with the men of earlier times. Because I notice that whenever the city goes after any of the men in politics for committing injustice they get angry and complain bitterly that they're suffering terrible things; after they've done many good things for the city, they're suddenly being ruined by it unjustly, as their speech goes.
C But the whole thing is false, because a leader of a city couldn't ever be unjustly ruined by that very city he leads—never once could it happen. It's liable to be the same thing with people who hold themselves up as politicians as with those who hold themselves up as sophists. Because the sophists, though they're smart in other respects, do this one ridiculous thing: while they claim to be teachers of virtue they often accuse their students of being unjust to them by cheating them out of their fees and not giving them any other
D thanks, when they've been treated well by them. And what could be a more illogical thing than this speech, claiming that people who've become good and just, with injustice removed from them by their teacher and justice taking it's place, commit injustice by means of that which they don't have? Doesn't that seem absurd to you, my comrade? You've well and truly forced me into talking like a demagogue, Callicles, by not being willing to give answers.

Callicles: And you're the one who can't speak unless someone answers you?

E *Socrates:* It looks like I can. I'm extending my speeches a long way now, anyway, since you're not willing to answer me. But good fellow, tell me, for the sake of Friendship, doesn't it seem to you to be illogical for someone who claims to have made someone good to criticize him because, after becoming and being good thanks to him, he's then depraved?

Callicles: It does seem that way to me.

Socrates: And you do hear such things being said by those who claim to educate people into virtue?

520A *Callicles:* I do. But why should you speak about worthless people?[59]

Socrates: And why should *you* speak about people who claim to be leading the city and taking care that it will be the best it can be, who then in turn accuse it, whenever it happens to suit them, of

58 This is the only hint in the dialogue at what may have become of Callicles. Alcibiades became a scapegoat for Athenian anxiety while he was at the height of his popularity and power. Callicles' public career may have ended before it began.

59 Sophists were traveling teachers who claimed not to impart skills but to make their students excellent people. Native Athenians considered themselves better able than any learned foreigners to do that for their children. In Plato's *Meno* (91B-95A), Anytus displays the typical attitude.

being depraved? Do you imagine they're any different from those others? You blessedly happy fellow, a sophist and a rhetorician are the same thing, or something close to it and very much alike, as I was saying to Polus, and it's from ignorance that you imagine the B
one, rhetoric, to be something completely beautiful while you look down on the other. The truth is that sophistry is more beautiful than rhetoric to the same degree that lawmaking is more beautiful than judging, and gymnastic training than doctoring. And I'd imagine public speakers and sophists are the only ones who have no room to complain about the very thing that they themselves educate, that it's vicious toward them, or else by that same speech they'll also be accusing themselves at the same time of having been of no benefit to those they claim to benefit. Isn't that the way it is?

Callicles: Quite so. C

Socrates: And no doubt it's likely that they're the only ones who would have room to give away the favor without a fee, if they were speaking the truth. Because anyone who's received any other favor, such as becoming fast thanks to a trainer, might possibly cheat him of his due, if the trainer had given it to him freely and hadn't agreed on a fee, and gotten the cash as nearly as possible at the same time he imparted the speed. Because I don't imagine it's from slowfooted- D
ness that people behave unjustly, but from injustice—right?

Callicles: Yes.

Socrates: And if someone takes that away, injustice, there's no fear that anything unjust will ever be done to him, but to him alone it's safe to give away that favor freely, if in reality anyone were capable of making people good. Isn't that so?

Callicles: I'd say so.

Socrates: It's likely on that account, therefore, that it's not a shameful thing for someone to take cash for giving other sorts of advice, such as about housebuilding or the rest of the arts.

Callicles: Likely so. E

Socrates: But as far as *this* activity is concerned, about how someone might be the best possible and manage his household and city the best, it is conventionally regarded as a shameful thing to refuse to give advice unless someone gives one cash—right?

Callicles: Yes.

Socrates: Because it's clear that this is the reason: that this favor alone makes the one who's well treated desire to do good in return, so that it seems to be a beautiful sign if the one who does good by this favor is done good to in return, and it's not a beautiful sign if he's not. Is that how these things are?

Callicles: It is. 521A

Socrates: Then which way of taking care of the city are you urging me toward? Draw the line for me. Is it that of doing battle with the Athenians, like a doctor, so they'll be the best they can be, or is it being like a menial servant, and joining in with them for gratification? Tell me the truth, Callicles, because you're being just if, the same way you began by speaking frankly to me, you finish up by saying what you think. Now speak well and like a well-born man.

Callicles: Then I say it's being like a menial servant.

B *Socrates:* Therefore, best-born of men, you're urging me to be a panderer.

Callicles: Call it being a Mysian,[60] Socrates, if that gives you more pleasure; because unless you do these things—

Socrates: Don't tell me what you've said repeatedly, that anyone who
wants to will kill me, so I won't have to say back that a worthless
person would be killing a good one. And don't say that he'll take
away whatever I have, so I won't have to say back that once he's
taken it he won't have a clue about how to use it, but just as he took
C it from me unjustly, so too when he's got it he'll use it unjustly, and
if unjustly shamefully, and if shamefully badly.

Callicles: The way it seems to me, Socrates, is that you believe not one of these things could happen to you, as if you lived in isolation and couldn't be dragged into court by some quite possibly vicious and degenerate human being.

Socrates: Then I'm a truly senseless person, Callicles, if I don't imagine
that in this city, anyone whatever might happen to have that happen
to him. *This*, however, I know for sure, that if I do go into court in
D danger of any of these things you speak of, it will be a worthless
person who drags me in—because no decent person would drag
a human being who'd done no injustice into court—and there'd be
nothing strange about it if I were to be put to death. Do you want
me to tell you why I foresee that?

Callicles: Quite so.

Socrates: I believe I'm one of a few Athenians, not to say the only one, to
make an attempt at the political art in the true sense, and the only
one of the present day to be actively engaged in political matters.
Seeing as how I'm not speaking with a view to gratification when
I make the speeches I make on each occasion, but with a view to
E what's best and not most pleasing, and I'm not willing to do what
you recommend, "those fancy subtleties,"[61] I won't have anything
to say in the courtroom. The same speech I was making to Polus
pertains to me, because I'll be judged the way a doctor would be
judged among children on the accusation of someone who cooks
tasty food. Just consider what such a person, caught in these circumstances, could say in his defense if someone were to accuse him

60 A race of people thought of as fit only for the lowest and most unmanly activities, probably the tribe of Lydians to which I. 155 of Herodotus's *History* applied most. In his exasperation, Callicles is saying, in effect, "Let's drop the rhetoric where life or death choices are at stake."

61 See 486C.

by saying, "Children, this man here has done a lot of bad things
even to you yourselves, and he corrupts the youngest among you
by cutting and burning, and he makes you helpless by shrivel- **522A**
ing you up and choking you, giving you the most sharp-tasting
things to drink and forcing you to go hungry and thirsty, not like
me, who feasted you on lots of pleasing things of all kinds." What
do you imagine a doctor caught up in this sort of trouble would
have to say for himself? Or if he told the truth, "I was doing all
these things, children, in the interest of health," how big a howl
of protest do you imagine such judges would make? Wouldn't it
be a huge one?

Callicles: Possibly.

Socrates: You'd better believe it. And don't you imagine he'd be in a
state of complete helplessness about what he should say? **B**

Callicles: Quite so.

Socrates: I know, though, that I too would suffer an experience of
that sort if I went into court. Because I won't have any pleasures
to say I've furnished them with, which they regard as favors and
benefits, though I feel no envy either of those who provide them
or those they're provided to. And if anyone claims that I corrupt
younger people by making them feel helpless, or insult their elders
by making sharply pointed speeches either in private or in public,
I won't be able to tell the truth—"I say and do all these things in **C**
the interest of justice, and that's precisely *your* interest, men of the
jury"—or say anything else. So probably I'll suffer whatever happens to come to pass.

Callicles: Does that seem to you, then, Socrates, to be a beautiful condition for a person in a city to be in, when he's in that plight and
powerless to stand up for himself?

Socrates: Yes, Callicles, if that one thing belongs to him that you've
repeatedly agreed about: if he's stood up for himself by having said **D**
or done nothing unjust toward human beings or gods. Because this
has been agreed by us over and over to be the most powerful way
of standing up for oneself. Now if someone were to refute me by
proving that I'm powerless to stand up for myself or for anyone
else with *that* sort of help, I'd be ashamed, whether I'd been refuted
in front of many people or few, or even alone by one person alone,
and if I were to die on account of that sort of powerlessness, I'd be
deeply distressed. But if I were to meet my end for lack of a pandering sort of rhetoric, I know for sure that you'd see me endure
my death as something easy. Because no one is afraid of dying **E**
itself, unless he's completely and totally irrational and unmanly;
he's afraid of being unjust. Because arriving in the realm of Hades
with one's soul weighed down with a lot of injustices is the utmost
of all evils. And I'm willing to make you a speech, if you'd like, to
show that's the way things are.

523A *Callicles:* Seeing as how you've finished everything else, just finish that too.

Socrates: Then listen to an ever so beautiful speech, as people say. You'll
consider it a myth, I imagine, but I consider it a speech, because I'll
be telling what I'm about to say as something true. Because just as
Homer tells,[62] Zeus, Poseidon, and Pluto divided up the rulership
among themselves when they took it over from their father. Now
in Cronos's time there was this law concerning human beings, and
it's still in effect now and always among the gods, that any human
B being who'd gone through life in a just and pious way would go off
when he died to the Isles of the Blessed to live in complete happiness
apart from evils, while any who'd lived in an unjust and godless
way would go to the prison house of punishment and just penalty
which people call Tartarus. In Cronos's time, and while Zeus still
newly held his reign, the judges of these people were living, while
they too were living, giving judgment on that day on which they
were going to die, so the judgments were decided badly. So Pluto,
and those in charge of the Blessed Isles, came and said to Zeus
C that undeserving human beings were constantly coming to them
in both places. So Zeus said, "Well, I'll put a stop to that. Because
the way the judgments are being judged is bad. That's because
those who are judged are judged," he said, "with their clothes on,
since they're alive. So many people," he said, "who have deplorable
souls are decked out in beautiful bodies and families and riches,
and when the judgment takes place, lots of witnesses come with
D them to testify that they've lived their lives justly. So the judges
are overly impressed by these things, and at the same time, they
do the judging with their clothes on, with eyes and ears and the
whole body acting as a veil in front of their own souls. All these
things get in their way, both their own coverings and those of the
ones who are being judged. So first," he said, "they're to be stopped
from knowing their death ahead of time, because now they have
E foreknowledge of it. So Prometheus has been given the word to
put a stop to that in them. Next, they're to be judged while naked,
stripped of all those things, because they need to be judged when
they're dead. The judge too needs to be naked, dead, gazing upon
the soul itself with the soul itself, immediately upon the death of
each person, when he's bereft of all his kinspeople and has left
behind on earth all that adornment of his, so the judgment may
be just. So knowing all this before you did, I made sons of mine
524A judges, two from Asia, Minos and Rhadamanthus, and one from
Europe, Aeacus. So when they've died, they'll do the judging in

62 In the *Iliad*, XV, 187 and following. Socrates adds a couple of details later from Book XI of the *Odyssey*, and others from Hesiod, but the story he tells is pure invention. The details give a flavor of myth and legend to an image that in some way sums up the *logos* that has unfolded.

the meadow where three roads meet and a pair of roads carry on, one to the Isles of the Blessed, the other to Tartarus. Those from Asia, Rhadamanthus will judge, and those from Europe, Aeacus will judge; to Minos, because of his elder rank, I shall give the right of rendering final judgment, in case the other two are unable to resolve any point, so that the judgment on the journey of human beings may be as just as it can be."

That's what I've heard, Callicles, and what I believe to be true. B
And from these speeches, I reason out that something like this follows: Death, it seems to me, is precisely nothing other than a separation from each other of a pair of things, the soul and the body. Therefore, when they're separated from each other, each of them keeps its condition not much lessened from what belonged to it when the human being was alive, with the body having its own nature, and the care and experiences it's had, all plainly vis- C
ible. For instance, if anyone's body was big by nature or nurture or both when he was alive, his corpse will also be big when he's dead, and if it was fat, it will be fat after he's died too, and so on with other things; and if he made a practice of wearing long hair, his corpse will also be long-haired. Also, if anyone was always getting whipped, and had traces of his beatings as festering sores on his body while living, either from whippings or other wounds, then also when he's dead his body is there to see with these marks on it. Or if anyone's limbs were broken or twisted when he was living, these same things are also plainly visible when he's dead. In a word, D
what he'd prepared his body to be while living is plainly visible when he's dead as well, either every one of those things or most of them, for some time. Therefore, this exact same thing seems to me to be the case with the soul too, Callicles. Everything in the soul is plainly visible when it's made naked, stripped of the body—the things belonging to its nature and the experiences the human being had in his soul as a result of his pursuit of every activity. So when they come before the judge, before Rhadamanthus in the case of E
those from Asia, Rhadamanthus stops them and gazes upon the soul of each, not knowing whose it is; but often when he's taken hold of the Great King or of some other king or emperor, he sees that there's nothing healthy in the soul, but it's been thoroughly whipped and filled with festering sores by false oaths and injus- 525A
tice, sores which every one of its acts has left as a blot on the soul, and everything is crooked as a result of lies and hypocrisy, and nothing is straight because of an upbringing without truth. And he sees the soul filled with disproportion and ugliness as a result of license and luxury and insolence and lack of self-control in its actions. And seeing that, he sends that soul off in disgrace directly on the way to the place of detention where, upon its arrival, it's to endure the appropriate sufferings.

B And it's appropriate for everyone who's undergoing punishment, when he's punished in the right way by anyone else, either
to become better and profit from it or to become an example for
others, so that others who see him suffering the things he suffers might be afraid and become better. And the ones benefited
by paying the just penalty at the hands of gods and humans are
those who commit curable transgressions; still, the benefit, both
here and in Hades' realm, comes to them through grief and pain,
C because it's not possible to get rid of injustice in any other way. But
it's from the ones who commit the most extreme injustices, and
by means of such injustices become incurable, that the examples
come; they themselves can no longer be profited in any way since
they're incurable, but others are profited as they see them undergoing, throughout all time, the greatest, most grievous, and most
frightening sufferings for their transgressions, literally hung up
there in the dungeon in Hades' realm as examples, displays, and
D warnings to those among the unjust who are continually arriving. I
claim that Archelaus will also be one of these, if Polus is telling the
truth, as will anyone else who's a tyrant of that sort, and I imagine
most of those examples have come from tyrants, kings, members of
dictatorial groups, and people active in the affairs of cities, because
they, on account of their authority, commit the greatest and most
unholy transgressions. Homer too bears witness to this, since he's
E depicted kings and dictators, Tantalus and Sisyphus and Tityus, as
those being punished in Hades' realm through all time, while no
one has depicted Thersites,[63] or any other private person who might
have been depraved, as someone incurable, afflicted with great
punishments. I believe that's because he didn't have any authority,
and for that reason he was more fortunate than those who did have
526A authority. Really, Callicles, it's from among the powerful ones that
the exceptionally depraved human beings come, though nothing
prevents good men from also turning up among them, and any who
come along are exceptionally worthy of being admired. Because it's
a difficult thing, Callicles, and worthy of abundant praise, when
someone who comes into a position with great license for committing injustice lives out his life justly; but there are a few people of
that sort, since they've turned up both here and elsewhere, and I
imagine they'll continue to do so, people who are beautiful and
B good at that virtue of administering justly whatever anyone turns

63 A loudmouth, smart-aleck foot-soldier in the *Iliad* (II, 211-277). Though Thersites was unworthy of everlasting torment, he was worthy of Socrates' notice in this dialogue, perhaps because his words in public assemblies were described as lacking measure in length (*ametroepês*), lacking order in arrangement (*epea akosma*), and lacking judgment in content (*akritomuthe*). The three souls who do suffer torments in Hades are in *Odyssey* XI, 576-600.

over to them, and there was one in particular, Aristides[64] the son
of Lysimachus, who became quite famous to the rest of the Greeks.
But most of those who exercise power, you most excellent fellow,
turn out bad. So as I was saying, when that judge, Rhadamanthus,
gets hold of any such person, he doesn't know anything else about
him, not who he is or what family he comes from, except that he's
someone depraved. And when he sees that, he sends him off to
Tartarus with a mark on him signifying whether he seems to be
curable or incurable, and when he arrives there, he suffers what's C
appropriate. And when, on occasion, he sees a soul that has lived
piously and in company with truth, that of a private man or anyone
else, and especially, I claim, Callicles, that of a philosopher who's
been active in his own concerns in life and hasn't meddled in other
people's business, he's struck with admiration and sends it off to
the Isles of the Blessed. And Aeacus does the same things as well,
with each of the two holding a rod, while Minos sits overseeing
them, he alone holding a golden scepter, as Homer's Odysseus D
claims he saw him,

> Holding a golden scepter, declaring what's rightful to the spirits of the dead.

So, Callicles, I'm persuaded by these speeches, and I look out
for the way I might display my soul to the judge in the healthiest
possible condition. So saying goodbye to the honors that come
from most human beings, I'll try, by a training in the truth, to be
in my very being the best I have the power to be, both to live that
way, and, when I die, to die that way. And I exhort all other human E
beings, as far as is in my power, and in return for your exhortation, I exhort you in particular toward this life and this form of
combat, which I claim is the equal of all forms of combat here, and
I blame you for the fact that you won't be able to come to your own
defense when the trial and judgment I was speaking of just now
are before you, but when you come to that judge, Aegina's son,[65] 527A
when *he* grabs you and takes you, you'll have your mouth hanging
open and your head swimming there no less than I will here, and
maybe someone will give you an insulting slap upside the head,
and heap abuse on you in every way.

Now this probably seems to you to be a myth, like something told by an old woman, and you look down on it, and there'd be nothing surprising about looking down on it if after searching we were in

64 Called Aristides the Just, he was an Athenian famous for assessing the monetary amounts paid by the cities of the Delian League so fairly that no one could suggest any way of improving them. He was ostracized early in his career, helped Athens in the Persian War even during his ostracism, returned to spend his life exercising power in the highest offices in the city, and died in poverty.

65 Aeacus, judge of European souls.

some way or other able to find anything better and truer than it.
But as it is, you see that the three of you, who are the smartest of
B the Greeks of our time, you, Polus, and Gorgias, can't demonstrate
that one ought to live any other life than this one, which is plainly
advantageous in the other realm as well. But out of so many speeches,
of which the rest have been refuted, this speech alone stands undisturbed: that committing injustice is what one ought to take precautions against more than against suffering it; that more than anything,
a man ought to take care not to seem to be good but to be so, both
in private and in public; that if anyone becomes bad in any respect,
he ought to be disciplined, and this is the second best thing after
C being just, becoming so and paying the just penalty by accepting
discipline; that every sort of pandering ought to be avoided, with
regard to oneself or to others, with regard to a few people or a large
number; and that the way one ought to make use of rhetoric, and
every other activity, is always toward the end of what's just.

So if you're persuaded by me, follow me to the place where, once
you've arrived, you'll be happy both while you live and when you've
died, as our speech indicates. Let anyone look down on you as senseless, and hurl abuse at you, if he wants to, and yes, by Zeus, *you* have
D the guts to let him give you that insulting slap, because you won't
suffer anything terrible by it if you're beautiful and good in your
very being, training yourself in virtue. And then, once we've trained
ourselves in that way, that's the time when, if it seems to be right,
we'll apply ourselves to politics, or we'll deliberate then on whatever
might seem good to us, when we're better at deliberating than we
are now. Because it's a shameful thing for people in the condition
we now appear to be in to turn around and be brash, as if we were
really something, when things never seem the same to us about the
E same things, even when these are the greatest things—that's how far
our lack of education goes. So let's take as a guide the speech that
has now made its appearance in our presence, which indicates to
us that this way of life is best, to live and to come to death training
ourselves in justice and the rest of virtue. Let's follow this way, and
exhort others to it, not that way you put your trust in and exhort me
to, because it's not worth anything, Callicles.

ARISTOTLE'S *RHETORIC*: CHAPTER SUMMARIES

BOOK I RHETORICAL SPEECH: its nature, its kinds, and the opinions it is based on

Chapter 1

There is an art of rhetoric centered on the study of enthymemes, persuasive arguments, in the same way dialectic is a preparatory study of demonstrative philosophic arguments. The current books called "arts of speeches" deal only with incidentals and not with the central activity of rhetoric. In lawcourts and legislative assemblies, there is not sufficient time or common ground for teaching or for a common pursuit of knowledge, but things that are true or just have an inherent persuasiveness. A study of common opinions and possible arguments from them gives one the means to see the better course in any situation requiring a decision, and to counteract weaker arguments.

Chapter 2

Since artful rhetoric is not manipulation into conclusions but the showing of evidence for them, the study of the art requires seeing what is available to be shown. An artful speech will show not only reasons for believing something to be factual or true, but also grounds for trusting the character of the speaker and for holding certain attitudes toward others. The two means by which all of this is done are enthymemes, which reason about matters of opinion, and examples, which suggest an interpretation of facts. Enthymemes argue from likelihoods, rather than from necessary or demonstrable premises, and by way of signs, rather than necessary inferences, and the arguments they use apply to any sort of subject matter.

Chapter 3

There are three forms of rhetoric. In the courtroom, speeches are made about past matters of fact, for the sake of attaining justice. In public assemblies, speeches give advice about future actions, for the sake of securing advantage.

On ceremonial occasions, speeches are made to display what is worthy of praise and admiration among human beings, to encourage the ongoing striving for what is beautiful in life as the highest end of political communities.

Chapter 4

Advisory speaking deals with everything communities deliberate about, most of which falls under five headings: revenues and expenses, war and peace, the defense of borders, imports and exports, and making laws to govern communal life.

Chapter 5

All advice about what is advantageous to a community aims ultimately at the happiness of its citizens. An artful advisory speaker must have thought through those things that are generally agreed to be necessary component parts of happiness. These are sketched out.

Chapter 6

In addition to happiness, everything chosen for its own sake is good, and all means to those ends are advantageous. Conventional signs of what is good are reviewed.

Chapter 7

Advisory speeches often dispute over which of two things is the greater good. Various general ways of arguing this, and examples of their use, are given.

Chapter 8

The greater good in any city will be measured in relation to the end taken as primary in the form of government by which it is ruled: freedom in democracies, wealth in oligarchies, education and the maintenance of a customary way of life in aristocracies, and security in both legitimate and tyrannical monarchies.

Chapter 9

Speeches for display single out for praise the virtues generally agreed to be parts of a beautiful character, and reserve the highest honor for those virtues seen as beneficial to others, such as justice, courage, and generosity. Other virtues of character worthy of high praise are temperance and greatness of soul, the latter being a sense of one's own worth that leads to great deeds; the highest virtues of intellect are wisdom and practical judgment. Exaggeration of all sorts is appropriate in these speeches, where facts are not in dispute and the aim is to inspire.

Chapter 10

Courtroom speeches deal with acts of injustice, including all types of harm done willingly in violation of law, whether written or unwritten. All faults of character, whether settled vices or mere weaknesses, lead people to treat others unjustly, even when those committing the unjust acts are not unjust people. People are not responsible for actions of their own that result from luck, nature, or force; they are responsible for everything they do as a result of habit, reasoning, spiritedness, or desire. Willing action is always for the sake of some apparent good or pleasure.

Chapter 11

The apparent pleasures that motivate unjust acts all seek sudden intense changes of feeling, some related to the body, others to the imagination.

Chapter 12

People commit injustices in various circumstances in which they think they can get away with them, against those who seem easy to take advantage of.

Chapter 13

All people have a notion that some things are naturally unjust, even when no written law forbids them, though there is disagreement about particular cases. There is also room for disagreement about acts that appear to violate the letter of the law; for instance not all taking of the property of others is theft. Speeches of accusation or defense must make clear what constitutes injustice in the circumstances at issue. And holding a lawbreaker strictly accountable for any act of injustice is not always the best or the decent thing for a community.

Chapter 14

Acts of injustice differ in degree, and penalties should be adapted to them.

Chapter 15

Courtroom speakers need to deal with various kinds of evidence that exist prior to and independently of their own arguments. One is the written law itself, which may be ambiguous or outdated. Another comes from contemporary witnesses, who may have something to gain by their testimony, or from notable people of the past, whose judgments in similar situations are known. Written documents may be of more or less importance. Evidence obtained by torturing slaves is not necessarily truthful. And there are various ways to interpret the fact that one of the parties has voluntarily taken an oath, or has refused to take one.

BOOK II. DESIGN OF SPEECHES: passions and predispositions of audiences and techniques of argument

Chapter 1

Whatever the merits of the arguments in a rhetorical speech, they will finally be judged by human beings, who will form some estimate of the speaker's character and trustworthiness, and who will have passions and predispositions that influence the way they regard the people and things argued about. While the passions vary from one person to another, there are typical feelings that accompany each kind, types of people toward whom they are felt, and typical occasions that give rise to them. An artful speaker needs to have studied these in order to show an audience when any particular passion is or is not appropriate.

Chapter 2

Anger is a desire for revenge for any perceived belittling of oneself or of anything felt as one's own. Belittling is shown by contemptuous dismissal, spiteful thwarting, or insolent humiliation. Any unfulfilled desire or passion leaves someone prone to anger. The feeling of anger can turn pain into pleasure through the imagining of revenge.

Chapter 3

The quieting or turning aside of anger produces calmness, and can replace a desire for revenge with a feeling of leniency.

Chapter 4

Liking someone is a desire for the good of that other person. Hostile feelings extend beyond anger and include a dislike of general classes of people, such as thieves and informers. Hatred also differs from anger; the former is incurable and is not satisfied by inflicting pain but only by seeing someone dead. It is possible to show people that those they like or dislike are not truly their friends or enemies.

Chapter 5

Fear is painful agitation from imagining an impending evil of a painful or destructive sort. It is generally frightening to be at risk of coming into anyone else's power. Confidence is inspired by anything that shows that there is nothing or little to be feared from an apparent enemy or danger.

Chapter 6

Shame is painful agitation at one's own bad deeds, even those merely intended, if they are of a kind that brings disrepute. Taking advantage of those who are helpless or poor is an example, as are all actions indicative of vice. Shirking of responsibilities expected of people of one's sort, and going along with the misdeeds of others can also bring shame. But actions committed in the presence of people one does not respect bring no shame.

Chapter 7

Charitable feelings incline people to help those in need, and seek no benefit in return. The magnitude of a charitable act has reference to the need, even if the service rendered is small.

Chapter 8

Pity is pain felt at a destructive or painful evil suffered by, or about to be suffered by, someone who does not deserve it. It is felt by those who feel that they themselves, or those close to them, are vulnerable to suffering in the same way, but it is not felt by those who are wrapped up in their own present misery. Pity is driven out by a feeling of horror, but is enhanced by vivid evidence of suffering placed before people's eyes or conjured up in their imaginations.

Chapter 9

Righteous indignation is the exact opposite of pity, a pain felt at undeserved prosperity. Like pity, it is a mark of good character, unlike envy, which is a painful agitation at the prosperity of others like oneself, whether they deserve their good fortune or not. Envious people are maliciously pleased when others lose their prosperity. Righteous indignation is more likely to be felt when undeserved prosperity is newly acquired. A speech that arouses righteous indignation blocks the feeling of pity.

Chapter 10

Envy does not involve any desire to have the things others do, but is pain at the mere fact that they have them. Those who are envious may have great prosperity themselves, but feel others get honor more appropriate to themselves, or gained with too little effort.

Chapter 11

Emulation is a feeling that is positive in those respects in which envy is negative. People who feel emulation are pained at the good and honored things belonging to others like themselves, not because those others have them but only because they themselves do not. It is characteristic of the young, and of those who may already have prosperity but desire to show they are worthy of it. The opposite of emulation is contempt.

Chapter 12

The predominant age, state of character, or condition of fortune in an audience or portion of an audience will influence its attitudes and passions. The young are dominated by desires, and are quick to anger. They love honor, but particularly the honor that comes from winning any sort of competition. They do not love money, and they prefer beautiful deeds to advantageous ones. They are trusting and full of hope, and easily moved to shame, to pity, or to laughter. Friends are more valued in youth than at any other time of life. Their errors come from excess and overenthusiasm. They feel certain about their opinions, and are apt to be unjust to others out of insolence.

Chapter 13

Experience has led the old to be uncertain about things, to assume the worst about others, and to expect little out of life. Their loves and hates have less vigor. They incline toward the vices of selfishness: stinginess, cowardice, and a lack of shame. They prefer advantageous deeds to beautiful ones. They live in memory rather than in hope. Their anger and desires have little strength, and this makes them appear temperate. They are not insolent, but tend to be malicious. They are inclined toward pity, not, like the young, from a love of humanity, but from a sense of their own weakness. They are full of complaints.

Chapter 14

Those in the prime of life are less subject to the excesses that characterize the young and the old. They are neither overconfident nor overfearful, and not particularly trusting or distrustful. They incline toward a balance of the advantageous and the beautiful, and to a mean between thrift and wastefulness. They combine the courage of youth with the temperance of old age. The peak of life for the powers of the body is in one's early thirties, for the powers of the soul in one's late forties.

Chapter 15

Good birth and distinguished ancestry lead people to be ambitious for honor. Nobility belongs only to those whose lives live up to the distinction of their ancestors, but most people who are well born turn out to be second-rate people. Extraordinary human beings are born from time to time, and their offspring are no better than anyone else, so gifted families always tend to degenerate.

Chapter 16

The rich tend to take their riches as the measure of goodness, and to become insolent and haughty. They are extravagant and ostentatious, and believe they deserve to rule. In sum, they are fortunate fools, but the newly rich have these vices to a greater extent and in a worse form than do those whose wealth is of long standing, since there is an opportunity for the latter to become educated in the decent use of wealth. The rich can be unjust either through insolence or from self-indulgence.

Chapter 17

Powerful people tend to be more ambitious, manly, and energetic than those who are merely rich. If the former commit injustice it is on a grand scale. Good fortune in general can make people arrogant and inconsiderate, but it can also make them devout, in gratitude to whatever divine power they view as responsible for their own prosperity.

Chapter 18

At this point, midway through Book II, the Rhetoric has dealt with the ends, opinions, and premises that differ for different types of speeches, and the passions and predispositions that differ in different types of audiences. It remains to discuss "topics," ready-made arguments that can be adapted to speeches on any subject and before any audience, and to discuss tactics of argumentation involved in all use of enthymemes and examples. The next chapter will address the most general topics likely to be of use in the three main kinds of speeches, those involving exaggeration for speeches for display, past facts for courtroom speeches, and future possibilities for advisory speeches.

Chapter 19

Various ways of arguing for the possibility of something, from the possibility of other things and from other kinds of signs, are reviewed. Arguments are given that make it likely, from other facts and signs, that something has in fact happened; these can also be extended to the likelihood that something will happen in the future. Arguments for the greater good were discussed above in Book I, Chapter 7, in connection with advisory speeches; the same arguments can be adapted for use in speeches for display.

Chapter 20

Examples are either taken from historical facts or made up. Made-up examples may be analogies, such as those commonly used by Socrates, or fables like those of Aesop. It is easier to find a fable precisely suited to the matter at hand, but in advisory speeches, historical examples are more effective. All examples work best when enthymemes have been given first, and the examples follow them as confirmation of their conclusions. If the examples stand alone or come first, a number of them must be given.

Chapter 21

Maxims are weighty-sounding generalizations about matters of action, packed into pithy sentences. If they go against popular opinion, they need explanation either incorporated in them or added afterward. If they are well known or self-evident once stated, they may be very terse or even spoken in riddles. Clichés are appropriate if they are to the point, since they make the point seem obviously true. Maxims of one's own that contradict authoritative sayings may be useful to show one's character or passion, since they reveal the universal basis of one's choices. Unsophisticated audiences love maxims that generalize their own opinions.

Chapter 22

Enthymemes ought not to reason from too far back or to include steps that are obvious; they should reason from things that are familiar and near at hand, and not appeal to all reputable sources but only those held in repute by those in the audience. The speaker must have available information relevant to the matter at hand, and keep his arguments pertinent rather than generic. Enthymemes may show directly from things that are agreed that something is or is not so, or they may be counterarguments to the enthymemes of one's opponent.

Chapter 23

Twenty-eight topics are compiled and presented with a wealth of illustrations from rhetoricians and poets. When there is a choice between using a topic directly or in the form of a counterargument, the latter is more effective, since it puts opposite conclusions side-by-side in a form easily taken in. The most effective enthymemes of all are those the audience sees coming as soon as they begin, or sees the point of as soon as they are complete, as long as they are not superficial, since people are pleased with themselves for grasping what the speaker has presented.

Chapter 24

Nine topics are presented that appear to form enthymemes but are fallacious. These use the language and have the form of syllogisms when nothing can in fact be concluded from them. Enthymemes establish only likelihood and never necessity, but they are still sound arguments. Fallacious enthymemes are illusions or tricks to make a weaker argument seem stronger. A speaker who has studied the common types of fallacies can expose them, and any audience can see what is wrong with them.

Chapter 25

Counterarguments differ from direct arguments only by making use of opposing opinions as premises, and all the same topics apply to them as well. A second form of refutation is by raising an objection that makes the opponent's argument fail without need for a counterargument. If the opponent's argument depends on a universal statement, one contrary instance defeats it, but if it depends on a likelihood, an objection is insufficient to defeat it, though it may fool the audience. To show that something is unlikely requires an abundance of examples to the contrary. Arguments from signs are always open to objection, unless the sign is of the infallible type that is a criterion for the conclusion.

Chapter 26

There are no special arguments for exaggerating and minimizing things. Just as counterarguments are the same in form as direct arguments, and objections can be stated to any inference or assumption, any argument that shows something to be the case may be modified to show that it is more the case, or less the case, than one might have thought.

BOOK III. PRESENTATION IN SPEAKING: wording and arrangement

Chapter 1

The things that make a speech persuasive need to be put into words, and those words need to be spoken aloud. Giving a speech is a performance: attention to melodiousness, rhythm, and variations of the loudness of one's voice is necessary if one is to convey feeling effectively. It should be good enough if the way a speech is delivered causes no annoyance to distract from its content, but rhetoric deals with opinion, and opinions are influenced by the effect a speech has on the imagination and the pleasure it gives a listener. Skill at performance is something that has to be present by nature, but effective wording is a matter of art, and can be studied. The earliest rhetorical style to be made into art, that of Gorgias, was based on poetic wording, which is impressive to uneducated people but not appropriate to the occasions of civic speeches. Even the tragic poets gradually abandoned a style that was not suited to conversation. An ornate style of rhetoric like that of Gorgias is therefore an inappropriate imitation of an obsolete kind of poetry.

Chapter 2

The virtue of wording is to be clear, and to be neither above nor below its subject in the dignity of its tone. The use of prevalent words brings clarity, while a use of out-of-the-ordinary wording elevates the tone. The use of the latter must be unobtrusive if it is to avoid seeming contrived. Metaphors can give distinction to wording without departing from a conversational tone; eccentric, compound, and made-up words need to be used more sparingly. Appropriate metaphors can be clear, pleasing, and unfamiliar all at one time, and can be chosen to adorn or disparage the things they name. Well chosen metaphors bring the thing spoken of before one's eyes.

Chapter 3

Four sorts of wording do not come off. Examples are given of compounded words, eccentric words, descriptive epithets, and comic or tragic metaphors that call attention to themselves rather than conveying anything clear. All these can come across as ridiculous.

Chapter 4

All metaphors can be worded as similes. The latter need to be used less frequently, since they have a poetic feel.

Chapter 5

Primarily, all wording in speeches needs to be grammatical and not vague or ambiguous. What is easy to read is easy to say and clear to a listener.

Chapter 6

There are various ways of making wording more weighty or more succinct. Weightiness can be increased indefinitely by describing something through attributes it does not possess.

Chapter 7

Appropriate wording cannot use offhand language for weighty matters or solemn language for ordinary ones. It cannot attach ornamentation to run-of-the-mill things without becoming comical. Language appropriate to the feelings the things described call forth makes an audience sympathize with the speaker, and conveys a sense of the kind of person the speaker is. If a speaker overuses language laden with feeling, he can soften the effect by apologizing for it, but he should never lay on any feeling too thick with vocal and facial enhancements of his words. Harsh things can be more persuasive when said in a mild tone. Wording that would otherwise be ridiculous may be effective at moments when the speaker has roused the audience to a pitch of feeling; such faults may also be relieved of offense by irony.

Chapter 8

The pattern of wording in a speech ought never to be strictly metrical, but must not lack rhythm. Meter in a speech seems contrived, and distracts the listener from the content of what is said, but rhythm enhances the definiteness of the content. A suitable rhythm makes a sentence feel complete.

Chapter 9

Definiteness and completeness of wording are produced not only by the rhythm of its sounds, but by the way its content is composed. A periodic style of composition is the most pleasing to listen to and easiest to understand. A period is a stretch of wording that has a beginning and end in virtue of its meaning; it is easy to foresee as it unfolds, easy to remember when it is complete, and easy to take in at one time in one's understanding. It has a length that does not pull the listener up short or leave him behind. A larger period may be built up out of clauses that are themselves periodic. Successive clauses that contain any sort of contrast form an antithesis, and if the two clauses are of equal length it is a balanced antithesis. These are especially pleasing because contraries side-by-side are easily grasped, and seem to demonstrate something. A similarity in sound at the beginnings or ends of the clauses reinforces the effect.

Chapter 10

Elegance is the quality that belongs to wording that makes us learn something quickly. A metaphor has greater impact than the same thing worded as a simile because the hearer has the pleasure of making the connection. Elegant arguments are those in which the point is not obvious before they are complete, and not still obscure when they are ended, but clear as soon as they end or just afterward. Antitheses and metaphors are the most highly regarded forms of wording, and especially metaphors that place things right before our eyes. A number of elegant illustrations are given.

Chapter 11

In order to bring things before the eyes, metaphors must involve activity. Some metaphors based on accurate analogies make us understand something but not picture anything. Homer in particular could make lifeless things come to life by making them actively present to us. Philosophy too requires a good eye for what is alike in things that are not obviously related to one another. Elegant effects often combine metaphor with misdirection, making a point more striking by the use of surprise. The wording of anything is improved if it can be made brief and antithetical, because it will pack more learning into fewer words. Elegant and appropriate uses of ambiguities, similes, and hyperboles are discussed.

Chapter 12

Written speeches need precision in their wording, but extemporaneous or competitive speaking requires skill at performance. Faults of grammar or needless repetitions are detrimental to written work, but can go over well in performance. Repetitions of the same thing, with slight variations of wording and tone of voice, can give the impression that more is being said, an effect that can also be achieved by successive brief clauses strung together without conjunctions. Performance counts for more than matters of detail in speeches before large public assemblies; precision counts for more in lawcourts before smaller juries or a single judge; speeches for display put the highest premium on precise wording, since they continue to achieve their aims as written works after the ceremonial occasions are over. A speech that is clear will always be pleasing to the listener if it strikes an appropriate mean in the elevated or conversational tone of its wording, in length, in the use of customary and unfamiliar terms, and in its blending in of rhythm, so long as all these aspects of wording are chosen suitably to the situation.

Chapter 13

Every rhetorical speech has two main parts, a statement and a demonstration, since the speaker needs to lay out what is to be shown and then make it persuasive. At most a speech has four parts, if these two are preceded by an introduction and followed by an epilogue. The many divisions of speeches given names in current treatises are either subdivisions of these or distinctions without differences.

Chapter 14

An introduction to a speech paves the way for what follows. In speeches for display, speakers commonly follow the example of flute-players, who use anything they happen to play well as a prelude before the main performance. On a ceremonial occasion, a speaker can praise or blame anything, and then make a connection to his subject. In a public assembly, a speaker may state general advice and give some example of its application before moving on to the particular subject he is to address. In a courtroom, the speaker may begin with some appeal to the audience, and should always give the listeners some indication of where his argument will go. A speaker for the defense should clear away prejudice in an introduction, but a speech of accusation should reserve anything prejudicial to the defendant for an epilogue, where it will be remembered better. Some speakers begin by encouraging the listeners to be more attentive; others, with weak arguments, begin by trying to distract them with jokes. Both tactics are inappropriate. Distraction will work only with listeners who would not follow an argument well in any case, and encouragements to attentiveness are needed later, when attention has slackened. What is needed in an introduction is a summary statement of the matter at hand. In a public assembly, not even that is needed ordinarily, since everyone knows what has brought them together.

Chapter 15

A courtroom speaker may attempt to dispel prejudice against a defendant by any sort of excuse, or by shifting the same sort of prejudice onto the accuser, or by speaking in general about the distortion of facts by prejudice. One may arouse prejudice by appealing to irrelevant circumstances, or by undercutting someone's good qualities by some pointed or repeated reference to a bad one.

Chapter 16

A narrative of facts need not be consecutive or complete. Speeches for display can pick out relevant facts, in any order, to back up whatever points are being made. Facts that are well known need only be alluded to, without narration. In courtroom speeches, the length and detail of narratives should be determined in the same way as any other aspect of a speech: enough to make all the points helpful to one's case without straining a listener's memory. The common advice that all such narratives should be rapid makes no sense. Details should be chosen to reveal those choices that show someone's character to be good or bad, and in ways that convey feeling. Narrative details can also convey the trustworthiness of the speaker, but this should be done unobtrusively. A telling detail that the audience is familiar with can make other things one says more persuasive. Narration of facts can be useful at various places in a speech and not just at the beginning.

Chapter 17

The main argument of a courtroom speech should focus on what is in dispute, whether the thing alleged happened, whether harm was done, whether it was serious, or whether it was just. The last three points admit of legitimate excuses based on ignorance or difference of opinion, but a dispute of the first sort always means someone must be lying. The main argument before a public assembly will make use of past examples to show what is likely to happen in the future. There is little need to demonstrate anything in speeches for display, unless the facts are hard to believe or credit for them is generally given to the wrong person. No speaker should ever use a long series of enthymemes; the listener's attention should be kept where persuasion is most needed. No argument should be given for anything the audience already believes, or about anything for which arousing feeling or revealing character matters most. Precision of argument is never as important as showing oneself to be honest, but there is most room for exact demonstration in courtroom speeches, since the law itself can be the starting point for strict argumentation. Counterarguments make their conclusions clearest to an audience, and these can be made preemptively if one speaks first; the speaker who goes second needs to begin with counterarguments to clear the way for a receptive hearing of his own arguments. Instead of praising oneself, or speaking abusively about one's opponent, one can put things into the mouths of others, and instead of putting every argument in the form of an enthymeme, one may recast some in the form of general maxims.

Chapter 18

The most effective time to pose a question to an opposing speaker is just after he has finished speaking, when one well-chosen question can make some absurdity result from what he has said, or force him to equivocate. The one who is asked a question can argue that the question is ambiguous, and go on at length to deflect the conclusion his opponent is trying to set up. The questioner should ask no further questions if he gets the conclusion he is seeking. Gorgias rightly pointed out that it is always possible to undercut an opponent's seriousness by a joke, or his joking by seriousness.

Chapter 19

The concluding section of a speech should reinforce the various impressions the speaker wants to produce, and remind the audience of the main points of his argument, showing that he has done what he promised at the beginning, and contrasting his argument with that of his opponent.

ARISTOTLE
RHETORIC

BOOK I

Chapter 1.

Rhetoric is a counterpart[1] of dialectic; for both are concerned with 1354a
the sorts of things that all people in common discern in some manner, and not confined to any one branch of knowledge. And hence all people participate in some manner in both; for everyone to some extent makes an attempt to test and to support an argument, and to make a defense and an accusation. Most people do these things either in a random way or by a habituation that comes from practice, but since they admit of being done both ways, it is evident that it would also be possible to do them in a methodical way, for it is possible to see[2] the cause on account of which people attain their end, some by habituation and others by chance, and everyone would agree immediately that such a thing is the work of an art.

Now one might say that those who have composed the current "arts of speeches"[3] have not even provided a part of the art; for it is

---

1 Literally an antistrophe, a stanza in a choral ode chanted in the same metric pattern as the preceding stanza, and danced in the same steps, but in the opposite right or left direction across the stage. Dialectic is understood by Aristotle to be the study of rigorous reasoning that begins from starting points not evident in their own right, but widely accepted on the basis of popular or authoritative opinions (*Topics* 100a 30-b 24). Aristotle's choice of the word *antistrophos* here echoes 464B-465D of the *Gorgias*, where Socrates calls rhetoric a counterpart for the soul of what cooking tasty food does for the body.

2 The word is *theôrein*; see 1355b 25 and footnote.

3 Handbooks giving instructions for making speeches in court were common in Aristotle's time. Aristotle is using the word "art" in the plural as a name for such books. Below, he coins the verb *technologein*, "make a speech-art," first used at 1354b 17, for what their writers do.

the means of persuasion alone that are intrinsic to the art, while the other things are accessories, and they say nothing about enthymemes,[4] which make up the body of persuasion. For the most part they busy themselves instead with things that are extraneous to the matter at hand; for prejudice and passions of the soul such as pity and anger are not concerned with the matter at hand, but have to do with the juror.[5] So if all trials were conducted the way they are now in some cities, especially in those with good laws, these writers would have nothing whatever they could say; for while all people believe the laws ought to make this pronouncement, some put it into effect as well and prohibit speaking outside the matter at hand, as in the Areopagus.[6] And they are right to make this the custom, for one ought not to lead the juror astray by provoking him into anger or envy or pity, since that would be as if someone made that very thing crooked that he was about to use as a ruler. Moreover, it's evident that there is nothing appropriate for a party to the dispute to do outside of showing[7] that the fact at issue is or is not so, and has or has not happened; as to whether it's a great or small matter, or just or unjust, the juror surely ought to form his own judgment as far as the lawmaker has not determined it, and not be instructed by the parties in dispute.

Now the most appropriate thing for laws that are laid down rightly is to determine everything that can be determined themselves, and to leave as little as possible up to those doing the judging; first,
1354b because it is easier to find one or a few people than many who use practical judgment well and are capable of making laws and adjudicating them, and next, because legislation comes about after people have considered things for a long time, while judgments of cases are made on the spur of the moment, so that it is difficult for those who judge them to do a beautiful job of coming up with what is just and advantageous. But the most important thing of all is that the judgment of the lawmaker is not on a particular matter, but is concerned with future and universal matters, while a member of an assembly or a juror is giving judgment about definite things immediately pres-

4 The word *enthumêma* refers to anything with a connection of thought in it. Aristotle calls it a "rhetorical syllogism" (1356b 4-5). In the formal logic of our time, a syllogism is any set of two premises and a conclusion, and an enthymeme is a syllogism with one premise left out. Aristotle confines the word syllogism to arguments in which the premises are evident in their own right, or are consequences of other such premises, and uses the word enthymeme instead when any of the premises are merely probable, or only signs of other things.

5 The word here is *dikastês*. In Athens, a large panel of ordinary citizens was chosen to decide each case as both jury and judge.

6 The Athenian court that tried those accused of murder, and a few other serious crimes.

7 The verb is *deiknumi*. Aristotle singles out *deixis*, argument from evidence, as the proper function of rhetoric. This falls short of strict and conclusive demonstrative reasoning, *apodeixis*, but goes beyond the mere arousal of passion or prejudice.

ent; for them, love and hate and private advantage are often directly involved, so that they are no longer capable of seeing adequately what is true, but their private pleasure or pain clouds their judgment. On other matters, then, as we are saying, the laws ought to make the judge authoritative over as few things as possible, but as for what has or hasn't happened, will or won't be, and is or is not the case, it is a necessity to leave these things up to the judges, for the lawmaker is not capable of foreseeing them.

And if these things are so, it is clear that all those who set out rules about the other things, such as what one needs to have as an introduction or a narrative, and each of the other parts, are making a speech-art out of things extraneous to the matter at hand; for they concern themselves in them with nothing other than how they will make the judge be a certain way, but they show nothing about the means of persuasion intrinsic to the art, and that is what might make someone become skilled with enthymemes. For this reason, even though the same way of proceeding applies to speaking in public assemblies and in lawcourts, and the business of the public assembly is of greater beauty and greater civic importance than that involved in private transactions, they say nothing about the former, but they all try to make a speech-art concerned with pleading in court, because speaking of extraneous matters is of less effect in public assemblies, and speaking in the assembly, because it has more to do with the common interest, is less able to work mischief than courtroom pleading. For in public assemblies, the judge is making a judgment about his own interests, so that there is no need to do anything other than to demonstrate that things are the way the one making the proposal claims, but in courtroom pleadings this is not sufficient, but winning over the listener is effective; for the decision is about other people's interests, so since they look at things from their own perspective and listen for their own pleasure, they give themselves over to the parties in dispute rather than judging them. This is why, as I said before, the law in a number of places prohibits saying things extraneous to the matter at hand, but in the assembly the judges themselves are sufficiently on guard against that.

But since it is clear that the way of proceeding intrinsic to the art is concerned with the means of persuasion, and persuasion is a kind of demonstration (because the time that we are persuaded most is when we suppose that something has been demonstrated), and a rhetorical demonstration is an enthymeme, and this, to put it simply, is the most decisive means of persuasion, and an enthymeme is a syllogism, and it belongs to dialectic, either as a whole or to some part of it, to look at what concerns every sort of syllogism alike, it is evident that the person who is most able to see what a syllogism consists of and how it comes about would also be most skilled with enthymemes, once he has also grasped what sorts of things an enthymeme is about and what differences it has from logical syllogisms. For it belongs to the same power to see what is true and what is similar[8] to what is true, while at the same time, human beings are adequately directed toward what is true by nature, and for the most part hit upon the truth. Hence, having a good sense for accepted opinions belongs to someone who has a similar sense for the truth.

So the fact that others make a speech-art for things extraneous to the matter at hand, and the reason why they turn their attention more toward courtroom pleading, are clear. Rhetoric is useful, though, because things that are true and things that are just are by nature stronger than their opposites, so if decisions do not come out the appropriate way, it is necessary that they have been made weaker by them,[9] and this is deserving of condemnation. Also, in speaking before some people, it would not be easy to be persuasive even if we had the most precise knowledge, because a speech based on knowledge is something that belongs to teaching, but with some people this is not possible; it is necessary instead for means of persuasion and speeches to be made by way of things shared in common, as we said also in the *Topics*[10] on the subject of dealing with the multitude. Also, one needs to be capable of being persuasive about opposite things, exactly as in the case of syllogisms, not in order that we might act on both (since one ought not to be persuasive about corrupt things), but so that the way things are might not go unnoticed, and in order that, if someone else uses arguments unjustly, we ourselves might have the means to refute them. None of the other arts reasons to opposite conclusions; dialectic and rhetoric are the only ones that do this, because they are both concerned equally with opposites. The underlying matters, though, are not on an equal footing, but things that are true and things that are better are always easier to reason to, and, to put it simply, more persuasive. And besides these things, it would be
1355b absurd if being incapable of defending oneself with the body were a shameful thing, but it was not shameful to be incapable of doing so with speech, which is more distinctive of a human being than the use of the body. As for the claim that someone using such a power with

8 The following sentence shows that the things similar to truth Aristotle has in mind are accepted opinions (*endoxa*). Hence he is not speaking of deceptive or illusory appearances of truth, but of beliefs which hold the same rank among things subject only to opinion that truth holds among things subject to demonstration and knowledge.

9 Reading *autôn* as in the manuscripts rather than the editorial emendation *hautôn* in Ross's text, and understanding "they" as the things that are true and just and "them" as their opposites. The standard condemnation made of the sophists (see *Gorgias* 520A and footnote), and *not* of rhetoricians, was that they made the weaker speech or argument the stronger. In Aristophanes' *Clouds*, a father wants Socrates to teach his son how to make the weaker speech, which can overturn the stronger by arguing in favor of unjust things (882-884).

10 At 101a 31-34.

speeches might do great harm, this applies in common to all good things except virtue, and most of all to the most useful things, such as strength, health, riches, and skill at leading armies; for one might confer the greatest benefits by using these justly and do the greatest harm by using them unjustly.

It is clear, then, that rhetoric is not about any definite class of things but is like dialectic, and that it is useful, and that its work is not to persuade but to see the means of persuasion that are available on each matter; this is how it is with all other arts as well, since the job of the doctor's art is not to make someone healthy, but to bring him along as far as is possible in that direction, because even for people who are not capable of gaining health, it is still possible to do a beautiful job of providing treatment. And besides these things, it is clear that it belongs to the same power to see what is persuasive and also what appears to be persuasive, just as with dialectic and what forms a syllogism and what appears to form a syllogism, because sophistry is present not in the power but in the intention, except that here one person will be a rhetorician on the basis of knowledge and another on the basis of intention, while someone is skilled at dialectic not on the basis of intention but on the basis of the power. And let us now try to speak about the way of proceeding that belongs to rhetoric, about the manner in which and the means by which we shall attain the ends we propose. So again, as if from the beginning, let us speak of the remaining matters after we have defined what it is.

Chapter 2.

Let rhetoric, then, be a power of seeing[11] what is capable of being persuasive on each subject. For this is not the work of any other art, because each of the others is instructive and persuasive about what belongs to it, as the doctor's art is about things that are healthful and diseased, and geometry about the attributes that go along with magnitudes, and arithmetic about numbers, and similarly with the rest of the arts and kinds of knowledge. But rhetoric seems to be capable of seeing what is persuasive about any given thing, one might say, and this is why we claim that the artful character it has is not concerned with any special definite class of things. And among the means of persuasion, some are inartful and others artful. By inartful ones, I mean those that are not provided by us but are already present, such

11 The word is *theôrein*, "beholding," used by Aristotle for contemplative thinking, and for the power of recognizing things not resting on reasoning but from which reasoning must begin. The choice of word emphasizes that Aristotle understands the art of rhetoric not as a set of rules for persuasive procedures, but as, first of all, a theoretical study of what becomes "visible" or evident in persuasive speeches; correspondingly, the activity of the persuasive speaker is not getting people to do something, but getting them to see something, a showing or *deixis* (1354a 27, 1356a 4). This translation attempts to stay close to the simple notions of seeing and showing that Aristotle takes as the central tasks of rhetoric.

as witnesses, evidence obtained by torture, written agreements, and everything of that sort, and by artful ones those that are capable of being prepared by us by a methodical procedure; so one needs to make use of the former, and discover the latter.

1356a Of the means of persuasion provided by way of speech, there are three forms, for some are in the character of the speaker, some consist in putting the hearer into a certain disposition, and some are present in the speech itself by showing or appearing to show something. Persuasion is by means of character whenever the speech is spoken in such a way as to make the speaker trustworthy; for we are more persuaded, and more quickly, by decent people, about all matters without exception, and completely so in matters in which there is nothing precise but there is divided opinion. But even this ought to come about through the speech, and not because the speaker has a prior reputation for being a certain sort of person; for it is not the way some of the speech-art makers assume in their "arts,"[12] that the decency of the speaker contributes nothing to his persuasiveness, but character, one might say, has in it just about the most decisive means of persuasion. Persuasion is by means of the hearers whenever they are led on into passion by the speech, for we do not render our judgments the same way when grieved as when delighted, or when friendly as when hostile; it is on this and only this matter, we claim, that the current speech-art makers make any effort to exert themselves; what concerns each of these attitudes will be made clear when we speak about the passions. And persuasion is by means of speech whenever we show something that is true, or appears so, from things that are persuasive on each subject.

And since the means of persuasion are conveyed through these things, it is clear that grasping them belongs to someone capable of reasoning about and seeing things that pertain to states of character, to virtues, and thirdly to passions, what and of what sort each of the passions is, and by what means and in what manner it arises; so it follows that rhetoric is a sort of outgrowth of dialectic and also of the study that has to do with states of character, to which it is just to apply the name of politics. This is why rhetoric even slips into a disguise[13] in the shape of politics, and those who claim to have the former lay claim to the latter, in some cases from a lack of education, in some from false pretenses, and in some from other human failings. For as we said when we began, rhetoric is a certain part and likeness of dialectic, since neither of them is a knowledge of the way things are in connection with any definite subject, and each is a certain sort of power of providing arguments.

---

12 The translation of this clause follows the manuscripts rather than Ross's editorial emendation.

13 The verb *upoduesthai* is a reference to the *Gorgias*, 464B and following.

So as for the power belonging to them, and how they stand in relation to each other, pretty much enough has been said. And of the ways of showing or appearing to show something, as in dialectical arguments as well, similarly here there is induction,[14] syllogism, and 1356b
apparent syllogism; for an example is an induction, an enthymeme is a syllogism, and an apparent enthymeme is an apparent syllogism. I call an enthymeme a rhetorical syllogism, and an example a rhetorical induction. All speakers who produce persuasion by showing something do so by examples or enthymemes, and nothing besides these; so if it is a necessity in all cases that showing anything whatever is done by reasoning syllogistically or inductively (and this is evident to us from the *Analytics*),[15] it is necessary for the former pair to be the same as the latter. What the difference is between an example and an enthymeme is clear from the *Topics* (for syllogism and induction have previously been spoken of there), namely, that to show that something is a certain way in a number of similar instances is called induction in dialectic and example here, and when, certain things being the case, something else besides these follows from these by their being the case either universally or for the most part, this is called a syllogism in dialectic and an enthymeme here. It is also clear that each of the two forms of rhetorical practice has something good about it; for what was said in the *Methodics*[16] applies similarly to them, since some rhetorical speeches are suited to examples and others to enthymemes, and likewise some rhetoricians are good with examples and others good with enthymemes. Speeches that rely on examples are no less persuasive, but those that are full of enthymemes get a stronger reaction; we'll give the reason later,[17] and say how one needs to use each of them, but for now let us determine more clearly what pertains to these things themselves.

14 The word *epagôgê* is translated "induction" here only with reluctance. Aristotle defines the word as "the transition from particulars to universals" (*Topics* 105a 14), but he never uses it to mean a mere generalization made acceptable by an accumulation of particulars. The universal is something intelligible, wholly and precisely present in a single perceptual experience of a particular, and for grasping it, a single instance is sufficient, even if more facilitate its discovery. Nothing needs to be built up from separate pieces of evidence since acts of *epagôgê* "reveal the universal through its being evident in the particular" (*Posterior Analytics* 71a 8). But what Aristotle means by an example (*paradeigma*) in rhetoric is an alleged fact or invented illustration, which may serve as one type of sign that something general is true. The distinction between *epagôgê* and *paradeigma* is between two types of example, one strict and reliable, the other approximate and at best probable, in keeping with the counterpoint between dialectic and rhetoric, but translating them as "induction" and "example" seems the least confusing choice.

15 *Prior Analytics* 68b 10-14; *Posterior Analytics* 71a 1-11. The reference to the *Topics* in the next sentence is to 100a 25-27 and 105a 14-19.

16 A lost work listed in some ancient catalogues of Aristotle's writings.

17 Especially at 1400b 29-33.

Since what is persuasive is persuasive to someone—and is persuasive and credible either immediately by itself, or by seeming to be shown by means of things of that kind—and since no art investigates the particular thing, as for instance the doctor's art considers what is healthful not for Socrates or Callias but for a person or persons of a certain kind (for this is intrinsic to the art while the particular is an infinite[18] and unknowable thing), rhetoric will not look at the particular opinion accepted by, say, Socrates or Hippias, but instead that which is accepted by people of a certain kind, the same way dialectic does. For the latter does not reason from things taken at random (since even to confused people, things appear to be certain ways), but from things that have need of argument, and rhetoric reasons from things that people have already been accustomed to deliberate about. Its job is concerned with the kinds of things we deliberate about but have no arts for, among the kinds of listeners who are not capable of taking many things in view together or of reasoning from a distant starting point. And we deliberate about things that appear to admit of being two different ways; for no one deliberates about things that cannot have been, or turn out to be, or now be otherwise, if he believes they are of that sort, since it would be of no use.

It is possible to form syllogisms and draw inferences either from things reasoned out beforehand or from things not reasoned out, but requiring a syllogism because they are not accepted opinions; but it is necessarily the case that the former type of reasoning is not easy to follow because of its length (since the one judging is assumed to be a simple person), while the second is not persuasive because it is not from things agreed upon or from accepted opinions. So it is necessary for the things about which an enthymeme is a syllogism, and an example is an induction, to be those that in most circumstances admit of going different ways, and for them to be based on few premises, often fewer than the first syllogism would have. For if any of the premises is well known, there is no need to state it, since the hearer adds that himself; for instance, to show that Dorieus won a competition in which the prize was a crown, it is sufficient to say that he won at the Olympic games, and there is no need to add that the Olympic games carry the prize of a crown, since everyone knows that.

And since few of the premises on which rhetorical syllogisms are based are necessarily so (for most of the things decisions and investigations have to do with admit of going different ways, because the things people deliberate about and investigate are things they act on, while all actions are within the class of things of that kind, and one might almost say none of them is by necessity), and things that happen and are possible for the most part are necessarily reasoned out from

18 Aristotle's point is not that there are infinitely many particulars, and one cannot know them all, but that each one of them has infinitely many interconnections and cannot be fully known.

other things of that kind, while necessary things are reasoned out from necessary things (and this too is evident to us from the *Analytics*),[19] it is clear that while some of the premises from which enthymemes are stated are things necessarily so, most are things that are so for the most part; and enthymemes are based on likelihoods and signs, so it is necessary for the former pair to be the same as the latter.[20]

A likelihood is something that happens for the most part, though not in the unqualified sense in which some people define it,[21] but as applied to things that admit of going different ways; it has the relation to the thing about which it is likely that the universal has to 1357b
the particular. Among signs, one sort has the relation that one of the particulars has to the universal, but the other has the relation that one of the universals has to the particular. Of these, a necessary sign is a criterion, but the non-necessary kind has no name to indicate the difference. By "necessary," I mean signs from which a syllogism comes about, and hence a sign of this sort is a criterion, for whenever people think it is not possible to refute what has been said, they believe they are offering a criterion that it has been conclusively demonstrated, since a boundary and a conclusion are the same thing in the ancient tongue.[22] The kind of sign that is as the particular to the universal is, for example, like this: if one were to say that, since Socrates was wise and just, it is a sign that the wise are just. This is a sign, but a refutable one, even if what is said is true, since it does not form a syllogism; but if one were to say, for example, that since someone has a fever, it is a sign that he is sick, or that since a woman has milk, it is a sign that she has given birth, this is necessary. Among signs, that is what a criterion alone is, for only it, if it is true, is irrefutable. The kind of sign that has the relation of the universal to the particular is, for example, if one were to say that, since someone is breathing rapidly, it is a sign

19 There are various relevant passages in both works, especially *Prior Analytics* I, 8 and 13.

20 That is, since there are only two sorts of premises in rhetorical reasoning, the likelihoods and signs about to be described, and the likelihoods all belong to the for-the-most-part category, any rhetorical premises that are necessarily true must be signs, though Aristotle will refine this point by distinguishing two kinds of signs. He is continuing to work out the parallels between rhetoric and dialectic; at 1356b 10-11 he matched up enthymemes and examples with syllogisms and induction, and here he uses the same wording to match up the necessary and contingent premises of dialectical syllogisms with the signs and likelihoods used in enthymemes. The "sameness" of the pairs is not an identity in either case, or rhetoric would simply be dialectic rather than an antistrophe to it.

21 What happens for the most part includes everything that happens by nature, but the fact that rain is likely in winter or scorching heat in late summer (*Physics* 198b 34-199a 3) would be a matter studied by some art other than rhetoric. Aristotle is restricting the sense of likelihood relevant here to matters that human actions can cause to happen in one way or another.

22 "Criterion" translates *tekmêrion* and "conclusively" translates *peparasmenon*. Their roots *tekmar* and *peras* originally both referred to a boundary marker.

that he has a fever. And this too is refutable, even if it is true, because it is also possible for someone who does not have a fever to be short of breath. What, then, a likelihood is, and what a sign and a criterion are, and how they differ, have now been stated, but in the *Analytics*, distinctions are made about them more clearly, and the reason why some are incapable of forming syllogisms and others can be put in syllogisms is given.[23]

It has been stated that an example is an induction, and what sorts of things it is an induction about has been said. It does not have the relation of part to whole, of whole to part, or of whole to whole, but of part to part,[24] like to like; whenever both fall under the same class of things, but one of the two is better known than the other, it is an example—for instance, that Dionysius, by demanding a bodyguard, was plotting a tyranny, because Peisistratus had demanded a bodyguard earlier when he was plotting, and when he got it he became a tyrant, as did Theagenes among the Megarians. And all the others whom people know about become examples for Dionysius, when they do not yet know whether he makes the demand for this reason; they all fall under the same universal, that someone who is plotting a tyranny demands a bodyguard.

1358a The materials from which the means of persuasion that seem to be demonstrative are argued have now been described. But the most important distinction among enthymemes, and the one that has gone most unnoticed by just about everyone, is one that also applies to the way dialectic proceeds with syllogisms; for some enthymemes reflect a rhetorical procedure just as some syllogisms reflect a dialectical procedure, while others reflect other arts and capacities, both the ones there already are and also others not yet fully comprehended. Hence it also goes unnoticed by their hearers that by sticking to the latter manner of speaking, they cross the line out of rhetoric and dialectic. This assertion will be more clear if it is stated in more detail. What I mean is that dialectical and rhetorical syllogisms are concerned with what we call topics; these are common to things having to do with justice or with physics, with politics or with many subjects that differ from it in kind, such as the topic of the more and less.[25] For there will be no more syllogisms to be made or enthymemes to be stated from this about matters of justice than about matters of physics or anything whatever, even though these differ in kind. But there are also as many special topics as come from the premises that have to do with each

23 *Prior Analytics* II, 27.

24 Whole (*holon*) and part (*meros*) are meant here in the same sense as universal (*to katholou*, what applies to a whole class of things) and particular (*to kata meros*, what applies to part of a class) in 1357a 1 above.

25 A topic is a ready-made argument; the topic of the more and less is described at 1397b 12-19. Roughly, it is any argument of the form, if *a* is the case, then *b* must be the case all the more so, or if *a* is not the case, even less could *b* be the case.

specific kind and general class of things; for instance, there are premises having to do with physics from which there is no enthymeme or syllogism that has to do with matters of ethics, and others having to do with the latter from which there will be none concerning physics, and this holds similarly in all cases. The common topics will not make anyone knowledgeable about any class of things, since they are not concerned with any underlying subject, but with the special topics, the better anyone is at selecting premises, the more he will be producing, without realizing it, a knowledge different from dialectic and rhetoric. For if he hits upon its starting points, his speech will no longer be dialectic or rhetoric, but that kind of knowledge whose starting points he has. Most enthymemes that are stated are drawn from these specific kinds of premises, the particular and special ones, and fewer from the common topics. So just as in the *Topics*,[26] a distinction needs to be made here too, among enthymemes, between the specific kinds and the topics from which they are taken. By specific kinds, I mean the special premises of each class of things, and by topics, those common to all things alike. So let us first take up the kinds of rhetoric, so that once we have distinguished how many there are, we may take up the elements and premises connected with them separately.

Chapter 3.

The specific kinds of rhetoric are three in number; for that's how many kinds the hearers of speeches belong to. For a speech is comprised of three things—the speaker, that about which he speaks, and 1358b
the one to whom he speaks—and it is to the latter, namely the hearer, that its end is related. And it is a necessity for the hearer to be either a spectator or a judge, and a judge either of things that have happened or things that are going to happen. A member of an assembly is someone who judges about things that are going to happen, a juror about things that have happened, and a spectator about the ability of the speaker, so that there would necessarily be three kinds of rhetorical speeches, advisory, for the lawcourt, and for display.[27] Of advice, one sort is exhortation, the other warning; for those who give advice in private and those who address assemblies in common always do one of these things. In a trial, one sort of speech is accusation, the other defense;

26 This is apparently a reference to chapter 9 of the treatise now known as *On Sophistical Refutations*, understood as a ninth book of the *Topics*.

27 The last kind of speech is *epideixis*. The word was commonly used for the showy style of speaking indulged in by professional private teachers and paid public advocates. (See, for example, Plato's *Greater Hippias*, 282B-C, and Thucydides' *Peloponnesian War*, III, 42.) At the beginning of the *Gorgias*, forms of the word are used several times by various speakers to refer to what Gorgias does, but at 467C, Socrates transforms its meaning by challenging Polus to display the evidence for his contentions. Aristotle adopts that transformation; he takes *epideixis* as *deixis* (see footnote to 1354a 27) addressed to an audience that is not under an obligation to make a practical decision.

for it is necessary that the parties in dispute do one or the other of these. Of speech for display, one sort is praise, the other blame. The time that belongs to each of these kinds is the future for the advisory speaker (since he gives advice about things that are to be, either by exhorting or warning), the past for the courtroom speaker (since he always makes either an accusation or a defense about things that have been done), and in speech for display, the present is the most decisive (since everyone gives praise or blame in regard to existing circumstances) though speakers often make additional use both of past things by recalling them and of future things by foreseeing them in imagination.

The end is different for each of these, three for the three kinds. For the advisory speaker, it is what is advantageous or harmful, since someone who exhorts is advising something as best, and someone who warns is warning against something as worse; other things, that it is just or unjust, beautiful or shameful, they take in as side-issues to that. For courtroom speakers, it is what is just or unjust; they take in other things as side-issues to those. And for those engaged in praising and blaming, it is what is beautiful or shameful; they bring other things back to refer to these. A sign that the end for each kind is what has been said is that sometimes people might not dispute the other matters; for instance, someone pleading in court might not dispute that the thing happened or that he did harm, but he would never agree that he committed an injustice, or there would be no need of a trial. Similarly, advisory speakers often give way on other matters, but would never agree that they are advising disadvantageous things or warning against beneficial ones; but often they pay no attention to the fact that it is unjust to enslave their neighbors or people who have done no injustice.[28] Similarly too, those engaged in praising and blam-
1359a ing do not consider whether someone has performed advantageous or harmful actions, but often they even make it a matter of praise that he did some beautiful thing in disregard of what was profitable to himself; for example, they praise Achilles because he went to the aid of his companion Patroclus in the knowledge that he would have to die, though it was possible for him to live. For him, a death of that sort was a more beautiful thing, though living was advantageous.

From what has been said, it is clear that it is necessary to have propositions about these matters in the first place, and rhetorical propositions are criteria, likelihoods, and signs, for a syllogism is made up wholly of propositions, and an enthymeme is a syllogism composed

28 The manuscripts have the word *not* before "unjust" in this sentence, but it is deleted by Ross and other editors. Classic statements of both versions of the principle may be found in Thucydides' *Peloponnesian War.* In the Melian dialogue (V, 89), a nameless Athenian representative argues that the injustice of destroying the people of Melos is beside the point, and in the Mytilenian debate (III, 44), Diodotus argues that the justice of destroying the people of Mytilene is irrelevant to Athens' interests.

of the propositions mentioned. And since impossible actions cannot be performed and cannot have been performed, but only possible ones, and it is not possible for things that have not happened and will not happen either to have been performed as actions or to be performed as actions in the future, it is necessary for the advisory speaker, the courtroom speaker, and the speaker for display to have propositions about what is possible and impossible, and about whether something has or has not happened and will or will not happen. Also, since all of them, those who praise and blame, those who exhort and warn, and those who accuse and defend, try to show not only the things that have been mentioned, but also that the good or bad thing, or the beautiful or shameful thing, or the just or unjust thing is a great or small matter, either in speaking of them in their own right or in comparing them to one another, it is evident that it would be necessary also to have propositions about greatness and smallness, and what is greater or lesser, both universally and about each sort of thing, such as what is a greater or lesser good, or injustice, or act of justice, and similarly with the rest. The things about which one must necessarily get hold of propositions, then, have been stated; after this, distinctions need to be made about each of them as a special matter, namely, what advice has to do with, what speeches for display have to do with, and third, what court trials have to do with.

Chapter 4.

The first thing to be taken up, then, is what sorts of good and bad things an advisory speaker gives advice about, since it is not about them all but as many as admit both of happening and of not happening; as for those things that either are or will be the case necessarily, or are incapable of being the case or happening, there is no advice about them. In fact, it is not even about all things that admit of happening or not, since there are some good things among these that happen by nature or from chance, about which giving advice is of no use. But it is clear that advice is concerned with everything there is deliberation about, namely, all the things that are of such a nature as to be traceable back to us, and of which the source of their coming into being is up to us. We investigate things up to that point at which we discover 1359b
whether they are possible or impossible for us to do. Now it is not required on the present occasion to seek to enumerate each of these particulars with precision, and to divide up into specific kinds the things people are in the habit of consulting about, and to go on to make definitions about them as far as possible in accord with truth, because that doesn't belong to the rhetorical art but to one more amenable to knowledge and truth. And far more subjects than it properly studies have been given over to it nowadays, for what is true is exactly what we said before, that rhetoric is composed of a knowledge of analytics and of that part of politics that has to do with types of character, and

is similar in some respects to dialectic and in others to sophistical arguments. To the extent one tries to make either dialectic or this art into a kind of knowledge rather than a power,[29] he will unwittingly obliterate their nature by the transformation, re-making them into knowledge of some underlying subject matter rather than of arguments only. All the same, let us now mention as many things as it is useful to distinguish, while still leaving the investigation of them to the branch of knowledge that has to do with politics.

For it is pretty much the case that of the things about which everyone deliberates and which advisory speakers address, the most important ones are exactly five in number, and these have to do with finances, war and peace, and also guarding territory, imports and exports, and lawmaking. So someone who is going to give advice about finances needs to know what the sources of income of the city are and how many it has, so that if any has been neglected it may be added, and if any is too small it may be increased, and also about all the city's expenses, so that if any is unnecessary it may be subtracted, and if any is too large it may be made less. For it is not only by adding to what belongs to them that people become wealthier, but also by subtracting from what they spend. And it is not only possible to get a general view of these things from experience in private matters, but also necessary to be inquisitive about things that have been found out by others, for the purpose of advising about them.

Concerning war and peace, one needs to know the city's power, both how much is already available and how much is capable of becoming available, as well as what sort is available and what is capable of being added, and also what wars the city has fought and how it has fought them. And it is necessary to know these things not only about one's own city but also about those on its borders and with which it might be expected to go to war, so that it might stay at peace with the stronger ones and have it be up to itself whether it goes to war with the weaker ones. It is also necessary to know their powers, and whether they are like or unlike its own, for it is also possible to get the better of them or come off worse on that score. And in addition to these things, it is necessary to have studied not only the city's own wars but also how those of other cities have ended up, for similar things naturally come from similar causes. Further, concerning guarding territory, one must not be unacquainted with how the guarding is done, and must also know the size of the guarding force, the form it takes, and the locations of the guard posts (and this is impossible for someone who has no experience of the territory), so that if the guarding force is too small it may be added to, and if any of it is unnecessary it may be taken away and protect places that are more suitable. Also, concerning food, one needs to know how much is sufficient for the

29 See the first sentence of Chapter 2 above.

city, and what sort, including both the food grown by it and what is imported, and which items they need to export as well as which ones they need to import, in order for contracts and treaties to be made for them; for there are two kinds of people whom it is necessary to keep the citizens from incurring blame against: those who are stronger and those who are useful for these purposes.

With a view to safety, it is a necessity to be able to see all these things, and not least, to have an understanding of lawmaking; for the preservation of the city is in its laws, so that it is necessary to know how many specific forms of government there are, what is advantageous to each, and what things each is naturally destroyed by, among both the things inherent in it and those opposed to it. As for being destroyed by things inherent in it, I mean that outside of the best form of government, all the others are destroyed when they become slack or rigid; democracy, for instance, becomes weaker not only when it is slackened in such a way that it comes in the end to oligarchy, but also when it is made extremely rigid. In the same way too, a hooked nose and snub nose not only come to the mean by being slackened, but also, when they become extremely hooked or snub, they get to such a condition that they do not even seem to be noses.[30] And it is useful for lawmaking not only to understand what form of government is advantageous by looking at past events, but also to know the forms of government in use among other peoples, and what sorts fit what sorts of people. So it is evident that for lawmaking, travels around the earth are useful, since it is possible to grasp the laws of various nations from them, and for political advice, the investigations contained in writings about the deeds of those nations, but all these things are work for the study of politics and not of rhetoric. The most important matters with which someone who is going to give advice needs to have 1360b
an acquaintance, then, are this many. But let us speak again about the things on the basis of which one needs to give exhortations and warnings on these and other matters.

Chapter 5.

For just about every person in private and all people in common there is a certain target they are aiming at in the things they choose and avoid, and this, to state it in sum, is happiness and its parts. So for the sake of example, let us take up what happiness, simply stated, is and what its parts consist of, for all exhortations and warnings deal with this and with the things that are directed to this and opposed to it; for it is necessary to perform the actions that provide for this or

30 A rigid adherence to democracy, then, untempered by any non-democratic laws or practices, would result in something that no longer seemed to be a city. Aristotle defines democracy below, at 1365b 30-31, as a form of government that chooses its officials by lot, so that even elections, which make distinctions among better and worse qualified citizens, would be a slackening of pure democratic practices.

for any of its parts, or make them greater rather than less, while not performing actions that destroy or impede them or produce their opposites. So let happiness be good activity combined with virtue, or self-sufficiency in living, or the most pleasant life consistent with safety, or abundance of possessions and bodies[31] along with the power to protect and make effective use of them, since everyone pretty much agrees that happiness is one or more of these things.

So if happiness is that sort of thing, it is necessary that the following are parts of it: being well born, having many friends, having good friends, riches, having good children, having many children, having a good old age, and also the virtues of the body (such as health, beauty, strength, size, athletic power), reputation, honor, luck, and virtue; for this is the way one would be most self-sufficient, if these goods, both within himself and external, were to belong to him, since there are no others besides these. Those within himself are the ones that have to do with the soul and the ones in the body, and the external ones are being well born, friends, possessions, and honor; also, we believe he must attain to positions of power and have luck, since his life would be safest in that way. Let us, then, in a similar fashion, also grasp what each of these is.

Now in a nation or a city, being well born is to be the original inhabitants of the land, or ancient ones, and for the first ones to have been conspicuous leaders and for many of those descended from them to have been conspicuous for admired qualities; in private life, being well born is either from the father's side or the mother's, with legitimacy from both, and as with the city, with the first ancestors being notable for either virtue, or riches, or something else held in honor, and with many conspicuous young and older men and women coming from the family.

Having good children and having many children is not unclear. In
1361a a community, it means that the youth are plentiful and good—good in respect to the virtue of the body, such as size, beauty, strength, and athletic power, while in the soul, temperance and courage are the virtues of the young. In private life, having good children and many children means there are many such children of one's own, both female and male; of the females, the virtue of the body is beauty and size, and of the soul, temperance and a love for work without slavishness. In private life and in a community alike, one must seek to have each of the things of this sort present in both men and women; because those

31 Probably meaning slaves, and possibly also livestock. The first definition given (*eupraxia met' aretês*) approximates the one Aristotle arrives at dialectically in Book I, Chapter 7 of the *Nicomachean Ethics* (*energeia kat' aretên*, 1098a 16-17); those that follow become increasingly more remote from it. The last is the least defensible, but is also probably the most widespread opinion, which is what rhetoric must begin with and work with. The crudeness of the word "bodies" in this context is surely deliberate.

among whom the condition of women is debased, as it is among the Spartans, are, just about to the extent of half, not happy.

The parts of riches are a plentiful supply of money and land, possession of estates outstanding in number, size, and beauty, and also possession of conveniences, slaves, and livestock outstanding in number and beauty, with all of these safe, suited to freedom, and useful. Things that are fruitful are more useful, while those that are for enjoyment are more suited to freedom (and by fruitful I mean those that bring income, by enjoyable, those from which nothing of any worth comes, aside from the use of them). The measure of safety is what is possessed in such a place and such a way that the use of it is in one's own control, and of being owned, when it is in one's control to make it over to another or not (and by making over to another I mean giving or selling). Universally, being rich lies in using more so than in possessing, for the being-at-work and being-in-use of such things are the riches.

Good reputation is being taken by everyone as a person of serious stature, or as the sort of person who has something that everyone, or most people, or good people, or sensible people aspire to. Honor is a sign of a good reputation for doing good, and those who are honored justly and the most are those who have performed good works, not that someone who has the power to do good is not honored as well. Doing good leads either to safety, and to whatever is responsible for its being present, or to riches, or to any other goods of which the acquisition is not easy, either in general or at a certain place or time; for many people seem to attain honor for small things, but places and times are responsible for it. The parts of honor are sacrifices, memorials in verse or without verse, privileges, special plots of land, front row seats, tombs, portraits, maintenance at public expense, barbarian practices such as obeisance by prostration and stepping off paths, and gifts precious to various peoples. For a gift is both the giving of a possession and a sign or honor, and hence both money-lovers and honor-lovers desire them, since they both get what they want, 1361b
because it is a possession which money-lovers desire and also has in it an honor which honor-lovers desire.

The virtue of a body is health, but health of such a kind that people can be free of distress while using their bodies, since lots of people are healthy the way Herodicus[32] is said to have been, people whom no one would consider happy in their state of health, since they give up everything human, or most everything. Beauty is different at each stage of life. In a youth, beauty is having a body fit for exertions, both for a running track and involving force, and which is pleasant to look at for enjoyment; that's why those who compete in the pentathlon are

32 An athletic trainer described in Plato's *Republic* (406A-B). He was sickly himself, and devised a regimen for himself and others that made maintaining health their full-time occupation and worry.

the most beautiful, because they are naturally adept at force and speed at the same time. The beauty of someone in his prime is related to the labors of war, but involves being pleasant-appearing along with fearsomeness; of someone old, it is related to being sufficiently fit for necessary exertions, and not painful to see, on account of not having any of the disfiguring ills that afflict old age. Strength is a power of moving someone else around the way one wants, and for moving someone else it is necessary that one either pull or push or lift or press down or compress him, so that the strong person is strong by doing all or some of these things. The virtue of size is to be greater than most in height, girth, and breadth to just such an extent that one's motions are not made slower by the excess. The virtue of a body for athletic contests is a combination of size, strength, and speed (and someone speedy *is* strong); for someone with the power to fling his legs a certain way and move with speed and for distance is adept at running, someone with the power to press and hold down is adept at wrestling, and someone with the power to throw a punch is adept at boxing; someone with both the latter powers is adept at no-holds-barred wrestling, and someone with them all is a pentathlete.

Having a good old age is a slow process of aging with a freedom from pain; for if someone has aged quickly, or gradually but with pain, he is not aging well. That is a matter of bodily virtues and luck, for without being free of disease and strong, one will not be without suffering and pain, and without luck he could not stay that way long. There is also a certain other power of longevity apart from strength and health, for many people who lack the virtues of the body are long-lived, but giving a precise account of these matters is of no use for what concerns us now.

Having many friends and having good friends are not unclear once a definition of a friend has been given, and that is: a friend is the sort of person who is active in bringing about things he believes are good for someone, for that person's sake. Someone who has many people of that sort has many friends, and someone whose friends are also good men has good friends.

Good luck involves good things of which chance[33] is the cause,
1362a when either all, or most, or the most important of them come along or are present all along. And chance is a cause of some things for which there are also arts, and of many things in which art is not involved, for instance the things of which nature is the cause (though chance also admits of being contrary to nature); for art is a cause of health, but nature of beauty and size. In all cases, the sorts of good things that come from chance are those that are an occasion for envy. And chance is also a cause of good things that are beyond accounting for:

33 The word *tuchê* is sometimes used by Aristotle for all chance results of the complex interactions of other causes, and sometimes confined to chance that happens to affect human beings; in the latter instances it is sometimes translated here as luck.

for example, if the rest of the brothers are ugly but one is beautiful, or everyone else fails to see a treasure but one person finds it, or if an arrow hits a bystander but not the person aimed at, or if, the only time someone didn't go somewhere he always frequented, others who went just that one time were killed. For all such things seem to be matters of good luck.

Concerning virtue, seeing as how the most appropriate place for it is the one that has to do with praises, it is best left to be defined when we give an account of praise.[34]

Chapter 6.

It is clear, then, what one needs to be aiming at in exhortations for the future or present, and in warnings, since they are against the opposites of those things. But since the target immediately before for someone giving advice is what is advantageous (for people deliberate not about the end but about the means to the end, and these are things advantageous in regard to actions, and what is advantageous is good), what needs to be grasped would be the elements that go into something good and advantageous, taken simply.

So let the good be that which is chosen itself for its own sake, and for the sake of which we choose something else, and at which all things that have sense perception and intelligence aim (or would if they were to get intelligence), and all the things that intelligence would give over to each and all the things that intelligence in each case does give over to each; for the good for each thing is that which, when it is present, puts that thing in a sound and self-sufficient condition, and its good is its self-sufficiency along with the things that tend to produce or preserve such things and the things from which such things follow, as well as the things that prevent and destroy their opposites. Something follows in two ways, either simultaneously or subsequently; for instance knowing is subsequent to learning, but living is simultaneous with being healthy. And what tends to produce something has three senses, as being healthy produces health, as food produces health, and as gymnastic exercise does, because for the most part it produces health. With these things laid down, it is necessary that both gains of good things and losses of bad ones are good, for not having the bad is simultaneous with the one and having the good is subsequent to the other. That is also necessary in the cases of gaining a greater in place
of a lesser good or a lesser in place of a greater evil; for by the amount 1326b
that the greater exceeds the lesser, to that extent it becomes a gain of the one or a loss of the other. It is also necessary for the virtues to be a good thing (for those who have them are in a sound condition as a result of them, and they also tend to produce good things and lead to actions, but what each virtue is and what kind it is needs to be spoken

34 Book I, Chapter 9.

of separately for each),[35] and for pleasure to be a good thing; for all animals desire it by nature, and so it is necessary for both pleasant things and beautiful things to be good, since the former tend to produce pleasure, while among beautiful things, some are pleasant and others are themselves chosen in virtue of themselves.

To speak of them one by one, it is necessary for the following to be good things. Happiness, since it is both chosen in virtue of itself and self-sufficient, and we choose everything else for its sake. Justice, courage, temperance, greatness of soul, magnificence, and other active conditions of that sort, since they are virtues of a soul. Health and beauty and things of that sort, since they are virtues of a body and tend to produce many things, as health tends to produce both pleasure and life, which is why it seems to be the greatest good, because it is responsible for two of the things most honored by most people, pleasure and life. Riches, since that is the virtue of acquisition and tends to produce many things. A friend and friendship, for a friend is chosen in virtue of himself, and also tends to produce many things. Honor and reputation, for they are both pleasant and tend to produce many things, and for the most part the possession of the things for which people are honored goes along with them. The power of speaking and of action, for all such things tend to produce many good things. Also natural giftedness, memory, ease of learning, quickness of mind, and all such things, since these powers tend to produce good things. Similarly, all kinds of knowledge and all arts. And life, for if no other good thing were to follow from it, it would still be chosen in virtue of itself. And justice, for it is something advantageous in common.

These, then, are pretty much the things agreed to be good; but among the disputable ones, syllogisms are based on the following points. That of which the opposite of bad is good. Also that of which the opposite is advantageous to one's enemies; for example, if being cowards is the most advantageous thing for one's enemies, it is evident that courage is the most beneficial thing for the citizens. And generally, the opposite of what one's enemies want and take joy in appears to be beneficial; this is why it was said "Priam would surely be delighted."[36] But this is not always the case, though for the most part it is, for nothing prevents the same thing from sometimes being
1363a advantageous to opposite sides; hence it is said that evils bring human beings together, whenever the same thing is harmful to both sides. That of which there is no possibility of excess is good, but whatever is greater than it ought to be is bad. And that for the sake of which

35 See 1366b 1-22.

36 At the quarrel between Achilles and Agamemnon that begins the *Iliad* (I, 255). The two quotations a few lines below are from Bk. II of the *Iliad* (160, 298), on the futility of going home without Helen after ten years of fighting. The proverb has something to do with spilling a drink that took labor to fetch when it is on the point of being served.

a lot has been suffered or spent, for it is already an apparent good, and such a thing is accepted as an end, and an end worth a lot, and the end is what is good. Hence these things were said: "she would be something for Priam to boast of," and "it is a disgraceful thing to stay so long," and also the proverb about the pitcher at the door. And something that a lot of people aim at, and is obviously fought over, for that which everyone aims at was said to be good, and a lot of people gives the appearance of being everyone. And what is praised, since no one praises what is not good. And what enemies and worthless people praise, for it is just as if everyone were already in agreement if even those who have come off badly from it are in agreement about it; for it is because it is something obvious that they would be in agreement, just as it is worthless people on whom their friends cast blame and their enemies do not (which is why the Corinthians presumed they had been insulted by Simonides when he wrote "Troy finds no fault with the Corinthians"). And what any good man or woman with practical judgment has shown a preference for, as Athena did for Odysseus, Theseus for Helen, the goddesses for Paris, and Homer for Achilles.

And in all cases, things that are chosen, and people choose to do the things that have been mentioned, and also to do bad things to their enemies and good to their friends, and to do what is in their power. The latter has two senses, referring both to things that can happen and to those that happen easily; and easy things are those that happen either painlessly or in a short time, since what is difficult is marked by either pain or extent of time. And what goes the way people want; and they want either nothing bad or something less bad than good (and this will be the case when the price to be paid is either unnoticed or small). And deeds that are peculiarly theirs and no one else's and exceptional, for in that way the honor is greater. And deeds especially fitted to themselves; and of this sort are deeds appropriate to their family and power, and deeds they believe they have fallen short in, even if they are minor, since they nevertheless choose to perform these actions. And deeds that are readily accomplished, since they are in their power and easy; and deeds that everyone, or most people, or people like them or inferior to them have succeeded at are readily accomplished. And deeds that will delight their friends or be hateful to their enemies. And those actions that people they admire choose to perform. And deeds they are naturally gifted for or experienced at, since they believe they will succeed at them easily. And deeds no worthless person chooses, for these are praised more. And deeds they happen to have a longing for, since they are not only pleasant but also seem to be better. And most of all, each sort of people chooses deeds 1363b
related to the things they are devoted to, as those who love winning choose what will bring victory, honor-lovers what will bring honor, money-lovers what will bring money, and the same way with the rest.

The means of persuasion concerning what is good and advantageous need to be grasped from these things.

Chapter 7.

But since often when people agree that both of two things are advantageous, they dispute over which is more so, the next thing to be spoken of would be concerned with the greater good and what brings more advantage. Let what is so much and beyond it be exceeding and what is contained within be exceeded; let greater and more numerous always be relative to less, and great, small, many, and few be relative to the size of most things, and let what exceeds be great and what falls short be small, and the same way with many and few. Now since we call something good that is itself chosen for its own sake and not for the sake of anything else, and something that all things aim at and would choose if they were to get intelligence and practical judgment, and what tends to produce, to preserve, or to follow upon such things, and since an end is that for the sake of which other things are done, and what has these attributes relatively to a certain person is good for him, it is necessary that more than one of these things, or more than some lesser number, when that one or that lesser number are counted in among them, would be a greater good; for it exceeds them, and what is included within something is exceeded.

And if one thing that is greatest exceeds another thing that is greatest, things of the first kind also exceed those of the second; and for all kinds that exceed other kinds, the greatest in the one also exceeds the greatest in the other. For instance, if the largest man is larger than the largest woman, then men in general are also larger than women, and if men in general are larger than women, then the largest man is also larger than the largest woman; for the general kinds that exceed and the greatest members within them are in proportion. And when this follows upon that, but not that upon this, and follows either simultaneously, successively, or in potency, *that* exceeds *this*, for the use of the thing that follows is included in that of the other. Living follows simultaneously upon being healthy, but not the latter upon the former, knowing follows successively upon learning, and stealing follows upon desecrating a temple in potency, since someone who desecrates a temple would steal from it. And things exceeding the same thing by a greater amount are greater, since they are necessarily greater even than that greater amount. And things that tend to produce a greater good are greater, for that is what was meant by being something that tends to produce something greater. And when the thing tending to produce something is greater, the thing produced is likewise greater; for if something healthy is more choiceworthy and a greater good than something pleasant, then health is also greater than pleasure.
1364a And what is more choiceworthy in virtue of itself is greater than what is chosen not in virtue of itself; for instance strength is greater than

something healthy, since the latter is not chosen for its own sake, but the former is, which is what the good meant.

And if one thing is an end while another is not an end; for the latter is chosen for the sake of something else, but the former for the sake of itself, as gymnastic exercise is chosen for the sake of the body's well-being. And that which has less additional need of any other thing or things, since it is more self-sufficient; and what has additional need of fewer things or of things easier to get has need of less. And when this is not present without that, or is not capable of coming into being, but that is without this, the one without the need is more self-sufficient, and is thus manifestly a greater good. And if something is a source, and another is not a source, or is a cause, and the other is not a cause,[37] for the same reason; for without a cause and source a thing is incapable of being or coming into being. And of two sources, what comes from the greater source is greater, and of two causes, what comes from the greater cause is greater; and conversely, the source of what is greater is the greater of two sources, and the cause of what is greater is the greater of two causes. So it is evident from the things that have been said that there are two ways for something to appear greater; for it will seem greater both if it is a source and the other thing is not, and if it is not a source and the other thing is, since the end and not the source is greater. In this way, Leodamas, making an accusation against Callistratus, said the one who gave advice committed a greater injustice than the one who performed the action, since it would not have been performed if he had not advised it; then again, against Chabrias, he said the one who performed the action committed a greater injustice than the one who gave the advice, since it would not have happened if there had been no one to perform the action, because it is for the sake of this that someone hatches a plot, for people to carry it into action.[38]

And something that is more scarce is a greater good than something plentiful, as gold is in comparison to iron, even though it is less useful, since its possession is a greater thing on account of being more difficult. But in another way, what is more plentiful is greater than what is more scarce, for the frequent exceeds the rare, and hence it is

37 In a strict sense, Aristotle uses the word cause (*aition*) only for first causes, and as synonymous with the word for source (*archê*), but *aition* can be used for anything in any way responsible for something else, and apply to intermediate or incidental steps in a causal series.

38 Callistratus and Chabrias were tried for their involvement in the loss to the Thebans of a town on the border of Athenian territory. The example illustrates the point made in Chapter 2, that rhetoric deals with matters that admit of being decided in opposite ways. The reader may be reminded of the story of the lawyer who argued that his client had an alibi for the time the car was stolen, and had the owner's permission to use it anyway, and in any case it was already dented before he drove it.

said, "Water is best."[39] And what is more difficult is generally greater than what is easier, since it is more scarce, but in another way, what is easier is greater than what is more difficult, for that is the way we want things. Also that of which the opposite or the lack is greater. And virtue is a greater thing than the lack of vice, and vice than the lack of virtue, for the former member of each pair is the complete condition of which the latter is an incomplete version. And those things that lead to more beautiful or more shameful deeds are themselves greater, and those deeds that come from greater vices and virtues are greater, since as the causes and sources are to one another, so are their effects, and as the effects, so are the causes and sources. And those things of which an excess[40] is more choiceworthy or more beautiful, as seeing acutely is more choiceworthy than smelling acutely (since sight is also
1364b more choiceworthy than smell), and acting on the basis of passionate devotion to one's companions is a more beautiful thing than acting on the basis of passionate devotion to money, so that passionate devotion to companions is also more beautiful than passionate devotion to money. And the other way around as well, excesses of better things are better, and excesses of beautiful things are more beautiful. Also those things for which the desires are more beautiful or better, since greater longings are for greater things; and if the things they are for are more beautiful or better, the desires are better and more beautiful as well, for the same reason.

And the things that the more beautiful or more serious kinds of knowledge are concerned with are also more beautiful and more serious, for the truth about something has the same standing as the knowledge of it, and each kind of knowledge has command of what belongs to it. And the kinds of knowledge concerned with more serious and more beautiful things are proportionate to them for the same reason. And it is a necessity that what people with practical judgment—either all, or many, or most, or the best of them—would judge or have judged to be a greater good is that way either simply or in the respect in which it accords with the judgment they made about it. This is a point that applies in common to other things as well: for what anything is, and to what degree, and of what kind, are the way knowledge and practical judgment would say they are. But we have been speaking about good things, for the good was defined as what something that acquired practical judgment would choose in

39 The beginning of Pindar's first Olympian ode. The full line continues, "but gold is a blazing fire."

40 Most translators shy away from translating this word accurately here, out of a misunderstanding of the praise of the mean in Aristotle's ethics. Although courage, for example, is always a mean between cowardice and rashness, there is no such thing as too much courage. Aristotle in fact says in the *Nicomachean Ethics* that the mean involved in the virtues of character is always also an extreme (1107a 23). One who has virtue of character recognizes a potential action as beautiful in itself, and choiceworthy apart from any considerations of pleasure or advantage.

each case; it is evident, then, that the greater good is the one practical judgment more-so says it is. Also what is present in better people is a greater good, either simply or in the respect in which they are better; for instance courage is a greater good than strength. Also what a better person would choose, either simply or in the respect in which he is better, for instance to suffer injustice rather than commit it, since a more just person would make that choice.[41] Also what is more pleasant in comparison to what is less pleasant, since all things pursue pleasure and long for having pleasure for its own sake, and the good and the end were defined by these things; and what is more free of pain or pleasant for a longer time is more pleasant. Also what is more beautiful in comparison to what is less beautiful, since the beautiful is either what is pleasant or what is chosen in virtue of itself.[42] Also those things people themselves more-so want to be responsible for, either for themselves or for friends, are greater goods, while those people want less to be responsible for are greater evils. Also more enduring things in comparison to those of shorter duration, and things that are more constant rather than more unreliable, for the use of enduring things is greater on account of time and that of constant things on account of one's wishes, for the use of something constant is more available whenever people want it.

And the way things are with one of a set of cognate terms, or one of a set of inflected forms of the same term, also follows for the rest; for instance if it is more beautiful and more choiceworthy to do something courageously rather than temperately, then courage is also more choiceworthy than temperance, and to be courageous than to be temperate. Also what all people choose in comparison to what not all people choose, and what more people rather than fewer choose, since the good was what everything aims at, so that what is chosen more is a greater good. Also what parties in dispute or enemies claim is a greater good, or people who are judging or those whom they pick out, for in the former case it is as if all people were claiming it, and in the latter, as if the authoritative and knowledgeable people were. Sometimes something that everyone has a share in is greater, since it would be a disgrace not to share in it, but sometimes something that no one or few share, since it is more scarce. Also things that get more praise, since they are more beautiful. And the same way with things that get greater honors, since it is as if honor were a certain measure of worth; and things that get greater penalties. And things greater than those agreed to be or appearing to be great. And the same things appear greater when divided up into parts, since a greater number

41 See *Gorgias*, 469C.

42 This pair of criteria for the beautiful may be compared with the different but related pair that Socrates offers in the *Gorgias*, in 474C-475B. Aristotle refines what he means by the beautiful below at 1366a 33-34.

of things has an appearance of exceeding. Hence the poet says the following[43] persuaded Meleager to rise up:

> All the evils that come to human beings whose city
>   is conquered
> The men are annihilated, fire levels the town,
> Other people carry off their children.

Also putting things together and building one on another, as Epicharmus[44] does, for the same reason as dividing up, since the putting together shows the excess as large, and because it makes something appear to be a source and cause of great things. And since what is more difficult and more scarce is a greater thing, opportune occasions, stages of life, places, times, and powers make things great; for if an action is beyond one's power, age, or equals, if they had been in the same situation, place, or time, it will have magnitude among beautiful, good, or just things, or their opposites. Hence the epigram[45] about the Olympic victor,

> Before, holding a rough harness across both shoulders,
> I used to carry fish from Argos to Tegea.

And Iphicrates used to extol himself by speaking of the conditions from which he started out. And what springs from oneself is greater than what is acquired, since it is a more difficult accomplishment; hence the poet says, "self-taught am I." And the greatest part of something great; for instance Pericles said in the funeral oration that for the youth to be taken from the city was as if the spring had been stolen away from the year.

And things useful in a greater time of need, as in old age and in sickness; and of two useful things, the one nearer to the end; and what is useful to oneself rather than useful simply; and what is in one's power rather than what is not in one's power, since the former is useful to oneself and the latter not; and things involved in the end life aims at, since ends are more important than means to an end. And
1365b things that pertain to truth rather than to opinion; and the defining mark of what pertains to opinion is what one would not choose if it were going to be unnoticed. Hence too, it would seem to be more choiceworthy to have something good done to one rather than to do good to someone else, since one will choose the former even if it goes

43 *Iliad* IX, 592-594.

44 See note to *Gorgias* 505E. The technique of building things up by steps suggests a series of effects causing greater and greater effects, as in the familiar nursery rhyme that begins "For want of a nail the shoe was lost..."

45 In the following series of examples, the epigram is a fragment from Simonides, Iphicrates was an Athenian general who rose from the lower class of citizens, the poet is Phemius in the *Odyssey* (XXII, 347), and the simile made by Pericles is not contained in Thucydides' version of his most famous funeral oration.

unnoticed, but it is not thought that one would choose to do good unnoticed. Also all the things people want to be present rather than seem so, since they pertain more to truth; hence too, people claim that justice is a small thing, because it is more choiceworthy for it to seem than to be present, but that is not so with being healthy. Also things that are more useful for many purposes, such as for living, for living well, for pleasure, and for performing beautiful actions; hence, the greatest things seem to be riches and health, since they have all these uses. Also what is more free of pain and accompanied by pleasure as well, since there is more than one good, because both pleasure and freedom from pain are present in it. And of two goods, the greater is the one which, when added to the same other thing, makes the whole greater. And things whose presence is not unnoticed in comparison with those that go unnoticed, since they put the truth forward; hence being rich would obviously be a greater good than seeming rich. And what is held most dear, both by those who have that thing alone, and by those who have it among others; hence the penalty is not the same if someone puts out the eye of a one-eyed person as if he had put out an eye of a person with two eyes, since he has robbed him of the thing he held most dear.[46]

So the things on the basis of which one needs to bring forward persuasive arguments in giving exhortations and warnings have pretty much been stated.

Chapter 8.

The greatest and most decisive of all the things that contribute to being able to be persuasive and to do a beautiful job at giving advice is to have a grasp of all forms of government, and to distinguish the characters of the people and customary practices in each, and the things advantageous to them. For everyone is persuaded by what is advantageous, and what is advantageous is what preserves the form of government. Also, a declaration made by the ruling authority is decisive, and the ruling authorities are differentiated in accord with the forms of government; as many forms of government as there are,

46 There is a famous Biblical example of this principle in King David's response to the parable of the one ewe lamb, told to him by Nathan the prophet in 2 Samuel 12, verses 1-7.

so many are the forms of ruling authority. And there are four[47] forms of government—democracy, oligarchy, aristocracy, and monarchy—so that the ruling and deciding authority would be some part of these, or the whole of them. Democracy is a form of government in which the ruling offices are distributed by lot, oligarchy one in which people hold them on the basis of property qualifications, and aristocracy one in which they depend on education; I am speaking of the education established by custom, for those who rule in an aristocracy are people who have remained faithful to customary practices. These necessarily appear to be the best people, which is where this form of government
1366a has gotten its name. Monarchy, in accord with its name is a form of government in which one person is in authority over everyone; of these, the sort that follows some prescribed order is kingship, and the unlimited sort is tyranny.

And one must not fail to note the end sought by each form of government, since people make choices in reference to the end. And the end sought by democracy is freedom, by oligarchy riches, by aristocracy the things that have to do with education and customary practices, and by tyranny self-preservation. So it is evident that the kinds of human character, customary practices, and what is advantageous to each must be differentiated in relation to its end, if in fact people make choices in reference to that. And since persuasive arguments come about not only from demonstrative speech, but also from speech that reveals character (since it is because the speaker appears to be a certain sort of person that we trust him, that is, if he appears to be good or good-willed or both), it would be necessary for us to have an understanding of the kinds of character that belong to each of the forms of government; for the kind of character that belongs to each is necessarily the most persuasive when addressed to each. And these kinds of character will be grasped by way of these same ends, since one's character is manifest as a result of a choice, and one's choice is made in reference to one's end.

So the future or present things we need to strive for in making exhortations, and the things among which we need to find persua-

47 In the *Politics* (III, 7), Aristotle says there are three forms of government, rule by one, few, or many, each of them having a degenerate form that rules for the sake of the private interests of the ruler or rulers, with tyranny as the degenerate form of kingship, oligarchy as that of aristocracy, and democracy as that of "polity." The last named is a constitutional government that has prescribed roles for all classes of citizens in office holding and decision making, as in Athens under the constitution drawn up by Solon. In Plato's *Republic*, five forms are recognized, reflecting aspects of human character, aristocracy and kingship being treated as one form with a trivial distinction based on how many people are present with outstanding qualifications to rule, the Spartan form of government in which ruling is based on earning honor being given the name timocracy to distinguish it from oligarchy in which it is based on owning property, and democracy and tyranny being regarded as those lowest forms in which the passions of the mob or of one demagogue have been unleashed. Here, in accord with the purposes of rhetoric, Aristotle is using only those distinctions widely made within popular opinion.

sive arguments having to do with what is advantageous, and also the means and manner for us to be equipped to deal with the kinds of character and customary practices in the various forms of government, to an extent commensurate with the present occasion, have been stated; these things are investigated with precision in the *Politics*.

Chapter 9.

Let us next speak about virtue and vice, and about what is beautiful or shameful, for these are the things someone who praises or blames has in view. And as we speak about these things, at the same time it will turn out that those things will also become clear on the basis of which we will be assumed to be people with character of a certain sort, which was a second means of persuasion; for based on the same things, we will be able to present both ourselves and someone else as trustworthy in regard to virtue. And since it often happens, without seriousness or even with it, that someone praises not only a human being or a god, but also lifeless things or any of the other animals at random, premises about these things too must be grasped in the same way, so that we may also say enough about them to serve as an example.

Now the beautiful is that which is praised as being choiceworthy on account of itself, or is good and is pleasant because it is good,[48] and if this is the beautiful, it is necessary that virtue is something beautiful, since it is praised for being good. And virtue is thought of[49] as a power of providing and safeguarding good things, as well as a power of conferring many great benefits, in fact all sorts of benefits in connection with all things. The parts of virtue are justice, courage, **1366b** temperance, magnificence, greatness of soul, generosity, practical judgment, and wisdom. And the greatest virtues would necessarily be those that are most useful to others, if in fact virtue is a power of conferring benefits, and for this reason people give the most honor to those who are just and courageous, since the one virtue is useful to others in war, and the other in both war and peace. Next is generosity, since such people give freely and do not get into disputes about money, which other people make their highest aim. Justice is a virtue

48 The second formulation rules out what is good solely because it is pleasant, as the first rules out anything that is advantageous, or choiceworthy as a means to an end. The idea of the beautiful in this sense is more common in ancient Greek, but we have it in our language and our time as well, whenever we speak of an unselfish or impractical action as a beautiful thing to do. We, like Aristotle, mean that its goodness simply shines forth. See also the note to 1383b 17 below.

49 Like the discussion of happiness in Chapter 5 above, and that of the forms of government in Chapter 8, the discussion of virtue here is based on popular opinion and not on the conclusions Aristotle arrives at dialectically in other works. In the *Nicomachean Ethics*, virtue is understood as what makes up human character in such a way that one's choices may achieve one's own happiness; doing good to others and following the law are consequences of it and not the things that govern it.

through which each person has what belongs to him and what is in accord with the law; and injustice is that through which people have things that belong to others, and things not in accord with the law. Courage is that by which people are capable of performing beautiful actions in dangerous situations, and as the law prescribes, and are willing to serve the law, and cowardice is the opposite. Temperance is a virtue through which people conduct themselves in the way the law prescribes in relation to the pleasures of the body, and self-indulgence is the opposite. Generosity is a beneficent disposition concerning money, and stinginess is its opposite. Greatness of soul is virtue disposing one to do things of great benefit, and magnificence is a virtue disposing one to produce great things in expenditures; smallness of soul and chintziness are their opposites.[50] Practical judgment is a virtue of thinking in accord with which people have the power to deliberate well about the good and bad things that were mentioned as influencing happiness.

What has to do with virtue and vice in general, then, and with their parts, has been stated sufficiently for the present occasion, and what has to do with the rest is not difficult to see; for it is obvious that the things that produce virtue are necessarily beautiful (since they are in accord with virtue), and so are the things that come from virtue, and the signs and deeds of virtue are things of that sort. And since these signs and the sorts of things that are done and suffered by a good person are beautiful, it is necessary that all things that are deeds of courage or signs of courage or have been done courageously are beautiful, and so are just things and deeds performed justly (but not things suffered justly, for in this one case alone among the virtues, something with the attribute "justly" is not always a beautiful thing, but in the case of being punished, it is a more shameful thing to suffer justly than unjustly), and the same way with the rest of the virtues. And all those things for which the prize is honor are beautiful, especially those for which it is honor instead of money, and those choices upon which someone acts not for his own sake, and things that are good simply, all the things someone does for his country in disregard of his own interest, and things that are good by their nature
1367a and not good for oneself, since one does things like that for his own sake. Also, all those things that are more capable of being present after one is dead than while one is alive, for things present during life have more about them that is for one's own sake. Also, all those deeds that are for the sake of others, since they are less for the sake of

50 Under the name magnificence, Aristotle refers to expenditures on a grand scale by private citizens for public buildings, monuments, and entertainments, when they are made not for ostentation but with good taste and judgment. Analogously, the great-souled man is someone with a lofty idea of the dignity and importance of his own actions, when that idea is well-founded; he is not a politician hungry for constant expressions of honor but someone who will offer his service to the community only when a great occasion arises to which only he is equal.

oneself. And all things that make others prosper rather than oneself, and especially those who have done good to one, since that is just. And things done out of kindness, since they are not for oneself. And the opposites of things people are ashamed of, for they feel shame at saying, doing, and even intending to do shameful things, as Sappho has portrayed in a poem,[51] when Alcaeus says

> I want to say something, but shame is holding me back,

and she goes on

> If your desire was for good or beautiful things,
> And your tongue wasn't pregnant with something evil
> to say,
> Shame would not be weighing down your eyes,
> And you'd be speaking of things that were just.

Things people are anxious but not fearful about are beautiful things, since they experience this toward good things that lead to a good reputation.

And the virtues and deeds of those who have a more serious stature by nature are more beautiful, such as those of a man in comparison to those of a woman. And things that cause enjoyment for others rather than for oneself; this is why a just deed and justice are beautiful.[52] And taking vengeance on one's enemies rather than reconciling with them, because repayment in kind is just and what is just is beautiful, and it befits a courageous person not to be bested. Victory and honor belong among the beautiful things, since they are choiceworthy even when they are fruitless, and display an extreme degree of virtue. And things worthy of remembrance are beautiful, the more so the more memorable they are; also things that follow someone who is no longer living and to which honor is attached, and extraordinary ones that belong to one person alone are more beautiful since they are better remembered. And useless possessions, since they are more befitting free people. And there are special sorts of beautiful things that belong to each group of people, and are signs of what is praised among them; for instance, among the Spartans it is a beautiful thing to have long hair, since it is the sign of a free person, because it is not easy for someone with long hair to do any sort of menial work. And

51 The word used for shame in the Sappho fragment is *aidôs*, while the word Aristotle has just used is *aischunê*. He treats the two as interchangeable, but the latter is the more intense feeling, producing a painful blush, while the former is the modest attitude expressed in downcast eyes. See Bk. II, Chap. 6 below.

52 In the *Nicomachean Ethics*, the notion of the beautiful is conspicuous by its absence from Aristotle's discussion of justice, though in that work he repeatedly speaks of the beautiful as the end that governs all virtue of character (1115b, 12-13, 1122b 6-7). He may be thinking here especially of the kind of justice he calls decency (*epieikeia*) in Book V, Chap. 10, of that work and in Chap. 13 below; the decent person looks beyond the strict requirements of law and gives more, and demands less, than would be due.

it is not a beautiful thing to work at any servile art, since it befits a free person not to live at the promptings of someone else.

For purposes of praise and blame, the thing to do is to take attributes that approximate the ones that are present as being the same things: for example, to take an overcautious person as cool and calculating and a foolish one as trustworthy, or an unfeeling person as mild-tempered. And each person is always to be taken as having what is best from among the attributes that go together: for instance, a hot-headed and frenzied person as being forthright, and an arrogant
1367b one as being magnificent and grand, and people in excessive conditions as being in the conditions of the virtues, as for instance a rash person as courageous and a wasteful person as generous. For it will seem that way to most people, and be reinforced at the same time by a false inference about the cause; for if someone is prone to take risks where there is no necessity, much more would it seem that he would where there is a beautiful reason, and if he gives lavishly to people at random, much more would it seem that he would to his friends, since the excess of the virtue would be to do good to everyone.[53] Consider also those among whom the praise is given—for just as Socrates used to say, it is not difficult to praise Athenians among Athenians—and that one needs to speak as though what is held in honor among each group of people, whether Scythians, Spartans, or philosophers, were actually present. And in all cases, one needs to draw what is held in honor toward what is beautiful, since it is at least in that neighborhood; so too are things in accord with what is fitting, for example, if they are worthy of one's ancestors or of what one has accomplished before, since attaining additional honor is accounted as happiness and is a beautiful thing. This is especially so if one goes beyond what is fitting to something better and more beautiful, for instance if someone

53 The last clause is the false inference; a wasteful person can't recognize when lavish giving is good and appropriate, but people might take him to be even more generous than ordinary generosity would call for. The misunderstanding of the way virtue is a mean (see also note to 1364a 37) affects most scholarly commentary on Aristotle as well as ordinary popular opinion. Generosity is not a certain moderate amount of lavish giving, in a range quantitatively marked off between stinginess and wastefulness, but a reliable recognition of all the circumstances that make giving right (*Nicomachean Ethics* 1120a 23-26). So while people in general might take evidence of wastefulness as proof of generosity, or evidence of rashness as proof of courage, Aristotle regards the truth as just the opposite. Whether he is recommending taking advantage of people's misunderstandings in this way is not clear. If so, then he regards deceptive rhetoric used merely for praise on ceremonial occasions as acceptable, but it may be that even in these cases what he is recommending is an awareness on the part of the student of rhetoric of a technique widely used. Where most translations have Aristotle saying "one ought to" or "one must" do so-and-so, what he writes in many cases is an impersonal verbal adjective ending in *–teon*, meaning more precisely "the thing to be done," or "the thing necessary for the purpose."

is restrained in good fortune and great-souled in misfortune,[54] or is a better and more forgiving person when he has become more powerful. To this effect are the remark of Iphicrates, "What I came from, to what!" and the line about the Olympic victor, "Before, holding across both shoulders a rough..." and that of Simonides,[55]

> She who was from a father, a husband, and brothers,
> tyrants all.

Since praise is based on actions, and an action in accord with a choice is particularly a mark of a person of serious stature, the thing that needs to be done is to try to show that someone was acting in accordance with choice. And it is useful for him to appear to have engaged in such action many times; hence things that happened incidentally and by luck need to be taken as part of his intention, since, if one brings forward many similar instances, that will seem to be a sign of virtue as well as of choice. Praise is speech that manifests greatness of virtue, so it is necessary to display actions as having that character. An encomium, though, is about deeds.[56] The surrounding things, such as good birth and education, play a role in persuasion, since it is likely that good offspring come from good parents and that a person raised a certain way is of that sort, and so we also make encomiums upon the people who perform the actions. And deeds are signs of the active condition of one's character, since we would make an encomium even upon someone who had not performed any actions, if we believed him to be the sort who would. Congratulating someone on his blessedness or happiness are the same as one another, but not the same as praise and encomium, but just as happiness encompasses virtue, so too congratulating someone on his happiness includes praise and encomium. And praise and advice have a common form, since those things one might propose in giving advice become encomiums when **1368a**
the wording is changed, so when we've got what one ought to do, or what sort of person one ought to be, it is necessary for those who state these things as proposals to make a change in the wording and

54 *Nicomachean Ethics*, 1100b 30-33: "Something beautiful shines through when one bears many and great misfortunes calmly, not through insensitivity but through good breeding and greatness of soul."

55 For the first two quotations, see 1365a 11-15 above and the footnote there; the line of Simonides is from his praise of Archedice, daughter of Hippias, an Athenian tyrant.

56 Virtues are reliable states of character for which Aristotle invents the wonderful word *ametakinêtos* (*Nicomachean Ethics* 1105a 33) to indicate that they are conditions of stable equilibrium rather than of rigid adherence to principle. People may sometimes act in ways that would be characteristic of some virtue, even by deliberate choice, without possessing the virtue itself. Aristotle here confines the general word for praise to laudatory speeches about character; for laudatory speeches about deeds he appropriates a name that applied to songs sung in Bacchic celebrations upon the return of a military victor to his home village, encomium (like comedy) being derived from the word for village, *kômê*.

redirect it. For example, that one ought not to pride oneself on things due to luck, but on things due to oneself, when worded in that way, has the force of a proposal, but in the following way it is praise: "he is one who prides himself not on things that belong to him due to luck, but on things due to himself." So whenever you want to praise someone, see what you would propose, and whenever you want to propose something, see what you would praise. And the wording will necessarily be opposite since something that is a prohibition in the one case is changed in the other case to something that is not a prohibition.

And many kinds of exaggeration need to be used, as in a case when someone has been the only one, or the first, to do something, or is one of few, or even has done it most, since these are all beautiful things. Also there is exaggeration based on times and occasions, and for that which may be beyond what the situation calls for. Also if someone has accomplished the same thing successfully many times, since this is a great thing and would seem not to be by luck but due to the person himself. Also, if things used as incentives and honors have been invented and devised on account of that person, as they were for Hippolochus, who was the first upon whom an encomium was made, and for Harmodius and Aristogeiton, to whom a monument was set up in the marketplace. And something similar may be done even in opposite cases; if you do not have enough that applies to the person himself, then compare him to others, which is exactly what Isocrates[57] used to do, because of his unfamiliarity with speaking in lawcourts. And one needs to compare someone with people of high repute, since that tends to augment him, and if he is better than people of serious stature, that is a beautiful thing. Exaggeration comes in reasonably in speeches of praise, since it has to do with preeminence, and preeminence is among the beautiful things; hence even when one cannot compare someone to people of high repute, one still ought to compare him to other people, since preeminence is thought to be an indication of virtue. And among the forms of speaking common to all speeches, exaggeration is always best suited to speeches for display, since they take up actions that are agreed about, so what remains is to adorn them with magnitude and beauty. Examples are best suited to advisory speeches, since we judge what is going to happen by making

57 Isocrates was an influential Athenian teacher of rhetoric who derived his style from that of Gorgias and his opinions from those of Socrates (see Plato's *Phaedrus* 278A-279B). He was a speechwriter but did not speak as an advocate in court himself. There is some discrepancy among the manuscripts as to whether Aristotle wrote "unfamiliarity" or "familiarity," but the former seems more likely since comparisons to enhance someone's reputation would be of little use in a courtroom but of great use in speeches of praise made for display on ceremonial occasions. Of the people mentioned in the previous sentence, Hippolochus is unknown apart from this reference, and Harmodius and Aristogeiton were Athenians regarded as political martyrs for killing the brother of the tyrant Hippias.

surmises based on what has happened before, and enthymemes are best suited to speeches in lawcourts, because what happened, since it is unclear, is especially open to causal and demonstrative reasoning.

So this is pretty much everything on the basis of which speeches of praise and blame are made, and the sorts of things to which one needs to look in praising and blaming, and the things from which encomiums and speeches of censure drawn. For when we've got these, the things opposite to them are obvious, and blame is based on those opposites.

Chapter 10.

The next thing to speak of would be what concerns accusation **1368b**
and defense, and how many and what sorts of premises there are on the basis of which one needs to make syllogisms. Now one needs to grasp three things: one is what and how many things people commit injustice for the sake of, a second is the sorts of dispositions of the people who commit it, and a third is the sorts of people they commit it upon and the conditions they are in. So after defining committing injustice, let us speak of them in order.

Let committing injustice be doing harm willingly contrary to law. And there is a particular law and a common law.[58] By particular, I mean the written law by which people are governed, and by common, all those unwritten laws that seem to be agreed to by everyone. And the things people do willingly are all those they do knowingly without being forced. Now the things people do knowingly are not all done by choice, but all things done by choice, they do knowingly, since no one is unaware of what he chooses.[59] The things on account of which people choose, contrary to law, to do harm and do base things are vice and lack of self-restraint. For if certain people have one or more faults of character,[60] they are also unjust in connection with that about which their characters happen to be at fault; for instance, a stingy person will be unjust about money, a dissipated one about pleasures of the body,

58 Aristotle is using the last phrase not in the sense it acquired in English legal tradition, which codified the ways custom had come to have the force of law, but as equivalent to the phrase "natural law," coined originally by Thomas Aquinas (*Summa Theologiae* I-II, Q. 91, A. 2; Q. 94). In the *Nicomachean Ethics*, Bk. V, Chap. 7, Aristotle calls the law that is common in this sense natural justice.

59 *Nicomachean Ethics* 1111b 6-10: "A choice is obviously something willing, but they are not the same thing, as what is willing covers a wider range, since children and the other animals share in willing acts but not in choice, and we speak of things done on the spur of the moment as willing acts, but not as things done as a result of choice."

60 Aristotle is here using the word *mochthêria* (usually a synonym for *kakia*, vice) to include both vice and lack of self-restraint. Someone with a vice has a bad character in that respect, having deliberately chosen to be that way, while an unrestrained person has a weak character, not wanting to act the way he does but having never exerted himself to form his character the opposite way. Aristotle heaps up the examples to show that any fault of character, however minor or however remote from injustice it may seem, makes someone treat others unjustly.

a person with a soft character about taking easy options, a coward about dangers (because they leave those who share the dangers with them in the lurch on account of their fear), an ambitious person will be unjust for the sake of honor, a sharp-tempered person from anger, a lover of victory for the sake of winning, a bitter person for revenge, a foolish person from being misguided about what is just and unjust, a shameless person from contempt for opinion, and similarly with each of the others about each of the underlying faults of character. But the things having to do with these matters are evident, some of them from what has been said about the virtues, and the rest from what will be said about passions. What remains to speak of is the purpose for which people commit injustice, the condition they are in, and who it is that they treat unjustly.

First, then, let us distinguish what and what sorts of things people are longing for and fleeing from when they turn their hands to committing injustice; for something that clearly needs to be considered by an accuser is how many and what sort, from among those things everyone aims at in committing injustice upon those around him, are present in his courtroom opponent, while the defendant needs to consider how many and what sort of them are not present. Now of all the actions all people perform, some are not their own doing and others are. Of those that are not their own doing, some are actions they perform by luck, and the rest are by necessity, and of those by necessity, some are by force and others by nature, so that all the actions people perform that are not their own doing are from luck, by force, 1369a or by nature. Those that are their own doing, and for which they are themselves responsible, are either from habit or from appetite, some of the latter from rational and others from irrational appetite. Wishing is an appetite for something good (since no one wishes for anything except when he believes it to be something good), while anger and desires are irrational appetites, so that there are necessarily seven causes through which people perform all the actions they perform: luck, nature, force, habit, reasoning, spiritedness, and desire. To break down actions further on the basis of age, states of character, or anything else would be overly fastidious; for if it incidentally belongs to young people to be prone to anger or full of desires, they act on such impulses not on account of their youth but on account of anger and desire. Nor is action caused by riches or poverty, but it is incidental to people who are poor to desire money because of their lack of it, and to those who are rich to desire unnecessary pleasures because they have the means to pay for them; but they too will act on account of desire rather than on account of riches and poverty. Similarly, the just and the unjust, and all the others who are said to be acting from their states of character, will act from the same causes, from either reasoning or passion, though the ones will be acting on account of favorable states of character and passion and the others from opposite states. It does, of course, turn out that the consequences that follow from the favorable states of character are of the same sort they are, and those that follow from the other kind are of their sort; for a temperate person, as an immediate consequence of being temperate, is accompanied by favorable opinions and desires about the things that are pleasant, while the opposite sort of opinions and desires about those same things equally accompany the self-indulgent person. Hence, while distinctions of these kinds need to be left aside, consideration needs to be given to what sorts of things are the usual consequences of what others; for if someone is pale or dark skinned, or tall or short, there is no fixed consequence that follows such things, but if someone is young or old, or just or unjust, that already makes a difference. And in all cases, consideration needs to be given to any incidental attributes that make a difference in the character of human beings; for instance, whether one seems to oneself to be rich or poor, or lucky or unlucky, will make some difference. We will speak of these things later,[61] then, but for now let us speak first about the remaining matters.

The sorts of things that happen by chance are those of which the cause is indefinite, that happen not for the sake of anything, neither always nor for the most part, and not in a regular pattern; what pertains to them is evident from the definition of chance. Things that happen by nature are those whose cause is within themselves and follows a regular pattern; for they always turn out the same way, or do so for the most part. As for the exceptions to the natural pattern, there is no need to go precisely into the question whether they happen in accord with nature or have some other cause, though it would seem that chance is responsible for this sort of thing too. Things that happen by force are those that are done contrary to their own desire or reasonings by the people who perform the actions. The things that are by habit are those that people do because of having done them many times. Things done by reasoning are those that seem, on the basis of the goods that have been mentioned, to be advantageous, either as ends or as means to an end, when they are done by reason of being advantageous; for even self-indulgent people do some advantageous things, though not because they are advantageous but for pleasure. Vengeful acts are committed out of spiritedness and anger; but revenge and discipline[62] are different things, since discipline is for the sake of the person who undergoes it, but revenge is for the sake of the person who inflicts it, to get satisfaction. What anger is will

61 Chapters 12-17 of Book II consider the ways various stages of life and advantages of birth and fortune influence the thinking of a speaker's audience.

62 The word is *kolasis,* used frequently in the *Gorgias* (as in 505B-C), where it is meant to point to the worthwhile kind of rhetoric Socrates himself practices, which is disciplinary (*kolastikos*) as opposed to the pandering (*kolakikos*) kind he accuses Gorgias and his followers of using.

become evident in the chapters that concern passions.[63] Those things that appear pleasant are done from desire; and what is familiar and habitual is included among pleasant things, for there are many things that are not pleasant by nature that people do with pleasure because they are accustomed to them.

So gathering together all the actions people perform by their own doing, one may say that they either are good or appear good, or else are pleasant or appear pleasant. And since people willingly perform those actions that are their own doing, but perform the actions that are not their own doing unwillingly, everything they do willingly would either be good or appear good, or else be pleasant or appear pleasant, since I am also counting getting rid of evils or apparent evils or exchanging a greater evil for a lesser among good things, because they are all preferable in one way or another, and likewise counting getting rid of pains or apparent pains or exchanging a greater pain for a lesser among pleasant things. Therefore it is the things that are advantageous and the things that are pleasant that need to be grasped, how many and of what sort they are. Now what is advantageous has been spoken of above,[64] among things pertaining to advisory speeches; let us now speak of what is pleasant. And on each subject, it is necessary to regard definitions that are neither unclear nor precisely correct as being at the right level.

Chapter 11.

Let it be adopted as our hypothesis that pleasure is a certain kind of motion of the soul, a sudden and perceptible resettling into its proper natural condition,[65] and that pain is the opposite. And if
1370a this is the sort of thing pleasure is, it is evident that something that produces the stated condition is pleasant too, while something that destroys that resettling, or produces its opposite, is painful. So it is necessary that going into a condition in accord with its nature is pleasant in most cases, and especially so whenever the things that go on as a result of that condition have been restored to their own natural state. Habits too are necessarily pleasant, because what is habitual becomes, at some point, just like something natural, since

63 Bk. II, Chap. 2.

64 In Chapter 6.

65 A sudden, rather than gradual, restoration of the soul's normal state is perceptible and is felt with pleasure. This is not what Aristotle believes pleasure is. The last sentence of the preceding chapter is a warning not to take it as a claim to truth, and this chapter begins by emphasizing that it is merely a hypothesis adopted for a particular purpose, namely to explore the apparent pleasures sought by people who commit crimes. In Book VII, Chapter 14, of the *Nicomachean Ethics*, Aristotle discusses the illusion involved in the belief that the only pleasures are strong, sudden returns from painful conditions. His own opinion is that pleasure is never a motion or change at all, but a steady awareness any animal has when its soul is at work, unimpeded, in the ways that fulfill its nature.

habit resembles nature; for something that happens often is close to something that happens always, and nature goes with "always" the way habit goes with "often."[66] What is unforced is also pleasant, since force is contrary to nature; this is why what is necessary is painful, and it has rightly been said,

> Everything that's a matter of necessity is naturally
> a nuisance.

Worries, exertions, and stresses are painful, because they are necessary and forced, unless they become habitual; if they do, habit makes them pleasant. And their opposites are pleasant, which is why taking it easy, freedom from work, freedom from worry, amusement, relaxation, and sleep are among pleasant things, since none of them has anything to do with necessity. And everything for which one has a desire in him is pleasant, since desire is an appetite for what is pleasant. Of desires, some are irrational, and others are combined with reason. I call irrational all the things people desire not as a result of making any assumption about them, and of this sort are all desires that are said to be natural, like those that are present on account of the body, such as the thirst and hunger for nourishment, the particular form of desire for each form of nourishment, desires related to tastes, to sexual activity, and to objects of touch in general, as well as to smell, hearing, and sight; and all the things people desire as a result of being persuaded are combined with reason, for people desire to see or acquire many things from hearing about them and being persuaded.

And since being pleased consists of perceiving a certain feeling, and imagination is a certain kind of weak perception, then some imagining of what a person remembers or anticipates would always be present as an accompaniment in someone who is remembering or hoping; and if this is the case, it is evident that there would also be pleasures for people at the same time that they are remembering and anticipating, since perception is present as well. So it is necessary that all pleasant things be either in the perceiving, as present, or in the remembering, as past, or in the anticipating, as future, since people perceive things that are present, remember things that are past, and anticipate things in the future. So memories are pleasant, and not only 1370b
those of things that were pleasant at the time when they were present, but even some of things that were not pleasant, if, later, what came after them was beautiful or good. And it is out of this experience that the following things[67] were said:

---

66 Aristotle never says what was later sometimes attributed to him, that habit is "a second nature." In the *Nicomachean Ethics* (1152a 32-33) he quotes lines from Evenus of Paros (also the author of the line about matters of necessity just below) that say that habit ends up being the nature of human beings.

67 The first, from Euripides' lost play *Andromeda*; the second *Odyssey* XV, 400-401, slightly misquoted.

> But it is truly pleasant to remember troubles after one is saved from them,

and,

> Afterward, a man takes delight even in his sorrows,
> Remembering, he who has suffered and done many things.

The reason for this is that not having an evil is also pleasant; so are all those things in our anticipations that appear to give enjoyment or benefit in a big way when present, and to give the benefit without pain. In general, those things that give enjoyment when present are, for the most part, pleasant both when anticipated and when remembered. This is why even being angry is pleasant, as Homer too wrote about spirited anger,[68]

> Which is sweeter by far than dripping honey,

for no one gets angry at anyone who appears to be out of his power to get revenge on; at those who are far above them in power, people either get less angry or do not get angry at all.

A certain pleasure goes along too with most desires, for people enjoy a certain feeling of pleasure either in remembering that they have attained it or in hoping that they will attain it; for example, people afflicted with thirst during fevers get enjoyment from remembering times that they were drinking and from anticipating drinking again, and people in love get enjoyment from talking about, writing about, and constantly doing something having to do with the one they love, because when they are recollecting the beloved in all such things they feel like they are having the perception. This is where the beginning of love comes from for everyone, when they not only delight in the person when present, but also when absent, though remembering also brings them pain at not being with him;[69] but even in grief and mourning a certain pleasure comes into it, for while there is pain over his not being present, there is a pleasure in remembering and somehow seeing the person and what he did and what he was like. And for that reason it was reasonable to say this,[70]

> He spoke in that way, and moved them all to a yearning for crying.

Getting revenge is pleasant too, for anything it is painful not to attain is pleasant to attain, and when people who are angry do not get revenge they feel a pain of unsurpassable intensity, but they take joy in anticipating it. Winning is also pleasant, not only for people

68 *Iliad* XVIII, 109.

69 The preceding clauses are a bit scrambled in the manuscripts, but the thought is roughly clear; on the gender of some of the pronouns, see the note to *Gorgias* 481D.

70 *Iliad* XXIII, 108 and *Odyssey* IV, 183.

who love victory but for everyone, because an imagination of superior excellence comes with it, and everyone has a desire for that, either mildly or intensely. And since winning is pleasant, there is necessarily also pleasure in forms of play that are combative or argumentative 1371a
(since there is a lot of winning in them), as well as in games of dice, ball, gambling in general, or checkers. And it is similar with serious sports, since some become pleasant once someone is experienced in them, while others are pleasant right away, such as the chase and hunting of every sort, because wherever there is striving there is also winning. Hence too, arguing in court and competitive debating are pleasant for people who have experience and ability. Honor and good reputation are among the most pleasant things, because they make everyone imagine that he is the sort of person who has serious stature, and more so when he believes the people who say so are telling the truth. People of this sort would be neighbors rather than people far away, fellow citizens familiar with them rather than people from somewhere else, contemporaries rather than posterity, sensible people rather than fools, and numerous people rather than few; for those mentioned are more likely to be telling the truth than their opposites, since with people for whom one has a very low opinion, as one would for children and animals, one does not care about their honor or one's reputation with them at all, not for the sake of the reputation anyway, but if at all, for some other reason.

A friend is also included among pleasant things, since feeling love is pleasant (for no one would be a wine lover if he did not get enjoyment from wine) and being loved is pleasant too. For there is an imagining involved in that experience that something good is present in oneself that everyone who perceives it desires; and to be loved is to have affection shown toward oneself for one's own sake. And being admired is pleasant for the sheer honor of it. Even to be pandered[71] to by a flatterer is pleasant, since a flatterer is in appearance an admirer, and in appearance a friend. And doing the same things often is pleasant because what one is accustomed to is always pleasant; to change is pleasant too, because changing happens in the course of nature, since to have the same thing going on all the time makes for an excess of the established condition, which is why it was said,[72]

> Change in all things is sweet.

And for this reason people and things that turn up after some time are pleasing, since that is a change from the present, and at the same time what turns up after some time is rare. Learning and being in a state of wonder are pleasant for the most part, for in wondering

71 This is the word Socrates uses in the *Gorgias*, starting at 463A-B, for the usual practice of rhetoricians.

72 In Euripides' *Orestes*, line 234.

there is a desire to learn, so that the thing wondered at is desired, and in learning there is a settling into our natural state.[73] To do good and to have good done to one are both among pleasant things; having
1371b good done to them is an attaining of things people desire, and doing good is having a superior position, both of which are things people long for. And because anything that tends to do good is pleasant, it is also pleasant for people to help their neighbors get back on their feet and make up for the things they lack. And since it is pleasant to learn and to be in a state of wonder, whatever is associated with that is necessarily pleasant as well, such as a work of the imitative arts like painting, sculpture, and poetry; and anything that is skillfully imitated is pleasant, even if the thing imitated itself happens to be unpleasant, since that is not the thing one gets enjoyment from, but rather the inference that this image is that thing, so that one ends up learning something. Sudden reversals and narrow escapes from dangers are also pleasant, because they are all sources of wonder. And since anything in accord with nature is pleasant, and things that are akin are related to each other in accord with nature, all things that have a kinship and likeness are for the most part pleasant, such as one human being to another, one horse to another, and one young person to another. This is where the proverbial sayings come from: "agemate delights agemate," "always the like," "beast knows beast," "birds of a feather," and everything else of that sort.

And since everything that is like and akin to oneself is pleasant, and each person himself bears this relation to himself most of all, everyone is necessarily a lover of self to a greater or lesser extent, because all such conditions are present in relation to oneself most of all. And since all people are lovers of self, the things that are their own are necessarily pleasant to everyone, such as their deeds and words, and this is why people for the most part have a love for flattery, for those who are in love with them, for honor, and for their children, since their children are their own work. And completing anything that is lacking is pleasant because that comes from their own work. And since it is most pleasant to be in authority, it is also pleasant to be thought to be wise, since having good judgment contributes to exercising authority, and wisdom is a knowledge of many wondrous things. Also, since people are for the most part lovers of honor, it is necessarily also pleasant to be disapproving of their neighbors, and to be in authority over them, and to spend one's time in that in which one is thought to be at one's best; as the poet[74] too says, he presses on to that,

73 *Physics* 247b 17-248a 3: "It is by the settling down of the soul out of its native confusion that it comes to be something with intelligence and knowledge...For some it is settled and calmed down by nature itself, for others by other people."

74 The poet is Euripides; the lines are a slight variation from some quoted by Callicles in the *Gorgias*. See 484E and note.

Giving it the greatest part of each day,
So that he succeeds at being his best.

Similarly, since amusement and every form of relaxation are among pleasant things, laughter is also among pleasant things, and the things one laughs at are necessarily pleasant too, whether people or words 1372a
or deeds. Distinctions about the things one laughs at are made elsewhere, in the *Poetics*.[75] So let these things have been said about the things that are pleasant, and the things that are painful are obviously their opposites.

Chapter 12.

Those are the things for the sake of which people commit injustice; let us now say what condition they are in when they commit it, and who their victims are. They commit it when they believe it is possible for the thing to be done and in their own power to do it, if they believe they can go undetected in the action, or if not undetected not pay the just penalty, or pay it but have the penalty be less than the gain to themselves or to those they care about. Now the sorts of things that appear possible and impossible will be stated in what comes later,[76] since they apply in common to all speeches, but those who most of all believe it to be in their power to commit injustice without penalty are people who have ability at speaking, have practical skill, have experience in various conflicts, if they also have a lot of friends and are rich. They believe they have this power most of all if they themselves are in the classes of people mentioned, but failing that, also when they have friends or servants or partners of those sorts belonging to them, since by these means it is possible for them to act, go undetected, and not pay the just penalty. Also, if they are friends of those who suffer the injustice or of the judges, since friends are not on guard against being treated unjustly, and also seek to reconcile rather than prosecute, while judges are indulgent with people who are their friends, and either let them off completely or give them small penalties.

People apt to go undetected are those who are the opposite of the things complained of, for instance a weak person in a case of assault, someone poor and ugly in a case of adultery. Also apt to go undetected are things right out in the open under people's eyes, since they are not guarded against because no one would expect them at all. Also things so great and of such a sort that not a single person would expect them, since these are not guarded against either, because everyone takes precautions against the usual things, as with illnesses; with injustices too, what no one has ever been afflicted with, no one takes precautions

75 At 1448b 36-38 and 1449a 32-37, the subject matter of comedy is distinguished from ridicule of particular people known to the audience and from debased or ugly things that would cause pain to any audience.

76 Bk. II, Chap. 19.

against. Also people who have no enemy or many of them; the one sort believe they will go undetected because of not being watched for, and the other sort go undetected because it does not seem they would attempt anything with many watching for them, and because they have the defense that they would not have undertaken it. And people who have either means or places for concealing things, or are well supplied with ways to dispose of things.

For those who do not go undetected, people commit injustice because there is a possibility of avoiding a trial, or putting off the time of it, or corrupting the judges. And for those who get a fine, there is a possibility of avoiding payment in full or putting off the time; or it is possible that, from a lack of means, one has nothing to lose. And there are those for whom the gains are obvious or large or
1372b near at hand, while the penalties are small or not apparent or far off. There is also injustice for which there is no punishment equal to the benefit, as is thought to be the case with tyranny. And there are those for whom the injustices are profits in hand, while the penalties consist only in disgrace. And there are those for whom on the contrary the injustices lead to something praiseworthy; for instance, if it turns out at the same time that one gets revenge for a father or mother, as Zeno did, while the penalties involve money or exile or something of that sort. People commit injustice for both reasons and in both conditions, even though they are not the same but opposite in their characters.[77] And people commit injustice if they have often gone undetected or not been penalized, or if they have often failed to achieve it (for in such circumstances too, just as in those of war, there are some people of the sort who keep going back into the fight). Also, those for whom something pleasant, or some gain, is right at hand, while the pain or the penalty comes later; people who lack self-restraint are like that, and a lack of restraint can be present toward all the things people desire. Also those for whom, on the contrary, something painful or the penalty is there right away, while the pleasure or benefit comes later and is more lasting; people who are self-restrained and have better judgment pursue things of that sort.[78] And some because it is possible for them to seem to have acted as a result of chance, or necessity, or nature, or habit, and generally to have made a mistake instead

77 Aristotle distinguishes between an unjust act and an unjust person (*Nicomachean Ethics* 1134a 17). His example here, and the Zeno he refers to, are unknown, but presumably his meaning is that the revenge itself is a beautiful and decent thing but involves injustice of a lesser sort. See the notes to 1367a 20 above and 1372b 18 below for references to Aristotle's distinction between two kinds of justice.

78 Some translations suggest wrongly that Aristotle is speaking of people with some degree of temperance or wisdom, but he is referring to those who have not formed the virtues of character that would permit them to make good choices, but have enough sense and self-control to make bad ones for long-term pleasures or gains. Their characters are weak rather than bad or vicious, but not so weak that they can never resist something they desire when it is at hand.

of committing an injustice. And some because it might be possible to get a lenient judge.[79] Also some because they are in need, but people are in need in two senses, either in need of something necessary, as the poor are, or in need of something excessive, as the rich are. And some commit injustice because they are extremely well thought of or extremely badly thought of, the one sort because they would not be thought to have done it, the other sort because they would not be thought of any the worse for it.

So those who put their hands to unjust acts are in these conditions, and those they commit them against, and in what sorts of ways, are the following: those who have what they need, either for necessities, for excess, or for enjoyment, both far away and near them, for from the latter the taking is quick and from the former the revenge is slow, as it would be for people who plunder the Carthaginians. And those who are not careful or watchful but trusting, since all such people are easy to take things from. And people who are easygoing, because it takes a diligent person to bring a prosecution. And people who are shy, since they are not apt to be belligerent about matters of gain. And people who have had injustice done to them by many and not prosecuted them, since these are the proverbial Mysian pickings.[80] And those who have never or often had injustice done to them, since both sorts are off their guard, the one sort thinking it would never happen, the others that it would not happen again. And those who have been slandered, or who are easy to slander, because such people either do not choose to prosecute, for fear of the judges, or cannot persuade them, being so disliked and resented. And those toward whom people have the excuse that their ancestors or they themselves 1373a
or their friends either did harm or meant to, either to them or to their ancestors or loved ones, since as the proverb says, an excuse is the only thing wrongdoing needs. And both their enemies and their friends, since it is easy to do so to the latter and pleasant to the former. And those with no friends, and those who are not skilled at speaking or at action, since they either make no attempt to prosecute, or reconcile, or accomplish nothing. And those for whom it is unprofitable to waste their time looking out for a judgment or payment, such as foreigners or people who have to work for a living, since they settle for a small amount and are easily make to drop the prosecution. And those who have committed many injustices themselves, or injustices of the same sort that are done to them, since it seems pretty close to being a case where no injustice is done when someone suffers some injustice of the same sort that he too was in the habit of committing; I mean, for example, if someone were to assault a person who habitually treated

79 "A lenient judge" translates *ho epieikês*, a decent person, in the sense described in Bk. V, Chap. 10, of the *Nicomachean Ethics*, one who does not insist on a justice involving rigid rules but looks to what is best in the totality of circumstances.

80 Like taking candy from a baby; see note to *Gorgias* 521B.

others with humiliating violence.[81] And those who either have done harm to them, or have wanted to, or want to, or are going to do so, since there is something both pleasant and beautiful about it, and it appears pretty close to doing no injustice. And those whose suffering would please one's friends or people one admires or is in love with, or one's bosses, or generally the people one's life revolves around. And those in whose case there is a chance of getting leniency.[82] And those whom one has prosecuted or had previous rifts with, the way Callippus did in affair of Dion,[83] since such cases too appear pretty close to doing no injustice. And those who are about to suffer injustice from others if one does not commit it oneself, since there is no more time to deliberate; this is the reason it is said that Aenesidemus sent the cottabus[84] prize to Gelon, who had just enslaved a city, since the latter had got in first on what he himself was intending. And those by committing injustice to whom, one will be enabled to perform many just actions, on the grounds that the injustice is easily cured, the way Jason the Thessalian said he had to commit some injustices so he could also do many just things.[85]

People commit the injustices that all or many others are in the habit of committing, since they believe they will get forgiveness. And they commit thefts that are easy to conceal, such as thefts of things that are quickly used up like edible things, or of things easily changed in shape or color or mixture, or things easy to get out of sight in many places, such as portable things that can be tucked away in small spaces. Also, they take things that the one stealing them already has many things similar to and indistinguishable from. And they commit injustices that the sufferers would be ashamed to speak of, such as violations of the women in their households, or on themselves or their sons. And those in which someone who prosecuted them would seem too fond of lawsuits, such as minor offenses and those for which there is forgiveness. These, then, are pretty much the conditions people are in when they commit injustices, the sorts they commit, the sorts of people they commit them upon, and the reasons they commit them.

81 The last phrase translates the verb meaning to commit *hubris*. In Athenian law it was regarded as a much more serious crime than simple assault, and could be a capital offense. In Bk. II, Chap. 2, below (1378b 23-25), Aristotle defines it as causing injury and pain in a way that disgraces the other person, not for revenge but for the mere pleasure of cruelty.

82 See 1372b 18-19 and note. Here, Aristotle is apparently thinking of people who would overlook the injustice done to themselves.

83 Callippus was involved in the assassination of Dion, of Syracuse in Sicily, and argued in his defense that Dion would have killed him if he had not acted first.

84 A Sicilian game played at drinking parties; both men were tyrants of Sicilian cities.

85 The reader is reminded that the reasoning is that of those who commit crimes. The Jason cited as the source of this omelet-without-breaking-eggs argument is another tyrant.

Chapter 13.

Let us divide up all unjust and just acts, starting first from the following point. 1373b The things that are just are distinguished in relation to two kinds of law and also in relation to people understood in two ways. I mean that there is a particular law and a common law: particular law is that determined by each group of people for themselves, and this is either unwritten or written, and common law is that which comes from nature.[86] For there is something that all people have a notion of as naturally just and unjust, even if there is no unanimity or agreement among them, and it is such a thing that Sophocles' Antigone is obviously speaking of in saying that it is a just thing, though forbidden, to bury Polyneices, since that is just by nature:

> For this is not something of today or yesterday, but for
> ever and ever
> It has its life, and no one knows where it came to light.

This is also the sense in which Empedocles speaks about not slaughtering anything with the breath of life in it, because it is not that this is just for some people and not just for others,

> But what is lawful for everyone under the wide watchful
> Sky stretches unbroken through the boundless light of day,

and the sense in which Alcidamas says in the *Messeniacus* "the god has left everyone free; nature has made no one a slave."[87] And there is a twofold distinction as regards people, since the things one ought to do and not do are defined in relation to the community or against one of those in the community. Hence unjust and just actions consist in committing injustice or doing justice in two ways, either to one definite person or to the community. Someone who commits adultery or assault is doing injustice to some definite person, but someone who does not serve in the army is doing injustice to the community.

Now that all acts of injustice have been divided up, some being against the community and some against another person or persons, let us go back again to what it is to suffer injustice[88] and speak of that. Now to suffer injustice is to have unjust things done to one by someone who acts willingly, for committing injustice was defined before as a willing act. And since necessarily the person suffering the injustice is

86 See the note to 1368b 7. Aristotle begins there with the broad distinction between written and unwritten laws, but adds a bit more precision here by noting that particular laws can also be unwritten. This is not an inconsistency, as some have thought.

87 The lines from *Antigone* are 456-457. Those from Empedocles are a fragment from *Purifications*, one of his two long philosophic poems. Alcidamas is said to have been a pupil of Gorgias; the words quoted are missing from the manuscripts, but are incorporated in the text by Ross from another source. The Messenians praised in his speech regained their freedom after three centuries of slavery as Spartan helots.

88 See 1368b 6-7.

harmed and suffers harm done willingly, the kinds of harm are evident from the things said earlier, for the things that are good and bad in their own right were stated above, and it was stated that willing acts are those done by people who know what they are doing; so it is necessary that all accusations are concerned with either the community or a private person, and are made against one who was either ignorant and unwilling or willing and knew what he was doing, and in the latter case either from choice or on account of passion. What has to do with spiritedness will be spoken of in the chapters on the passions; what sorts of actions are performed by choice, and the conditions people are in when they perform them, were stated above.

1374a But since often people admit to having carried out an action but disagree with either the indictment or what the indictment is for, agreeing, for example, to having taken something but not to having stolen it, or to having hit someone first but not to having used outrageous violence, or to having had sex with someone but not to having seduced her, or to having stolen something but not to having committed sacrilege (since it was not something dedicated to a god), or to have used land they did not own but not public land, or to having had discussions with the enemy but not to having committed treason—for these reasons it will be necessary to give definitions of these things as well, of what theft, violent outrage, and adultery are, so that if we want to show that they do or do not apply, we will be able to make clear what is just. In all such cases, the dispute is over whether someone is unjust and hence depraved or not unjust, because depravity and the committing of injustice are present in the choice, and such words as violent outrage and theft have an implied reference to intentional choice. For if one hits someone, he does not in all instances commit a violent outrage, but only if it is for the sake of something such as shaming the other person or giving himself pleasure. And if one takes something secretly, he does not in all instances commit theft, but only if it is to someone's harm and to appropriate it for himself. And in the rest of the cases as well, things are similar to the way they are in these.

And since there were two forms of just and unjust things (some with respect to written, others to unwritten laws), those which the laws proclaim have been discussed, but there are two forms of the unwritten ones. One sort are things that involve a surpassing of virtue or vice, and for them there are reproaches or praises and expressions of dishonor or honor, and awards (for example, for having gratitude to someone who has done you a favor, for doing a favor in return to someone who has done one, for being quick to come to the help of one's friends, and whatever else is of that sort), and the other are things left out of the law that is particular and written. For the decent thing seems to be just, and a decent thing is something just that goes beyond the written law. This sort of thing happens in some cases willingly, in

others unwillingly, on the part of the lawmakers, unwillingly when it escapes their notice, and willingly when they are not able to make a distinction but are under the necessity to speak in universal terms about something that is not universal but is the case for the most part, and about those things that are not easy to distinguish owing to the limitlessness of cases; an example is how big and what sort of iron implement does bodily harm, since a lifetime would leave one still counting them up. So if that is indeterminate, but there is a need to make a law, it is necessary to speak in simple terms, and thus if someone who has on a ring lifts his hand[89] or hits anyone, by the written law he is subject to punishment and commits an injustice, but by the 1374b
truth of the matter he does not commit an injustice, and that is the decent thing to decide.

And if the decent thing is what has been said, it is clear what sorts of things are and are not decent, and what sorts of people are not decent, because when there are things for which one ought to make allowances, that is the decent thing to do, and not to consider mistakes and injustices worthy of the same punishment, or even mistakes and misfortunes. Misfortunes are unforeseeable and do not come from faults of character, mistakes are not unforeseeable and not from badness,[90] and injustices are not unforeseeable and are from badness. It is a decent thing to make allowances for human failings, and to look not to the law but to the lawmaker, and not to the word but to the thought of the lawmaker, not to the action but to the intention, not to the part but to the whole, and to consider not the sort of person someone is at a moment but the sort of person someone always was and is for the most part. And it is a decent thing to remember the good things done to one more than the bad, and the good things done to one more than the good things one has done, and to put up with receiving injustice, and to be willing to resolve matters by word rather than by deed, and want to go to arbitration rather than to a trial; for the arbitrator looks at what is decent, but the judge looks at the law, and the arbitrator was devised for that reason, so that the decent thing may prevail. Let what concerns things that are decent be marked out in this way.

89 Even without striking a blow, one could be considered guilty of assault with a deadly weapon. There was a recent instance in which a child was suspended from school for having a key-ring ornament in the shape of a gun.

90 The middle category is the interesting one. The translation assumes that Aristotle is using the word *mochthêria* the way he did at 1368b 14 (see note there), for both badness and weakness, and shifts to *ponêria* to refer to bad character alone. Hence a mistake (*hamartêma*) is either a failure of knowledge in a good person (as in tragedy) or a failure to resist temptation in a weak person. The decent person would have to judge first the character of the accused and then the degree of temptation before excusing an action. The translation departs from Ross's edition in dropping a clause from the end of this sentence that is not in all the sources, and that seems to violate the distinctions the sentence lays out.

Chapter 14.

Unjust acts are greater to the degree the injustice they come from is greater; that is why the slightest things can be the greatest injustices, as in the accusation Callistratus made against Melanopus, that he shortchanged the temple builders by three half-pennies of a dedicated offering. The case of justice is the other way around. These things are so as a result of what is present in potency, because someone who has embezzled three dedicated half-pennies would also commit any injustice whatever. So the greater injustice is sometimes judged in this way, but sometimes from the harm done. And an unjust act is greater for which there is no equivalent penalty, but all penalties are too little, and so is one for which there is no cure, since it is difficult or even impossible to deal with, and one for which it is not possible for the one who suffered it to obtain a legal penalty, for it is incurable since a legal penalty is both a disciplinary measure and a cure. An unjust act is also greater if the one who suffered and had the injustice done to him punished himself greatly, since it is just for the one who committed it to be punished with something even greater; for instance Sophocles,[91] when he was speaking as an advocate on behalf of Euctemon, who had cut his own throat after he had suffered a violent outrage, said he would not set a lesser penalty than the one the victim had set on himself. An unjust act is greater if someone has been the only one to commit it, or the first, or is among few who have done so. And making the same mistake over and over is a great offense. So is anything on account of which preventive and punitive measures are sought and devised; in Argos, for instance, one on whose account a law is passed is punished, as well as people on whose account a prison is built.[92]

And the more brutal an unjust act is, the greater it is. So is one that results from more premeditation. Also one that makes people who hear of it feel more fear and pity. And the rhetorical means of showing this are of this sort: that someone has reneged on or violated many commitments, such as oaths, pledges, assurances, and marriage vows, since that is an overload of multiple acts of injustice. And an act of injustice is greater when committed in the place in which those who commit injustice are given their punishments, which is the very thing perjurers do; where would they not commit injustice, if they do so even in the lawcourt? And acts of injustice are greater for which the disgrace is greatest; and they are greater if they are committed against that person by whom one was benefited, since he does more than one injustice, because he does harm and also fails to do good. And acts of injustice that go against the unwritten standards of justice are greater, since it is the mark of a better person to be just without

91 Probably not the poet, but a political figure mentioned also at 1419a 26.

92 This seems to mean that Argos imposed an extra punishment for causing the trouble and expense of providing for punishing the original crime.

compulsion, and the written laws are enforced by compulsion, while the unwritten ones are not. But in a different way, acts of injustice are greater if they go against the written laws, since anyone who commits injustice in matters subject to fear and penalties would also commit injustices not subject to penalties. So what has to do with greater and lesser injustice has been stated.

Chapter 15.

The next thing is to run through the so-called inartful means of persuasion that were mentioned,[93] for these belong to courtroom speeches in particular. They are five in number: laws, witnesses, written agreements, evidence obtained by torture, and oaths. Let us speak about laws first, then, and how they need to be used both in exhorting and warning and in accusing and defending. For it is clear that, if the written law is opposed to the fact, use needs to be made of the common law and of what is more decent and more just, because "in one's best judgment"[94] means not to use the written law exclusively, and because what is decent always endures and never changes, any more than the common law does, since it comes from nature, while the written laws change frequently. This is where the things said in Sophocles' *Antigone* come from,[95] for she defends herself on the grounds that she carried out the burial contrary to Creon's law but not contrary to the unwritten law, 1375b

> For this is not something of today or yesterday but for
> ever and ever...
> And I was not about to pay that penalty because of
> any man...

Also it may be argued that what is just is true and advantageous, but what seems just is not, so that what is written is not law, since it does not do the job of the law. And that the judge is like an assayer of silver, to distinguish between counterfeit and true justice. And that it is the mark of a better man to use and stand by the unwritten laws rather than the written ones. And if a law anywhere is opposed to a well-regarded law, or even to itself, as for instance one law sometimes demands that whatever is contractually agreed upon is binding while another forbids making a contract contrary to the law, or if a law is ambiguous, then one may turn it and see which way of taking it fits what is just or advantageous and then use that. And if the facts on the basis of which the law was enacted are no longer in effect, but the law is, an attempt needs to be made to make this clear and to do battle against the law on this point. But if the written law

93 See 1355b 35-39.

94 A phrase in the oath taken by Athenian juror-judges.

95 Line 456, quoted above at 1373b 12, is here followed by 478.

is in accord with the fact, what needs to be said is that "in one's best judgment" is not for the sake of deciding contrary to the law, but so that one may not be in violation of the oath if he is ignorant of what the law means. Also that no one chooses what is good simply, but what is good for himself. Also that not using a law is no different from not establishing it. Also that in the other arts, there is nothing to be gained by "outsmarting the doctor," since the doctor's mistake does not do as much harm as getting in the habit of disobeying the one in authority, and that looking for ways to be wiser than the laws is just what is forbidden in the laws that are praised. Let distinctions about the laws be made in this way.

As for witnesses, witnesses are of two sorts, ancient and recent, and among the latter, some are in jeopardy along with the one accused and others outside it. By ancient witnesses I mean poets and all other notable people whose judgments are well-known. The Athenians, for instance, used Homer as a witness concerning Salamis, and the people of Tenedos just recently used Periander of Corinth against those of Sigeum.[96] Cleophon also used the elegies of Solon against Critias, saying that his family had been out of control from of old, for otherwise Solon would never have composed the line

> Do me a favor and tell red-haired Critias to obey his father.

1376a So people of this sort are witnesses concerning things of the past, but those who interpret oracles are witnesses concerning future things—Themistocles, for example, invoking the "wooden wall" to say a naval battle had to be fought.[97] And also proverbs, like those mentioned,[98] are testimony; for instance, if someone is giving advice against making a friend of an old man, a proverb bears witness to this,

> Never do a favor to an old man,

or to killing the sons whose fathers had also been killed,

> Thoughtless as a child is he who leaves alive the sons
> of fathers slain.

---

96 In the catalogue of ships in Bk. II of the *Iliad* (lines 557-558), Homer had linked Salamis with the Athenians, and Athenian representatives appealed to this centuries later to win a territorial claim over the Megarians. Periander of Corinth had arbitrated a dispute over Sigeum (in Asia minor) about two hundred years before Aristotle's time, but the later event is unknown.

97 When two oracles from Delphi had predicted disaster for the Athenians, Themistocles restored their morale, and advanced his project to make them a naval power, by declaring that ships would be the unbroken wooden wall that would be their only protection. Herodotus tells the story in his *History*, VII, 140-144.

98 Aristotle has appealed to a few himself, in Chapters 10-12 above. The second one cited below is attributed to Stasinus, an early poet. One of the most famous remarks in Machiavelli's *The Prince* (Ch. 17) goes Stasinus one better: "men sooner forget the deaths of their fathers than the loss of their patrimony."

Recent witnesses are those notable people who have made judgments about anything, since their judgments are useful to those engaged in a dispute about the same matters; for example, Euboulus, in the lawcourts, used against Chares what Plato had said to Archibius, that to admit to being depraved had become common in the city. Recent witnesses also include those who would be in jeopardy along with the accused if they seemed to be lying. Such people are witnesses only to these things: whether something happened or not, and whether something is the case or not. As to what sort of thing it is, such as just or unjust, advantageous or disadvantageous, they are not witnesses at all; outsiders are more credible about those things, and ancient witnesses are the most credible, since they cannot be corrupted. As corroborations of testimony for someone who has no witnesses, what is to be said is that one should judge on the basis of likelihoods, that this is the meaning of "in one's best judgment," that it is not possible for likelihoods to engage in deception for money, and that likelihoods are not convicted for false testimony; for one who has witnesses, what is to be said against someone who does not is that likelihoods are not subject to legal action, and that there would be no need of witnesses if it was sufficient to look at things on the basis of arguments.

Some witnesses have to do with oneself, others with the other party to the dispute, and some have to do with the fact, others with the person's character, so it is obvious that it is never possible to be at a loss for a useful witness; for if there is no witness to the fact, either in agreement with oneself or in opposition to one's adversary, there are still character witnesses, either to one's own decency or to one's adversary's baseness. The other things relating to a witness, whether he is a friend, an enemy, or in-between, whether he has a good reputation, a bad reputation, or one in-between, and all the other distinctions of that kind are to be argued on the basis of the exact same sorts of topics from which we also make enthymemes.

About written agreements, there is a use for arguments to the extent of magnifying their importance or knocking them down, to make them either credible or without credibility—credible and bind- 1376b
ing if they work to one's advantage, and the opposite if the advantage belongs to the other party to the dispute. For making them credible or without credibility, there is no difference from the way of proceeding with witnesses, since written agreements are credible as a reflection of what sorts of people they are who sign them and keep them. When it is admitted that there is a written agreement, if it is on one's side it needs to be magnified in importance, since an agreement is a private and particular law, and while agreements do not make a law binding, the laws make agreements in accord with the law binding; in general, the law itself is a kind of agreement, so anyone who fails to credit an agreement or nullifies it is nullifying the laws. Also, most of our willing transactions are carried out in accordance with agreements,

so if these become nonbinding, the usefulness of human beings to one another is destroyed. The other arguments that fit the situation are there to be seen on the face of it.

But if the agreement is opposed to one's side and with the other party to the dispute, then in the first place, those same things fit the situation that would if one were fighting against an opposing law, for when we believed one ought not to obey the laws if they are not rightly laid down and those who made them were in error, it would be absurd to say it is necessary to obey agreements. Then too, what is to be said is that the judge is the arbiter of justice, so it is not what was agreed that needs to be looked into, but what is more just, and what is just is not something that can be twisted out of shape by fraud or compulsion (since it is natural), but agreements are affected by both fraud and compulsion. In addition to these things, one needs to consider whether the agreement is opposed to any of the written or common laws, and among the written ones, either one's own or foreign laws, and then whether it is opposed to other later or earlier agreements, since it may be that the later ones are binding and the earlier ones not, or that the earlier ones are rightful and the later ones were tainted by fraud, whichever way might be useful. One needs to look also at what is advantageous, in case the agreement is opposed to the judges[99] in any point, and any other such issues, since these are similarly easy to see.

Evidence given under torture is one sort of testimony, and it seems to have credibility because a certain compulsion is attached to it. So it is not difficult to see what it is possible to say about these matters, by which to magnify their importance when they are to one's advantage,
1377a to the effect that these are the only truthful witnesses; and when they are opposed and with the other party to the dispute, one may undo their effect by stating what is true about the class of evidence given under torture as a whole, that people under duress tell lies no less than truths, both those who stand up under it to avoid telling the truth and those who make false allegations readily to put an end to it more quickly. One ought to have examples to bring up of things that have happened in such cases that the judges know about. (And one ought to say that testimonies given under torture are not true. For many thick-headed and tough-skinned people who are also strong in soul hold out nobly against force, while others who are cowardly

99 There is a modern example of an American university that was originally endowed to offer free education to white males. Its founder's will was voided by the courts on all these points without any specific laws to the contrary, when its terms became disadvantageous financially and against public policy.

and timid nerve themselves up before seeing any force, so that there is nothing credible in evidence given under torture.)[100]

Concerning oaths,[101] there are four possibilities to distinguish: one either proffers an oath and takes one, or does neither, or does one and not the other, and in this case either proffers an oath but does not take one, or takes one but does not proffer one. In another sense there is a case in addition to these, if this oath has already been sworn by oneself or by the other party.

If someone does not proffer an oath, he may say that people easily swear falsely, and that someone who has sworn an oath does not make restitution, but he assumes that people will condemn those who have not sworn one, and that this risk, the one involving the jurors, is the better one to take, since he trusts them and not the other person. If he does not take a proffered oath, he may say that an oath is a substitute for money, and that if he were dishonest he would have sworn it, since it's better to be dishonest for some profit rather than none, and he'd get a profit from having sworn but none from not having sworn; so his not having sworn would be due to virtue rather than to avoid perjury. And Xenophanes' remark fits the situation, because "this is no fair challenge, from an impious person to a pious one"; it's as if a strong man were to be challenged to hit a weak man or not hit him. But if he takes the oath, he may say that he trusts himself but not the other person. What he needs to declare, by turning Xenophanes' remark around, is that this is the way for it to *be* fair, if the impious man proffers the oath and the pious one swears it, and that it would be a terrible thing not to be willing to swear an oath himself on matters on which he considers it right for others to swear one in order to be judges. If he proffers an oath, he may say that it is a pious thing to be willing to turn the matter over to the gods, and that his opponent ought not to need any other judges since he is giving the decision over to them, and that it is absurd to be unwilling to swear an oath about matters on which he considers it right for others to swear.

And since it is evident how the argument needs to be made in each particular case, it is also evident how it needs to be made when they are linked in pairs, such as when one is willing to take an oath himself but not proffer one, or if he proffers one but is not willing to
take one, or if he is willing to take one and to proffer one, or not will- 1377b
ing to do either. Since by necessity the situations are a combination

100 The sentences in parenthesis are missing from most manuscripts but present in an otherwise reliable one. They are accepted as genuine by Ross, but generally considered to be a later addition to the text. Torture was routinely used to make slaves testify against their owners.

101 Before a case came to trial, either party could call upon the other to take an oath. The challenger proffered both the words of the oath and the divine witness by whom the other party was to swear. This practice had an effect similar to our lie-detector tests; it could lead to an out-of-court settlement, or its results could be used at trial for or against either party.

of the cases mentioned, the arguments too must be a combination of those mentioned. And if there has already been a contradictory oath sworn by himself, an argument may be made that this was not perjury; for committing an injustice is a willing act and to perjure oneself is to commit an injustice, but acts resulting from force or fraud are unwilling. In this case, then, the conclusion must be drawn that committing perjury is also something in one's thinking and not in one's mouth. But if there was a contradictory oath sworn to by one's opponent, one may argue that someone who does not stand by things he has sworn to makes everything null and void, and it is for this reason that those who apply the laws have taken oaths: "They think it right for all of you to stand by the oaths you've sworn when you judge them, when they themselves do not stand by theirs," and whatever else one might say to make a bigger point of it. So let this much be said about the inartful means of persuasion.

BOOK II

Chapter 1.

The foregoing are the things on the basis of which one needs to 1377b
exhort and warn, praise and blame, and accuse and defend, and the sorts of opinions and premises that are useful for persuasive speeches about them. For enthymemes deal with them and come from them, involved in speechmaking in each particular class of speeches. But since rhetoric is for the sake of a judgment (because in deliberations people make judgments and a trial *is* a judgment), it is necessary not only to look to the argument, so that it will be demonstrative and persuasive, but also to present oneself as a certain sort of person and prepare for a certain sort of judge; for it makes a big difference as far as persuasion is concerned, in deliberations especially and secondly in trials, what sort of person the speaker appears to be, and how his hearers assume he is disposed toward them, and moreover, whether they themselves might happen to be disposed in some particular way. The sort of person the speaker appears to be is more useful in deliberations, and the way the hearer is disposed is more useful in trials, because things do not appear the same to those who feel friendship as to those who are hostile, nor do they appear the same to those who are angry as to those who remain calm, but appear either altogether different or different in magnitude. For to someone who feels friendship for 1378a
the one about whom he makes the judgment, the latter seems to have committed either no injustice or a small one, but to someone hostile to him it seems the opposite; and to someone who desires something and is hopeful about it, if it is something that is going to be pleasant, it appears to him both that it is going to happen and that it is going to be a good thing, but to someone who is apathetic or disgruntled it looks the opposite.

Three things are responsible for making the speakers themselves be believed, because that is how many things there are, apart from demonstrative arguments, on account of which we feel trust. These are judgment, virtue, and goodwill.[102] For people go wrong in the things they speak of or give advice about by reason of all these or of any one of them, since they either have incorrect opinions on account of a lack of judgment, or while having correct opinions do not say what seems true to them on account of vice, or, if they are of good judgment and decent but not good-willed, it is possible for that very reason for them to fail to give the best advice they know how to give; besides these there are none. It is a necessity, therefore, that anyone who seems to have all these attributes will be trusted by his hearers. The things on the basis of which one might appear to be of good judgment and high moral stature need to be gathered from the distinctions

102 This trio of attributes should be compared with the one Socrates offers in 486E-487E of the *Gorgias*, in a different but related context.

that were made about the virtues, since one might present himself as such on the basis of the same things he would use to present someone else in that way; good will and friendship need to be spoken of in a discussion of the passions.[103]

The passions are all those sources of change on account of which people differ in their judgments that are accompanied by pain and pleasure; examples are anger, pity, fear, and everything else of that sort, as well as their opposites. And with respect to each of them, it is necessary to make a threefold division; I mean, with respect to anger for example, what sort of disposition makes people prone to anger, whom they tend to get angry with, and on what sorts of occasions, since if we had two of these, but not all of them, it would be impossible to produce anger, and similarly in the other cases. So just as we have drawn up propositions applicable to the things discussed earlier, let us do so about these matters as well, and let us divide them in the manner described.

Chapter 2.

Let anger be understood as a desire, accompanied by pain, for revenge for a perceived belittling of oneself or anything of one's own, when that belittling is not appropriate.[104] And if this is anger, it is necessary that the one angered is always angry at some particular person, such as Cleon, and not just at a human being, and because that
1378b person has done something, or is about to do something, against him
or something of his, and that a certain pleasure follows every feeling of anger from the anticipation of getting revenge. For it is pleasant to

---

103 This discussion begins here and continues through Chap. 11. In the sense in which the word is used here, the *pathê* are described in the *Categories* (9b 34-10a 10) as temporary passive qualities of the soul. In English, in the late 18th century, David Hume notes at the beginning of Bk. II of his *Treatise of Human Nature* that a "vulgar and specious" distinction confines the word passion to the violent emotions and the word emotion to the softer passions. This translation follows the primary philosophic tradition that speaks of the whole range of feelings as the passions.

104 This may seem to be an arbitrary narrowing of a group of related feelings that takes many different shapes. There are several reasons for Aristotle's precision. First, he typically seeks to understand things meant in more than one sense by looking for the primary instance, of which the rest are modifications. What he offers here is a definition in the sense of a delimiting, not a formulation meant to substitute for every use of the word *orgê*, a philosophic and not a lexical definition. In the *Nicomachean Ethics* (1125b 29-31, 1108a 7-8), he invents the word *orgilotês*, proneness to anger, for the extreme state of someone who flies off the handle on any and every sort of provocation. The particular case of negative feeling against persons unknown for unfair treatment of people unconnected with oneself (say, the rulers of some third-world country who live in luxury on the foreign aid meant for their poverty-stricken subjects) would be properly called *nemesis*, a righteous indignation discussed separately in Chap. 9 below. Anger is understood by Aristotle as an immediate and irrational response to anything felt as a hostile encroachment on oneself or one's own, governed by *thumos*, the spiritedness that fueled the wrath of Achilles against Agamemnon, referred to in the lines quoted just below. The broader category of hostility in general (*echthra*) is discussed at the end of Chap. 4 below, beginning at 1382a 1.

imagine one will attain things one desires, and no one desires things that are obviously impossible for him, but the one who is angry desires things possible for him. Hence it was beautifully said[105] of spirited anger,

> It is a thing much sweeter than dripping honey
> As it swells in men's chests,

since a certain pleasure goes along with it for this reason, and because people dwell in their thoughts on getting revenge; so the imagining that then arises produces a pleasure just as in dreams.

And since belittling is a putting to work of an opinion to the effect that something appears worthless (since we think that bad things and good things, and things that tend in those directions, are worth taking seriously, but we take as worthless those things that are not at all, or only slightly, either way), there are three forms of belittling: contempt, spitefulness, and insolence.[106] Someone who shows contempt for another person belittles him, since it is things people believe are worthless that they have contempt for, and worthless things that they belittle; and someone who treats another person with spite appears to belittle him, since spite is a thwarting of someone's wishes, not to gain anything for oneself but so that person will not gain it. So since it is not for any gain for oneself, one is belittling the other person, for it is clear that one does not expect the other to do one any harm, because then one would be afraid and not belittle him, or to do one any good worth mentioning, because then one would be taking thought about how to be his friend. And someone who behaves insolently to another person also belittles him, since insolence is the doing or saying of things that bring shame to the person who suffers them, not to get anything out of it oneself other than to have it happen, just to get pleasure from it, for people who are acting in retaliation are not being insolent but vengeful. What is responsible for the pleasure felt by insolent people is that they believe they are showing a greater superiority by behaving maliciously (and this is why young people and rich people are insolent, since they think that in being insolent they are being superior).

105 *Iliad* XVIII, 109-110; see also above, 1370b 12.

106 The three attitudes form an ascending scale, as Aristotle spells out. The last of the three is *hubris*, used in Chaps. 12 and 13 of Bk. I in its legal sense for an outrage, or humiliating violation of another person. Here it includes speaking and gestures as well. The sense in which the word hubris has been brought into English, primarily by high-school English teachers, to mean something like being too big for one's britches, does not reflect the element of cruelty that is always present in Aristotle's use of the word.

Dishonor is part of insolence, and someone who dishonors another person belittles him, since what is worthless has no honor as either good or bad; this is why Achilles, when he gets angry, says[107]

> He has dishonored me, for after taking away my prize
> he keeps it himself

and

> As if I were some tramp with no honor,

as if these were the reasons he was angry. People believe they deserve to be shown great respect by those who are inferior to them in family,
1379a in power, in virtue, and generally in any attribute in which they themselves have any great superiority, as a rich person has over a poor one in money, a rhetorically skilled person over someone not fluent at speech in speaking,[108] a ruler over someone ruled, and a person who deserves to rule over someone who deserves to be ruled. This is why it was said,

> Great is the angry spirit of kings supported by Zeus

and

> Yet even afterwards he still holds a grudge,

since they are provoked on account of their superiority. A person also expects respect from those he believes he should be well treated by; these are people he has treated well himself, or is treating well, or intends or intended to, or whom anyone has treated well through him or anyone close to him.

So it is already clear from these things what the condition is of the people themselves who are angry, as well as who it is they are angry at and for what reasons. For they themselves are angry when their feelings are hurt; anyone feeling pain desires something, so if anyone deals any sort of blow to his getting it immediately, say to his drinking if he is thirsty (and similarly, even if he does not, if he appears to do that same thing), or if anyone acts in opposition to him, or does not act in support of him, or bothers him in any other way when he is in this condition, he is angry with them all. That is why people who are sick, poor, in love, in thirst, and in general in the grip of unfulfilled desire, are prone to anger and easily aroused, especially against those who belittle their present distress—a sick person, for example, at those who belittle his illness, a needy person at those who belittle his

107 *Iliad* I, 356 and IX, 648, spoken by Achilles; the two lines quoted next are II, 196 and I, 82, referring to Agamemnon.

108 The *Gorgias* begins by showcasing Gorgias's assumption of superiority on this ground, and Polus's eruption of anger in 461B is a precise depiction of what Aristotle describes here. One comic aspect of the scene is that Polus, sputtering with rage on behalf of the honor of skilled speakers, loses all his skill at speaking.

poverty, someone in a war at those who belittle the war, a lover at those who belittle love, and similarly with the rest. For each person has the way paved for his own anger by the passion that is already present. And the anger is still greater if he happened to be expecting the opposite, for something far beyond expectation causes more pain, just as something far beyond expectation causes more delight if things happen the way one wants them to. Hence too, the sorts of times and seasons, dispositions and ages for being easily moved to anger are evident, as well as where and when they occur; and when people are in them to a greater degree, they are also more easily moved.

People themselves are easily moved to anger, then, when they are in these conditions, and they are angry at those who ridicule, mock, and jeer at them (because they are showing insolence), and at those who do them harm in any sorts of ways that are signs of insolence; the harm is necessarily of a sort that is neither in retaliation for anything or of benefit to those who do it, for that in itself makes it seem to be done out of insolence. People are also easily moved to anger by those who speak ill of and look down on things that they themselves treat with the utmost seriousness; for instance, people who take pride in philosophy get angry at those who are contemptuous of it, and people who take pride in their looks get angry at those who are contemptuous of that, and similarly in other cases. And these responses are far more intense when people secretly suspect that they do not really possess these things, either not at all or not very strongly, or that they are 1379b
not thought to, for whenever they firmly believe they are superior in those things for which they are mocked, they pay no attention to it. And they get angry at their friends more than at those who are not their friends, since they believe they deserve to be better treated by them than by those who are not friends. And they get more angry at those who are accustomed to treat them with honor or respect, if they back off and do not show them these regards, for they believe they are being looked down on by them too, since otherwise they would keep doing the same things. People also get angry at those who do not return favors, or do not pay them back in equal measure, and at those who do anything in opposition to them, if they are people of lesser standing, for all such people appear to be showing them contempt, the latter as if they were opposing inferiors, the former as if the favors were from inferiors.

And people get more angry at those who are of no account, if they belittle them in any way, for it was assumed that anger arises from belittling and at those from whom it is inappropriate, and it is appropriate for people of lesser standing *not* to engage in belittling. And people get more angry at their friends if they do not speak or act well toward them, and still more if they do the reverse, and also if they fail to notice when they need something, as Antiphon's Plexippus did[109] in his *Meleager*; for not noticing is a sign of belittling someone, since we do not fail to notice what involves people we respect. Also, people get angry at those who rejoice over their misfortunes, and in general at those who are in good spirits when they themselves are suffering misfortunes, since this is a sign either of an enemy or of someone who belittles them. And they get angry at those who are unconcerned if they give them pain; this is why people get angry at those who bring them bad news. And people also get angry at those who listen to reports of their faults or witness them, since that makes them look like they are belittling them or being hostile to them, because friends share one's sorrows, and all people who witness their own faults feel sorrow.

People get still more angry at those who belittle them, if they do so in the presence of five sorts of people: people they feel rivalry with, people they admire, people by whom they want to be admired, and either people around whom they feel shame or any of those who feel shame around them. They also get angry at those who belittle people of a sort that it would be shameful for them not to defend, such as parents, children, wives, and those they rule; also at those who do not give them the gratitude they deserve, since the belittling goes beyond what is seemly; also at those who are ironic[110] about things they take seriously, since irony is something that shows contempt; also at those who do favors for other people if they do not do favors for them, since this too shows contempt, in not considering one worthy of things everyone is worthy of. Forgetfulness, even of names, for example, is also something that produces anger, despite being about something so slight, since forgetfulness too seems to be a sign of belittling, because forgetfulness comes from carelessness, and carelessness is a sort of belittling.

1380a So at the same time, it has been stated at whom people get angry, what condition they themselves are in, and what sorts of things cause it. And it is evident that, by one's speech, one might need to prepare people to be of the same sort as those feeling prone to anger, and to present one's opponents as guilty of those things which cause people to get angry and as being the sort of people they get angry at.

Chapter 3.

Now since getting angry is the opposite of calming down and anger is the opposite of calmness, what needs to be taken up is the condition people are in when they are calm, who it is toward whom

109 It is not clear from the Greek who was angry at whom, and the play is not extant. The translator's guess is based upon the fact that the legendary Meleager was notorious for his rage.

110 See 489E of the *Gorgias*, where Socrates and Callicles trade this reproach.

they feel calm,[111] and what makes them calm down. Let calming down be understood as a settling and quieting of anger. If, then, people get angry at those who belittle them, and belittling is an intentional act, it is clear that they are calm with those who do not do any of that, or who do so unintentionally, or at least appear that way. They are also lenient toward those who meant to do the opposite of what they did, and with those who behave the same sort of way toward themselves, since it does not seem that a person himself would belittle himself. And they are lenient toward those who admit to belittling them and feel remorse about it, since they calm down from their anger as if the other person's being pained at what he had done got them justice. There is a sign of this in the way household slaves are disciplined, since we discipline more strongly those who talk back and deny what they have done, but our spirits stop being angry at those who admit they are being disciplined justly. The reason is that denying things that are obvious is shamelessness, and a lack of shame shows belittling and contempt; at any rate, if we feel great contempt for people, we have no shame toward them. People are also lenient toward those who show humility and do not talk back, because they seem to admit to being in an inferior position, and people in an inferior position feel fear, and no one who is afraid of someone belittles him. Even dogs make it clear that anger stops toward those who show humility, by not biting people who squat down. And people are calm with those who behave with seriousness when they themselves are serious, for they seem to take them seriously and not show contempt. And they are lenient toward those who have shown them greater kindness. And toward those in need who ask them for help, since they are more humble. People are lenient with those who are never insolent, mocking, or belittling toward anyone, or not toward honest people, or not toward people of their own sort. In general, one ought to look at things that cause leniency on the basis of their opposites, and people do not get angry at those they fear or in whose presence they feel shame, as long as they are in those states, since it is impossible to be afraid of someone and angry at him at the same time. And at those who have done something out of anger, people are either not angry at all or less so, since they do not appear to have acted because of belittling; for no one who is angry at someone belittles him, since belittling is unaccompanied by pain, while anger involves pain. And people are 1380b
lenient toward those who feel shame in their presence.

111 Aristotle is using an array of words derived from the root of the adjective *praos*. The process that reverses getting angry is best called calming down in English, and calmness is a good name for the state opposite to anger, but much of the chapter deals with an attitude toward others that is more than just an absence of anger. When the context of the word *praos* calls for it, this translation will use forms of the word "lenient" to indicate an inclination to excuse offenses. Some older translations use forms of the word "mild" for all cases, but greater accuracy seems achievable with a sacrifice of uniformity.

And it is clear that people are calm when they are in a condition opposite to being angry, as when they are in a state of playfulness, laughter, feasting, prosperity, achievement, satisfaction, and in general in a state of freedom from pain, or pleasure without insolence, or wholesome anticipation. People are also calm when their anger has gone on a long time and is not fresh, since time puts an end to anger. And an act of revenge taken first against a different person puts an end even to a greater anger against someone else. This is why Philocrates gave a good reply when the populace was angry at him and someone asked him, "Why don't you defend yourself?" "Not yet," he said. "When, then?" "When I see someone else getting vilified." For people become calm when they have used up their anger on someone else, which is what happened with Ergophilus; for even though the people were more infuriated with him than with Callisthenes, they let him off, because they had passed a death sentence on Callisthenes the previous day.[112] People are also lenient when they feel pity, and when someone has suffered a greater evil than those who are angry would have inflicted, for they believe it is just the same as if they had taken revenge. And when people believe they themselves are in the wrong and are suffering justly, no anger arises at something just, since they no longer regard themselves as being treated inappropriately, and that is what anger was taken to be. And this is the reason why one ought to make an explanation first in speech, for then even slaves are less upset about being disciplined.

And people are lenient when they think someone will be unaware that the retaliation came from them and what it was for, because anger has to do with oneself as a particular person, as is clear from its definition; this is why the poem has it right in the words,

> Say it was Odysseus, sacker of cities,

since there would have been no revenge if the other was unaware by whom and for what it was happening.[113] Hence people do not stay angry either at others who are unaware of it or at the dead, since they have suffered the ultimate penalty and will not be pained by or even

---

112 Philocrates and Callisthenes made peace agreements with Macedonia, about 20 years apart, that were unacceptable to the Athenian people; Ergophilus was an Athenian commander who led a failed battle against Thrace. Aristotle's point is that delay in answering a charge can improve an accused person's chances with a jury. Machiavelli takes the same principle several steps further as applied to absolute monarchies, in Chap. VII of *The Prince*; he describes the way Cesare Borgia, after he had used Ramiro d'Orca to impose order on the Romanga, had him cut in half and placed on display in a public square.

113 The line is IX, 504, of the *Odyssey*. If Odysseus had kept quiet, the blinded Cyclops could not have endangered the men on his ship by throwing a boulder at them, and could not have called down the curse that eventually got all Odysseus's companions killed. Aristotle is not saying it was right of Odysseus to make the taunt, but that it was right of Homer to understand how anger works. This perspective shows how much alike the stories of Odysseus and Achilles are in Homer's handling of them.

aware of the anger, which is what those who are angry desire. This is why, in connection with Hector, the poet,[114] wanting Achilles to put an end to his anger against a dead man, says well,

> In his rage he is tormenting senseless earth.

So it is clear that it is on the basis of these topics that people need to argue when they want to make others lenient, preparing them to be that way by presenting those they are angry at as people to be feared, or deserving of a sense of shame, or as having done them favors, or as having acted unwillingly, or as greatly pained at the things they have done.

Chapter 4.

Let us say who people like and hate and why, after we have defined love[115] and liking. And let liking be understood as wanting someone to have the things one believes are good, for that person's sake and
not one's own, and to have what is apt to bring that about as much as 1381a
possible. A friend is someone who likes another person and is liked in return, and those who believe this is the case between them believe that they are friends. These things being assumed, a friend is necessarily someone who shares in pleasure in good things and shares in pain at distressing things for no other reason than on account of the other person. For all people feel joy when the things they want happen, and feel pain when opposite things do, so that their pains and pleasures are signs of their wishes. So those for whom the same things are good and bad, and who are friends and enemies toward the same people, are friends, since it is necessarily the case that they want the same things, so that someone who wants the exact same things for another person as for himself appears to be a friend to that person.

And people like those who have done good either to them or to those they care about, if the things they have done are of great magnitude, or if they have done them wholeheartedly or at such times as were critical, and for the sake of the beneficiaries themselves, and they also like those they believe want to do good to them. And people like their friends' friends, and those who like the people they themselves like, and those who are liked by those whom they like, and those who are enemies of their own enemies, and who hate those they themselves

114 Homer puts the words in the mouth of Apollo (*Iliad* XXIV, 54).

115 The word is *philia*. In the *Nicomachean Ethics*, it plays an enormous role as the topic of Bks. VIII and IX, where Aristotle argues that it supercedes justice in uniting people and provides the bridge between the virtues of character and intellect in one's development as a whole human being. There it clearly means friendship, though Aristotle also uses it (reluctantly) in Bk. IV, Chap. 6 for a minor social virtue one might call amiability. In his primary discussion of *philia* in that work, he distinguishes it from the mere state of feeling that he calls *philêsis* or affection (1157b 28-29). Here *philia* is used for a feeling that can be aroused in a persuasive speech, that can make one feel toward another person the way one would toward a friend or family member.

hate, and who are hated by those whom they hate; for to all these, the same things appear to be good as appear so to them, so that they want what is good for them, which is exactly what was taken as the mark of a friend. Also, people like those who are inclined to do good in matters of money or safety, which is why they honor those who are generous, courageous, and just; and they assume that those who do not live off others are of this sort, and that includes people who make a living by working, among whom are those who live by farming, and most of all, in comparison to the rest, those who work their own land. And they like those who are temperate, because they are not unjust, and those who stay out of other people's business, for the same reason.

People like those with whom they want to be friends, if *they* plainly want it, and this includes those who are good by reason of virtue as well as those who have good reputations, among either all people, or the best sort, or those admired by them, or those who admire them. And they also like those who are pleasant to live among and to spend time with, and these include those who are easygoing, do not nag others about their faults, and are not ardently competitive or persistently contentious (since all such people are combative, and combative people appear to want things that oppose others), as well as those who are adroit at teasing and being teased, for in both cases people are eager for the same thing as their neighbor, that they be able both to take jokes and make jokes agreeably. And people like those who praise their good attributes, especially those they fear they
1381b do not possess. They also like those who are clean in appearance, in clothes, and in life as a whole. And they like those who are not critical either of their faults or about the good they have done them, since both are ways of browbeating people. And they like those who are not mindful of past wrongs and do not hold onto grievances, but are easily reconciled, because they believe they will be the same way toward them that they take them to be toward others. And they like those who neither engage in malicious gossip nor even know any evil about their neighbors or associates, but only good things, for that is what a good person does. And they like those who do not resist them when they are angry or urgent about something, for such people are combative. And they like those who hold them in serious regard in any way, such as admiring them and taking them to be of serious stature and welcoming their company, especially those who feel that way about the things they themselves most want to be admired for, or taken seriously about, or seem pleasant on account of.

People like those who are like themselves and have the same interests, so long as they do not become boring, and if their livelihood does not come from the same source, since in that case it becomes a matter of "potter versus potter."[116] And they like those who desire the same things—things, that is, which it is possible for them to share at the same time; if not, the same thing happens in this case too. And people like those around whom they are comfortable enough not to be ashamed of things on account of their opinion—people, that is, whom they do not look down on—and also those around whom they *are* ashamed of things on account of something true. And people like, or want to be friends with, those with whom they feel an ardent rivalry for honor, or those by whom they want to be emulated but not envied. And they like those whom they would assist in good projects, so long as that is not going to result in greater evils for themselves. And they like those who show the same sort of affection for absent friends as for the ones who are present; that is why everyone likes those who feel that way about friends who have died. In all cases, people like those who have strong affection for their friends and do not abandon them, for the good people they like best are those who are good at being friends. And they like those who have no pretenses toward them, and this includes those who even tell them their own faults. For it was noted that around friends, we are not ashamed of things on account of their opinion, so if someone who *is* ashamed does not feel friendship, someone who is not ashamed seems likely to be feeling friendship. And we like those who are not frightening to us, with whom we feel confident, for no one likes a person he is scared of. Companionship, living in the same place, ties of kinship, and all such things are forms of friendship. A favor is something that tends to produce friendship, especially doing one without being asked and not making a display of having done it, for in that way it appears to be for the other person's own sake and not done for any other reason.

It is clear that the way to see what concerns hostility and hatred is 1382a
from their opposites. Anger, spitefulness and slander are things that produce hostility. Anger comes from things done against oneself, but hostility arises even without anything directed at oneself, for when we take the notion that someone is a certain kind of person, we hate him. And anger is always directed at particular people, such as Callias or Socrates, but hatred also applies to classes of people, for everyone hates a thief or informer. And anger is curable by time, while hatred is incurable; the former is a desire for pain, the latter for evil. For someone who is angry wants to see the other person suffer, but in the other case that makes no difference, and while all painful things are observable, the greatest evils are the least observable, namely injustice and bad judgment, since the presence of vice is not painful. The former feeling is also accompanied by pain, while the latter is not, since someone who is angry is pained and someone who feels hatred is not. The former may feel pity under many circumstances, but the latter pities no one,

116 Hesiod, *Works and Days*, 25-26: "Potter has a grudge against potter, carpenter against carpenter, beggar against beggar, and singer against singer."

since the former wants the person he is angry at to suffer in return, while the latter wants the person he hates not to exist.

It is evident from these things, then, that it is possible to demonstrate that people are enemies or friends and make them be so when they are not, to refute those who claim they are, and, when people are in dispute because of anger or hostility, to bring them over to whichever side one chooses.

Chapter 5.

What sorts of things and persons people fear, and the condition they are in when they feel that way, will be evident from the following. Let fear be understood as a certain pain and agitation from the imagining of an impending evil of a destructive or painful sort. For people are not afraid of all evils, for instance that they will become unjust or stupid, but only those evils with the potential for great pain or destruction, and those only if they do not appear far away but so near as to be about to happen, since people do not fear things that are exceedingly remote. All people know that they will die, but because it is not imminent, they give it no thought. So if this is what fear is, then necessarily all such things as appear to have the potential to inflict great destruction, or to do harm that extends to causing great pain, are feared. Hence even the signs of such things are feared, since the fearsome thing appears imminent. For this is danger: the approach of something feared. And the hostility or anger of those who have the power to do something about it are signs of this kind, since it is apparent that they are willing and able to do something, and consequently near doing so. Injustice that has power is another such sign, since
1382b an unjust person is unjust by choice. Another is virtue that has been treated with insolence, when it has power, since it always chooses to act when it suffers insolence, and in this case it has the power. Another is fear in people who have the power to do something about it, since that sort of person is necessarily in a state of preparedness.

And since most people are worse rather than better,[117] unable to resist a chance to gain, and cowardly amid dangers, it is for the most part a frightening thing to have oneself at the mercy of anyone else, so for someone who has done some terrible thing, those who share the knowledge of it are feared by him, either to turn him in or to leave

117 This is explained by what follows, as referring to human weakness rather than deliberate vice. Aristotle regards both vice and virtue as uncommon conditions that involve the consistent choice and sustained discipline required to form a character. In Bk. VII of the *Nicomachean Ethics*, he describes the more common human condition as one of relative restraint or lack of restraint on the occasion of each new opportunity for pleasure or pain that crops up, and says that most people maintain an in-between position, even though the scale is more heavily weighted to the worse side (1150a 15-16); that would seem to imply that the effort must be correspondingly stronger to the better side. Like the thing he describes, Aristotle's assessment of human nature is a balanced one.

him holding the bag. And those who have the power to do injustice are feared by those who are vulnerable to having injustice done to them, since for the most part human beings commit injustice when they have the power to. And those who have suffered injustice, or regard themselves as having suffered it, are objects of fear, since they are always on the lookout for an opportunity. Those who have committed injustice are also feared when they have power, since *they* are afraid of suffering retaliation, and that sort of thing was set down as something frightening. Those who are one's rivals for the same things, that cannot be possessed by both at the same time, are also feared, since people are always at war with those of that sort. Those who are feared by people stronger than oneself are also frightening, for if they would be capable of harming the stronger ones, all the more would they be capable of doing harm to oneself. Also frightening, for the same reason, are those whom people stronger than oneself are afraid of. And those who have brought down people stronger than oneself, and also those who have attacked people weaker than oneself, are already frightening in the former case or, in the latter, will be when they have increased in strength. Among those who have had injustice done to them, and among enemies and those one grapples with, it is not the hotheads and loudmouths who are to be feared, but those who are calm, peaceful, and unscrupulous; they go unnoticed when they are nearby, so it can never be evident that they are out of range. And all frightening things are more frightening when there is no chance for those who have transgressed to set things right, either because that is completely impossible or because it is not up to themselves but up to their opponents, as are things for which there is no help in defending oneself, or none that is easy to come by. As a way of putting it simply, frightening things are all those that arouse pity when they happen to others, or are on the point of happening.

One may say that the foregoing are pretty well the most important things that are frightening and that people fear; let us now say what condition the people themselves are in who are afraid. Now if fear includes an expectation of undergoing some devastating suffering, it is obvious that no one who believes he is not going to suffer any such thing is afraid, either of those things he does not believe he will suffer or of those people by whom he does not believe he will suffer them, or at any time when he does not believe he will suffer them. By necessity, then, those who are afraid are people who do believe they will suffer some such thing, and they fear those by whom they believe they will and the things they believe they will suffer, when they believe they will. But people who are, or think they are, in the 1383a
midst of great prosperity do not believe they will suffer (and hence they are insolent, disparaging of others, and reckless, and what makes them that way is either riches, bodily strength, a multitude of friends, or political power), and neither do people who regard themselves as

having already suffered every kind of terrifying affliction, when all feeling toward the future has grown cold, as though they already had it battered out of them. Some hope of being saved from the thing causing their agony has to be left; a sign of this is that fear makes people deliberate, and yet no one deliberates about things that are hopeless. So that shows the sort of attitude it is necessary to get people into, on occasions when it would be better for them to be afraid, the realization that *they* are just the sort who will suffer (since other and greater people have suffered too), and to show that people of their sort are suffering and have suffered, at the hands of the sort of people they did not believe would do that, and suffered things which, and at times when, they did not believe they could.

And since it is evident what fear is, and what things are feared, and, for each sort of people who are afraid, what condition they are in, it is also evident from this what being confident is, and the sorts of things people are confident about, and how they are disposed when they are confident. That which gives confidence is the opposite of that which causes fear, so that the hope of things that secure safety is combined with an imagining that they are nearby, while those that cause fear are either not present or far away. Both the distance of terrifying things and the nearness of things that bring safety are confidence-inspiring, and confidence is present when remedies and sources of help are many or sizable or both, when people have neither suffered nor committed injustice, when they have either no competitors at all or none with any power, or those who have power are their friends who have either conferred or received benefits, or there are either more competitors or more powerful ones, or both, for whom the same things are advantageous as for oneself.

People are confident themselves when they are in the following conditions: when they believe they have had success at many things and have not suffered, or have often gotten into terrifying situations and have escaped them. For there are two ways in which human beings come to be untroubled, either by not having been put to the test, or by having the means to get through them, just as, in dangers at sea, both those who have not experienced a storm and those who, from experience, have the means to get through one, feel confident about what they are to undergo. People are also confident when those like themselves, or inferior to them, or whom they believe they are superior to, find nothing to be afraid of, and they believe they are superior to any people if they have conquered them or their superiors or equals. And people are confident when they believe they have more or more powerful possessions of the sort in which a superiority
1383b makes people feared, and that includes abundance of money, strength of body and of friends, of lands, and either all or the most important kinds of equipment for war. And people are confident when they are in a state of having done no injustice to anyone, or not to many

others, or not to those from whom anything is to be feared, and generally when things stand well with them in matters that pertain to the gods, with respect to omens, charitable giving, and other things. For anger inspires confidence, and being treated unjustly when one has done no injustice produces anger, and it is assumed that the divine power helps victims of injustice. And people are confident when, in undertaking anything, they believe that they will either succeed at it or at least suffer no harm. And what pertains to things that inspire fear and confidence has been stated.

Chapter 6.

What sorts of things make people feel ashamed or shameless, and in whose presence, and what their condition is, will be clear from the following. Let shame be understood as a certain pain or agitation over bad deeds, present, past, or future, that appear to bring one into disrepute, and let shamelessness be a certain belittling and indifferent attitude toward these same things. So if shame is as defined, then necessarily shame is felt at bad deeds, either in oneself or of people one cares about, that seem to be ugly.[118] All deeds that result from vice are of this sort, such as throwing down one's shield and running away, which comes from cowardice; or embezzling money left in trust, which comes from injustice; or having relations with women whom one ought not, or where or when one ought not, which comes from self-indulgence; or profiting from petty or ugly sources or from helpless people, such as the poor or the dead (about which there is the proverb about looting a corpse), which comes from base profiteering and miserliness; or not helping someone in money matters when one is able to, or helping less than one could, or accepting help from those with lesser resources, or borrowing when it will seem like begging, or begging when it will seem like asking for repayment, or asking for repayment when it will seem like begging, or praising things one will seem to be begging for, and doing so none the less after one has failed to get them, all of which are signs of miserliness, while giving praise when people are present is a sign of flattery; or overpraising good qualities and glossing over bad ones, or grieving to excess in the presence of someone in grief, and all the other things of that sort, which are signs of flattery; or not submitting to labors that older people
or those who are frail or in higher positions of authority, or generally 1384a
those less capable, do undergo, all of which are signs of softness; or to accept favors from another person, and do so often, and still com-

118 The words for beautiful and ugly in ancient Greek (*kalos* and *aischros*) were used more widely for deeds, as opposed to bodily appearance, than we use them in English, but we have exactly the same usage, as when a parent says to a child who has done something generous, "That was a beautiful thing you did," or to one who has done something spiteful, "Don't be so ugly." Shame (*aischunê*), and all the words related to it, are built on the root meaning ugly. See Aristotle's definition of the beautiful in Bk. I above, at 1366a 33-34.

plain about the person who did the favors, all of which are degrading signs of a small soul; or talking all the time about oneself, holding forth and claiming for oneself things done by others, which are signs of braggadocio. And similarly with the deeds that come from each of the other vices of character, and the things that are signs of them or resemble them, since they are ugly and shameless things to do. And it is shameful not to take part in those beautiful things that everyone, at least everyone—or most everyone—like oneself does take part; and by "like" I am speaking of those who are alike in nationality, citizenship, age, family connections, and generally those of equal standing, for it is already shameful, for example, not to take part in education to the same extent, and in other things like that. And all these things are more shameful when they appear to be one's own fault, since that makes them appear, from that point on, to be more a result of vice, once one has become responsible oneself for one's past, present, and future attributes. And people feel shame when they have things done to them of a sort that brings them dishonor or reproach, and also after such things have happened and when they are about to happen; these include yielding one's body, or acquiescing in shameful practices, and being violated is among them. Yielding to dissipation can be both willing and unwilling, though yielding to force is unwilling; submitting without resisting comes from unmanliness or cowardice.

These things, then, and things of these sorts, are what people are ashamed of, and since shame is an imagining involving disrepute, and is felt for the sake of that very thing rather than for any consequences, and since no one cares about an opinion except on account of those who hold the opinion, then necessarily shame is felt in relation to those whom people have regard for; and they have regard for those who admire them, those whom they admire, those by whom they want to be admired, those toward whom they feel rivalry, and those whose opinion they do not have disdain for. And people want to be admired by, and admire, all those who have anything good that is highly prized, or those who are just the ones who have control of anything they themselves feel an overwhelming need for, as lovers do; they feel rivalry toward those like themselves; and they respect as truthful the opinions of people with good judgment, such as their elders and educated people. And things that happen in front of people's eyes and out in the open cause more shame (from which comes the proverb about embarrassment[119] being in the eyes); this is why people feel more ashamed before those who will always be around them and
1384b those who watch over them, because they are under their eyes in both

119 The word is *aidôs*, an attitude of modest respect for the opinion or the privacy of others, as opposed to the burning shame felt at one's own ugly behavior implied by *aischunê*. The proverb, as found in a fragment from Euripides' *Cresphontes*, more likely refers to an inability to meet the eyes of someone before whom one feels embarrassed.

cases. And people are more ashamed in the presence of those who are not culpable on the same grounds, since it is apparent that they look at things the opposite way; and in the presence of those who do not have a forgiving attitude toward apparent offenders, since it is said that no one is indignant at his neighbors about those things that he himself does, so it is clear that what he does get indignant about are things he does not do; and in the presence of those who tend to broadcast things to many others, since there is no difference between not talking about something and not thinking it worth talking about. The people who do broadcast others' faults are those who have suffered injustice, from being on their guard against it, and those who are malicious gossips, since, if they even talk about people who have done no wrong, all the more will they talk about those who have. And people are more ashamed in the presence of those whose pastime is to dwell on the faults of their neighbors, the way jokesters and comic poets do, since they too, in a way, are spreaders of malicious gossip. They are also more ashamed in the presence of those they have never disappointed, since the position they occupy is the same as being admired, and this is why they feel shame toward those who are asking them for anything for the first time, since they have never yet gained a bad reputation among them for anything; this is the case with people just now wanting to be one's friends (since they have only seen one's best side, which is what was good about Euripides' reply to the Syracusans[120]), and also applies to those old acquaintances who are not aware of any faults.

People feel shame not only at the aforementioned shameful deeds themselves, but also at the signs of them, not only at engaging in sexual acts, for instance, but also at the signs of it, and they are ashamed not only of doing shameful things but even of talking about them. And they are ashamed not only in the presence of the people who have been described, but likewise in that of those who might make things known to them, such as their servants and friends. But they feel no shame at all around those whose reputation for being truthful they greatly disdain (since no one is ashamed around small children or animals), nor do they feel shame over the same things around acquaintances as around those they do not know, but over things that seem shameful on true grounds around acquaintances, and over things that seem that way according to convention around strangers.

And it is when in the following situations that they themselves would feel shame: first, if any of those we said were the sort around whom people are ashamed were present with them. These were those admired by them, or who admire them, or by whom they want to be admired, or from whom they need some service they will not get if they are in disrepute. And these are either the ones who see them

120 This is taken to refer to a caution to the Syracusans not to reject an alliance with the Athenians when they were just beginning to feel the need of their help.

(which was Cydias's point in his speech to the assembly, about giving out land on Samos, when he insisted that the Athenians imagine the Greeks all standing around them in a circle, seeing and not just hearing how they voted), or such people as are nearby or will find out about it. This is why, at times when people are in misfortune, they do not want
1385a to be seen by those who look up to them, since these are their admirers. People would also feel shame whenever they have past deeds or acts of their own, or of their ancestors or any others with whom they have any close connection, on which they would bring disgrace, and generally on behalf of those on whom they themselves would bring shame; these include those mentioned as well as any people their own actions would be a reflection on, people whose teachers or advisors they have been, or any others like themselves there may be with whom they compete for honor, since many things that people do and refrain from doing come from feeling shame toward others of that sort. And they feel it more strongly when they are going to be seen and to go around openly with those who are aware of their shameful deeds. That is the reason the poet Antiphon, when he was about to be beaten to death at the order of Dionysius,[121] seeing those who were to be executed with him hiding their faces as they went through the gates, said "Why are you hiding? Because one of these people might see you tomorrow?"

These then are the observations that pertain to shame; as for shamelessness, it is obvious that we shall have plenty of material from their opposites.

Chapter 7.

Toward whom people have charity, on what occasions, and what condition they themselves are in, will be clear once we have defined charity.[122] So let a charitable act, in the sense in which people are said to have charity, be understood as service done for someone in need, with nothing in return and not so that there will be anything for oneself, but only for the other person. The charity will be great if that person is greatly in need, or needs important or difficult things, or on occasions of importance or difficulty, or if the one giving it is the only one or the first one to do so or gives it most. Needs are cravings, especially cravings for things that bring pain when they are not attained. And desires such as love are of this sort, as are the desires

121 Tyrant of Syracuse, in Sicily. There are differing accounts of what Antiphon said to offend him.

122 The noun *charis* can mean graciousness, a gracious act, or gratitude. At 1381b 35 above it was translated "a favor" as between one friend and another. In this chapter it has to do with deciding when someone has or has not acted freely to relieve someone else's need, so that, by implication, a jury or political assembly might be persuaded to treat them as they treat others. The emphasis on need seems to restrict it to charitable acts, within the wider class of favors and gracious gestures.

involved in distress or danger to the body, for a person in danger or in pain feels desire. This is why those who stand by someone in poverty or exile have shown charity even if they render only small services, like the person who gave someone a mat in the Lyceum, because of the magnitude of the need and occasion. It is necessary, then, that the service have reference to things of that same kind, or if not, to equal or greater ones. So since it is obvious for whom and on what occasions a charitable act is performed, and what condition those who perform it are in, it is clear that it is from these materials that arguments need to be prepared, showing that some people either are or have been in that sort of pain and need, and that others have been of service to them in some such way in such a time of need, or are being so.

It is obvious too what would take the charitable motive out of something and make people uncharitable. It is either because they are 1385b
performing or performed the service for their own sake (which is not what charity was), or because it fell out that way by chance, or compulsion played a part in it, or because they were giving something back rather than simply giving it, whether they knew that or not—either way it is something in return for something, and in that case it could not be an act of charity. And it needs to be considered in all the ways a thing can *be* something, for an act of charity is what it is because of being either a particular thing, of a certain magnitude or a certain sort, or at a certain time or place. And it is a sign of being uncharitable if one has failed to do us some lesser service, or has done the same or equal or greater ones for our enemies, since it is clear that these are not for our sake either, or if he has done services knowing they are worthless, since no one admits to needing worthless things.

Chapter 8.

What pertains to being charitable and being uncharitable has been stated. Let us now speak of the sorts of things that arouse pity, who it is that people pity, and what condition they themselves are in when they do so. Let pity be understood as a certain pain at an apparent evil of a destructive or painful sort, when it strikes someone who does not deserve it, an evil which one might expect to suffer oneself, or that someone close to one might, and all this when it appears near at hand. For it is clear that someone who is going to feel pity must to begin with be the sort of person that he imagines could suffer some evil himself, or that someone close to him could, and an evil of such a kind as was stated in the definition, or one like it or pretty close to it. Hence people who have been completely ruined feel no pity (for they do not believe they can suffer anything more, since they have already suffered it), and neither do people who consider themselves to be at the pinnacle of happiness—they are insolent instead, for if they believe they are already in possession of all good things, this clearly includes an inability to suffer any evil, which is one of the good

things. People who do regard themselves as the sort who might suffer are those who have already suffered and come out of it; the elderly, on account of their judgment and experience; the weak, and even more so the more cowardly ones; the educated, since their reasoning is the best; those who have parents, children, or wives, since these are parts of themselves and vulnerable to suffering the things mentioned; those who are not in a passionate state of a manly sort, such as anger or confidence (since these are reckless about the future), and not in an insolent disposition either (since they too are reckless about suffering anything) but in between the two,[123] and not greatly afraid either. Those who are driven to distraction feel no pity because they are wrapped up in their own suffering. Also, to feel pity, one needs to believe there are some decent people, since one who believes there
1386a are none will think everyone is deserving of evil. In general, then, someone feels pity when he is disposed to recall that the same sorts of things have happened either to himself or to someone close to him, or to anticipate that they may happen to him or his.

The condition people are in when they feel pity has been stated, and the things for which they have pity are evident from the definition: all painful and distressing things that bring destruction are pitiable, and all that bring any sort of ruin, and all evils of any magnitude for which chance is responsible. The things that are ruinous and destructive are deaths, injuries and abuses to the body, old age, diseases, and starvation, and the evils for which chance is responsible include a lack or scarcity of friends (which is why it is a pitiful thing to be torn away from one's friends and fellow countrymen), deformity, debility, loss of limbs, the turning up of any evil from a source from which something good would be expected to arise, especially when such a thing happens repeatedly, the coming to pass of something good only after one has suffered (as when honors for Diopeithes from the Great King were delivered after he was dead), and either having nothing good at all come to pass or getting no enjoyment out of it once it has come.

These and things like them, then, are the occasions on which people feel pity, and they have pity on those who are known to them, unless they are exceedingly close to their own household. About the latter, they are in the same condition as when those things are about to happen to themselves, which is why Amasis did not cry over his son when he was being led off to be killed, so people say, but did cry when he saw his friend begging,[124] since that was pitiful but the other was horrifying. What is horrifying is a different thing from something

123 The insolent disposition is cruel, and anger is a spirited reaction against insolence. The insolent person considers no one worthy of his pity, and the angry person considers the insolent one as having forfeited his claim to be worth any.

124 The story is told in Herodotus' *History*, III, 14, not about Amasis, but about his son who succeeded him as King of Egypt.

pitiful; it drives out pity and is often felt[125] as its opposite, since people no longer feel pity when the horrifying thing is near them. People pity those like themselves in age, in character, in specific states of character, in standing, and in family, for in all these cases there is a greater appearance of something that might also happen to them, since in general and here as well, one should grasp that whatever things people fear as applied to themselves, they pity when they happen to others. And since it is sufferings that appear near at hand that arouse pity, and those that are thousands of years away in the past or future, that people neither anticipate nor remember, they either feel no pity over at all or not in a similar way, it necessarily follows that those who enhance the effect by gestures, tone of voice, clothing, and histrionics in general are more pitiful. For they make the evil appear near at hand, putting it before the eyes as either imminent or recent, and things that have just happened or are just about to happen are more pitiful from the shortness of time. For the same reason, signs also make things more pitiful, such as the clothing, and anything else like that, of people who have suffered, and actions and words and anything else belonging to people in a state of suffering, such as those who are dying. And it is most pitiful of all when those who are in such a critical condition are people of serious stature. All these things make the pitiful element greater by appearing near at hand, both because of its being undeserved and because the suffering is appearing in sight of our eyes.

Chapter 9.

The feeling called righteous indignation is most exactly opposed to feeling pity, for compared to being pained at undeserved adversity, being pained at undeserved prosperity is in one manner its opposite, and it also stems from the same state of character. For both passions are marks of good character, since one ought to share the grief of those who fare badly without deserving it and pity them, and be indignant at those who fare well without deserving it, because it is unjust for something to happen contrary to what is deserved. Hence we attribute the feeling of righteous indignation even to the gods. And it might seem that envy too is in a certain manner the opposite of feeling pity, as though it were closely allied with or even the same as being indignant, but it is something different. For envy too is an agitated state of pain, and it is directed at prosperity, but not because the person is undeserving but just because he is one's equal or is like

125 The word is *chrêsimon* which ordinarily means "useful"; the translation draws on a possible but unlikely meaning within the verb from which the adjective is derived. I am not at all confident of having grasped Aristotle's meaning, and the "not" in the following clause is not in the manuscripts, but inserted by Ross and other editors. My guess is that there is some way to construe the two clauses that would make sense of both anomalies, but I haven't found it.

oneself. What needs to belong to all these feelings alike is that they do not refer to anything else that may happen to oneself but are felt toward one's neighbor himself, since it would no longer be envy in the one case, or righteous indignation in the other, but fear, if the pain and agitation is present on account of feeling that there will be something bad for oneself as a result of the prosperity of the other person. And it is clear that feelings of a contrary sort will go along with these. For someone who is pained by those who undeservedly suffer adversity will be pleased or at least not pained at those who suffer adversity the opposite way; no honest person, for example, would be pained when those who commit patricide or other bloody murders meet with punishment, since one ought to rejoice at such things, the same way one would when people do well in accord with what they deserve. For both things are just and make a decent person rejoice, since he must hope that what happens to someone like him will happen to him as well. And all these feelings are marks of the same state of character, while their opposites are marks of the
1387a opposite state, since the same person who is envious is also malicious, because someone who is pained when something happens or is present must necessarily be happy when that same thing is lost or destroyed. Hence all these things are blockages to pity, even though they differ for the reasons mentioned, so that all of them alike can be used to make things not be pitied.

So let us speak first about feeling righteous indignation, who it is people feel it toward, on what occasions, and the condition they themselves are in when they feel it, and then speak of the other feelings after that. And what has been said makes the matter clear, for if feeling righteous indignation is being pained at someone who appears to be prospering without deserving to, it is obvious first of all that it is not possible to be indignant at all good things, since if someone is just or courageous, or acquires any virtue, no one is going to be indignant at that (since people are not pitied for the opposites of these attributes either), but at riches and political power and things of that sort, things which, to put it simply, good people and people who by nature have such goods as high birth, beauty, and that sort of thing are deserving of. And since what is of long standing has an appearance somewhat close to what is natural, as between those who possess the same good thing, people necessarily feel more indignation at those who happen to have newly attained it and are prospering on account of it. For those who are newly rich cause more annoyance than those who have been rich a long time and on account of their family, and similarly with those who have ruling offices, those who are powerful, those who have many friends, or who are fortunate in their children and anything else of that sort. And it is similar if some other good thing comes to them on account of those. For here too the new rich are more annoying than the old rich, when they gain ruling positions, and similarly in the other cases. The reason is that the one sort seem to have things that are properly theirs while the other sort do not, since something that has always appeared a certain way seems true, with the result that other people are thought to have things they are not entitled to. And since each good thing is not deserved by just any random person, but there is a certain proportion and something fitting in things (as for instance beauty of weapons is fitting for a courageous person rather than for a just person, and distinguished marriages are fitting for the well-born rather than for the newly rich), if someone who is good does not attain what is fitting, that is something to be indignant about. So too when a lesser person gets into contention with a greater one, especially among those with the same distinction, which is why the following[126] was said,

> He steered clear of battle with Telamonian Ajax,
> For Zeus would have been indignant with him if he fought
> with a better man.

So, too, if the distinction is not the same and a lesser person contends 1387b
with someone who is greater in any respect whatever, say a musician[127] with a just person, since justice is a greater excellence than music.

It is clear from these things, then, who it is people are indignant with and what their reasons are, since they are these and others like them. People are inclined to be indignant if they themselves happen to be worthy of the greatest goods or happen to possess them, since it is not a just thing for those unlike them to be considered worthy of goods like theirs; and secondly if they happen to be good and of serious excellence, because that means they judge things well and hate injustices; also if they are ambitious and crave certain positions, especially when they are ambitious for those positions that others have attained without deserving. In general, those who believe that they themselves are worthy of things that others are unworthy of are inclined to be indignant toward those people about those things. Hence slavish, worthless, and unambitious people are not inclined to be indignant, since there is nothing they believe themselves to be worthy of. And it is evident from the foregoing discussion what sort of people it is about whom one ought to be happy, or at least not distressed, when they are unfortunate, fare badly, and fail to attain things, since the opposites of the things mentioned are clear from them. Hence if the speech puts the judges into this attitude, and shows that those who expect to be pitied, and the things they expect to be

126 The first line is *Iliad* XI, 542; the second is not in any manuscripts we have, but may have been part of an ancient oral tradition.

127 The word *mousikos* could also mean someone refined or cultured, educated in the arts inspired by the Muses. One might imagine a modern example of a literary celebrity criticizing a public figure noted for personal integrity over a matter of public policy.

pitied for, are unworthy to get any and deserve to get none, it makes it impossible for the judges to have pity on them.

Chapter 10.

It is also clear on what occasions people feel envious and of whom, and what condition they are in, if envy is a certain pain at the prosperity of those like oneself in regard to the good things mentioned, not in order to get anything for onself but just because they have it. The sort of people who will feel envy are the ones for whom there are, or appear to be, others like themselves, and by "like" I mean in race, family, age, traits of character, reputation, and possessions, and who are little short of having it all, which is why those who perform great deeds and enjoy good fortune are still envious, because they believe everyone is taking things that are theirs, and who are honored for any great distinction, and especially for wisdom or happiness. Ambitious people are more envious than unambitious ones, and so are those who consider themselves wise, since they are ambitious in regard to wisdom. In general, those who are desirous of reputation for anything are envious about that, and so are small-souled people, since everything seems great in comparison to themselves. The good things that make people feel envy have been stated: deeds and possessions in regard to which people are desirous of reputation or of honor or crave glory, and whatever things good fortune brings, are pretty much all sources of envy, especially the ones people themselves either crave or believe they ought to have, or the ones that put them a little ahead or a little behind others according to who possesses them.

And it is obvious who it is that people envy, since this has been stated along the way. They envy those near them in time, place, age, and reputation; hence it has been said[128]

> Kinship knows how to envy too.

They also envy those they feel rivalry with, since they feel it with the people who have been mentioned, while no one feels rivalry with people who are thousands of years away, or people of the future, or with the dead, or with those at the Pillars of Heracles,[129] or with those who they think of as far below in comparison with them or with others, or far beyond them, and they feel envy toward them in the same way and about the same sorts of things. And since people feel rivalry with their competitors, their rivals in love, and generally with those who are striving for the same things, it is necessarily these whom they envy most, the very thing meant by "potter versus potter."[130] And people envy those whose acquisitions or accomplishments are an unfavor-

---

128 In a fragment from Aeschylus.

129 The boundaries of the Straits of Gibraltar, an idiom for the edge of the world.

130 See 1381b 16 and note.

able reflection on them (and these are people near them and similar to them), since it is obviously their own fault that they do not attain what is good, and the consequent pain over this produces envy; and those who either have or have acquired those things that would be appropriate for them to have, or that they once possessed, which is why older people envy younger ones. And those who have spent a lot envy those who have spent little for the same things. And those who have attained something with difficulty or failed to attain it envy those who have attained it quickly. And it is clear on what occasions such people are happy, what people they are happy about, and what condition they are in, since the condition that makes them feel pain is the same condition that makes them feel pleasure at the opposite things. So if those who make the decision have themselves been brought into this condition, and those who expect to be pitied or to get something good are the sorts of people who have been described, it is clear that they will get no pity.

Chapter 11.

What the condition is of people who feel emulation, what sorts of things it involves, and whom it is felt toward are evident from what follows. For if emulation is a certain pain at the apparent presence, with people of a nature like one's own, of good things held in honor and possible to get for oneself, not because they belong to someone else but because they do not belong to oneself as well (which is why emulation is a decent passion of decent people, while envy is a base passion of base people, since the former sort of person, led by emulation, makes himself attain good things, but the latter sort, led by envy, makes his neighbor lose them), then it is necessarily those who regard themselves worthy of good things they do not possess who tend to **1388b**
feel emulation (and for things it is possible for them to get, since no one regards himself as worthy of things that appear impossible). It follows that the young and those with great souls[131] are of this sort. And so are those who have the sorts of good things that honored men deserve, which include riches, a multitude of friends, ruling positions, and things of that kind, for in the belief that it is the proper thing for them to be good people, they feel emulation for the sorts of good things that properly belong to those who maintain a state of good-

131 Greatness of soul (*megalopsuchia*) was a term in common use for anyone with an attitude of lofty superiority or disdain for petty concerns. In Bk. IV, Chap. 3, of the *Nicomachean Ethics*, Aristotle elevates it to the status of a major virtue, in those who rightly regard themselves as worthy of great things. In another work (*Posterior Analytics* 97b 14-26), he names Socrates and Achilles as great-souled men. The opposite vice of smallness of soul is mentioned above at 1384a 4.

ness.[132] Also, those whom others regard as worthy of something, and whose ancestors or kinspeople, or households, or race, or city are held in esteem for something, feel emulation for those things, since they think of them as being their own and regard themselves as worthy of them. And if it is good things held in esteem that are the objects of emulation, then necessarily the virtues are of this sort, and everything that is of benefit and service to others (since people honor those who perform such services and who are good), as well as all those good things one's neighbors get enjoyment out of—riches and beauty, for example, rather than health.

It is obvious too who it is people feel emulation toward, since it is those who have the things they feel emulation for and other things of a similar kind. These are the things that have been mentioned, such as courage, wisdom, and a ruling position (since rulers have the power to do good to many people, as do generals, rhetoricians, and everyone with that sort of power). Also emulated are those whom many people want to be like, or with whom many people want to be acquaintances or friends, or whom many people admire, or whom one admires oneself, and those about whom praises or eulogies are written by either poets or speechwriters. But people feel contempt for the opposite types, for contempt is the opposite of emulation, and looking down on someone is the opposite of looking up in emulation. And those who are in such a condition as to feel emulation for anyone or to be emulated must necessarily be contemptuous of those who have the bad attributes opposed to the goods ones that are emulated, for those reasons; this is why people often have contempt for those who are fortunate, when fortune comes to them in the absence of any of the good attributes held in esteem.

So those things by which the passions arise and are dispelled, from which the means of persuasion concerning them are derived, have been stated.

Chapter 12.

As for the kinds of people there are in respect to their characters, let us go over them next, in relation to passions, states of character, ages, and fortunes. By passions I mean anger, desire, and the sorts of things we have been discussing; by states of character, virtues and vices, and in connection with these, the sorts of things each type of person chooses and the ways they are inclined to act were stated earlier. The ages are youth, the prime of life, and old age; and by fortune
1389a I mean good birth, riches, political power, and their opposites, and good and bad fortune in general.

132 This cumbersome sentence seems to mean that even those who have all the advantages of birth and fortune aspire to live up to them, and to achieve the outward signs that they have done so. One may think of contemporary billionaires who seek to become as well known for philanthropy as for wealth.

Now the characters of young people are dominated by desires, and they are the sort who do whatever they desire. Among bodily desires, they are especially apt to be led by the desire for sex, and are unable to control it, but they are changeable and fussy in their desires, and though they desire things intensely, those desires quickly cease (for their wants are sharp but not extensive, like the thirsts and hungers of sick people). Spirited and quickly provoked, they are the sort who follow the promptings of anger, and they are overpowered by their spiritedness; for due to their love of honor, they cannot bear to be belittled, and lose their tempers whenever they imagine they have been treated unjustly. And while they love honor, they love winning more (for youthfulness desires pre-eminence, and winning is a sort of pre-eminence), and both of these more than they love money (for as Pittacus's quip to Amphiarus has it, they love money least who have not yet made the acquaintance of need). And they are apt to think well rather than badly of people, because they have not yet witnessed much depravity; they are also trusting, because they have not yet been deceived much, and filled with expectations, because the young are as overheated by nature as others are by drinking wine, and because, along with that, of not having experienced failure much. And they live in hope most of the time, since hope is for the future as memory is of bygone times, and for the young there is a lot of future and a short time gone by; for when life's day begins, there is nothing to remember and everything to hope for. And by reason of what has been said they are easily deceived (since they easily give way to hope), and more courageous as well (because they are spirited, which makes them not be afraid, and hopeful, which makes them have confidence, since no one is afraid when he is angry, and the hope of a good outcome is a source of confidence). They are also given to shame (since they have been educated only by conventional opinions, and they do not yet envision beautiful deeds of any other sort), and to greatness of soul (because they have not yet been humbled by life, and have not experienced necessities, and thinking oneself worthy of great things is greatness of soul, and this is the way a hopeful person thinks).

They prefer to perform beautiful deeds rather than advantageous ones, because they live by character more than by reasoning, and reasoning has to do with what is advantageous, while virtue has to do with what is beautiful. They love having friends and companions
more than those at other stages of life do, because they enjoy sharing 1389b
their lives with them and do not yet decide on anything with a view to advantage, and hence not on friends either. They err on the side of excess and overenthusiasm in all things, contrary to Chilon's motto[133]

133 "Nothing too much." This was one of the sayings carved on the temple of Apollo at Delphi, along with "Know thyself." Like Pittacus, mentioned above in this chapter, and Bias, mentioned in the next, Chilon was one of the ancients the Greeks called the Seven Sages.

(for they do "everything too much"—they love too much and hate too much and are the same way about everything else). They believe they know everything and are completely sure about it all (which is also responsible for the "everything too much"). The injustices they commit are due to insolence, not malice. They are full of pity because they assume all people are honest and better than they are (for they measure their neighbors by their own lack of malice and hence presume them to be undeserving of suffering). They love laughing, and therefore love being witty, for wittiness is educated insolence.

Chapter 13.

Such, then, is the character of the young, and in most respects those who are older and past their prime have characters that are made up of attributes pretty much the opposite of theirs. For just by having lived many years and having been deceived and mistaken more often, and because the greater part of human affairs are in a sorry state, they are not certain about anything and are less impressed with everything than one ought to be. They have beliefs, but do not know anything, and because of their doubts they always add "maybe" or "perhaps," and everything they say is like that; nothing is positively asserted. And they are malicious, for it is maliciousness to assume the worst about everything. Their distrust makes them suspect the worst, and they are distrustful because of their experience. For those reasons too, they neither love nor hate with much vigor, but following the advice of Bias, they love like people who are going to hate and hate like people who are going to love. They are small-souled on account of having been humbled by life, for they desire nothing great or out of the ordinary, but only the things that sustain life. And they are stingy, since property is one of the necessities, and they know by experience how hard it is to get and at the same time, how easy it is to lose. And they are cowardly and afraid of everything before it happens, since their constitution is the opposite of that of the young: they are chilled while the latter are heated, so that the old age paves the way to cowardice because fear is also a kind of chill. They love life, the more so on its last days because desire is for what is absent and what people lack is what they desire most. And their self-love is greater than it ought to be, for this too is a certain smallness of soul. And they live with a view to what is advantageous rather than to what is beautiful more so than
1390a one should, on account of being lovers of self. For the advantageous is good for oneself while the beautiful is good simply. And they are shameless rather than inclined toward shame, for since they do not have as much concern for the beautiful as for the advantageous, they pay no heed to the way things seem. And they hardly ever hope for anything, because of their experience (for the greater part of what happens is a sorry lot, since most things turn out for the worse) and also because of their cowardice.

They live in memory rather than in hope, for what remains of their life is short while what has gone by is long, and hope is for the future while memory is of bygone things. This is the very reason they are so excessively talkative, since they spend their time talking about the past because their pleasure comes from remembering. Their fits of temper are sharp but without strength, and their desires have either left off or lost strength, so that they neither feel desire nor act in accordance with it, but for gain. This is the reason people of that age give the appearance of being temperate, because their desires have slackened and they are enslaved to gain. And they live more by reasoning than in accord with character, since reasoning is concerned with what is advantageous and character with virtue. The injustices they commit come from malice, not from insolence. The old are inclined toward pity too, but not for the same reasons as the young; the latter are so from love of humanity, but the former from weakness, because they believe themselves to be close to suffering all kinds of things, and this was something that disposes people to pity. As a consequence, they are full of complaints, and they are not witty and do not love to laugh, since a complaining temperament is the opposite of a jolly one. Such are the characters of the young and the elderly, so since everyone is open to speeches addressed to his own sort of character and to people like himself, it is not unclear how people make use of speeches to give themselves and the things they say that sort of appearance.

Chapter 14.

For those in the prime of life, it is obvious that their character will be in between those of the other two ages; they eliminate the excess, and are neither greatly confident (for such a thing is indicative of rashness) nor overly fearful, but hold a beautiful position with respect to both, not trusting everyone and not distrusting everyone either, but judging instead by the truth of the situation, and living with a view not to what is beautiful or what is advantageous alone but to both, 1390b
and not to what is thrifty or what is wasteful but to what is fitting, and likewise in respect to spiritedness and desire, their temperance is combined with courage and their courage with temperance. For in the young and the old these are separated, since young people are courageous and self-indulgent while the elderly are temperate and cowardly. Speaking in a general way, whatever advantages youth and old age have in separation, they have paired together, and in whatever respects the other two ages are excessive or deficient, they hold the mean and fitting position between them. But while the body is at its peak from the age of thirty to thirty-five, the soul reaches its peak

about one year short of fifty.[134] So let this much be said about youth, old age, and the prime of life, and the sorts of character each has.

Chapter 15.

Next in order, let us speak about the goods that come from fortune, in particular those among them through which states of character turn out to be of certain sorts in human beings. Now an aspect of character in someone who has had a good birth is to be more ambitious for honor; for whenever anything is present, it is the usual practice for all people to accumulate more of it, and good birth is a legacy of honor from one's ancestors. Another character trait is to be contemptuous even of people similar to one's ancestors because the same things are held in higher honor and are easier to brag about when they happened farther back than when near the present. But while a good birth is one that results from the virtue of one's family, nobility results from not degenerating from that nature, and this is exactly what does not happen for the most part with those who are well born, most of whom are, instead, second-rate people. For in the generations of men, just as in what is brought forth by the earth, there is a certain harvest, and sometimes, when the stock is good, extraordinary men are produced for some time, and then things go back the other way. Gifted families degenerate into types of character marked more by mental instability, as were the decendants of Alcibiades and the elder Dionysius, while solidly reliable ones turn flighty or turn into sluggards, as did those of Cimon, Pericles, and Socrates.

Chapter 16.

The traits of character that go with riches are right on the surface for all to see; for being affected in some way by the possession of riches, people become insolent and haughty, since they have the atti-
1391a tude that they have everything that is good. Riches are some sort of valuation of the worth of other things, and so everything appears to be for sale in exchange for it. Rich people are extravagant and ostentatious: extravagant on account of luxury and the flaunting of their happiness, and ostentatious in bad taste because all people are in the habit of spending their time with what they love and admire, and because they suppose that other people are eager for the same things they are. At the same time, they come by this opinion reasonably, since lots of people are in need of what they have. This is the reason for what was said by Simonides to the wife of Hiero about the wise

134 These ages bear an interesting relation to those given by Socrates in Bk. VII of Plato's *Republic* (537E-540B) in his program for the education of the guardians of a city. The years from thirty to thirty-five are assigned to strenuous and intense participation in dialectic (as a counterpart to gymnastic training for the body), to be followed by a period of service to the city through age forty-nine, after which the candidate is ready for the completion of a philosophic education before taking a turn as one of the rulers.

and the rich when she asked whether it was better to become rich or wise: "Rich," he said, since, he said, one sees the wise spending their time at the doors of the rich.[135] Rich people also believe they deserve to rule, since they believe they have the things that make someone deserve to rule. The sum of the matter is that the character of a rich person is that of a fortunate fool. But there is a difference in their characters between those who have newly acquired riches and those who have been rich a long time: the newly rich have all the vices to a greater extent and in a worse form. It is just as if the newly rich person is uneducated about riches. The injustices the rich commit are not from malice, but in some cases from a tendency to be insolent, in others from an inclination to self-indulgence, which lead them, for instance, to assault or adultery.

Chapter 17.

With power too, most of the character traits are similarly pretty obvious. For power has some of the same ones as riches, and some better ones. For powerful people are more ambitious and more manly in their characters than rich people, since they aspire to those actions their power gives them the opportunity to perform, and they are more energetic on account of being in a position of responsibility, forced to look out for what affects their power. And they are dignified but not grave, for their rank gives them dignity enough, and so they are moderate about it, and dignity is a mild and graceful gravity. If they commit injustices they are no petty criminals but villains on a grand scale.

Good fortune in its separate forms contains the character traits of the people described (for the gifts of fortune that are thought to be the greatest tend in these directions), and in addition, good fortune makes one better off in regard to good children and good attributes
of body. And while people are more arrogant and inconsiderate as a 1391b
result of good fortune, one of the best character traits there is accompanies it, because such people are devout and have a special regard for the divine power, trusting it because of the things that have come to them from fortune.

So the things that pertain to the character traits that go with age and fortune have been stated, for the ones opposite to those mentioned are obvious from their opposites, such as the character of someone poor or unfortunate or powerless.

Chapter 18.

So, seeing as how the use of persuasive speeches is aimed at a judgment (for there is no further need of a speech about things we know and have made a judgment about), and this is the case even if

135 Simonides was a poet and was considered wise; Hiero was a tyrant and was definitely rich.

the one using the speech is giving an exhortation or warning to a single person, the way people do when advising or persuading someone (for that one person is nonetheless a judge, since whoever it is one needs to persuade is, to put it simply, a judge), and this is just as much the case whether one is speaking against opponents or against a proposition (for it is necessary to use the speech and refute the opposing arguments against which one is making it the same way as against an opposing speaker), and the case is the same even in speeches made for display (for the speech is composed with reference to the spectator just as for a judge, even though in general the only one who is a judge in an unqualified sense is someone judging the questions people bring into civic proceedings, where he is seeking to resolve how things stand with the facts in dispute or the proposals about which they are deliberating), and the types of character involved in advisory speeches in different forms of government have been spoken of earlier, the ways and means by which speeches need to be made suited to the listener's characters may be regarded as having been marked out.

And since there was a different end in view for each class of speeches, and opinions and premises concerning all of them have been collected from which those who are giving advice, making displays, or disputing opponents draw their means of persuasion, and materials from which it is possible to make those speeches suited to the listener's characters have been collected as well, and the distinctions that pertain to these have been made, what remains for us to do is to go through the topics common to them all. For it is necessary for all speakers to make additional use in their speeches of the matter of what is possible or impossible, and to try to show either that something will happen or that it has happened. Also, what has to do with magnitude is a topic common to all speeches, since everyone makes use of understating or exaggerating things in giving speeches of advice, of praise or blame,
1392a and of accusation or defense. And after these things have been determined, let us try to say anything we can about enthymemes in general, and about examples, so that, once the remaining matters have been added, we may provide what was proposed at the beginning. And among the common topics, the one most appropriate to speeches for display is exaggeration, as has been said; for courtroom speeches it is the topic of the past (since the judgment concerns past matters), and for advisory speeches it is that of the possible and the future.

Chapter 19.

First, then, let us speak about what is possible and impossible. Now if it is possible for one thing either to be or to come to be, its opposite would also seem to be possible; for instance, if it is possible for a human being to become healthy, it is also possible for him to get sick, since the same potency belongs to the opposite things, in the respect in which they are opposite. And if one thing is possible, then

so is something like it; and if a more difficult thing is possible, then so is an easier one. And if it is possible for a thing of great stature or beauty to come into being, it is also possible for that kind of thing to come into being in general, since it is more difficult for there to be a beautiful house than just a house. And if it is possible for the beginning of something to come into being, then the end is also possible, since no impossible thing can come into being or even begin coming into being; for the commensurability of the diagonal[136] could no more begin to come to be than come to be. And if the end is possible, the beginning is as well, since all things come into being from a beginning. And if it is possible for something more advanced in being or in generation to come into being, then something earlier in the process is also possible; for instance, if a man can come into being, a child can too (since that comes earlier in the process), but also if a child can come into being, a man can too (since the child is also a beginning). And things for which love or desire is present by nature are possible, since, for the most part no one loves or desires impossible things. And if there is a knowledge or art about some type of things, it is also possible for those things to be or come to be.[137] And all those things are possible whose source of coming into being is in people whom we can compel or persuade, those, namely, over whom we have power or authority or whose friends we are. And if the parts of something are possible, so too is the whole, and for the most part, if the whole is possible, so too are its parts; for if the front, top, and sides can come into being then so can a pair of shoes, and if the shoes, then a front, top, and sides as well. And if a whole general class consists of things 1392b
capable of coming into being, then a specific form of it can come into being as well, and if the form, then also the class; if, for instance, a ship can come into being then so can a battleship, and if a battleship, then also a ship. And if one of two things naturally related to each other is possible, so is the other; for example, if the double is possible, so is the half, and if the half, the double as well. And if something is capable of coming into being without art and preparation, all the more will it be possible by art and attentiveness, which is also why it was said by Agathon,

> While there are surely some things we have to do by art,
> Others just come to us from necessity and luck.

136 The incommensurability of the side and diagonal of a square was demonstrated by the Pythagoreans. It is Aristotle's usual example of a logical impossibility, used here merely as a negative illustration for arguments about practical possibilities. If someone claimed, for example, that there can be no democracy in a certain region of the world, the fact that formation of a democratic government had begun there would be sufficient proof that such a thing is not outside the realm of possibility. True impossibilities could never make the slightest appearance.

137 If a charlatan claimed to have some special knowledge or art, this would be a way of refuting his claim, if he could produce no evidence of results.

And if something is possible for those who are less skilled, weaker, or less intelligent to do, all the more is it possible for those who are their opposites, as Isocrates also said that it would be a terrible thing if he himself would be be unable to find out something when Euthynus had learned it. And it is clear that what pertains to the impossible is there to be seen from the opposites of the things mentioned.

Whether something has happened needs to be considered from the following points. First, if something with less of a nature to happen has happened, then something with more of such a nature would have happened too. And if something that usually happens later in a process has happened, then what is usually earlier has happened; if someone has forgotten something, for example, he also at one time learned it. And if someone was able and willing to do something, he did it, since all people, when they want to do something they have the ability to do, put it into action, since there is nothing standing in the way. The same thing is the case if someone wanted to do something and nothing external prevented it, if he was able to do it and was angry,[138] or if he was able to do it and desired it; since for the most part, what people desire to do, they do, if they are able to—the worse sort from lack of self-control and the decent ones because their desires are for decent things. And if someone was intending something, then he also did it, since the likelihood is that someone intending to do something does it. And if all those things have happened that naturally either lead to or are for the sake of something, that thing too has happened; for example, if there was lightning there was also thunder, and if someone has made attempts to do something, he has done it. And if all those things have happened that naturally come later in a process or are the things for the sake of something happens, then what comes earlier or is for the sake of the latter has also happened; for example, if there was thunder there was also lightning, and if someone did something, he has also made attempts. Of all these things, some happen this way by necessity and others for the most part. And what pertains to something's not having happened is obvious from the opposites of the things mentioned.

1393a What has to do with what will happen in the future is also clear from the same points. For what is in someone's power and wish will happen, as will those things that are in one's desire or anger or reasoning, combined with the power to do them, when there is also an impulse or intention to do them, since, for the most part, it is the things one intends that happen, rather than the things one does not intend. And if all the things that naturally happen earlier in a process have happened, so will what is naturally later, as when clouds gather, it is likely to rain. And if what is for the sake of something has happened,

138 This is the first explicit indication that the topic of this whole paragraph is intended to apply to speeches in a courtroom, as Aristotle mentioned at the end of the preceeding chapter.

that thing is likely to come into being too, as if there is a foundation, there will also be a house.

What has to do with greatness and smallness among actions, the greater and the lesser, and large and small matters in general, is obvious from things said by us above. For in the section on advisory speeches, there was a discussion of the magnitude of goods, and of what is greater and lesser simply, so since for each kind of speeches, the end set before it is a good, in the form of the advantageous, the beautiful, or the just, it is clear that arguments for exaggeration need to be taken from those materials by all speakers. To seek to go further beyond these things on the subject of magnitude and excess taken simply is to waste words, for in matters of action it is the particulars more than the universals that are decisive to the business at hand.

Let these things be said on the subject of the possible and impossible and whether something has or has not happened or will or will not happen, and also about greatness and smallness among actions.

Chapter 20.

What concerns the means of persuasion common to all speeches remains to be discussed, now that the particular topics have been spoken of. And the common means of persuasion are two in kind: example and enthymeme (for a maxim[139] is a part of an enthymeme). So let us speak first about example, since an example is similar to an induction[140] and an induction is a starting point. Examples are of two forms; one form of example is to describe events that have happened in the past, and one is to make them up oneself. Of the latter, one kind are analogies and another are fables, such as those of Aesop and the Libyan ones. A stating of facts is some such thing as if one were to say that it is necessary to make preparations against the King and not allow him to get his hands on Egypt, because in earlier times
Darius did not cross the sea until he had taken Egypt, but did cross 1393b
once he had taken it, and again Xerxes did not make his attack until he had taken it, and did cross over after he had taken it, so that if this King takes it too, he will cross over, and hence this is something that cannot be tolerated. An analogy is the sort of argument Socrates used, as if someone were to say that people chosen by lot ought not to be rulers,[141] since that would be the same sort of thing as if one chose athletes by lot, not the ones with the ability to compete but whoever won the lottery, or if whichever one of the sailors one chose by lot had to steer the ship, as if it had to be the lottery winner and not the one with knowledge.

139 Discussed in Chapter 21 below.

140 See 1356b 1 and note.

141 See 1365b 31-32. Socrates elaborates the "ship of state" analogy in Plato's *Republic*, 488A.

A fable is, say, that of Stesichorus about Phaleris or that of Aesop in defense of the demagogue. For when the people of Himera had chosen Phaleris as military dictator, and were about to give him a bodyguard, Stesichorus, after he had made his other arguments, told them a fable about how a horse had a meadow all to himself. When a stag came in and did a lot of damage to the pasture and the horse wanted to get revenge on the stag, he asked some man if he could join him in taking vengeance on the stag; the man said he would, on condition that the horse would take a bridle while he mounted on him holding javelins. When the horse agreed and the man climbed on him, instead of getting his revenge he himself became the man's slave. "Now see that you too," he said, "in your desire to get revenge on your enemies, do not suffer the same fate as the horse in the same way. For you have already taken the bridle by choosing a military dictator, and if you give him a bodyguard and let him climb up above you, you will at once become slaves to Phaleris." And Aesop, addressing an assembly in Samos, on behalf of a demagogue facing a death sentence, said a fox who was crossing a river was swept into a cleft in the rocks, and being unable to get out, she was in a bad way for a long time and had a lot of dog-ticks on her. A hedgehog was wandering by and when he saw her he felt sorry for her, and asked if he should pull the ticks off her, but she would not let him. When he asked why, she said "because these ticks on me are already full and are drawing little blood, but if you take these away, other hungry ones will come along and drink off the rest of my blood." "But, men of Samos, this man likewise is not doing you any more harm, now that
1394a he is rich, but if you put him to death, others will come who are poor and will ruin you by stealing what is left." Fables are well suited to public speaking, and they have this good point, that while it is hard to find similar events that have happened in the past, it is easier to come up with fables. One ought to make them up in the same way as analogies, if one is able to see the point of similarity, and philosophic pursuits make it easier to do that very thing. But while the examples that come from fables are easier to provide, those that come from past events are more useful to deliberate on, since things in the future for the most part resemble those in the past.

It is necessary to make use of examples as demonstration when one has no enthymemes (since persuasion comes from them), but as testimonies when one does have enthymemes, using the examples as a follow-up to them. When one puts them first, they seem like an induction, but induction is not appropriate for rhetorical speeches except in a few cases, but when used as follow-ups they are like testimonies, and a witness is persuasive in every situation. Hence, too, when one puts them first it is necessary to state a number of them, but for one who puts it at the end, one example is sufficient, since a single solid witness serves the purpose. How many forms of examples there are, then, and how and when they are to be used, have been stated.

Chapter 21.

As for speechmaking in maxims, once it has been said what a maxim is, it might best become clear on what subjects, when, and by whom it is appropriate for this style of speaking to be used in speeches.[142] A maxim is a declaration, but not one that concerns particulars, such as the sort of person Iphicrates is, but a universal one, and not about all universal matters, for instance that what is straight is the opposite of what is bent, but about those things that actions are concerned with, and what is to be chosen or avoided in taking action; since, therefore, the sort of syllogism that concerns such matters is an enthymeme, it is pretty much the case that the conclusions and premises of enthymemes, when taken out of the syllogism, are maxims. For example,[143]

> No man who is right-thinking by nature should ever
> Let his children be educated to be outstandingly wise.

That is a maxim; but when the reason and the "why" are added, the sum total is an enthymeme, as with,

> For apart from any other lazy inclination they acquire,
> They incur a resentful jealousy from their neighbors.

And this, 1394b

> There is no man who is happy in all things,

or this,

> There is no one among men who is free,

is a maxim, but add the next line and it is an enthymeme,

> For he is a slave either to money or to fortune.

So if a maxim is what has been described, there are necessarily four forms of maxim, since it will occur either with or without an addendum; the ones that need demonstration are all those that state something that goes against popular opinion or disputable, but those that have nothing against popular opinion in them lack addenda.

---

142 "Maxim" is an old-fashioned word, as are the words "gnomic" and "sententious" which describe this way of packing weighty-sounding generalizations into pithy sentences, but the style of speechmaking is perennial.

143 Most of the following examples are from Euripides, who does not use maxims more than Aeschylus or Sophocles, but is more likely to state a reason. The first two together are *Medea* 294-297, the third is a fragment from the lost play *Stheneboea*, the fourth and fifth are *Hecuba* 864-865, and the seventh is *Trojan Women* 1051. The sixth and ninth are sometimes attributed to Epicharmus, and the author of the eighth is unknown.

There are some among them that should necessarily have no addendum because it is already known, such as,

> The best thing for a man is to have his health; it seems
> that way to me anyway,

since it appears that way to most people, and there are others that are evident as soon as they are stated to those who look at the matter, such as

> No one is a lover who does not always love.

Of those with addenda, some are parts of enthymemes, like "No man who is right-thinking should…," and others have the force of enthymemes without being parts of enthymemes.[144] These are the ones that people hold in especially high regard, and they are all those in which the reason for what is being said is made evident, as in

> Being mortal, do not keep an immortal anger going,

For saying one ought not to keep it going is a maxim, but the addition "being mortal" is the reason why, and likewise with

> It is right for a mortal to think mortal thoughts,
> not immortal ones.

How many forms of maxim there are, then, and for what sort of use each is fitted, are clear from what has been said. For on matters that are disputable or against popular opinion, it is not fitting for them to lack an addendum, but it is possible to put the addendum first and use the maxim as a conclusion (as if one were to say "Since one ought not to incur jealousy or be lazy, I say it behooves one not to get an education"), or to say that first and say the preceding part after it. With things that are not paradoxical obscurities, it is fitting for the reason to be added as concisely as possible. In such cases, even
1395a laconic[145] terseness or speaking in riddles is appropriate, as if one says what Stesichorus said to the Locrians, that they ought not to be insolent, lest their cicadas do their singing from the ground. Speaking in maxims is fitting for those more advanced in age, on matters in which one is experienced; hence it is as unsuitable for someone not of such an age to speak in maxims as to tell stories, and on matters in which one is inexperienced it is foolish and shows a lack of education.

144 The four forms of maxim, then, are: lacking an added reason because it is already known, lacking one because it is self-evident as soon as stated, having one and stating it fully, and having one somehow incorporated in the maxim itself.

145 This common word comes from the name of the region surrounding Sparta. In his *Life of Lycurgus*, Plutarch says the Spartans were brought up to make their speech like their swords, short and sharp. The following example, laconic in style though not Spartan in origin, may be more obscure to us than it would have been to Aristotle's contemporaries, who would know well that cicadas sing in trees, and that armies that lay waste a city's lands burn down all the trees.

A sufficient sign of this is that it is country bumpkins who are most given to making up maxims and quick to show them off.

To speak in universal terms of what is not universal is most suited to bitter complaining and making things seem dreadful, either to start off with in these cases or after one has demonstrated the facts. One ought to use even overworked and clichéd maxims if they are to the point, since they seem to be right just by being clichés, as though everyone agreed with them; for instance,[146] for someone exhorting troops to face a danger without favorable sacrifices,

> One bird-omen is best: to fight for the fatherland,

or when they are the lesser force,

> The War God plays no favorites,

or to wipe out even the innocent children of the enemy,

> Thoughtless as a child is he who leaves alive the sons
> of fathers slain.

And some proverbs are also maxims, like the proverbial "Athenian next door."[147] And one ought to assert maxims even when they run counter to sayings that have taken on the status of public authority (by which I mean things like "Know thyself" and "Nothing too much"), whenever so doing is either going to make one's character appear better or make one's speech passionate. It is passionate, for example, if one should claim angrily, "It's a lie that one should know oneself; if this man knew himself, anyway, he would never have considered himself fit to be a general." It shows better character to say that one ought not, as people claim, to love as if they are going to hate, but instead to hate as if they are going to love. And one ought to make what one is choosing clear by the wording, or if not, to add the reason. One might say it this way: "It is not right to love the way people say, but as if one were always going to keep loving, since the other is the traitor's way." Or like this: "The saying is not to my liking, for a true friend ought to love as if he were always going to keep loving," and

146 The first two are from the *Iliad*, XII, 243 and XVIII, 309, the third, from the early poet Stasinus, was quoted at 1376a 7 above as a proverb.

147 An expression from the Peloponnesian wars, for a dangerous neighbor. The implicit maxim would be something like: you can't relax your guard with an Athenian next door.

"I don't care for 'Nothing too much' either, for one ought to go to extremes in hating evils."[148]

1395b Maxims have one great benefit in speeches that comes from a lack of sophistication in its hearers, since they love it when someone speaking in universal terms hits upon opinions which they hold in a particular case. What I mean will be clear from the following, which will make clear at the same time how one ought to hunt for maxims. As was said, a maxim is a universal declaration, and people love it when something they already happen to assume about a particular case is stated universally. For instance, if anyone happened to be afflicted with worthless neighbors or children, he might be especially receptive to someone who says that there is nothing more annoying than neighbors, or nothing more foolhardy than having children, so one needs to guess[149] what sorts of things they happen to have preconceived notions about, and then say something universal about them along those lines. So that is one use for speechmaking in maxims, and they have another, weightier use, because they make speeches reflect character. And those speeches in which a choice is evident have character in them. But all maxims do this because the person stating the maxim reveals the universal basis of his choices, so if the maxims are sound, they make the speaker appear as someone with a sound character.[150] Concerning a maxim, then, what it is, how many forms of it there are, how it needs to be used, and what benefit it has, let these things have been said.

Chapter 22.

Let us speak in general about the way one ought to seek out enthymemes, and after that about their topics, since each of these discussions takes a different form. Now it was said above that an enthymeme is a syllogism, what manner of syllogism it is, and in what respect it differs from those in dialectical arguments. For the conclusion ought not to be drawn from far back or by taking in all the steps, since the former is unclear on account of its length and

---

148 "Nothing too much" is Chilon's motto; see note to 1389b 4. The cynical saying about loving and hating is Bias's advice, mentioned at 1389b 23-25. The last suggestion of Aristotle in this paragraph is an ancestor (by way of Cicero) of Barry Goldwater's line at the 1964 Republican convention, "Extremism in defense of liberty is no vice; moderation in the pursuit of justice is no virtue." The professor who contributed the line to his speech is said to have telephoned friends, claiming the extremism issue would be dead as soon as the speech was heard. Aristotle's claim for this rhetorical tactic is more modest.

149 See *Gorgias* 463A, where Socrates names this as the special aptitude of rhetoricians.

150 Character (*êthos*) and choice (*proairesis*), the two central notions in Aristotle's *Nicomachean Ethics* are understood in relation to one another. Character is formed by choice, when one takes a stand in relation to feelings and to pleasure and pain; choice then has a stable basis in character, in which thinking and desire become united in view of an end. See also 1417a 16-36 below.

the latter is a waste of words by stating the obvious. This is also the reason uneducated people are more persuasive among crowds than educated ones are, just as the poets say the speech of the uneducated is music to the ears of the crowd, because people of the one sort make general arguments in universal terms, while the others argue from what they know and things near at hand. Hence one needs to argue not on the basis of all reputable sources but from a limited group of them, such as those that are held in repute by the judges or seem to 1396a
be people they approve of, because this is the way it appears likely for something to be clear to all or most people. And one ought not to draw conclusions only from necessary premises but also from things that are the case for the most part.

Now the first thing one needs to grasp is that it is necessary to have available all or at least some of the things pertinent to that subject one needs to speak and reason about, whether in political argumentation or in any other kind; if you have none, you have nothing to draw conclusions from. I mean, for instance, how would we be able to give advice to the Athenians about whether or not a war should be fought without having a grasp of what their forces are, whether they are naval or infantry or both, how many they are, what revenues, friends, and enemies they have, and then too what wars they have fought and how, and other things of that kind? Or how could we praise them if we had no idea of the naval battle at Salamis or the battle at Marathon or the things done by the descendants of Heracles or anything else of that kind? For all speakers praise people on the basis of beautiful attributes that belong to them or are thought to belong to them. Likewise, they blame people for attributes of an opposite kind, considering what there is of that sort that belongs to them or is thought to, for instance that they treated the Greeks like slaves and actually reduced to slavery men who had been their most valiant allies against the barbarian invader, the Aeginetans and Potidaeans, and anything else of that kind, any other such transgression that may belong to them. And in the same way, when people give speeches of accusation and defense they make those accusations and defenses from a consideration of the pertinent facts. It makes no difference whether it has to do with Athenians or Spartans, a human being or a god; one does the same thing. And if one is giving advice to Achilles, or praising or blaming him, or making an accusation or defense of him, the pertinent things about him or the things that are thought to be so need to be grasped, so we may argue from them, praising or blaming him if some beautiful or shameful thing is present, accusing or defending him if there is anything just or unjust, and giving advice if there is anything advantageous or harmful. And what has to do with any matter whatsoever needs to be handled in a way similar to these; on the subject of justice, for instance, whether it is or is not a good thing, one needs to argue from things that pertain to justice and the good.

So since everyone obviously demonstrates things in that way,
1396b whether his reasoning is more precise or more loose (since they do not take their arguments from all premises but from the ones that are pertinent on each subject), and since it is clear that it is impossible to show anything in any other way by means of a speech, it is obviously necessary, as is said in the *Topics*, to have first of all on each subject a selection of the most relevant matters the subject takes in, and when subjects come up on the spur of the moment, to seek things out in the same manner, not looking off into an unlimited array of things but into the things pertinent to what the speech is about, and getting a sketch of the most things that are closest to the matter at hand. For the more of the pertinent materials one has to work with, the easier it is to show things, and the closer they are to the matter, the more appropriate and less generic is what is shown. I mean by generic, praising Achilles because he is a human being and a half-god, or because he went on the expedition to Troy, since these things apply to many others as well, so that such a speech gives no more praise to Achilles than to Diomedes, but things that are attributes of no one other than Achilles are particular to him, such as having killed Hector, the best of the Trojans, and Cycnus, who prevented everyone from getting off the ships as long as he was unwounded, and the fact that Achilles was the youngest one to go on the expedition, and did so without being bound by an oath, and everything else of that kind.

So one manner of selecting material, and that which is primary, is by topics; let us now discuss the elements of enthymemes. By an element of an enthymeme, I mean the same thing as a topic. But let us first mention some things it is necessary to speak of first. For there are two forms of enthymemes: those of one form show that something is or is not so while those of the other are counterarguments, and they differ in the same way as a counterargument and a syllogism in dialectical reasoning do. An enthymeme that shows something is one that draws a conclusion from things that are agreed, but a counterargument draws conclusions that are not agreed to. And we pretty well have a grasp of the topics on each species of useful and necessary subjects, since a selection has been made of premises having to do with each of them, so that the topics one needs to draw on for enthymemes about what is good or bad, beautiful or shameful, or just or unjust are already available to us, and topics having to do with types of character, passions, and particular traits of character have been taken
1397a up in the same way. But let us now also take a different approach to all these arguments as a whole,[151] and state an array of examples of counterarguments, demonstrations, and of apparent enthymemes which are not enthymemes for the same reason that they are not syl-

151 The program for the rest of Bk. II is: a compilation of arguments not grouped by subject matter (Ch. 23), examples of different kinds of fallacious arguments (24), and strategies of refuting or minimizing an argument (25-26).

logisms. When these have been displayed, let us distinguish between refutations and objections, and sources from which one needs to bring them to bear on enthymemes.

Chapter 23.

(1)[152] One topic has to do with showing things by opposites. For one needs to consider whether an opposite belongs to an opposite, refuting the proposition if it does not and furnishing proof if it does.[153] For instance, the proposition that being temperate is good, because being self-indulgent is harmful. Or, as in the *Messeniacus*,[154] "If war is the cause of the present evils, it is necessary to set them right with peace." Or,

> If in fact when people act badly without meaning to
> It is unjust to descend into anger at them,
> Then when anyone acts well in any way by compulsion
> It is not fitting for him to be owed any thanks.

Or,

> But if in fact among mortals there is lying that is
> Trusted, you'd better believe the opposite too, that
> Lots of truths get no trust from mortals.

(2) Another topic has to do with showing things by similar grammatical inflections, since they have to go together or not in a similar way. For instance, the proposition that what is just is not good in every respect, since what is done justly would also be good in every respect, but as it is, being killed justly is not something one chooses.[155]

(3) Another topic has to do with showing things by mutually related items. For if doing something in a beautiful or just way pertains to one of them, undergoing it pertains to the other, or giving an order in the one case and performing the deed in the other. For instance, as Diomedon the tax-collector said about taxes, "If there's no disgrace in your selling them, there's none in our buying them."[156] And if "beautifully" or "justly" applies to the one something is done to, it also applies to the one who has done it. But it is possible to introduce a fallacy in this argument, for if someone undergoes something justly,

152 Aristotle does not number the topics in this chapter or the next. The numbers have been added by the translator for the convenience of the reader.

153 As the examples show, Aristotle means that a proposition can be tested by applying the opposite of its predicate to the opposite of its subject.

154 See the note to 1373b 18. The first of the two following sets of verses is of unknown origin; the second is a fragment from Euripides' lost play *Thyestes*.

155 This line of argument, and the limitations of the next one, escape the notice of the rhetorician Polus in the *Gorgias* at 476B and following.

156 It was common in the ancient world for governments to "farm out" the right to collect taxes to anyone rich enough to make the investment.

it is still perhaps not just for it to be done by you. Therefore there is need to consider separately whether the sufferer deserves to suffer and
1397b whether the doer has a right to do, and then to use the argument in whichever way it fits the situation. For sometimes the two are things not in accord in such a case, and nothing prevents it from being like that in Theodectes' *Alcmaeon*, where to the question "Was there none among mortals who found your mother abominable?" Alcmaeon says in reply, "One has to consider that by taking it in two parts," and when Alphesiboea asks how, he responds

> They judged it right for her to die, but not for me to
> have killed her.

But there was also the trial involving Demosthenes and the killers of Nicanor, where because it was judged that they could justly put someone to death, he was thought to have been put to death justly, and the one about the man who died in Thebes, in which the defendant insisted that it be judged whether it was a just man who died, since it would not be unjust to kill someone who would be dying justly.

(4) Another topic has to do with showing things by the more and the less. For instance, "If not even the gods know everything, then humans hardly could," since that is to say "If something doesn't belong to a thing to which it would apply more, it clearly does not belong to a thing to which it would apply less." And that someone who hits his father also hits his neighbors comes from "If something that applies less belongs, then something that applies more does too." For people are less apt to hit their fathers than their neighbors. So it can go that way, or "if something does not belong to a thing it applies to more..." or "if something does belong to a thing it applies to less..." according to what needs to be shown, whether that something does or does not belong. There is also the case in which something is neither more nor less, on the basis of which it was said[157]

> When your father deserves pity for having lost
> children too,
> Does Oeneus deserve none for having lost a glorious son?

Other examples of this are: if Theseus did no injustice, neither did Paris; or, if the sons of Tyndareus did no injustice, neither did Paris; and if Hector did no injustice to Patroclus, Paris did none to Achilles; and if no other possessors of arts are to be despised, neither are philosophers; and if generals, who are often killed, are not to be

157 A fragment from Antiphon's *Meleager*. In the following examples, Theseus had abducted Helen, the sons of Tyndareus (Castor and Pollux) had abducted women engaged to other men, and Hector had killed Patroclus in battle. The reference to the generals seems to mean that they are killed, not in battle but by Athenian juries who hold them responsible for losing battles; the point would be that sophists are despised for the harm their pupils sometimes do. Gorgias makes a similar argument about rhetoricians and boxing instructors at *Gorgias* 476C-477C.

despised, then neither are sophists; and "if a private citizen should care about the reputation of you people, you should care about that of the Greeks."

(5) Another topic has to do with showing things by considering the time, as, for instance, Iphicrates did in his speech against Harmodius, saying "If before I had done it, I had demanded the honor of getting a statue once I did it, you would have given it; will you not give it to me now that I have done it? Don't make promises when you expect something and then break them when you have gotten it." And again, it was said to the Thebans, to let Phillip pass through into Athenian 1398a
territory, because if he had demanded it before helping them against the Phocians, they would have agreed; it would be absurd, then, if they would not let him through because he gave up that chance and trusted them.

(6) Another topic has to do with showing something by turning things said against oneself on the one who said them, as in *Teucer*. But the way in which Iphicrates used it against Aristophon is different:[158] when he asked him whether he would have betrayed the fleet for money, and he said no, he then said, "You, who are Aristophon, would not have betrayed it, and I, who am Iphicrates, would?" But the other person has to be someone who seems more apt to commit an injustice; otherwise it would be obviously ridiculous, as it would if anyone else said this to Aristides, if he made an accusation, with the aim of discrediting the accuser. For the accuser always means to imply that he is a better person than the accused, so one has to counter this. But it is wholly absurd when anyone criticizes others for things he himself does or would do, or urges them to do things he himself does not and would not do.

(7) Another topic has to do with showing something by a definition, such as what divinity means: "Is it not a god or the work of a god? And surely whoever believes something is the work of a god necessarily also believes there *are* gods."[159] And the way Iphicrates showed that the noblest man means the best man, since nothing noble belonged to Harmodius and Aristogeiton before they did something noble, and so he himself was closer kin to them: "As for deeds at any rate, mine are more closely akin to Harmodius and Aristogeiton than yours are." And as is argued in the speech on Paris, that everyone would agree that disordered people are those who are not satisfied by

158 This might mean "is outstanding," since *diapherein* can mean either to differ or to surpass. *Teucer,* a lost play of Sophocles, may have contained a more ordinary example too familiar to need quoting.

159 This is an argument Socrates used to defend himself against the charge of impiety; see Plato's *Apology,* 27a and following. With the next example, on Iphicrates' origins, see 1367b 19 and note, and on his dispute with a descendant of the famous Harmodius, see 1397b 31. On the Archelaus mentioned in the last example in this section, see note to *Gorgias* 470D.

the enjoyment of one body. And then there is the reason why Socrates said he did not go at Archelaus' invitation, for he said it would be just as much an act of insolence to be put in the position of being unable to repay good as it would to be unable to repay evil. All these people reason by making definitions and getting at what something is in connection with the matters about which they speak.

(8) Another topic has to do with showing something by the number of meanings of a word, as in the chapter of the *Topics* on using them rightly.[160]

(9) Another topic has to do with showing something by a division. For instance, if there are three things for the sake of which all people commit injustice, since it is either for this one or that one or this other, and it is impossible for it to be on account of two of them, and they themselves are not even claiming it is for the third.

(10) Another topic has to do with showing something by induction. For instance, from the example of the Peparethian woman, to argue
1398b that women everywhere establish the truth about their offspring; for this happened to the Athenian rhetorician Mantias, when he was disputing the claim of his son, and the mother spoke out against him, and at Thebes, when Ismenias and Stilbon were in dispute, and the Dodonan woman revealed Thettaliscus as the son of Ismenias, and he was so regarded for that reason. And then there is this from Theodectes' *Law*: "if people do not turn over their own horses to those who have taken bad care of the horses of others, or their ships to people who have capsized the ships of others, and if it is like that in all cases, then those who have been bad at guarding the safety of others are not the sort to use for one's own." And the way Alkidamas argued that everyone honors the wise: "The Parians hold Archilochus in honor, at any rate, in spite of his foul mouth, and the Chians honor Homer, even if he was not their fellow citizen, and the Mytilenaeans honor Sappho, even though she was a woman, and the Spartans made Chilon one of their Elders, even though they least of any people were lovers of literary pursuits, and the Greeks in Italy honor Pythagoras, and the Lampsacenes buried Anaxagoras, even though he was a foreigner, and still honor him even now, and the Athenians flourished when they followed the laws of Solon and Spartans those of Lycurgus, and at Thebes, the city flourished at the same time that those in charge became philosophers."

(11) Another topic has to do with showing something by a judgment on the same matter, or a similar one, or an opposite one, especially if everyone always judged it that way, or if not, at least most people, or all or most of the wise or the good, or the present judges

160 The chapter in question is I, 15. "Using them rightly" translates *tou orthôs*, which is the only reading in any manuscript sources, but it may be an early copyist's mistake for *tou oxeôs*, "sharp," which is one of the first ambiguous words discussed in the *Topics* chapter.

themselves, or people whom they accept or whose judgment it is not possible to oppose (such as those who hold authority) or not seemly to oppose (such as gods, a father, or teachers). This is the way Autocles meant what he said to Mixidemides, "So it was seemly for the Dread Goddesses to submit to the lawful claims of the Areopagus, but not for Mixidemides."[161] Or Sappho, that dying is a bad thing, since the gods had judged it so; otherwise they would have died. Or the way Aristippus meant what he said to Plato, who, so he thought, had made some pronouncement too emphatically: "Surely our companion never said anything like that," meaning Socrates. And Hegesipolis asked the god in Delphi, after first consulting the oracle at Olympia, whether things seemed the same way to him as to his father, implying that it 1399a
would be shameful to say the opposite.[162] And that Helen was a woman above reproach, as Isocrates wrote, since Theseus judged her so, and similarly with Paris, because the judgment of the goddesses singled him out, and with Evagoras, that he was above reproach, as Isocrates said, since "Conon, at any rate, thought so when he was out of luck, since he went to Evagoras, passing by everyone else."[163]

(12) Another topic has to do with showing something by parts, as in the *Topics*, on the sort of motion the soul is, since it has to be this kind or that kind.[164] There is an example in Theodectes' *Socrates*: "What holy place has he profaned? Which gods has he not honored that the city believes in?"

(13) Another topic has to do with showing something by consequences, in exhorting or warning, accusing or defending, or praising or blaming, since in most cases it turns out that the same thing is accompanied by something good or bad. For instance, being envied is a bad consequence of education, but being wise is a good one. "Well then, one shouldn't get an education, since one shouldn't incur envy." "No indeed, one should get an education, since one should be wise." The *Art* of Callippus amounts to this topic, with the addition of the possible and the other things mentioned.

(14) Another topic applies when one needs to make an exhortation or warning about two things paired and set against one another,

161 An invocation of the precedent enshrined in Aeschylus's *Eumenides* that even the Furies abided by the judgment of the Athenian high court.

162 Aristotle apparently misspelled the name of the Spartan king mentioned in Xenophon's *Hellenica* (IV, 7.2) who consulted Apollo at Delphi only after having gotten the reply he wanted from Zeus at Olympia.

163 On Isocrates, see note to 1368a 20. Conon was a general who, afraid to go back to Athens after losing a battle, sought asylum from Evagoras, the king of Cyprus.

164 *Topics* 111b, 5-11. Aristotle identifies four kinds of motion in the *Physics*: change of place, qualitative or quantitative change, and change of thinghood or being; one can thus argue by a process of elimination, and leave it to an opponent to demonstrate any contention that the enumeration was incomplete. Aristotle himself considers the soul to be an activity or being-at-work rather than a motion; see especially 408b 1-32 of *On the Soul*.

using the method described in the preceding topic for both cases. It differs in that in the other case randomly related things are contrasted, but opposite things here. For instance, a priestess did not allow her son to be a public speaker, "For if you say things that are just," she said, "people will hate you, but if you say things that are unjust, the gods will." "But then one *should* be a public speaker, for when you say things that are just, the gods will love you, and when you say things that are unjust, people will." This is the same as the saying about buying the swamp with the salt; and when each of a pair of opposites has a good and a bad consequence, opposite each to each, this is criss-crossing.[165]

(15) Another topic, since people do not praise the same things openly and out of public view, but mostly praise just and beautiful things openly while privately wanting what is advantageous instead, has to do with trying to use those statements to draw the other conclusion. This topic is the most decisive way of confounding an opinion.

(16) Another topic has to do with showing something by those things that follow the same logic. For instance, Iphicrates, when people were requiring his son to do public service when he was younger than the appropriate age, just because he was tall, said that if they
1399b considered tall boys men, they would be voting next that short men were boys. And Theodectes, in his *Law*, said "You make citizens of mercenaries like Strabax and Charidemus for their decent behavior; will you not make exiles of those among the mercenaries who do irreparable harm?"

(17) Another topic has to do with showing something by the fact that the consequence of things would be the same. For instance, Xenophanes used to say that people who claim the gods were born are just as impious as those who say they die, since in both ways it follows that there is a time when the gods are not in existence. But this also involves taking what follows from each thing in a universal sense, as always being the same: "You are about to make a judgment not on Isocrates, but about a way of life, whether it is right to pursue philosophy," and giving earth and water is slavery, and joining in the common peace is following orders.[166] But each case is to be taken in whichever way serves one's purpose.

(18) Another topic has to do with showing something from the fact that people do not always choose the same thing later that they did

165 *Blaisôsis*, apparently meant to convey a figure both knock-kneed and pigeon-toed, since an original pair of branching alternatives has another branch on each side turning back toward each other.

166 "Giving earth and water" was a euphemism for collaborating with the invading army during the Persian War; some Greek cities sought to be spared by allowing the invaders to camp in their territory. The "common peace" was a euphemism for the capitulation of most of Greece to Alexander the Great.

earlier, but just the opposite. This enthymeme is an instance: "Can it be that we who when exiled fought in order to come back home are going to flee, now that we have returned, in order not to fight?" For at one time they would have chosen to stay even if it meant fighting, but at the other they would have chosen not to fight even if it meant not staying.

(19) Another topic has to do with showing something by claiming a thing is the case or happened for the sake of some end it might possibly be for or have happened for, for instance, if one were to give something to someone in order to cause pain by taking it away. This too is said from that point of view:

> For most people, it is not from bearing them any goodwill
> That the divine power grants them great prosperity,
> But so the calamities they get will be more conspicuous.

And so is this from Antiphon's *Meleager*:

> Not so they could kill the beast, but in order that
> they might
> Become witnesses to Greece of the excellence of Meleager.

And this from Theodectes' *Ajax*: that Diomedes singled out Odysseus not to honor him, but so that his follower would be a lesser man. For it is possible he did it for that purpose.

(20) Another topic, used in common by parties to a legal dispute and speakers giving advice, has to do with showing something by considering the things that impel and deter people, for the sake of which they act and avoid action. For these are things which one ought to act on if they are present, but not act if they are not, for example, if something is possible and easy and beneficial to oneself or to one's friends or harmful to one's enemies, even if it brings some penalty as long as the penalty is less than the thing gained; people are impelled to act on the basis of these things and deterred on the basis of their 1400a
opposites. And people make both accusations and defenses on the basis of these same things, basing their defenses on the deterrent factors and their accusations on the ones that impel action. This topic is the whole *Art* of both Pamphilus and Callippus.

(21) Another topic has to do with showing something by things that are believed to happen but are hard to credit, because they would not have been believed if they had not been the case, or been close to happening. There is even more reason to believe such things, because people assume things that either are the case or are likely, so if something is hard to credit and not likely, it would be true, since it is not on account of likelihood or credibility that it is believed to be so. For instance, when Androcles, of the Pitthean district of Athens, was making a speech attacking the law, after the people hooted at him for saying "the laws need a law to correct them," continued, "Well,

fish need to be salted, even though it's not likely or credible for them to need salt when they've grown up in saltwater, and mashed olives need olive oil, incredible as it may be for the things olive oil comes from to need olive oil."[167]

(22) Another topic for counterargument is to look for inconsistencies, if anything from among places, times, actions, and words is inconsistent, in the separate cases of one's opponent (for instance, "he claims he's your friend, but he was in on the conspiracy with the Thirty Tyrants"),[168] and oneself ("he claims I'm fond of lawsuits, but he can't demonstrate even one suit that I've taken to court"), and between oneself and one's opponent ("this fellow has never even made a loan, while I've even paid ransom for many of you").

(23) Another topic for people and actions that have been the subject of prior prejudice, or seem to be, is to explain the reason why things are not as they appear, since there *is* something that makes them appear that way. For instance, a woman who had given her own son to someone else was thought to be sexually involved with the young man because she kissed him, but when the reason was explained, the slander was brought to nothing. There is also an example in Theodectes' *Ajax* in which Odysseus explains to Ajax why he is a more courageous man than Ajax but does not seem that way.

(24) Another topic has to do with showing something from its cause: that if the cause is present, it is the case, and if not, not, for the cause and that of which it is the cause go together, and nothing is the case without a cause. For instance, when Thrasybulus made the accusation that Leodamas's name had been engraved on a pillar in the marketplace for treason, but had been scratched out at the time of the Thirty Tyrants, Leodamas said there was no possibility of that, since the Thirty would have trusted him more if his hostility to the democratic faction had been left inscribed.

(25) Another topic has to do with showing something by considering whether there could have been or could be another better way to go about something than what someone is advising or doing or has done, since apparently, if there is such a way, he would not have done what he did, since no one willingly and knowingly makes worse choices. But this is false, since it often becomes clear afterward how it would have been better to act, when it was unclear before the event.

(26) Another topic, when someone is about to do something opposite to other things that have been done, involves looking at them

167 One must make one's own judgment about Androcles' argument. Another example of this topic may be found in the book *Jacob Klein: Lectures and Essays* (St. John's College Press, Annapolis, Maryland, 1985), p. 311, to the effect that the traditional title of Plato's *Philebus* must be genuine, since Philebus speaks less than one out of every hundred of its lines.

168 A group of oligarchs installed as rulers of Athens after it lost the Peloponnesian War.

together. Xenophanes, for instance, when the Eleans asked whether or not they should make sacrifices and sing laments to Leucothea,[169] advised them not to sing laments if they assumed she was a goddess and not to make sacrifices if they assumed she was a human being.

(27) Another topic involves making an accusation or defense based on mistakes. For instance, in Carcinus's *Medea*, people make the accusation that she killed her children, who had at any rate disappeared (since Medea had made the mistake of sending her children away), and Medea makes the defense that she would not have killed the children but Jason, since not doing the latter would have been a mistake if she had also done the other. This topic and this form of enthymeme is the whole of the earlier version of Theodorus's *Art*.[170]

(28) Another topic is based on a name, as, for instance, the way Sophocles writes,

> Even the name you bear is obviously for iron,

and the way people are accustomed to speak in praise of the gods, and the way Conon used to call Thrasybulus "bold counselor," and Herodicus said to Thrasymachus "you are always a bold fighter," and to Polus "*you* are always a puppy," and of Draco the lawgiver that his laws were not those of a human being but of a dragon (for they were severe), and the way Euripides' Hecuba says about Aphrodite "the name of the goddess rightly begins like witlessness," and Chaeremon says Pentheus is named for his impending misfortune.[171]

In the realm of enthymemes, counterarguments are more highly regarded than demonstrations because a counter-enthymeme is a uniting of opposites in a brief form, and things put side by side are more evident to the hearer. But of all syllogisms, counterarguments and demonstrative ones alike, those that bring the most applause are the sort people see coming as soon as they begin, if they are not superficial (for at the moment that they grasp what is coming they are

---

169 Ino, the daughter of Cadmus, threw herself and her baby into the sea to escape her insane husband, and was given the name meaning "white goddess" in token of the belief that she had been deified.

170 Ross chooses a manuscript variant that would mean "This topic…is the whole art before Theodorus." The idea that this topic could be the whole of any approach to the rhetoric of defense may become plausible if one thinks of the way teenagers and other inexperienced people so often and so confidently meet accusations by saying, "Why would I do that? I would have done so-and-so instead."

171 Most of these names are simply repeated to convey their literal meanings, but Aphrodite's name shares the first two syllables of the other word, and Pentheus means roughly "the lamentable one"; what happens to Pentheus in Euripides' *Bacchae* is perhaps the grisliest ending in any classical tragedy. The line of Sophocles is a fragment of the lost play *Tyro* (and refers to Tyro's stepmother Sidero), and that of Euripides is 990 of the *Trojan Women*. The Polus referred to is the one depicted in the *Gorgias*; his name more often refers to a colt than to a puppy. Draco's laws made every crime punishable by death; he is said to have explained why by saying he had nothing more severe.

also pleased with themselves); and among those of the sort that they see after the fact, the most applauded ones are the kind that they get the point of as soon as they have been stated.

Chapter 24.

And since there can be a syllogism and also something that is not a syllogism but appears to be one, necessarily, too, there can be an enthymeme and also something that is not an enthymeme but
1401a appears to be one, seeing as how an enthymeme is a kind of syllogism. And there are topics among apparent enthymemes, one of which is attributable to wording, and one part of this is just like making a final statement in dialectical reasoning in the form of a logical conclusion when there has been no syllogism ("Therefore, so-and-so is not the case; therefore necessarily it is such-and-such"); among enthymemes, something tightly organized with balanced antitheses appears to *be* an enthymeme because that sort of wording is proper ground for an enthymeme, and it seems likely to be such a thing just by the design of its wording. For making statements in wording of a syllogistic form, it is useful to collect the upshots of a number of syllogisms, as that "he saved some, avenged others, and liberated the Greeks." For each of these has been demonstrated from other things, but when they are gathered together, it appears that some conclusion also comes out of them.

(1) And one topic involving apparent enthymemes is attributable to ambiguity; claiming, for instance, that a mouse is of serious stature, being the source, at any rate, of the most honored of all religious initiations, since the most honored of all religious initiations are the Mysteries.[172] Or if, in praise of the dog, someone were to bring in the one in the heavens, or the god Pan, because Pindar said

> Blessed art thou, whom Olympians call
> The many-formed dog of the Great Goddess,

or the fact that it is quite a dishonorable thing when there is no dog, and thus clearly it is an honorable thing to be a dog. Or to claim Hermes is the most sharing among the gods, since Hermes alone is called "a share."[173] Or that a word is the thing most highly valued,

172 The word for mouse (*mus*) differs in accent and meaning from the first syllable of the *mustêria* of the Eleusinian religion. This might be a bit like praising the bird called a cardinal for its importance to the Roman Catholic Church. In the following example, the Greeks called the Dog Star simply "the dog," and Pan, often depicted with features of a goat, was also called the dog of Cybele, or Mother Earth.

173 Hermes was the god of luck. A lucky find was called a *hermaion,* and it was customary for anyone who saw someone else make such a find to call out "a share!"

because good men are worthy not of money but of a good word, since "worth a good word" is not meant in a simple way.[174]

(2) Another topic involving apparent enthymemes has to do with saying something separated as combined or something combined as separated. For since things that are not the same often seem to be the same, one has to take it whichever way is more useful. This is Euthydemus's argument about, for instance, knowing that a battleship is in the Peiraeus, because he knows each part.[175] Or that someone who knows the letters knows the word, because the word is the same thing as its letters. Or claiming that, since a double amount of something makes someone sick, a single portion would not be healthy either, because it would be absurd if two good things are one bad one. So it is a counterargument in that form, but for showing something, it goes like this: two bad things could not be one good one. But the whole topic is fallacious. And again, there is Polycrates' remark about Thrasybulus, that he deposed thirty tyrants, since he adds them together.[176] Or there is the argument in Theodectes' *Orestes*, since it is made by taking things apart:

> It is a just thing, for any woman who murders her husband,

that she be killed, and just too for a son to avenge his father; "well 1401b
then, that's exactly what's been done." But maybe they are no longer just when combined. The fallacy could also be attributed to leaving something out, since he takes out the matter of by whom.[177]

(3) Another topic involving apparent enthymemes has to do with trumping up or undermining a case by horribilizing it. This is what happens whenever a speaker, without having shown that his opponent did something, exaggerates the deed. This makes it appear that the one who has the charge against him has not committed the offense, when he himself exaggerates the charge, or that he has committed it, when the accuser exaggerates the offense. Accordingly, there is no enthymeme, since the hearer falsely infers that the accused did or did not do something that has not been shown.

(4) Another topic involving apparent enthymemes uses a sign, since this too yields no syllogism, as if one were to say "Lovers are

---

174 The word that is not simple in meaning is *logos*. What is translated here as "worth a good word" is literally "worth a word," but means something like "estimable."

175 Euthydemus was a debater who won arguments with verbal trickery. This example is hard to reconstruct precisely, but it is the same gimmick as saying "the student, said the professor, is a fool" without reading the two commas.

176 Thrasybulus led the faction that restored democracy to Athens by defeating the pro-Spartan government ruled by thirty oligarchs, then asked for thirty times the reward he would get for overthrowing a tyrant.

177 The fallacy can be said to result from taking apart the two acts if one says a son is right to avenge his father, but not against his mother. It arises from leaving something out if one says a woman who murders her husband should be killed, as long as it is not by her son.

beneficial to their cities, for the love of Harmodius and Aristogeiton deposed the tyrant Hipparchus." Or if one said that Dionysius was a thief because he was depraved; this certainly yields no syllogism, since not every depraved person is a thief, although every thief is depraved.

(5) Another topic involving apparent enthymemes argues from something incidental. An instance is what Polycrates says about the mice, that they saved the day by gnawing through the bowstrings. Or if someone were to claim that being invited to dinner is the highest honor, because Achilles was enraged at the Achaeans in Tenedos for not inviting him. But he was enraged because they showed disrespect, and it was incidental that they did this by not inviting him.[178]

(6) Another topic involving apparent enthymemes is based on a consequent. In the speech on Paris, for instance, it is said that he was a great-souled man, because he despised the company of most people and spent his time by himself on Mount Ida, for since great-souled people are like that, he too would seem to be a great-souled man. Or that because someone dresses up and goes around at night, he is a womanizer, since that is what they do. A similar example is to say that beggars sing and dance in the temples, and the homeless are at liberty to live any place they want; since these things belong to those who are thought to be happy, then it might also be thought that those to whom they belong *are* happy. But the way they belong to them makes a difference, and hence this topic also falls in among those that leave something out.[179]

(7) Another topic involving apparent enthymemes is attributable to taking what is not the cause to be the cause of something's having happened, for instance, along with it or after it. For people assume what is after this is because of this, especially people who take part in politics, the way Demades, for example, claimed the policy of Demosthenes was the cause of all the troubles, since the war happened to come after it.

(8) Another topic involving apparent enthymemes is attributable to leaving out the when and the how. For instance, the argument that Paris took Helen justly, because the choice was given to her by her
1402a father. But this did not apply equally for all time, but to the first time, since the father's authority went up to that point. Or if someone were

178 The mice happened to save the Egyptians from Assyrian invaders, according to Herodotus (II, 141), and the flaring of Achilles' wrath before he even got to Troy is from a fragment of a lost play of Sophocles.

179 There are then at least three ways to characterize what is going on here. Aristotle first attributes it to arguing from the consequent: if A, then B, and B is the case, so therefore A must be true as well. The explanation of the happy homeless example shows that the flaw in such reasoning consists of slipping in the assumption that whenever B is a consequence of A, A is also a consequence of B. Whenever this converse is false, there is some restrictive condition left out of the original hypothesis; on what is left out of the greatness-of-soul example, see the note to 1366b 20.

to claim that hitting those who are free is an act of outrageous violence, since this is not so in every case, but only when someone is the first to injure the other person by putting his hands to him.

(9) Also, just as in debaters' arguments, an apparent syllogism comes about by mixing what is so simply and what is so not simply but in a particular case. In dialectical reasoning, for example, one may argue that nonbeing *is*, since nonbeing *is* nonbeing, and that the unknown is known, since it is known *that* the unknown is unknown; so too in rhetorical speeches, there is an apparent enthymeme from something that is not simply likely, but likely in a particular case. But it is not possible for this to be universal, as Agathon also says,

> One could probably say that this very thing is likely
> That many things that happen to mortals are unlikely.

For what defies likelihood does happen, so that what defies likelihood is likely too, and if that is so, there will be a likelihood of something unlikely. But this is not simply true, but just as in debaters' arguments, when someone fails to add in what respect something is true, in relation to what, and in what manner, that makes it misrepresentation, here too, the misrepresentation is due to something's being likely in a particular case but not simply. The *Art* of Corax is composed of this topic: "For if someone is not liable to the charge of assault, for instance because he is weak, he gets off because it is not likely, and if someone *is* liable to it, for instance because he is strong, he still gets off, because it is not likely that he would do something that was going to *seem* likely." And likewise in all other cases, since someone has to be either liable or not liable to the charge; so both arguments appear likely, but one *is* likely while the other is not simply likely, but likely under the restrictions mentioned. And this is making the weaker argument stronger; and this is why human beings were justly disgusted at Protagoras's pronouncement.[180] For it is false, and not a true but an apparent likelihood, and not present in any art other than rhetoric and debating.

Chapter 25.

What has to do both with things that are enthymemes and things that appear to be has been discussed, and the next thing to speak of following what has been said has to do with refutation. And it is

180 On making the weaker argument the stronger, see the note to 1355a 21 above, where Aristotle gives as a reason for studying rhetoric the prevention of this abuse. Protagoras's pronouncement was "A human being is the measure of all things," which Aristotle comments on in the *Metaphysics* (1062b 12 and following). Protagoras was unashamed to call himself a sophist; see Plato's *Protagoras*, 318D-E and 349A. Aristotle's use here of the word *anthropoi* (human beings) is a witty way of showing that Protagoras's famous saying refutes itself. Even likelihood is not a matter of mere seeming, but is measured by relevant circumstances, which the "art" of certain rhetoricians and debaters requires them to leave out.

possible to refute something by bringing up either an opposing syllogism or an objection. Now as for stating opposing syllogisms, it is evident that it is possible to make them on the basis of the same topics, since syllogisms are based on accepted opinions, and there are many opinions opposed to one another. And objections are brought up in four ways, as is said also in the *Topics*[181]: from the argument itself, or from something similar to it, or from its opposite, or from judgments already made. From the argument itself, I mean, for instance, if the
1402b enthymeme were to the effect that love is of serious worth, the objection could go two ways, either by making a universal statement that every form of lacking is bad, or by making the particular statement that one could not speak of Caunian love[182] if there were not also bad loves. And if, for instance, the enthymeme were to the effect that a good man does good to all his friends, an objection brought up from an opposite is "but a bad man does not do harm to all his friends." And if, for instance, the enthymeme is to the effect that those who have had harm done to them always feel hate, an objection from something similar is "but those who have had good done to them do not always feel love." As for judgments that have come from notable men, if, for instance, someone stated an enthymeme to the effect that one ought to have compassion on people who are drunk, since they commit their offenses in ignorance, an objection is that then Pittacus[183] does not deserve his high reputation, or else he would not have made it a law that the punishments are greater when anyone commits an offense while drunk.

Now enthymemes are argued on the basis of four things, and those four things are likelihoods, examples, criteria, and signs. Enthymemes based on likelihoods are those with conclusions drawn from things that either are or seem to be the case for the most part; the ones that come from examples are those that are argued from one or more similar cases, when one grasps something universal and then reasons to particulars; the ones that come from criteria are argued from something necessary and always the case; and the ones that come from signs are argued from something that is the case universally or in particular to conclude that something else either is or is not the case. And since something likely is what is the case not always but for the most part, it is obvious that it is always possible to refute an enthymeme of this sort by bringing up an objection, but the refutation is apparent but not always true. For someone who makes an objection proves that the thing is not necessarily so, but not that it is not likely. Hence too,

181 VIII, 10.

182 That is, incest. A single exception would constitute an objection to a universal claim.

183 One of the Seven Sages of early Greek times, a commoner elected dictator of Mytilene during a civil war. Aristotle mentions this decree of his with approval in the *Nicomachean Ethics* (1113b 30-33) and the *Politics* (1274b 18-23).

the person who makes a defense always has an advantage over the one who makes an accusation, on account of this fallacy. For since the accuser demonstrates his claim by means of likelihoods, and proving that something is not likely is not the same thing as proving that it is not necessarily so, and something that happens for the most part is always open to objection (for it could not be something that is always likely and at the same time be something that is always necessary), then when a refutation is made in this way, the judge supposes either that the charge is not likely or that it cannot be decided by him, but he is reasoning falsely, as we said. For he ought to be judging not only on the basis of what is necessarily so, but also on the basis of likelihoods, since that is what it means to judge "according to one's best judgment."[184] It is accordingly not good enough if someone proves that a thing is not necessarily so, but he has to prove that it is not likely. And this will follow if the objection instead is what happens for the most part. And it is possible for it to be more prevalent in two ways, either in time or in instances, and it is more conclusive if it is more prevalent in both ways; for if more things are that way more often, 1403a this makes it more likely.

Signs, and enthymemes stated by means of signs, are refutable even if they apply, as was said in the first chapters.[185] For the fact that no sign forms a syllogism is clear from our *Analytics*. And the same sort of refutation goes for enthymemes of the example form as for likelihoods, for if we have any one thing that is not like the example, it is proven that the conclusion is not necessarily so, even if more instances are like it or more often like it; but if more instances are more often like the example, one needs to combat it by arguing either that the present case is not the same or did not happen the same way, or at least that it has some difference. But it will not be possible to refute criteria and enthymemes of the criterion form for not forming a syllogism (and this too is clear from our *Analytics*), but it remains possible to show that what is said does not apply. But if it is obvious both that it does apply and that it is a criterion, such an argument at once becomes irrefutable, for once all of that is obvious, it is a rigorous demonstration.[186]

184 The quotation is from the oath taken by Athenian juror-judges, discussed also in Bk. I, Chap. 15, above.

185 That is, in the very definition of signs in Bk. I, Chap. 2. The next reference is to *Prior Analytics* II, 27.

186 I once heard a policeman at the scene of an accident say: "The tire marks show he turned right from the left lane. That's an illegal turn. We have to give him a ticket." The question whether any signs indicated any fault on the part of the other driver became irrelevant as soon as it was shown by an irrefutable sign that the first driver had committed an illegal act.

Chapter 26.

To exaggerate or minimize something is not an element of an enthymeme, since I mean the same thing by element as by topic. An element or topic is a tactic that applies to enthymemes on many subjects, but exaggerating and minimizing make enthymemes show that something is great or small, just as others show that something is good or bad, just or unjust, or anything else whatever. And these are all things about which there are syllogisms and enthymemes, so if none of these is a topic of an enthymeme, then neither are exaggerating and minimizing. Refutation is not a form of enthymeme either, that makes the enthymeme what it is. For it is clear that one makes a refutation by showing something or by bringing up an objection, and counterdemonstrates an opposite conclusion; for example, if someone showed that something happened, this shows that it did not, and if someone showed that something did not happen, this shows that it did. So this would be no difference, since both use the same tactics, and bring forward enthymemes to show that it is or is not the case. And an objection, as is said in the *Topics*, is not an enthymeme but the stating of some opinion from which it will be evident that someone has failed to make a syllogism or has assumed something false.

And since there are three things involved in speech that one has to be concerned with, let this much have been said on the subject of
1403b examples, maxims, enthymemes, and everything that pertains to thinking, both as to where we shall find a supply of them and as to how we shall refute them, what remains is to go over what concerns wording and arrangement.

BOOK III

Chapter 1.

There are three things involved in speech that one has to be con- 1403b
cerned with: the means of persuasion will constitute one of these, a second has to do with wording, and a third is how one should organize the parts of a speech. Now since what concerns the means of persuasion has been discussed, and how many sources they come from has been stated, that these are three, as well as what sorts they are and why there are only that many (for it is either because the judges themselves are affected in a certain way, or because they take the speakers to be people of certain sorts, or because something has been demonstrated, that everyone is persuaded), and enthymemes have been discussed, where one needs to provide them from (for there are specific subjects for enthymemes, and also general topics for arguing them), what concerns wording is the next thing to speak of. For it is not sufficient to understand the things one needs to argue; it is also necessary to understand how one needs to say them, and this contributes in many respects to making the speech appear to be of a certain sort.

So the first thing that was inquired about was the one that by its very nature came first naturally, the things themselves on the basis of which a speech has its persuasiveness, the second is putting those things into words, and there is a third among these things that has the greatest power but has never yet been dealt with, the matters having to do with performance. Even in tragedy and the reciting of epics it was neglected for a long time, because at first the poets themselves performed their own tragedies. Now it is clear that such a thing is involved in rhetoric too, just as in poetry, where Glaucon of Teos and some others have paid attention to it. This is something in the voice, the way one needs to use it for each state of feeling, such as when it should be loud, soft, or in between and how to use its tones, as high-pitched, deep, or in between, and what rhythm goes with each. For there are three things for people to consider, and these are loudness, melodiousness,[187] and rhythm. These are pretty much the things that get the prizes in competitions, and in just the same way that actors now have greater power than poets there, this is also the case in political contests, because of the corrupt condition of the citizens.

An *Art* concerned with these things has not yet been composed, since even the matter of wording was late in coming forward, and it

187 The accents in ancient Greek indicate rises and falls in pitch, but good public speakers in any language match the things they say to changes of pitch. A student of mine, Robert Abbot, once pointed out in a class that in the "I have a dream" speech, Martin Luther King was dropping the pitch of his voice a perfect fifth at the ends of some sentences. My colleague André Barbera tells me that the speech is delivered primarily on the recitation tone of B flat below middle C, and establishes a key of E flat.

1404a is thought to be something vulgar, which captures it beautifully. But since the whole business of rhetoric is directed at opinion, one has to make it a matter of concern, not because it is right but because it is necessary. The *just* thing would be to aim at nothing more in a speech than that it not cause pain, but not cause pleasure either, since it is just to argue one's side by means of the facts themselves, so that the other things extraneous to the demonstration are superfluous, but all the same, as has been said, they have great power, owing to the corrupt condition of the listener. And yet the matter of wording has some small necessary place in every sort of teaching, since it makes some difference in regard to making something clear to say it this way or that way, though not all that much; this is all a matter of imagination, and all relative to the listener, which is why no one teaches geometry that way. So when that matter does come in for notice, it will do the same thing it did for the skill of acting, and some writers have made an effort to speak of it to a small extent, such as Thrasymachus in his *Pitiful Cases*.[188] Being good at acting is in fact something that is present by nature, and not so much from art, but what has to do with wording is intrinsically a matter of art. Hence prizes also go to people with ability at that, just as they do to rhetorical speakers for performance, because written speeches are more apt to prevail on account of their wording than the thinking in them.

As is natural, the poets were the ones who first started the process going, for words are the medium of their imitation, and they had available the part of us best adapted to imitating, the voice. And so the arts of reciting and acting, and others as well, were also devised. And since the poets, though they were saying simple-minded things, seemed to cover themselves in glory by the way they used words, it was for this reason that the first style of wording that came along, such as that of Gorgias, was poetic. Even now, most uneducated people believe that such speakers give the most beautiful discourses. But this is not so; wording suited to a speech is different from that of poetry. And what has happened makes this clear, since even those who compose tragedies no longer use it the same way, but just as they changed over from tetrameter[189] verses to iambic, because, in comparison to the other meters, that is the one most similar to speech, so too they have given up those words that go beyond what is conversational, the ones the first poets adorned their works with, as those who compose in hexameters still do even now. Hence it is ridiculous to imitate people who no longer use that style themselves; so it is obvious that there is

188 In Plato's *Phaedrus* (267C), Socrates says of this book that "the mighty man from Chalcedon is the master of tear-jerking speeches."

189 The meter used in the satyr plays that pre-dated tragedies was trochaic tetrameter, the meter found in English in Poe's *The Raven* and Longfellow's *Song of Hiawatha*. See Aristotle's *Poetics*, 1449a 19-25, and see 1408b 36-1409a 1 and note below. The hexameter verse mentioned just below is the dactylic meter of epic poetry.

no need for us to be precise in speaking about everything that has to do with wording, but only about those things that have to do with the sorts of speeches we are talking about. What has to do with the other sort has been discussed in the *Poetics*.[190]

Chapter 2.

So let that be a look taken at those things, and let the virtue of 1404b
wording be defined as being clear—for since a word is a certain kind of sign, if it does not make anything clear, it will not be doing its proper work—and neither low-class nor above what the subject deserves, but appropriate. For poetic wording may not be low-class, but it is not appropriate for a speech. With nouns and verbs alike, it is the prevalent ones that make the wording clear, while the other sorts of words discussed in the *Poetics* keep it from being low-class but make it fancy, because shifting it away from what is prevalent gives it a more dignified appearance. For people feel the same way about wording as they do about foreigners and fellow citizens, so one ought to make one's language be out of the ordinary, because things that are admired are found among what is remote, and what is admired is pleasing. Now in verse, many things are composed in this way and there they are fitting (because the things and people its talk is about stand out more), but in plain speech they fit in much less often, since the subject matter stands out less. Even in poetry, if a slave or someone too young were to use pretty words, it would be too inappropriate, or if such talk were used on matters too minor; even in these writings there is a fitness to what is held back and what is enhanced.[191] Hence people need to do this sort of thing unobtrusively, and not seem to be speaking in a contrived manner but in a natural one (since the latter is persuasive and the former is just the opposite, because people are put off by it as if someone were up to some scheme, just as they are when people mix something into their wine); it is like the way Theodorus's voice is received, in contrast to those of other actors, since his voice seems to be that of the character who is speaking, while theirs have an alien feel. And the author's hand is well concealed when he composes with words chosen from ordinary language; this is exactly what Euripides does, and he was the first to show people the way.

Now since speech is made up of nouns and verbs, and nouns have as many forms as are examined in the writings on poetry, those among

190 Chapter 22. The references in the chapter below are to this chapter of the *Poetics* or to Chap. 21.

191 A good modern illustration of this point may be found in a comparison of Shakespeare's *Richard II* to his *I Henry IV*, written a year later. In the earlier play, every character sounds the same, all speak in verse, and all engage in the sort of wordplay the author uses in his sonnets. In the later play, there is a remarkable variety in the way prose and verse are used, and the way the characters are distinguished from one another by the words they use and the ways they use them.

them that are eccentric[192] or compound or made-up words need to be used infrequently and in few places; we will say later in what places, and the reason for being sparing in their use has been stated, that it crosses over from what is appropriate to what is too much. In the wording of plain speech, only a prevailing native word should be used, or a metaphor. A sign is that these are the only things everyone does use, since everyone makes use of metaphors in conversation, as well as native and prevailing words, so it is clear that if someone composes well, there can be an unfamiliar feel and it can still be unobtrusive and be clear, and this was the virtue of rhetorical speech. Among nouns, ambiguous words are useful to the sophist, since it is with them that he does mischief, but synonyms are useful to the poet; I am speaking of prevalent synonyms like "proceed" and "go," for both of them are prevalent words and they are synonymous with each other.

What each of these things is, how many forms of metaphors there are, and that metaphor is the most powerful element in poetry and in speech as well, have been stated in the *Poetics*, as we said. But it is in speech that one needs to work all the harder on metaphors, to the degree that speech, compared to verse, has fewer elements to help it achieve effects. It is metaphor most of all that has in it something clear, pleasant, and unfamiliar, and it is not something one can get from anyone else. But one needs to speak in fitting metaphors, as in fitting epithets. This will depend on proportion; if there is none, it will appear inappropriate, because discrepancies are most apparent when things are next to one another. One needs to consider what suits an old man the way a purple cloak might suit a young one, since the same clothes would not be appropriate; and if you want to adorn something, bring in a metaphor taken from the best things in the same class, but from the worst if you want to find fault. I am speaking, for instance (since there are opposite things in the same class), of saying that someone begging is praying or that someone praying is begging, because both are petitioners; that is doing the sort of thing described. This is why Iphicrates called Callias a beggar-priest instead of a torchbearer, and Callias said only an uninitiate would call him a beggar-priest and not a torchbearer; both minister to a god, but one in an honored role, the other in a dishonored one. And it is one thing to call actors panderers of Dionysus, but they call themselves "artistes"; these are both metaphors, one disparaging, the other the opposite. And pirates nowadays call themselves procurement specialists. Hence too, one is free to say that someone who committed an injustice made a mistake, or that someone who made a mistake committed an injustice, or that a thief took something or procured it. And what Euripides' Telephus says,

192 The Greek word is *glôtta*, here meaning something like jargon, "lingo." In the *Poetics* (1457b 1-6), it is explained as any use of a word not prevalent among its intended audience. Examples are given in Chap. 3 below.

Being lord of the oar, he landed on Mysia,

is inappropriate because it is too much for what the subject merits, and hence there is no hiding it. It is possible to go wrong even in the syllables of a word, if they are indications of an unpleasant sound; for instance, Dionysius the Brazen, in his elegies, referred to poetry as "the screeching of Calliope," because both are vocal utterances, but a metaphor for meaningless vocal utterances is a bad choice.

Further, one ought to take metaphors that are not remote but drawn from things that are related and similar in form to the nameless things that are being named, so that it is clear as soon as it is spoken what the relation is. For instance, in the celebrated riddle 1405b

I saw a man glue bronze on a man with fire,

the process has no name, but there is a certain kind of attaching in both cases, so it calls the applying of the cupping bowl[193] gluing. And in all cases, it is possible to get reasonably good metaphors out of well-made riddles, since metaphors are riddles, so it is clear that the metaphors are also well-made. And one ought to take metaphors from things that are beautiful; the beauty of a word, as Licymnius says, is in its sounds or in what it means, and there is ugliness in the same ways. And there is a third factor, that refutes a sophistical argument, since it is not the case, as Bryson says, that there is no such thing as ugly talking if saying something this way instead of that way means the same thing. This is false, for one way is more prevalent, more of a likeness, and more proper than another for making the thing come before one's eyes. Also, this or that word does not signify something with the same connotations, so that in this way too it must be granted that one is more beautiful or uglier than another. For both words may signify the beautiful or ugly thing, but not in the respect in which it is beautiful or ugly, or in the same respect but to a greater or lesser degree. So this is where metaphors are to be brought over from, from words that are beautiful in sound or in import, or to sight or some other sense. It does make a difference, for instance, to say "rosy-fingered dawn" rather than "purple-fingered," or still worse, "ruddy-fingered."

With epithets too, it is possible to make the attribution from something base or ugly, such as "killer of his mother," or from something better, such as "avenger of his father."[194] And Simonides, when the winner of a mule race offered him a small fee, was unwilling to write

193 A medical instrument which, when heated and placed over a small incision, drew out blood. In Chap. 22 of the *Poetics* the same example is used to show that putting together too many metaphors makes something into a riddle. Here the point is that the riddle is easily solved if the metaphors are closely related to the unnamed thing (which would in this case have been a more familiar procedure in Aristotle's time).

194 Applied to Orestes in Euripides' play of that name, 1587-1588.

a poem because it was distasteful to write poetry about half-donkeys, but when he was offered enough, he composed

> Happiness to you, daughters of storm-footed steeds!

even though they were daughters of donkeys too. Then too, there is the use of diminutive terms, and it is possible that the diminutive will make either the bad or the good of something less; this is the way Aristophanes, in the *Babylonians*, facetiously uses "goldlet" for gold, "cloaklet" for cloak, "insultlet" for insult, and "diseaselet" for disease. But one needs to be cautious in the use of both techniques, and keep a careful eye out for the mean.

Chapter 3.

Aspects of wording that do not come off[195] come in four varieties. One kind is involved in compound words, as when Lycophron names "the many-countenanced sky over the great-pinnacled earth" and "a narrow-passagewayed shore," or the way Gorgias names
1406a "pandering-beggar-bards who swear lies like an honest swearer," or the way Alcidamas writes "the soul full of wrath and the face growing flame-hued," "he believed their eagerness would be end-bearing," "he constituted the persuasion in his words as an end-bearing thing," and "the cerulean-hued bottom of the sea," for all these things appear poetic on account of the compounding. So this is one cause for an effect's not coming off, and another is the use of eccentric words, the way Lycophron calls Xerxes a "humongous man" and Sciron a "ransack man,"[196] and Alcidamas speaks of a "bagatelle in poetry," the "overweening way of nature," and "exacerbated by the unruly impulse of his thought."

A third sort involves using long, unseasonable, or frequent epithets. For while it is appropriate in poetry to speak of white milk, in speech some such things are too inappropriate, and others, when they are overused, stick out and make it obvious that poetic crafting is going on; one certainly ought to use them, because they take the wording out of the ordinary and make it unfamiliar, but one needs to aim at a mean, since this can do more harm than speaking casually. For while a casual style does not have anything well done in it, one that is overdone has something bad. This is why the writings of Alcidamas that do not come off make the impression they do; for he uses epithets not as seasoning but as a main course, so frequent, long, and obtrusive are they. It is never "sweat," for example, but "damp sweat," not "to the Isthmian games" but "to the festive assembly of the Isthmian games," not "laws" but "laws, the sovereign rulers of

195 Literally, "that are cold," that is, lifeless. This is usually translated as "frigidity" of style.

196 The adjective applies to one legendary highway robber the name of another, which sounds like it comes from a verb meaning to plunder or destroy.

cities," not "at a run" but "with a running impulse of his soul," not "to art school" but "betaking himself to nature's art school"; there are "the sad-faced cares of the soul," and a craftsman not of "popularity" but of "universal popularity," and a "dispenser of pleasure to his audience," and he hid not behind "branches" but "branches of the woods," and he covered up not "his body" but "his body's nakedness." And there is "the desire of his soul was anti-imitative" (which is a compound and an epithet at the same time, so that it is made into a piece of poetry), and "so extraordinary an extravagance of depravity." Thus by speaking poetically in an unfitting way, they bring in something ridiculous that does not come off, and that is unclear because of empty words; for when one throws more words at someone who already gets the point, what is clear is dissipated by being cast into the shadows. But people use compounds when there is no name for something and the word goes together easily, like time-wasting; but if **1406b**
there is a lot of this, it gets a completely poetic character. This is why compound wording is used most by dithyrambic poets (since they have a noisy style), but eccentric wording by epic poets (since their writing is stately and idiosyncratic), and metaphor in iambic verse (since these are used nowadays, as was said.)

And there is also a fourth sort of wording that does not come off that comes up in metaphors. For metaphors can be inappropriate too, some by being comical (for comic poets use metaphors too), others by being too solemn and tragic. And they become unclear when they are a big stretch; Gorgias, for instance, speaks of "green and bloodless actions," and says "you have reaped in evil the things you sowed in shame"—this is too poetical. And there is the way Alcidamas called philosophy "a fortress in the territory of the law," and the *Odyssey* "a beautiful mirror of human life," and speaks of someone who "contributed no such bagatelle to poetry." All these phrases are unpersuasive for the reasons stated. And what Gorgias said to the swallow, when it let its excrement go falling down on him, is in the best tragic tone: "Shame on you, Philomela." For there is no shame for a bird if it did that, but there would be for a maiden. So he did well to rail at her by addressing what she had been and not what she was.[197]

Chapter 4.

A simile is also a metaphor, since there is little difference. For when one says "like a lion he pounced," that is a simile, but when one says, "a lion, he pounced," that is a metaphor. For because both are coura-

197 Philomela was a girl who was transformed into a swallow.

geous, he referred to Achilles metaphorically as a lion.[198] The simile is useful in speech as well, but less often, since it is poetic. They need to be applied in the same way as metaphors, since they are metaphors that differ in the manner mentioned.

Here are examples of similes: what Androtion said about Idrieus, that he was like little dogs off their chains, since they attack and bite, and Idrieus was dangerous too when let out of his chains; and the way Theodamas likened Archidamus to a Euxenus who did not know how to do geometry, since, by the analogy,[199] Euxenus would be an Archidamus who could do geometry; and in Plato's *Republic*,[200] that people who strip corpses are like dogs that bite rocks but do not touch the one who is throwing them, and the one about the populace, that it is like a shipowner who is strong but a little deaf, and the one
1407a about poets' verses, that they are like people in the freshness of youth but without beauty, since the latter, when the bloom is off, and the former, when freed of meter, no longer look the same; and Pericles on the Samians, likening them to children who take the scrap of food but cry about it, and on the Boeotians, that they are like live-oaks, because oaks are cut down by means of their own kind of wood, and Boeotians are continually fighting one another; and the one Demosthenes made about the populace, that they are like people who get seasick once they get on the ships, and the way Demosthenes likened rhetoricians to wet nurses who gobble up scraps of food and smear the babies' lips with their spittle; and the way Antisthenes likened the emaciated Cephisodotus to incense, because he entertains people while wasting away. One is free to state all of these as similes or as metaphors, so it is clear that all those things that are well thought of when worded as metaphors will be so as similes as well, since similes with a word missing *are* metaphors.[201] And a metaphor that comes from an analogy is always necessarily reciprocal and applies to either one of the correlative terms; if, for instance, a drinking bowl is a shield of Dionysus, then it is also fitting for a shield to be spoken of as a drinking bowl of Ares.

---

198 *Iliad* XXII, 164. The "he," Homer, does not need to be named to a Greek audience. The extended simile was the most distinctive feature of Homer's style, imitated forever after by anyone who wanted to achieve a heroic or mock-heroic tone. W. P. Kinsella's *Shoeless Joe* may be mentioned as an example of a good recent novel that makes readers uncomfortable by a too-frequent use of similes.

199 The analogy is the geometrical proportion Archidamas:Euxenus :: ungeometrical:geometrical. Hence the insult would be directed at Euxenus, by a covert simile that his geometry will enable him to deduce.

200 469C-E, 488A-B, and 601A-B.

201 The word is *hôs*, meaning as or like.

Chapter 5.

So speech is made up of these materials, but the primary thing in wording is to speak grammatically,[202] and this involves five considerations. The first is in the matter of connecting words, if one is to fulfill the natural way they come before and after one another, the sort of thing some of them require, the way a *men* requires a *de* and an *egô men* requires a *ho de*.[203] And one ought to supply them one to another while someone still remembers, and not leave them hanging a long time or supply a connection before the connection that has to be there, for there are few places where that would be fitting. In "I for my part, when he told me, for Cleon had come begging and pleading, set out and took them along," more than one connection is inserted before the connection that completes the sentence. But if the interval that comes between the "I" and the "set out" is long, it is unclear. So one thing is to handle connecting words well, and a second is to speak in exactly appropriate words and not in words that are in the general vicinity. A third is not to use things that can be taken two ways, that is, if one does not deliberately make the opposite choice, which people do when they have nothing to say but still pretend to say something. Such people tend to say those things in poetic form, as Empedocles does; for what goes around in a big circle bamboozles people, and the hearers have exactly the same experience most people do with soothsayers. For when they say things that can be taken in two ways, people join in nodding in assent, as at

> Croesus, by crossing the Halys, will destroy a
> great empire.[204]

And since a sweeping statement is less subject to error, soothsayers 1407b
speak about a thing in general terms. For one can hit the result more often in the game "odd or even" by saying "odd" or "even" rather than exactly what number, and elsewhere by saying what will be the case rather than when, so those who deliver oracles do not include a specification of the time. All these things are exactly alike, and except for some such reason, this is something to avoid. A fourth point is the way Protagoras distinguishes the classes of words as masculine, feminine, and neuter, since it is necessary to keep these in agreement correctly too: "She having arrived, and she having said her say, left."

---

202 Literally, "to speak Greek," the common language underlying all local dialects, as people might once have said "to speak the King's English."

203 The particles *men* and *de* indicate contrasting clauses, phrases, or words. The most heavy-handed translation of them would be "on the one hand...on the other hand"; sometimes a translation may use "while" for the first and nothing for the second, or nothing for the first and "but" for the second. The *egô men* and *ho de* might be conveyed in English by mere emphasis: "*I* am a professor; *he* is a tutor."

204 A Delphic oracle reported by Herodotus (I, 53). The empire Croesus destroyed was his own.

A fifth involves naming the number correctly as many, few, or one: "They having arrived, they started hitting me."[205]

Overall, what is written needs to be easy to read and easy to say, and these amount to the same thing. And this is not present when there are a lot of connective words, or in things that are not easy to punctuate, like the sayings of Heracleitus. For punctuating the sayings of Heracleitus is work, because it is unclear which of two things something goes with, the one after or the one before it; for example, at the very beginning of the collection he says "Though this *logos*[206] is present always people end up without understanding," and it is unclear which of the two ways to punctuate the "always."[207] The following thing also produces a fault in wording: lack of agreement if you do not link two words to something that fits both. Seeing, for instance, is not applicable in common to a sound and a color, but perceiving is. There are also unclarities if you do not say what you are proposing, if you are intending to toss in a lot of things in between; for instance, "I intended, after talking with him, and this and that and the other, to go away," instead of "I intended, after talking with him, to go away, but then this and that and the other came up."

Chapter 6.

The following things contribute toward weightiness of wording. One is using a description instead of a word: not "circle," for instance, but "plane figure equally distant from the center." But for succinctness it is the opposite: using a word instead of a description. And should there be anything ugly or inappropriate, if what is ugly is in the description, using the word contributes to weightiness, and if it is in the word, using the description does. Another thing that contributes to weightiness is using metaphor and epithets to make something clear, with due caution against anything sounding poetic. Another is making many out of one, the way poets do; though there is only one shore, they say "to Achaean shores," and they say

Here are the manifold pages of my writing tablet.

---

205 In both examples it is the participles that must agree in gender and number with the nouns and verbs. Ancient Greek was called a participle-loving language, and their inflected endings carry so much information that they permit a compact and flexible style. A language like English that has to keep repeating pronouns has a clunkier sound and feel. Greek did not have separate forms for "few" in addition to plural and singular, but did have separate dual forms.

206 The untranslatability of the word *logos* in Heracleitus's fragments reflects an intentional impossibility in pinning down its meaning.

207 Ancient Greek was written without punctuation marks, as it was still primarily a spoken language. Modern editions of writings such as those of Plato and Aristotle are punctuated by the editors.

And there is not linking two things but using a preposition[208] for each: "of that wife of ours." But to say it succinctly, it is the opposite: "of our wife." And there is speaking with a conjunction, or if speaking succinctly, without a conjunction but not without a connection, for instance "having gone and having had a discussion," "having gone I 1408a
had a discussion." And Antimachus's trick of speaking of things something does not possess is useful, as he writes about Teumessus,[209]

> There is a windy little peak...

because one can expand something in this way indefinitely. And this is applicable to good and bad things alike for anything they are not, whichever way serves one's purpose, from which poets too get the names "melody without strings" or "without a lyre," since they apply them from negations. This is a well-regarded technique in metaphors stated by analogy, such as saying a trumpet is melody without a lyre.

Chapter 7.

Wording will have appropriateness if it conveys feeling and character and is proportioned to its subject matter. There is proportion when it is worded neither in an offhand way on weighty matters nor in a solemn way on run-of-the-mill matters, and no ornamentation is attached to a run-of-the-mill word. Otherwise it has the appearance of comedy, like what Cleophon writes, for some of the things he said were just about as if one were to speak of a fig tree as "her royal highness." Feeling is conveyed when, if there is outrageous insolence, the wording is that of an angry person, or if there are sacrilegious and shameful things, it is that of a person disgusted and hesitant even to speak of them, or if there are praiseworthy things, they are spoken of with delighted admiration, or if they are pitiable, with dejection, and similarly in the other cases. People also credit the fact if the wording is proper to it, because the soul falsely concludes that someone is telling the truth because they feel that way in such circumstances; so even if things are not the way the speaker says, they believe the facts are that way, and the hearer always sympathizes with someone whose speech is full of feeling, even when he is saying nothing. That is why many people strike their hearers with amazement when they are just making a lot of noise.

This way of showing things by signs also conveys character, when a fitting display accompanies each kind and active condition of character. By a kind I mean what goes along with age, such as a boy, a man, or an old man, or with a woman or a man, or with a Spartan or

208 In the Greek it is a definite article that is repeated. The example builds this technique on the last, and does not imply polyandry.

209 In the epic poem the *Thebaid*.

Thessalian; by active conditions, those things by which one is a certain sort of person in living his life, since it is not in accordance with every sort of active condition that lives are of certain sorts.[210] So if one speaks in words proper to an active condition, he will put forward a state of character. For a country bumpkin and an educated person would not say the same things or speak the same way. Some effect is also made on audiences by a tactic the speechwriters give us our fill of: "Who does not know?" "Everyone knows." For the listener agrees out of shame, so he can be part of what everybody else is in on.

1408b Using wording at the right or wrong moment is a common feature of all forms of speaking. And a remedy for anything overdone is the one commonly mentioned: one needs to put in one's own rebuke to oneself.[211] Then what is said seems to be true, since the speaker is plainly not unaware of what he is doing. Another remedy is not to have every device corresponding at the same time, so the hearer can have them concealed from him; I mean, for instance, if the words are harsh, not using the voice and facial expression that fits them, for otherwise each of them becomes obvious for what it is, but if one device is used and another is not, one can do the same thing unobtrusively. So if mild things are said in a harsh tone and harsh things in a mild tone they become persuasive. Compound words, a greater number of epithets, and foreign words are especially fitting for a passionate speaker, for people have sympathy when an angry person says some evil thing "stinks to high heaven" or calls it monstrous, and when he has already whipped up enthusiasm in his hearers by praises, reproaches, anger, or affection, the sort of thing Isocrates does at the end of his *Panegyric*: "fame and name," and "whoever had the guts." For people utter such words when full of enthusiasm, so audiences obviously accept them when they are in the same state. This is why such things are also fitting in poetry, since poetry is something inspired. So this is the manner in which they ought to be used, or else with irony, the way Gorgias does and like the speeches in the *Phaedrus*.[212]

Chapter 8.

The pattern of the wording ought not to be metrical but ought not to lack rhythm. The first sort of pattern is unpersuasive because it seems contrived, and at the same time it stands out; it makes the hearer

---

210 The primary active conditions (*hexeis*) Aristotle has in mind are the virtues and vices, stable ways of being that have to be formed by choices and effort, but he uses a simpler example here.

211 Particularly feeble examples of this, from someone about to use a cliché, would be "not to use a cliché, but..." or "to coin a phrase..."

212 In Plato's *Phaedrus*, Socrates makes two rhetorical speeches, the first in order to outdo the speechwriter Lysias in his own style, and the second as though Socrates were carried away by enthusiasm himself. Gorgias, at the end of his *Encomium of Helen* (see note to *Gorgias* 483E), says he wrote the speech for his own amusement.

be on the watch for a similar pattern when it comes again. It is like the way children anticipate the response to the bailiff's "Whom does the freedman choose as his advocate?" by yelling "Cleon." But speech that lacks rhythm is indefinite, and it ought to be definite, though not with the definiteness of meter; for what is indefinite is unpleasing and unknowable. But all things gain definiteness from number, and the number that belongs to a pattern of wording is rhythm, and the meters are cuts made from this. Hence a speech ought to have rhythm but not meter, since that would make it a poem. But the rhythm should not be precisely carried through, and this will be the case if it is used only to a certain extent.

Among rhythmic patterns, the heroic is solemn but not speakable without a chanted intonation, while the iambic is the very speaking style of ordinary people, which is why speakers utter iambs most often of all the meters, but there ought to be some solemnity that makes speech depart from the ordinary. The trochaic rhythm is too
herky-jerky, and the tetrameters show this, since the tetrameter has **1409a**
a stumbling pace.[213] That leaves the paean, which was used starting with Thrasymachus, though there was no name anyone had to call it by. But the paean is a third rhythm following on the ones mentioned, since its pattern is 3:2, while theirs are either 1:1 or 2:1, so it stands between the latter two ratios as 1½:1.[214] The other rhythms should be left out for the reasons mentioned, and because they are metrical, but the paean can be taken in, because it is the only one of the rhythms spoken of from which there is no meter, so that it is the most unobtrusive of them. These days one sort of paean is used both for beginning and ending a sentence, but the end ought to be different from the beginning, and the two forms of paean are the opposites of each other; one of them fits at the beginning, the way it is used, and this the one that starts with the long syllable and ends with three short ones, as in[215] "De´los-born or Ly´cian one," and "Gol´den-haired far-Dart´er, Zeus-child," and the other is reversed, with three short syllables starting it and the long at the end:

> Amid the land´ and all the wat´ers, over O´cean was
> the Night´.

213 Literally, Aristotle calls this rhythm "too much like doing the cordax," an obscene dance used in old comedies and left here to the reader's imagination. To see how trochees lurch along, with the stress accents of English, try to march to the pace of "Once upon a midnight dreary…" or "By the shores of Gitche Gumee…"

214 A Greek metric foot was based on syllable lengths, with a long syllable sounded for about twice the time of a short one, so that an alternation of long and short syllables in trochees or iambs would give a 2:1 or 1:2 temporal pattern. The dactyls and spondees in the heroic rhythm would both be 1:1 feet. The paean had three short syllables and one long.

215 The three following examples are from verses by Simonides. The first two are epithets of Apollo; the marked accents are all somewhat forced, and some slight liberties are taken in the translation of the third quotation.

And this last one makes an end, because a short syllable, by being incomplete, makes a line feel cut short. It ought to be cut off with the long syllable instead and be a clear ending, not because of a copyist who makes a punctuation mark, but because of the rhythm.

Chapter 9.

So it has been stated that wording ought to be properly rhythmic and not lack rhythm, and what rhythms make it properly rhythmic, and under what conditions. And it is necessary that the wording either be run on and unified by connecting words, like the preludes in dythyrambs, or be turned back and similar to the antistrophes of early poets. The strung-together form of wording is the ancient one, since in earlier times everyone used it, but not many do now. By "strung-together" I mean wording that has no end in its own right, unless the thing being said is finished. And it is unpleasing because of its indefiniteness, since everyone wants to have an end in view. This is why people run out of breath and collapse at the goal line, for while they see the boundary ahead of them, they do not lose strength before reaching it. So this is strung-together wording, and the turned-back form is composed in periods. By a "period" I mean a stretch of word-
1409b ing that has its own beginning and end in its own right, and a length easily taken in view together. This sort of wording is pleasing and easy to understand. It is pleasing because it has the character opposite to indefiniteness, and because the listener always thinks he has a grasp of something somehow bounded in itself, while it is unpleasing to be unable to foresee or wrap up anything; and it is easy to understand because it is easy to remember, and this is because what is worded in periods has number, which is the easiest of all things to keep track of in memory. This is also the reason why everyone remembers verse better than words that all run together, since verse has number to measure it. But the period needs to come to an end along with the thought, and not break off the way Sophocles' iambs[216] do,

This is Calydon land, Pelops' ground,

since, from the way the words are divided, it is possible to get an opposite impression, as though, in the case mentioned, Calydon were in the Peloponnese.

A period is either in clauses[217] or unbroken. A period in clauses is wording that is complete and divided and easy to say in one breath,

216 The line quoted is actually from Euripides' *Meleager*. The following line makes it clear that Pelops' ground is across the Straits of Corinth from Calydon, but the periodicity of the line makes one hear the last two words of the line first as an appositive to what precedes them.

217 The word *côlon*, from which we get the name of the punctuation mark, refers literally to a limb of the body, and can refer to phrases as well as clauses, as in some examples below.

not for each division but as a whole, and a clause is one or the other portion of this. I call wording "unbroken" when it is in a single clause. Neither clauses nor periods should be either curtailed or lengthy. Something short often makes the listener lurch; this necessarily happens when, while still hurrying forward to the measure which the words have as an inherent limit, he is pulled up short when the speaker stops, and a sort of lurch results from the jolt. But lengthy stretches cause the listener to be left behind, as happens when people do not turn back until they are past the end of the road, and leave those who are out walking with them behind; similarly, when periods are long they turn into a discourse or something like a dithyrambic prelude. Hence they become what Democritus of Chios made fun of Melanippides for composing,[218] when he wrote preludes where there should have been antistrophes:

> A man brings evils on himself when he brings evils
> on another,
> And the greatest evil from a long prelude is for the writer.

The same sort of thing also fits speaking in lengthy clauses. And clauses that are too short do not make up a period, so they pull the listener headfirst.

Wording in clauses either takes something apart or sets up an antithesis. An example that takes something apart is "I have often marveled at those who convened the public festivals, and at those who set up the athletic contests"; in each clause of an antithesis, either
one contrary is put in juxtaposition with the other or the same word 1410a
is linked with both contraries. For example, "they were benefactors to both, to those who stayed behind and to those who followed them out, for the latter they gained larger estates than they'd had at home, and for the former they left behind estates large enough"; staying behind and following are contraries, as are large enough and larger. And in "so both those who needed to get property and those who wanted to enjoy theirs..." enjoying and acquiring form an antithesis. There are also: "it often turns out in these situations that the wise fail and the foolish succeed"; "they were deemed worthy of the prize of valor right away, and gained supremacy at sea not long after"; "to sail across the mainland and march across the sea, bridging the Hellespont and dredging Athos"; "and though they were citizens by nature, their city was taken away by law"; "for some were lost miserably and others were saved disgracefully"; "and using Barbarians as servants privately while publicly ignoring the many allies who were slaves"; and "either to have it while living or to leave it behind after

218 The couplet parodies lines 265-266 of Hesiod's *Works and Days*, where the original second line is "And the greatest evil from an evil plan is for the planner."

dying."[219] And there is what someone said in the courtroom about Pitholaus and Lycophron: "These men sold you out when they were at home and now they've come here this way and bought you." All these examples do what was said, and this sort of wording is pleasing, because contraries are easy to grasp, and even easier to grasp when juxtaposed; they also look like a syllogism, since a counterargument is a bringing together of contraries.

So this sort of thing is antithesis, and balanced antithesis if the clauses are equal in length; there is assonance if each clause has extremities that sound alike. This necessarily occupies either the beginning or the end; at the beginning it always involves whole words, while at the end it involves either the final syllables, inflected forms of the same word, or the whole word. Examples[220] of such things at the beginning are "tillage he got, till-less by him," and

> Assuaged with gifts they expected to be; persuasion
> by words they looked for too.

At the end there are: "You'd have thought he hadn't fathered a baby, but that he himself had become one maybe," and "most in mopes and least in hopes." And with inflected forms of the same word, "Do you think he's worth casting in bronze, when he's not worth a penny in brass?" And with the same word, "When he was alive you were speaking nastiness, now you're writing nastiness." And there is assonance of syllables in "What would be so frightful if you saw a
1410b man who was idle?" And it is possible to have them all together in the same place, and for the same sentence to be a balanced antithesis, assonant at the ends. The ways of beginning periods have been pretty well itemized in the *Theodectea*. And there are also false antitheses, as in the line Epicharmus wrote,

> Sometimes I was at their place, sometimes I was with them.

Chapter 10.

Now that distinctions have been made concerning those things, what makes things that are said be elegant and well-regarded needs to be discussed. Now composing them is a task for either natural gifts or training; showing what they are is the task of this inquiry. Let us then describe and itemize them, and let our starting point be this: to learn something with ease is a pleasant thing for everyone, and words have

219 All the examples in this paragraph to this point are from Isocrates' *Panegyric*. The following one refers to two men who had assassinated a tyrant.

220 The first is a fragment from Aristophanes, the second IX, 526 of the *Iliad*, and the next five are unknown. The translations are sometimes made a bit loose to approximate the effects in the originals. The *Theodectea* is believed to have been a compilation made earlier by Aristotle himself. Another example of a balanced false antithesis might be "heads I win, tails you lose."

meaning, so those words that make us learn are the most pleasing. And whereas the meanings of eccentric words are unknown to us, we know the meanings of the prevailing ones; but metaphor most of all produces the effect we are discussing. For when someone speaks of old age as a withered stalk, he causes learning and recognition by way of the common genus, since both things have lost their bloom.[221] The similes of poets also do the same thing, so if one of them is done well, it appears elegant. For as was said above, a simile is a metaphor differing in the way it is put, and it is less pleasing because of the extra part; it does not say that this *is* that, so the soul does not have to search this out.[222] Necessarily, then, the elegant wording and the elegant enthymeme are the ones that make us learn quickly. Hence superficial enthymemes are not well-regarded (for by "superficial" we mean those that are obvious in every respect, with nothing that needs to be searched out), and neither are those in which we do not understand what is said; the well-regarded ones are those of which understanding arrives as soon as they are stated, if it was not present before, or else those which one's thinking lags a little behind. For with that sort of thing, learning takes place, but it does not with either of the first two kinds. So enthymemes of this sort are well-regarded for the thought in what is said; as for their wording, in the design of it, they are popular if they are stated by way of antithesis. For example, in "regarding the peace shared with others as a war on their private interests," war is in antithesis to peace.[223] Enthymemes are well regarded for their choice of words if they contain metaphor, and if this is neither so alien as to be difficult to see at a glance, nor so superficial that it makes nothing happen; and still more so if it puts the thing in front of our eyes, for one ought to be witnessing things that are happening rather than things in the future. Therefore one ought to aim at these three things: metaphor, antithesis, active presence.

Of the four kinds of metaphor, the most well-regarded are those 1411a
based on analogy,[224] the way Pericles said the way the youth who perished in the war had disappeared from the city was as if someone had stolen the spring from the year. And Leptines said, in reference to the Spartans, not to stand by and watch while Greece had one eye put out. And Cephisodotus was upset when Chares was eager to submit

221 *Odyssey* XIV, 213.

222 Aristotle does not object to extended poetic similes like those of Homer; he is speaking of the impact of a statement like "He is a fox," as compared to "He is like a fox," or "He is as sly as a fox." The best wording is the one that gets us to the intended place with the least prompting.

223 From Isocrates' *Panegyric*.

224 The other three kinds of metaphor, as described in Chap. 21 of the *Poetics*, transfer the name of something from genus to species (as saying a ship at anchor is standing), species to genus (as calling any large number of things 10,000), or species to species (as speaking of cutting an animal's throat as sucking out its life).

the accounts for the Olynthian war for audit, and said he was trying to get the audit done while he had the populace by the throat. And once when Cephisodotus was urging the Athenians on after they were provisioned for Euboea, he said they needed to get going with the promptness of a decree of Miltiades. And Iphicrates was upset when the Athenians made peace with Epidaurus and the coastal region, and said they had just had their pocket money for the war taken from them. And Peitholaus called the Paralus the cudgel of the populace, and Sestos the bread-basket of the Piraeus.[225] And Pericles called for getting rid of Aegina, the eyesore of the Piraeus. And Moerocles said he was no bigger a cheat than a certain respectable person he could name, who cheated people at thirty percent interest while he himself took ten. And there is Alexandrides' iambic verse about daughters who take their time on the way to marriage,

> These maidens of mine are overdue in the rent on
> their marriages.

And what Polyeuctus said about a certain Speusippus who was crippled, that he was incapable of keeping still, even though fortune had locked him up in stocks with his infirmity. Cephisodotus called battleships colorful millstones, and the Cynic used to call taverns the Athenian dining halls.[226]

And Aesion said that the city poured itself out into Sicily; this is a metaphor that puts its meaning right in front of the eyes,[227] and his "so that Greece resounded" is also a metaphor, and in a certain way it too is before the eyes. And there is the way Cephisodotus urged the people not to make their assemblies so many mob-scenes; Isocrates too refers to those who make mob-scenes at public festivals. And there is an example in the funeral oration, about why it was right for Greece to cut its hair at the gravesite of those who died at Salamis, since their own freedom was being buried alongside their virtue; if he had said it was right to cry because their virtue was being buried, that would have been a metaphor and right in front of the eyes, but "their own
1411b freedom alongside their virtue" has a certain antithesis in it. And the way Iphicrates said "the path of my words goes through the middle of Chares' deeds" is a metaphor based on an analogy, and "through the middle" puts it before the eyes. And saying that one is calling

225 The Paralus was one of two Athenian ships used for state functions, including conveying prisoners, and Sestos was the setting-off point for ships bringing grain from the Black Sea region to the Athenian port at the Piraeus.

226 Diogenes was *the* cynic. Spartan citizens ate in common dining halls, while Athenians had a different custom when they went out for meals.

227 At the height of the Peloponnesian War, the Athenians launched a major invasion of Sicily. Thucydides (*The Peloponnesian War*) describes the massive numbers of men and amounts of resources that set out in VI, 31. In VII, 84 he describes the defeated Athenian remnant that was being massacred in a Sicilian river, while fighting one another to drink the blood-filled water.

in dangers to defend against dangers is a metaphor before the eyes. And Lycoleon's comment on behalf of Chabrias, "they have no shame before the supplicant posture of his image in bronze," was a metaphor at that moment, not for all time, but right in front of their eyes, for the statue, a reminder of his deeds for the city, pleads for him in his danger, the lifeless thing coming to life.[228] And "training themselves in every way to think small" is a metaphor, since to train is to increase something. So is "the god lit the intellect as a light in the soul," since both make things clear in some respect. And "we are not putting an end to the wars but postponing them," for both postponement and that kind of peace are putting things off. Also saying that the treaty is a trophy far more beautiful than those gained in wars, because they are for small things and single strokes of luck, while it is for a whole war, and both are signs of victory. Also that cities pay large bills in the censure of mankind, for a bill is a form of damages justly paid.

Chapter 11.

Now it has been stated that elegant things are said as a result of metaphor from analogy and by putting things before the eyes, but it needs to be said what we mean by "before the eyes," and what makes this happen. I mean that all those things that signify activity put something before the eyes; for instance, saying a good man is a square guy is a metaphor, since both are perfect in their kinds, but it does not signify activity. But there is activity with "having the prime of life coming into full bloom," and "you, like a free-ranging animal," and "as the Greeks shot to their feet"; "shooting" is an activity and a metaphor, since it means something is quick.[229] And there is the way Homer has made use of metaphor in many places to make lifeless things come to life. In them all, the way he produces active presence is highly regarded, as in the following examples[230]:

> Back to the plain rolled the shameless stone,
> The arrow flew,
> Flying eagerly, 1412a
> They stuck in the ground, still longing to glut themselves
> on flesh,

and

> The spearpoint leapt into his chest, quivering with
> excitement.

---

228 There was a statue in the marketplace of Chabrias himself, in a kneeling posture, commemorating a victory in battle, and visible from where the trial was held.

229 The last example is from Euripides' *Iphigeneia at Aulis*, line 80.

230 The first five are *Odyssey* IX, 598, and *Iliad* XIII, 587; IV, 126; XI, 574; and XV, 541. The sixth is *Iliad* XIII, 799, comparing marching troops to waves advancing on a shore.

In all these examples, something is made to appear actively at work, by being brought to life, for being shameless and quivering with excitement and the rest are activities, and Homer has applied them by way of metaphor based on analogy. For as the stone is to Sisyphus, so is a shameless person to the one being shamelessly treated. And he does the same things with lifeless objects in his highly regarded similes as well:

> Arched, white-crested, some in front, more upon
> more behind.

For he makes everything be in motion and be alive, and activity is motion.[231]

And one ought to take metaphors, as was said above, from things that are appropriate and not obvious, the way that, in philosophy too, it is the mark of someone with a good eye to recognize what is alike even in things far removed from one another. Archytas, for instance, said an arbitrator and an altar are the same, since both are destinations to which someone who has suffered injustice goes for refuge. Or if someone were to say an anchor and a hanging basket are the same, since both are the same sort of thing, but differ with respect to what is above and below. And to say the cities were put on a level footing involves something that is the same in things far removed, what is equal on a surface and in power.

And the greatest number of elegant effects are the result of metaphor combined with misdirection. For it becomes more evident in what respect one learns something when it goes against a disposition toward the opposite, and the soul seems to say "How true, and yet I missed it." In the case of quips, the elegant ones result from not meaning what one is saying, as in Stesichorus' remark that the cicadas would be singing to themselves from the ground.[232] And well-made riddles are pleasing for the same reason, for learning and metaphor are involved, and what Theodorus calls speaking in innovative ways. This happens when something is paradoxical and not, as he puts it, "by our prior" opinion,[233] but like the turns of phrase in things that make us laugh (which jokes are capable of doing even by a turn in a letter, since it surprises us) and in poetic verses. For they do not go the way the listener assumes they will, in, for instance, "he marched on with his feet shod in frostbite," which one imagines will

---

231 The last clause is not strictly true, as Aristotle demonstrates in Bk. IX, Chap. 6, of the *Metaphysics*. The distinction between motion (*kinêsis*) and activity (or being-at-work, *energeia*) is at a level of precision that goes beyond anything relevant to rhetoric, and is ignored here just as it was ignored earlier in this work in the definition of pleasure adopted for rhetorical purposes at the beginning of Bk. I, Chap. 11.

232 See 1395a 1 and note.

233 Aristotle seems to be giving Theodorus credit for a cute turn of phrase in *pros tên emprosthen*.

say boots. But this has to be clear at the moment it is said. The turn of a letter makes a word not have the meaning it has, but that of a word it turns into. For instance, in Theodorus' remark to Nicon the harpist, "something's bothering you," he is only pretending to say 1412b
"bothering," and being tricky, since he means something else. So it is pleasing only to someone who understands it, since if one does not get the meaning of being a Thracian, it will not seem so elegant.[234] There is also "you want to destroy him." Both need to be said appositely, and so too with such elegant remarks as saying that being first at sea was not the first of the evils for the Athenians, since they profited from it. Or as Isocrates has it, that the city's being first *was* the first of its evils. Both ways, something one does not imagine it will say is what is said, and one recognizes how it is true. For there is nothing clever in saying "first" is "first," but he doesn't mean it that way but differently, and the "first" that the other version denies is not the one it asserts, but a different one.[235]

In all these things, if the word is applied appositely by an ambiguity or a metaphor, then it works well. For instance, in "Madden is maddening," an ambiguity is alleged, but appositely if the man is unpleasant. And there is "don't be more of a stranger than you have to be"; "no more of a stranger than you have to be" is the same thing as "a stranger doesn't have to be a stranger forever," since it also means "alien." The same thing is involved in the celebrated line of Anaxandrides,

> It's a beautiful thing to die before doing anything
> deserving death.

For this is the same as saying "it's a worthy thing to die when one is not worthy of dying," or "it's a worthy thing to die when death is not the worthy thing." Now the form of wording in these is the same, but the fewer words it has and the more antithetical it is, the more highly regarded it will be. The reason is that there is more learning from something put antithetically, and it happens more quickly as a result of brevity. And something always needs to apply to the person it is said about and be said rightly, if what is said is to be true and not superficial; for it is possible to have these things separately, as in "one ought to die without having done any wrong," or "a worthy man ought to marry a worthy woman," which are not elegant. But

234 Ross "dubiously" substitutes the verb *thraxei* for the *thrattei* the manuscripts have. It could then be separated into two words with the pronunciation of the vowels changed; the turn of a letter, by adding a descending pitch and an iota-subscript sound to the alpha, would change "something is bothering..." into "...are a Thracian." An earlier commentator (Cope) explains the joke as meaning Nicon's playing is no better than that of a Thracian slave girl. In the next example, "destroy" (*persai*) is some sort of pun on Persian women, but its exact meaning has been lost.

235 The same word *archê* meant both "empire" and "beginning."

something will be elegant if it has both qualities at the same time: "it's a worthy thing to die when one is not worthy of dying." And to the extent it has more such qualities, so much the more elegant will it appear, for instance if the words are metaphors and the metaphors are just so, and it is an antithesis and a balanced one, and it has active presence.

And as was said in the discussion above about well-regarded similes, they are, in a certain manner, metaphors, since the statement of them always consists of two things, as in a metaphor based
1413a on analogy. We say, for instance, "a shield is the drinking bowl of Ares," or "a bow is a chordless lyre." In this form, then, they do not state something simply, but to say the bow is a lyre or the shield is a drinking bowl is the simple form. And people make similes this way too: a fluteplayer stands like an ape, or a person with a squint is like a sputtering lamp (since both are squeezed together). And the simile is well made whenever the metaphor is, since it is possible to make a simile that a shield is like a drinking bowl of Ares, or a ruin is like a rag of a house; and there is the simile Thrasymachus made when he saw Niceratus bested by Pratys at reciting, with his hair long and still dirty, by saying he was a Philoctetes bitten by Pratys.[236] It is in these details most of all, when they do not handle them well, that poets produce flops, and they are well-received when they do handle them well—when they get a correlation, I mean: "he carries his legs like twisted parsley," or "like Philammon sparring with a punching bag." All such things are similes, and the fact that similes are metaphors has been mentioned many times. Proverbs are metaphors too, from species to species; if, for instance, someone brings home something himself, in the belief that it is a good thing, and then it does harm, people say "he's like the Carpathian with the hare," since they both suffered in the way described. As for what makes things that are said elegant, then, and how, the reason has pretty much been stated.

Well-regarded hyperboles are also metaphors, like the one about the fellow with the black eye: "you would have thought he was a basket of mulberries." For his cheek is purplish, but this exaggerates it greatly. "Something like this-or-that" becomes a hyperbole by a change in the wording. "Like Philammon sparring with his punching bag" becomes "you'd have thought he was Philammon fighting with his punching bag," and "carrying his legs like twisted parsley" becomes "you'd have thought he didn't have legs but stalks of parsley, they were so twisted." There is something adolescent about

236 Philoctetes was abandoned by the Greeks on the way to Troy, on a deserted island, when he was bitten by a snake. Sophocles' *Philoctetes* takes place about ten years later, when he is wild-looking, with his wound still festering. Niceratus may have recited Philoctetes' central speeches as a competition piece.

hyperboles, since they show intensity of feeling, and this is why angry people[237] use them the most:

> Not even if he gave me as many gifts as there are grains
>   of sand and dust...
> I wouldn't marry a daughter of Agamemnon, son of
>   Atreus,
> Not even if her beauty rivaled Aphrodite who shines
>   like gold,
> And her accomplishments rivaled those of Athene.

Hence, it is unsuitable for an elderly person to speak in hyperboles, **1413b**
but Athenian rhetoricians make considerable use of them.

Chapter 12.

But one ought not to overlook the fact that a different wording fits with each kind of rhetoric. What is suited to a written speech is not the same as what suits debate, and the same wording is not suited to both a public assembly and a lawcourt. And it is necessary to have knowledge of both, since one involves knowing how to speak grammatically, the other how to avoid being forced to keep silent when one wants to put one's opinions out to others, which happens to people who have no skill at writing. Wording suitable for writing is the most concerned with precision, while that which is suitable for debate is the most concerned with performance (and with two forms of this, to convey character and to convey feeling). This is why actors are always hunting for plays with these qualities, and poets for actors with these skills. Poetry meant to be read gets a following; an example is that of Chaeremon, who is as precise as a speechwriter, and among dithyrambic poets there is Licymnius. If one puts the speeches side by side, those of the writers appear thin in contests, while those of speakers, however well delivered, appear unskillful when one has them in one's hands. The reason is that in the contests, the ones concerned with performance are fitting, and hence, when the performing is taken away, they are not doing their proper work and appear foolish. For instance, missing conjunctions and frequent repetitions of the same thing are rightly disapproved of in written work, but not in debate; rhetoricians tend to do these things too, since they go well with performance.

But it is necessary to vary the way one says the same thing, as if this very thing guides the way one performs: "This is the man who robbed you; this is the man who cheated you; this is the man who tried to carry out the ultimate betrayal." It is also the sort of thing Philemon the actor used to do in Anaxandrides' *Battle of the Old Men*, when he would talk about Rhadamanthus and Palamades, and in the business

237 The pre-eminent angry man in literature is Achilles, and the lines below are his, *Iliad* IX, 385, 388-390.

about "I" in the prologue to *The Pious Ones*. For if one does not do that sort of thing when acting, he becomes "the man lumbering around with a wooden beam." And it is the same way with missing conjunctions: "I came, I met, I begged." It is necessary to do some acting and not speak as though saying one thing in the same character and tone. And passages lacking conjunctions have a certain further peculiarity; a lot seems to be said in a given time, because a conjunction makes many things into one, so obviously when it is taken out, the one thing, on the contrary, will be many. Hence it makes for exaggeration: "I
1414a came, I discussed, I pleaded," (which seems like a lot of things); "he ignored everything I said." This is what Homer too is intending to do in "Nireus in turn, from Syme...Nireus, son of Aglaia...Nireus, who was the most handsome."[238] For if many things are said about someone, then he is necessarily referred to many times, so if he is referred to many times, it also seems that many things are being said. So through this fallacy Homer has enhanced someone mentioned only on one occasion, and made him famous without saying a word about him anywhere thereafter.

Wording suited to public assemblies is in every way like scene-painting, since the bigger the crowd is, the farther off is the view, and hence in both cases precise details are a waste of effort and make things appear worse. But wording that suits a lawcourt is more precise, and more so still if it is addressed to a single judge, since that gives the least scope for rhetoric, because it is easier for him to take in at a glance what is appropriate to the matter at hand and what is alien to it; the trappings of a contest are absent, so the decision is pure. This is why the same rhetoricians are not well-regarded in all these forums; where performance counts most, there is the least precision in it, but that is the place where a voice counts, and a big voice counts most. The wording in speeches for display is the most suited to writing, since being read is part of its work, with that for the lawcourt second. To take apart wording any more than this, and say it ought to be pleasing or magnificent, is a waste of effort. Why should it be that rather than be temperate or generous, or have any other virtue of character there may be? It is perfectly clear that the things already described will make it be pleasing, if indeed the virtue of wording has been rightly defined. For what other purpose does it need to be clear and not low-class but appropriate? If it is wordy, or cut short, it is not clear; it is obvious that the mean is fitting. And the things that have been described will make it pleasant if it is well blended with the customary and the unfamiliar, with rhythm, and with the persuasive element that comes from what suits the situation. What has to do with wording has been discussed, then, as it concerns all speaking in

238 *Iliad* II, 671-673.

common and each kind in particular. What is left is to speak about the arrangement of a speech.

Chapter 13.

There are two parts to a speech, since it is necessary to state the matter it concerns, and to demonstrate it. Hence stating it without demonstrating it or demonstrating it without stating it are both impossible, since anyone who makes a demonstration demonstrates *something*, and anyone who sets out a statement sets it out for the sake of demonstrating it. One of these parts is the laying out of the statement, the other is making it persuasive, the same way someone might make a division between a problem and a demonstration. But nowadays people make a ridiculous set of divisions, for a narrative presumably belongs only to a courtroom speech; how could there be a place for the sort of narrative they speak of in a speech for display or for a public assembly, or rebuttals to an opponent, or an epilogue **1414b**
to demonstrations? And in speeches for public assemblies, an introduction, weighing of opposing arguments, and recapitulation come up at times when there is a controversy, since this often involves accusation and defense, but giving advice does not entail this. Furthermore, an epilogue does not even belong in every courtroom speech, if, for instance, the speech is short or the matter it concerns is easy to remember, since it comes in to take out some of the length.

The necessary parts, therefore, are the laying-out and persuading. These are the proper ones, and at most there are an introduction, laying-out, persuasion, and epilogue. For rebuttals to an opponent are part of the persuasion, and weighing opposing arguments is an expansion of one's own argument, and thus a part of the means of persuasion, since someone who does this is demonstrating something; but the introduction is no part of this, and the epilogue is not either, but only serves as a reminder. If one keeps making such divisions the way those around Theodorus used to do, there will be the one narrative and also a post-narrative and a pre-narrative, and both a counter-argument and a counter-counter-argument. But one ought to impose a name only when speaking of something that has a form of its own and a differentiation; otherwise it becomes empty and silly, like what Licymnius does in his *Art*, making up names for straightaheading, offleading, and outbranching.

Chapter 14.

The introduction is the beginning of a speech, what a prologue is in poetry and a prelude in flute-playing, for all these are the sort of beginnings that pave the way for what follows. And a flute prelude is similar to the introduction in speeches for display, since flute-players also begin by playing whatever they are good at and connecting it with the lead-in to the piece, and one ought to write the same way in speeches for display, saying straight off whatever one likes, then getting to the lead-in and making a connection with it, which is exactly what everyone does. An example is the introduction to Isocrates' *Helen*, since sophistical debaters have nothing in common with Helen, but even if one gets off the subject with it, it is fitting for the whole speech not to be monotonous.

What is said in the introductions to speeches for display can be drawn from praise or blame. Gorgias, for instance, in his *Olympic* speech, praises those who instituted the public festivals, saying "you are worthy of being widely admired, men of Greece," while Isocrates blames them because they honored bodily excellence with prizes but made no award to those who use their intelligence well. It can also be drawn from advice, saying for instance that one ought to honor those who are good, so he himself goes on to praise Aristides, or honor the sort of people who are not well-regarded but not unworthy, but whose goodness has been obscured, like Priam's son Paris; this speaker is
1415a giving advice. Then too, it can be drawn from introductions to courtroom speeches, that is, from the appeals to the listener to be tolerant if the speech has to do with anything paradoxical or difficult or talked about often by many people, like Choerilus's line,

> These days, when every subject has already been taken.

So the introductions to speeches for display are drawn from these materials, from praise, blame, exhortation, warning, and appeals to the listener, and the lead-in has to be either alien to the speech or proper to it.

What one needs to grasp about the introductions to courtroom speeches is that they have exactly the same import as the prologues of plays and the introductory portions of epic poems. Those of dithyrambs are like those of speeches for display: "For your sake and for the sake of your gifts and loot." But in dramatic prologues and epics it is a sample of the story, so people may know in advance what the story is about and not have their thoughts left in suspense, since what is indeterminate causes confusion; so someone who puts the beginning in the listener's hand, so to speak, lets him follow the story by holding on to it. This is what the following[239] are for:

> Sing, goddess, the wrath...
> Tell me, muse, of the man...
> Lead me to another story, how out of the land of Asia
> A great war came into Europe...

Tragic poets too reveal what the drama is about, if not straight off in a prologue the way Euripides does, then somewhere at least, like

239 The beginnings of the *Iliad*, the *Odyssey*, and an epic on the Persian Wars by the same Choerilus quoted in the previous paragraph complaining that all poetic subjects had been used up before his time.

Sophocles' "My father was Polybius."[240] And comedy does the same thing. This, then, is the most necessary and proper job of the introduction, to reveal what the end is for the sake of which the speech is made, and this is why there is no use for an introduction if the speech is clear or brief.

The other forms of introductions people use are remedial, and common to speeches of all kinds. What is said in these deals with the speaker, the hearer, the subject, and the opponent. About oneself and one's opponent, it deals with the sorts of things that refute or produce prejudice. But these are not handled the same way; things dealing with prejudice are treated first by a defendant, but in an epilogue by an accuser. The reason why is not obscure; it is necessary for a defendant, when he is about to introduce himself, to clear away obstacles, so prejudice has to be refuted first, but the one attacking him needs to do his attacking in an epilogue so people will remember it better. What deals with the listener comes from making him favorably inclined or from making him angry, and sometimes from making him attentive or just the opposite; for it is not always to one's advantage to make him attentive, which is why many speakers try to lead people into laughter. Everything will lead to a readiness to be instructed if one wants it to, and especially seeming to be a decent person, since people pay more attention to them. They are attentive to things that 1415b
are important, that specially concern them, that incite their wonder, or that are pleasing, and hence one ought to impart the idea that the speech is about things of those kinds. But to make them inattentive, one ought to impart the idea that the subject is of small importance, that it has nothing to do with them, or that it is painful.

But it should not be overlooked that all such things are extraneous to the argument, for they are aimed at a low class of listener who listens to things outside the matter at hand, since, if he is not of that sort, there is no need for an introduction, other than just enough to state the matter in summary fashion, so that, like a body, it can have a head. What is more, making people attentive is a need common to all parts of a speech if it is needed at all, since attention slackens more everywhere else *but* when things are starting out; hence it is ridiculous to assign this to the beginning, when all the listeners are paying the most attention. Therefore, when the moment is right, one ought to say, "and pay attention to me now with all your mind, for it is in your interest no less than in mine," or "I'm about to tell you a thing such as you have never yet heard, so strange and wonderful." This is, as Prodicus used to say, tossing the listeners some of the fifty-buck stuff when they start to nod off. But it is obvious that this is not directed

240 *Oedipus Tyrannus*, line 774, about halfway through the play. This is a play that depends on concealment, but when the main character begins revealing his hidden history, he does so like a good speaker.

at the listener in his capacity as a listener, since in the introductions everyone is arousing prejudice or allaying fears:[241]

> My lord, I will not say that I come with speed.
> Why the preamble?

People do this when they have a weak case, or seem to, since it is better to spend their time anywhere other than on the matter at hand, which is why slaves do not give answers but speak in circumlocutions and preambles. The means one ought to use to make people favorably inclined have been discussed, along with each of the other things of that kind; and since it has been well said,[242]

> Grant that I come among the Phaiakians befriended
> or pitied,

these are the two things one should aim for.

In speeches for display, one ought to make the listener think he is included in the praise, either himself or his family or his way of life, or in some other way, for what Socrates says in the funeral speech[243] is true, that it is not difficult to praise Athenians among Athenians, but among Spartans it is. Introductions to speeches before public assemblies are derived from those of courtroom speeches, though in the nature of things they have them least; for certainly people know what they are about, and the subject needs no introduction, other than on account of the speaker himself or his opponents, or if people do not take the matter to be of the degree of importance you want them to, but either more or less. In that case it is necessary either to arouse or allay prejudice, or to exaggerate or minimize the matter, and for the sake of these things an introduction is needed. Or it may be for
1416a the purpose of ornamentation, since speeches seem hastily slapped together if they do not have them. Gorgias's encomium of the Eleans is like that, for with no preliminary stretching or shadow-boxing he starts right off, "Elis, happy city."

Chapter 15.

As for prejudice, one approach is drawn from things one may use to dispel a scornful assumption (and it makes no difference whether anyone has stated it or not, so this is universally applicable); another topic would involve confronting the allegations one is disputing, either on the grounds that they are not the case, or that they did no harm, or not to that person, or not so much, or that there was no injustice, or not a big one, or no disgrace about it, or none of any magnitude.

241 The following lines are Sophocles' *Antigone,* 223, and Euripides' *Iphigenia Among the Taurians* 1162.

242 *Odyssey* VII, 327.

243 That is, in Plato's *Menexenus,* 235D.

These are the sorts of things that get disputed, as Iphicrates did against Nausicrates, for he said he did what Nausicrates alleged, and did him harm, but did not do any injustice. Or one who has committed an injustice may set off one thing against another, saying that if it was harmful it was still a beautiful thing to do, or if it was painful it was still beneficial, or something else like that. Another topic is to say what happened was a mistake, a piece of bad luck, or a matter of necessity, the way Sophocles said his trembling was not a ploy to seem old, as his attacker claimed, but from necessity, since it was not by choice that he was eighty years old. Or one may offset the deed with its motive, saying that one did not mean to do harm but so-and-so, or did not do that which one is being attacked for, but caused harm accidentally: "it would be a just thing to hate me if I had done it in order for that to happen."

Another topic may be used if one's attacker has been implicated in something similar, currently or previously, himself or through any of those close to him; and another if others are implicated whom people agree are not guilty of the thing one is attacked for—if, say, the claim is that one is a womanizer because he is a fussy dresser, then one may say that a certain party must also be one. Another may be used if the attacker or someone other than he has attacked other people, or they have been under suspicion the way one now is oneself without being charged, and they have been shown not to be guilty. Another topic involves counterattacking one's attacker, for it would be absurd if his words were trustworthy when he himself is not. Another topic applies if a judgment has already been made, as Euripides retorted against Hygiaenon in a suit for confiscation of property, when Hygiaenon accused him of impiety, saying he had composed a line encouraging people to break oaths, namely

> My tongue has sworn, but my heart was not in on
> the swearing.

He said Hygiaenon was committing an injustice by bringing into the lawcourts judgments that belonged in the Dionysiac competition, for he had given an account of his words there, or would give one if anyone wanted to make an accusation.[244] Another topic makes an accusation on the basis of the prejudice, saying how big an effect it has, and that this is because it causes judgments to be changed, and because it does not put its trust in the fact of the matter.

244 The line is 612 of the *Hippolytus*, which had taken first prize at the festival of Dionysus, where tragedies were performed as a religious observance. Hence, the judges there had implicitly found it free of impiety. Hippolytus in fact does keep his oath, as one may see from the lines beginning at 656. The reference to confiscation (*antidosis*) appears to mean that one of the two men was trying to get out of bearing the cost of some public benefaction by getting the debt levied against the other. The accusation of impiety would not have been the original cause of action, but an attempt to discredit Euripides during the trial.

1416b A topic shared by both sides is to argue from circumstantial indications; in the *Teucer*,[245] for instance, Odysseus says that Teucer is a relative of Priam, whose sister Hesione was, but Teucer says that his father Telamon was an enemy of Priam, and that he himself had not denounced the spies. Another topic for the one making the attack is to blame someone for a great fault concisely after going on at length praising some small thing, or after laying out many good points, to blame one thing that bears on the matter at hand. People who do these sorts of things are the most artful and the most unjust, since their endeavor is to use things that are good to harm someone, by mixing them with the bad.[246] And one common to attacker and defender: since the same action admits of being done for more than one reason, the attacker needs to impute an evil motive by taking it at its worst, while the defender takes it at its best; for instance, that Diomedes chose Odysseus, on the one interpretation, because of assuming he was the best man, and on the other, because he was not, but for being the only one who was no rival, since he was so worthless.[247]

Chapter 16.

Let that much be said about prejudice. As for narrative, in speeches for display, it is not consecutive but piecemeal. One does need to go over the actions the speech is based on, since the speech is a composite, containing one element that is not artful (since the speaker is in no way responsible for the actions), and another that is derived from art; this latter consists of showing either that something is the case, if it is hard to credit, or that it is of a certain sort or of a certain magnitude, or all these things. And the reason one sometimes ought not to narrate everything consecutively is that showing things that way makes them hard to remember; on the basis of these actions, the subject of the speech is courageous, on the basis of these others he is wise or just. And this sort of speech is simpler, while the other sort is like embroidery and not plain cloth. One need only remind people of well-known actions; hence many speeches have no need of a narrative, as when you want to praise Achilles, since everyone knows his acts, and one needs only to make use of them. But if the subject is Critias, there is need of a narrative, for not many people know about him.[248]

And the way people say nowadays that a narrative ought to be rapid is ridiculous. As someone said to a baker, when he asked

245 A lost play of Sophocles. Hesione was Teucer's mother.

246 George Kennedy aptly cites Antony's repetition of "Brutus is an honorable man" in his funeral speech in Shakespeare's *Julius Caesar*.

247 Book X of the *Iliad* depicts a brutal and successful night raid behind Trojan lines by two Greek warriors. Diomedes volunteers first and picks Odysseus as his partner, citing his determination and cunning as the reasons for his choice.

248 Something is missing from the manuscripts here, and the next paragraph concerns courtroom speeches.

whether he should knead the bread hard or soft, "Why can't you make it just right?" It is similar here, since one ought not to go on narrating at length any more than go on at length with the introduction or with making the persuasive arguments. Here too, what is right is not rapid or curtailed but in measure: this is a matter of saying as much as will make the fact clear, or as much as will make people take it to have 1417a
happened, to have done harm or injustice, or to have been as serious as you want them to consider it, or the opposite for the opposing speaker. And you should include in the narration anything that has a bearing on your own virtue (such as "I kept warning him not to abandon his children, always arguing for what was just"), or on the other person's vice ("but he answered me that there would be other children wherever he might be," which is the answer Herodotus says the Egyptian deserters[249] gave), or anything that will please the jurors. But the narrative of the defendant is shorter, since the things he is taking issue with are either that the thing happened, that it was harmful, that it was unjust, or that it was as serious as alleged, so time ought not to be wasted on what is agreed, unless anything in it points in that direction—if it suggests, for instance that the thing was done but was not unjust. Also, except for what excites pity or horror when narrated as going on in the present, one ought to speak of things as having happened in the past; examples are the tale told to Alcinous, which when addressed to Penelope is condensed into sixty lines, and also the way Phaÿllus handled the epic cycle, and the prologue of the *Oeneus*.[250]

The narrative should be designed to reveal a state of character, and this will be the case if we know what makes a state of character be what it is. One way to do this is to reveal the choice that was made, and by what sort of choice this is, what sort of character is present, and what sort of choice it is in turn by what sort of end it aimed at. The reason mathematical treatises do not involve states of character is that they do not involve choice; there is no that-for-the-sake-of-which in them. But Socratic dialogues do, since they talk about things of that kind. Other things indicative of character are the details that accompany each state of character, for instance that someone kept walking at the same time he was talking, for this reveals a self-assured and uncouth character. And character is not revealed by speaking in the way that reflects thinking, the way people nowadays write, but in the way that reflects the making of a choice: "I wanted it because that was what I chose; if I get no benefit from it, still it is the better thing." One way is that of someone with practical judgment, but the other is that of a good person, for the mark of someone with practical judgment is seen

249 Who went off to Ethiopia, leaving their families behind. See II, 30 of the *History*.

250 The original tale told to Alcinous by Odysseus fills Bks. IX-XII of the *Odyssey* and thousands of lines. The other two examples are unknown, apart from the fact that the *Oeneus* was by Euripides.

in the pursuit of something beneficial, while that of a good person is seen in the pursuit of something beautiful. And if the choice is something hard to believe, then add the reason, the way Sophocles does; an example comes from his Antigone,[251] who says she cared more for her brother than for a husband or children, because *they* could be replaced when they die,

> But with a mother and father already departed into the realm of Hades
> There will never be any other brother who can come to birth.

And if you have no reason to give, you can still say that you are not unaware it is hard to believe but you are just that way by nature; for people do not believe anyone does anything willingly except what is advantageous.

Speak also of things that convey feeling, narrating even those accompanying details that people know about that are particularly characteristic of yourself or the other person: "he carried himself off,
1417b glowering at me." And there is the way Aeschines said of Cratylus that he was hissing and shaking his fists. Details like these are persuasive, because these things which people know about those others become indicators of things they do not know. The greatest number of such details may be taken from Homer:

> So she spoke, and then the old woman covered her face with her hands,[252]

for when people are starting to cry, they hold their hands over their eyes. Introduce yourself right away as a certain kind of person, so people will be looking at you that way, and do the same for your opponent; but do this unobtrusively. One sees how easy this is from messengers, for we know nothing about them, but we still get some impression. But narration ought to be in many places, and sometimes not at the beginning.

In speeches before public assemblies, there is the least narrative, because no one can give a narrative of the future, but if there is any narration, let it be about the past, so that people will take better counsel about what comes later by remembering those things. One may

251 The lines quoted are 911-912 of the play of that name. Jebb, editor of an authoritative edition of the works of Sophocles (and also a translator of the *Rhetoric*), rejects as spurious a 16-line passage that contains these verses, attributing it to Sophocles' son, or "some other sorry poet" before Aristotle's time. His reason is that the lines are illogical, inconsistent with earlier statements by Antigone, and in spots ungrammatical. But Sophocles knows how to depict a character collapsing under the weight of a doom-laden choice, clinging to the last shreds of rationalization for a choice made out of sheer love and loyalty, and Aristotle knows how to recognize the authentic voice of a great poet.

252 *Odyssey* XIX, 361.

either be attacking or praising what was done, but at such moments one is not doing the job that belongs to an advisor. And if there is anything hard to believe in the narrative, one ought to promise right away both to give a reason and to get it all squared away the way people want it, the way Carcinus's Jocasta, in his *Oedipus*, is always making promises when the man who is looking for her son asks her questions, and there is also Sophocles' Haemon.[253]

Chapter 17.

Persuasive arguments ought to be like demonstrations, and since the matter in dispute is of one of four kinds, one ought to demonstrate it by applying the demonstration to the one that is disputed. If, for instance, it is disputed that something happened, in the trial one ought to bring in a demonstration of that most of all, but if what is disputed is that it did harm, of that, and the same way if the claim is that it was not so serious or that it was done justly. And if the dispute is about whether the thing happened, let it not go unnoticed that this is the only sort of dispute in which there is necessarily fraud on the part of one or the other person, since ignorance is not responsible for it, as it could be if there were some people in dispute about a matter of justice; so then some time needs to be spent on this, but not in the other cases. But as for the exaggeration in speeches for display, the bulk of it will be to the effect that things are beautiful or beneficial, since the facts have to be taken on trust; for people seldom bring in demonstrations of them as well, and only if they are hard to believe or if some other person gets the credit for them. In speeches before public assemblies, one may either dispute the fact that something will happen, or argue that even though what the opponent is calling for will happen, still it will not be just, or not beneficial, or not such a big matter. And one ought also to see whether he is lying about anything outside the main issue, since these have the appearance of criteria for concluding that he is lying about other things too.

Examples are more suited for use with public assemblies, enthymemes with lawcourts. For the former are dealing with the future, and so it is necessary to speak of examples from the past, while the latter are concerned with what is or is not the case, about which there is more demonstration and necessity, because something that has happened has a necessity to it. But one ought not to state a series of enthymemes but mix in other things; otherwise they undercut one another. For there is a limit to their amount:

253 The reference is usually taken to be to *Antigone* 683-723 (but see also 1418b 31-32 below); Haemon perhaps seems to promise to tell a story that will make Creon change his mind. But Aristotle could be thinking of the report of Haemon's death by a messenger who enters at 1152, but does not begin his narrative until 1196.

My friend, you've said as much as a sensible man should,[254]

not the sort of things a sensible man should. And do not look for enthymemes about everything; otherwise you will be doing the same thing some philosophers do, who make syllogisms to prove things that are better known and more reliable than the premises from which they argue. And when you are working to produce feeling, do not state an enthymeme, since the enthymeme will either drive out the feeling, or be delivered to no purpose; for simultaneous motions drive each other out, and make each other either indiscernible or weak. And when the speech is meant to convey character, one ought not to look for an enthymeme at the same time, since a demonstration does not contain either character or a choice. But maxims are to be used both in narrative and in persuasive argument, since they do convey character: "I gave it to him, even though I know those words, 'Don't trust anybody.'" And they are useful if one is speaking with feeling: "I have no regrets, even though I suffered injustice, for gain tips the scales to his side but justice to mine."

Speaking for a public assembly is more difficult than speaking in a courtroom, and reasonably so, because it is about something in the future, while there it is about something in the past, which is already known even to the soothsayers, as Epimenides of Crete used to say (for he practiced divination not about future events but about obscure past events); also, the law is the foundation for courtroom speeches, and it is easier to devise a demonstration when one has a starting point. Public assembly speeches do not contain many lengthy digressions, on one's opponent, say, or oneself, or to put feeling into them; they have such things least of all, unless someone is trying to change the subject. In that case, when at a loss, one ought to do something Athenian rhetoricians do, especially Isocrates, for even when giving advice he makes some accusation, against the Spartans for instance in his *Panegyric*, and against Chares in his speech on the allies.[255] And in speaking for display, one ought to intersperse praises through the speech the way Isocrates does, since he is always bringing in someone or other. And what Gorgias used to say, that speech never fails him, amounts to the same thing, for if he is speaking about Achilles, he praises Peleus, then Aeacus, then the god; likewise, if he is speaking about courage, either it produces this and that, or it has such-and-such an aspect to it. Someone who has demonstrations needs to deliver them not only demonstratively, but in a way that conveys character as well; but if you have no enthymemes, speak so as to convey character. In fact, it
1418b is more fitting for a decent person to show himself as honest than for his argument to be precise.

254 *Odyssey* IV, 204.

255 The usual title given to the latter is *On the Peace*.

Among enthymemes, counterarguments are more highly regarded than those that show something directly, because when anything produces a refutation it is more evident that it has reached a logical conclusion; for contraries are easier to discern when they are side-by-side. Rebuttals to one's opponent do not constitute a different form but are included among persuasive arguments, refuting things in some cases by objection and in others by syllogism. In advisory speaking and in court as well, the opening speaker ought to state his own persuasive arguments first, and after that meet the opposing arguments by refuting them and pulling them to pieces before they can be made. But if the case for the opposition has a lot to it, one ought to meet the opposing arguments first, the way Callistratus did in the Messenian assembly, for it was only after a preemptive refutation of this kind that he said the things he was going to say. The person who speaks later needs to argue first against the opposing speech, giving refutations and countersyllogisms, especially if the first speech has been well received; for just as the soul is not receptive to a human being when prejudice has been aroused, it is similarly not receptive to a speech if the adversary seems to have spoken well. So it is necessary to make room in the listener for the speech he is going to hear, and there will be room for it if you invalidate the previous one. Hence it is only after combating in this way all the points in it, or the most important ones, or those that were well received, or those that are easy to refute, that one should make one's own persuasive arguments:

> First I shall come to the defense of the goddesses…
> For Hera, I…

In these lines the speaker has touched on the most foolish point first.[256]

These things have dealt with persuasive arguments. On the subject of character, since some things one may say about oneself have something invidious, wordy, or contradictory in them, and some things one may say about another person contain something abusive or rude, one should make someone else say them, which is exactly what Isocrates does in his *Philippus* and *Antidosis*. It is also the way Archilochus casts blame, for in his invective[257] he makes the father say about the daughter,

256 The lines are 969 and 971 of Euripides' *Trojan Women*. Hecuba is the speaker, replying to Helen.

257 Literally, in his iambic poem. Iambic verse was the forerunner of comedy, and ridiculed particular people known to the audience. Archilochus had been engaged to the daughter, but her father broke it off; he got his revenge on both by putting attacks on the daughter in the mouth of the father. In the next example, he invents a character to deliver his own criticisms of wealth. The preceding examples from the two speeches of Isocrates are praises of himself that he attributes to others. The reference below to Sophocles' *Antigone* is to lines 683-723.

> There is nothing one cannot expect, nothing prevented by a sworn oath;

and he has the carpenter Charon who says at the beginning of an invective,

> Not for me the belongings of a Gyges,

and it is the way Sophocles represents what Haemon says to his father on behalf of Antigone as though others were saying it. And one ought to vary the enthymemes sometimes by making them maxims; for instance, "People with good sense should reconcile with those who are enjoying good fortune, since that's the way they can get the most out of it," which, in the form of an enthymeme, is "if one ought to reconcile when reconciliation would be most beneficial and one would get the most out of it, one ought to reconcile with people enjoying good fortune."

Chapter 18.

In regard to posing questions, the most opportune moment to do so
1419a is when the other person has already spoken, so that, when one more question has been asked, an absurdity results. Pericles, for instance, questioned Lampon about the celebration of the rites of the savior goddess, and when he replied that it was not possible for an uninitiate to hear about them, asked if he knew them himself; when Lampon claimed he did, Pericles asked "How, since you are an uninitiate?" A second opportune moment for posing a question is when one point is obvious, and it is clear to the questioner that his opponent will grant another point, but once he has gotten the one premise in response, he should not ask an additional question about the obvious one, but just state the conclusion, the way Socrates did; when Meletus claimed Socrates did not believe in gods, the latter, having asked whether he did speak of a certain divinity, then asked whether divinities were not either children of gods or something godlike, and when the former stated "They certainly are," said "Who believes there are children of gods but no gods?"[258] Another opportune moment is when one is about to show that his opponent is either saying opposite things or speaking paradoxically. A fourth is when the one answering has no option but to evade the question in a sophistical manner, for if he replies like that, "It is and it isn't," or "Some are and some aren't," or "In a certain respect it is, but in a certain respect it isn't," people will hoot at him for having no answer. But do not attempt to pose a question in any other circumstances, for if the opponent has an objection[259] to it, you will seem to have been defeated; for it is not possible to ask a lot of questions, due to the weakness of the listener, for the same reason that one needs to make enthymemes as compact as possible.

---

258 Plato's *Apology*, 27C.

259 Not just a protest, but a logical objection, as discussed at the beginning of Bk. II, Chap. 25, above, that exposes a faulty assumption behind the question.

But when a question can be taken in two ways, one ought to answer by making a distinction in its meaning, and not be concise, bringing in a refutation of seeming contradictions right away in reply before one's opponent asks the follow-up question or draws a conclusion, since it is not difficult to foresee where the argument is going. But this point is evident to us from the *Topics*, as are the available refutations.[260] And when a conclusion is drawn, if one's opponent forms the conclusion as a question, one ought to state a reason, the way Sophocles did when asked by Peisander whether it had seemed good to him, as it did to the rest of the constitutional committee, to establish the government of the Four Hundred. He said it did, and Peisander asked "What? Didn't their actions seem to you to be iniquitous?"; he said they did, and Peisander asked, "So then you took part in these iniquitous acts?" and he said "Yes, because there was no better alternative." And there was the Spartan who was called to account for his term as ephor, who when asked whether it seemed to him the other ephors had been justly put to death, said it did; he was asked "and did you not impose the same measures they did," and said he did, and when the other went on "then wouldn't it be just for you to be put to death too?" he said "by no means, since they did those things because they took money to, but I did them not for that reason but by my judgment." This is why one should ask no 1419b
further questions after the conclusion, and not put the conclusion as a question, unless the balance of truth is far to one's own side.

As for jokes, since they seem to have some usefulness in competitive speaking, and Gorgias was speaking rightly when he said one ought to defuse the seriousness of his opponents with a joke and their joking with seriousness, there is a discussion in the *Poetics* of the various forms of joking,[261] some of which are and some of which are not fit for use by a civilized[262] person, so one may choose what fits him. Irony[263] is a more suitable style for civilized people than clowning, since someone who is ironic is making the joke to his own standard, while someone who is clownish is making it to that of someone else.

Chapter 19.

The concluding section of a speech is made up of four elements: setting up the listener to be favorable toward oneself and unfavorable toward one's opponent; exaggerating and understating things; getting the listener into certain states of feeling; and reminding him of things. For after demonstrating that one is truthful oneself and one's opponent untruthful, it is natural to indulge in praise and blame and hammer

260 Bk. VIII, Chaps. 4-7

261 This is not in the extant portion.

262 Literally "free" as opposed to a slave or someone with the habits and tastes of a slave.

263 See the note to 489E of the *Gorgias*.

things home. And one needs to aim at one of two impressions: that one is good and one's opponent bad either on these particular matters or simply. And the things on the basis of which one needs to present this impression, the topics by which one needs to present people as being of serious worth or no worth, have been discussed.[264] And after that, since things have already been shown to be the case, it is a natural step to exaggerate or understate their importance; for one needs to acknowledge the facts if one is going to speak of the degree of their importance, since growth in bodies too is from the pre-existing parts. And the topics by which one needs to exaggerate and understate things have been set out above.[265] After these things, when the sorts of things one is dealing with and their degree of importance is clear, one needs to lead the listener to certain feelings. These are pity, horror, anger, hatred, envy, emulation, and antagonism, and these topics too have been discussed above,[266] so what remains is to remind people of what has previously been said. It is fitting to do this by the method people recommend for introductions, though it is not fitting there, since they are not right in saying that. For what they tell people to do is to say things a number of times so they will be easy to understand. Now in an introduction one should state the matter at hand in order that the point to be decided on will not be missed, but it is in the conclusion that one should go through the points by which it has been shown, hitting the high spots.

The point to start with is that one has delivered what one promised, so one needs to say what the promises were and how they were kept. And this may be articulated by a comparison with what one's opponent has done, by comparing the things both have said on the
1420a same point, either directly ("here's what he said about these things and here's what I said and why"), or from an ironic standpoint (such as, "he said that and I said this; now what would he have done if that's what he had shown, rather than what he did show?"), or in the form of a question ("what then has been shown?" or "what did *he* show?") So the conclusion may be made by a comparison either in that point-by-point fashion, or following the natural course by which things were argued, the way one's own arguments went and then in turn, if you want it, a separate reminder of the points in the opposing speech. And a lack of conjunctions in the wording makes a fitting finish, so it can be the topping[267] on a speech rather than a speech: "I've spoken; you've listened; you have it; you judge."

---

264 In Bk. I, Chap. 9, above.

265 In II, 19.

266 In II, 1-11.

267 "Topping on a speech" is an attempt to get at the etymological sense of the word *epilogos*, which has been translated up to this point as "concluding section." The exemplary ending Aristotle suggests, which here forms the topping on the whole of the *Rhetoric*, is adapted from the end of *Against Eratosthenes*, a speech written by Lysias.

GLOSSARY

Advisory speaking (*sumbouleutikê*) Artful speech before a public assembly, urging the undertaking of some action, measure, or policy as advantageous to the community, or warning against it as disadvantageous. One of the three main forms of rhetoric distinguished by Aristotle in Bk. I, Chap. 3, of the *Rhetoric*. Sometimes called deliberative speaking in other translations, but the activity of the speaker is advice (*sumboulê*), while deliberation (*boulê*) is the function of the assembly he addresses. Aristotle sometimes calls this form of rhetoric *dêmêgorikê*, public-assembly speaking.

Art (*technê*) The skilled, practised, know-how to achieve an end reliably, in any realm from horse-riding to shoemaking to doctoring to poetry to mathematics. In the *Gorgias*, Socrates raises the question whether rhetoric is an art (see note to 447C), and denies that what Gorgias and Polus say they do is an artful pursuit, claiming instead that it is a combination of guesswork and experience at pandering to the irrational desires and tastes of ignorant crowds (463A-465D). Aristotle begins Chapter 1 of the *Rhetoric* by arguing that rhetoric is obviously by its nature an art, whether anyone has ever pursued it artfully or not, since an end that some people achieve haphazardly, and others repeatedly but in ignorance, could be approached methodically by someone who had studied its causes. He begins Chapter 2 by making it clear that *he* means by rhetoric not mere practical skill at persuasion but an informed skill, based on the theoretical study (*theoria*) of all the causes that go into making an opinion persuasive by speech.

Assonance (*paromoiôsis*) Any similarity of sound in whole or part of a pair of words used at the ends or beginnings of successive clauses or phrases. Aristotle gives examples of this at the end of Book III, Chap. 9, of the *Rhetoric* as a technique that contributes to a periodic style.

Conclusion (*sumperasma*) A statement that is a necessary consequence of two other statements. When Aristotle refers to the final portion of speech (*epilogos*) as a conclusion, this translation of the *Rhetoric* always uses some such phrase as "concluding section," or once, at the very end of the work, "the topping on a speech."

Courtroom speaking (*dikanikê*) Artful pleading of a case in a court of law, in accusation or defense, over an alleged act of injustice. One of the three main forms of rhetoric distinguished by Aristotle in Bk. I, Chap. 3, of the *Rhetoric*. Sometimes called forensic speaking in other translations.

Demonstration (*apodeixis*) The activity by which the necessary truth of anything is made obvious. Aristotle does not use the word for the merely formal construction of arguments with logically necessary conclusions, but only for reasoning that reveals consequences of things things that are self-evident. Strict demonstration cannot have a central role in rhetorical speech, but it is the pattern that the most persuasive rhetorical argumentation approximates in enthymemes (1355a 3 and following).

Dialectic (*dialektikê*) The verb *dialegesthai* means to engage in conversation. At 448D-E of the *Gorgias*, Socrates contrasts it with rhetoric, as speech that respects the opinion of the person addressed. Speech that is like conversation, or *dialektikos*, would not merely praise or blame something but establish common ground by saying what it is. Hence the give and take of conversation may lead people to pursue the presuppositions and consequences of their opinions, and in other Platonic dialogues, such as the *Republic*, this activity is given the name dialectic. Aristotle uses the word dialectic for the primary philosophic activity, that goes beyond conversation to become an artful pursuit of knowledge from an origin in opinions. The argumentation of dialectic, as Aristotle understands it, must be strictly necessary and not probable. Dialectic differs from demonstration only in not yet having self-evident starting points in hand. If the subject matter one reasons about does not admit of knowledge but only of opinion that may be more or less well-grounded, Aristotle calls the activity rhetoric, the counterpart of dialectic.

Display (*epideixis*) In the beginning of the *Gorgias*, the word is used for what Gorgias does, which is to make speeches that put himself and his skill on display. At 467C of the dialogue, Socrates shifts its meaning by challenging Polus to display (*epideiknunai*) the evidence for his claims. Aristotle uses the noun and related words for one of the three main forms of rhetoric, described first in Bk. I, Chap. 3, of the *Rhetoric*, the kind that puts the virtues or vices of some person, group, or institution on display in a speech made on a public occasion. Other translations sometimes call it ceremonial rhetoric, but Aristotle names it not by its occasion but by its characteristic activity. Aristotle's examples of speeches for display include Pericles' funeral oration for the young men who died in the early fighting in the Peloponnesian War, a speech in praise of the Athenian way of life, and Isocrates' *Panegyric*, in praise of the founders of Athens' public festivals. Because they show evidence for the praise and blame they offer, such speeches must articulate something about what is beautiful or shameful in human life and action in order to put particular people or deeds on display as admirable or as deserving reproach. Hence these speeches can rise above their immediate occasions to address the goals of communal life. Examples from American history would include Lincoln's Gettysburg address and second inaugural and Martin Luther King's "I have a dream" speech.

Elegance (*to asteion*) The quality present in a statement that says something new to the hearer in a way that is vivid, striking, and easily grasped, without wasted words. One particularly elegant technique Aristotle singles out is balanced antithesis (*antithesis parisos*); see Chapters 9-11 of Book III of the *Rhetoric*.

Enthymeme (*enthumêma*) A syllogism based in part or whole on likelihoods or signs, rather than on things that are immediately evident or demonstrably necessary; in the merely formal logic of our time, the word is used to mean a truncated syllogism, with one premise left out for rhetorical effect, but for Aristotle, the only difference between an enthymeme and a syllogism is its content. The word is a general term for anything connected in thought; Aristotle uses it for the characteristic building block of a rhetorical speech, the closest thing the subject matter of rhetoric permits to strict demonstration, a display of evidence for an opinion that cannot be turned into knowledge.

Example (*paradeigma*) An alleged fact or made-up illustration used as a basis for a generalization from that particular to the universal, and a subsequent conclusion about the case under discussion; one type of what Aristotle calls argument by signs. A perceptible particular directly present, from which someone can grasp an intelligible universal, is called *epagôgê*, translated here as "induction" for the sake of the distinction from rhetorical examples, though the traditional use of the word induction is misleading in its suggestion that a universal conclusion can be built up out of an accumulation of particulars. See the note to 1356b 1.

Good (*agathon*) In the realm of human action, anything worthy of choice. In the *Rhetoric*, Aristotle distinguishes three kinds of good: the advantageous (*to sumpheron*), what is choiceworthy as a means to an end and is sought by deliberative assemblies; the just (*to dikaion*), by which each person does and has what properly belongs to him, subject to determination by courts of law; and the beautiful (*to kalon*), which is choiceworthy for its own sake (1366a 33) and is praised in speeches for display. In the *Gorgias*, Socrates argues in 474D-475A that what is beautiful is either pleasant or well-adapted to an end or both, in 495A-500E that the good is not the same as the pleasant, and in 503D-507A that the good of anything depends on an orderliness (*kosmos*); hence, Socrates concludes (507E-508A), the human good is rooted in *the* cosmos, the ordered whole which includes heaven and earth, gods and humans, justice and geometry.

Likelihood (*eikos*) Something that happens or holds true for the most part in the realm of human action and endeavor. Aristotle distinguishes this sense of likelihood from what happens for the most part in the natural realm (1357a 34-36), where causes are strictly knowable but operate with organic consistency rather than mechanical necessity. Scorching heat *will* be present in the latitudes of Greece in late summer when no countervailing circumstances prevent it, but a rigidly maintained democracy does not necessarily lead toward anarchy or tyranny (1360a 25-27). Rhetoric deals with those aspects of communal life that are inherently open to going in different ways, and is itself one factor in assuring or averting a likely outcome.

Means of persuasion (*pistis*) The word refers primarily to an enthymeme, or to a sign or likelihood on which an enthymeme is based, and Aristotle often uses it in that restricted sense, but he also applies it to anything in a speech that displays the speaker's character as trustworthy, or arouses appropriate feelings, or offers any kind of reinforcement to an argument. Documents offered in evidence in a trial, for instance, would be *pisteis* of a kind extraneous to the art of rhetoric.

Pandering (*kolakeia*) Playing to the tastes and desires of others for one's own advantage, Socrates' characterization of the rhetoric that Gorgias and Polus practice. The word is usually translated "flattery," but Greek had many other words (*areskeia, thôpeia, hêdulogia*) for the agreeable sort of sweet talk that might be used among equals for no ulterior purpose. The emphatic characteristic of a *kolax* is shamefaced servility, in the sharpest contrast to the mastery and honor claimed by Gorgias and Polus.

Passions, the (*ta pathê*) The entire array of temporary, passively induced, irrational states of feeling. The word covers mild feelings such as a favorable impression of the defendant in a trial as well as violent ones such as hatred. Chapters 2-11 of Book II of Aristotle's *Rhetoric* amount to a treatise on the passions, and he speaks often in the work of speech or wording designed to arouse feeling (*pathetikôs* or *pathetikê*).

Prejudice (*diabolê*) Unfounded negative opinions or feelings about a person or group that are already present before a rhetorical presentation begins. Aristotle also uses the word for an attack meant to arouse prejudice and for the slander contained in such an attack. Chapters 14 and 15 of his *Rhetoric* deal with ways a speaker can neutralize prejudice.

Rhetoric (*rhêtorikê*) Introduced as an uncommon word in 448D of the *Gorgias*. *Rhêtôr* was a common word for a skilled public speaker, and rhetoric would be the name of his skill, whatever that may be. Gorgias, in Plato's dialogue, calls it a mastery over speeches and consequently over other people (452E); in his own *Encomium of Helen* (sections 10-11), he calls it witchcraft, a hypnotic art that molds false but potent speeches. Socrates calls it pandering, the manipulation of crowds in a servile rather than masterful way, but he leaves open the possibility of a more admirable kind of rhetoric. Numerous manuals of techniques for successful speaking had been written with the title *Art of Speeches*. Aristotle coins the verb *technologein*, "to make a speech art," or perhaps even "speech-art-mongering," for what is done in these books; he considers them all to dwell on the periphery of a central activity they say nothing about. Rhetoric, according to Aristotle, is the study of all the things that make an opinion persuasive, a dialectical inquiry applied to non-dialectical subjects, those that do not admit of knowledge, but do admit of opinions that can be shown to rest on better or worse evidence.

Showing (*deixis*) The presentation of evidence for an opinion, the central and characteristic activity of rhetorical speaking, according to Aristotle (1354a 26-28), to which all the other things a speaker does to be persuasive are accessories. It is what makes rhetoric more than the merely showy kind of showing-off (*epideixis*) that was the specialty of Gorgias, but also marks it as less than the demonstration (*apodeixis*) possible in mathematics.

Sign (*sêmeion*) Anything, particular or universal, which is for the most part an indication that something else is the case. A sign is a source of inference from one likelihood to another. If a ruler asks for a bodyguard, that is a sign that he may be plotting to become a tyrant. In the special case in which a sign invariably indicates that something else is the case, as a fever indicates that someone is unwell, Aristotle calls it a *tekmêrion*, translated here as criterion. (See 1357b 1-36 and 1403a 2-15.)

Speech (*logos*) A discourse spoken to a group of people, but the word also names the whole array of connections of meaning that underlie a language and allow a speaker to be understood. The word *logos* has perhaps the richest range of meaning of any word in ancient Greek, but the two meanings just given may be taken as the focal ones. They are the two fixed points around which the *Gorgias* revolves, from the moment when Gorgias declares that he has a mastery over *logoi* (449E), and Socrates asks in response about the variety of subjects human beings approach by means of the *logos*. Socrates' repeated declarations of his own preference for following the *logos* where it leads illustrate his fundamental opposition to those who attempt to force *logoi* into shapes that suit their predetermined purposes. To capture the echoes of this theme, that are everywhere in the *Gorgias*, this translation almost always renders *logos* as "speech," even when other English words might come closer to its various uses in their contexts.

Speech-art making (*technologein*) A word Aristotle coins (1354b 17) for the industrious production of manuals of rhetorical tricks, each of which went by the name *Art of Speeches* (*technê tôn logôn*), but none of which, according to Aristotle, contains any part of that art (1354a 11-13). Liddell and Scott missed the joke and thought the word was extending the meaning of another verb (*diorizein*) used in proximity to its first occurrence; they gave their stamp of authority to the unimaginative conjecture "bring under the rules of art, systematize" and subsequent translation and commentary have followed their lead.

Syllogism (*sullogismos*) The building block of demonstration, consisting, according to Aristotle, of two propositions that are either self-evident or necessary consequences of things that are self-evident, and a conclusion that necessarily follows from them. The word is used today for any pair of premises with a conclusion, but if the premises lack necessity, Aristotle would call such an argument an enthymeme.

Topic (*topos*) A ready-made argument that can be adapted to many situations. The word does not refer to the subject-matter of the argument, and is hence misleading in English, but its use was so well established before Aristotle's time that he does not define it, and the plural of it is his title for his study of dialectic, traditionally called in English the *Topics*, to which he refers often in the *Rhetoric*. The literal meaning of *topos* is "place," and it is used for a metaphorical location in a filing system, the spot to which one turns for an argument that does not have to be devised anew on every occasion.

INDEX

Page references are to the standard pagination printed in the margins. The Stephanus numbers 447A-527E refer to the Gorgias, *and the Bekker numbers 1354a-1420a to the* Rhetoric. *The letter n following an entry indicates a footnote.*